PostgreSQL Skills Development on Cloud

A Practical Guide to Database Management with AWS and Azure

Venkateswara Vadlamani

Apress®

PostgreSQL Skills Development on Cloud: A Practical Guide to Database Management with AWS and Azure

Venkateswara Vadlamani
Rancho Palos Verdes, CA, USA

ISBN-13 (pbk): 979-8-8688-0816-6   ISBN-13 (electronic): 979-8-8688-0817-3
https://doi.org/10.1007/979-8-8688-0817-3

Copyright © Venkateswara Vadlamani 2024, corrected publication 2025

This work is subject to copyright. All rights are reserved by the Publisher, whether the whole or part of the material is concerned, specifically the rights of translation, reprinting, reuse of illustrations, recitation, broadcasting, reproduction on microfilms or in any other physical way, and transmission or information storage and retrieval, electronic adaptation, computer software, or by similar or dissimilar methodology now known or hereafter developed.

Trademarked names, logos, and images may appear in this book. Rather than use a trademark symbol with every occurrence of a trademarked name, logo, or image we use the names, logos, and images only in an editorial fashion and to the benefit of the trademark owner, with no intention of infringement of the trademark.

The use in this publication of trade names, trademarks, service marks, and similar terms, even if they are not identified as such, is not to be taken as an expression of opinion as to whether or not they are subject to proprietary rights.

While the advice and information in this book are believed to be true and accurate at the date of publication, neither the authors nor the editors nor the publisher can accept any legal responsibility for any errors or omissions that may be made. The publisher makes no warranty, express or implied, with respect to the material contained herein.

    Managing Director, Apress Media LLC: Welmoed Spahr
    Acquisitions Editor: Shaul Elson
    Development Editor: Laura Berendson
    Coordinating Editor: Gryffin Winkler
    Copy Editor: Mary Behr

Cover image by Michael Siebert from Pixabay (pixabay.com)

Distributed to the book trade worldwide by Springer Science+Business Media New York, 233 Spring Street, 6th Floor, New York, NY 10013. Phone 1-800-SPRINGER, fax (201) 348-4505, e-mail orders-ny@springer-sbm.com, or visit www.springeronline.com. Apress Media, LLC is a California LLC and the sole member (owner) is Springer Science + Business Media Finance Inc (SSBM Finance Inc). SSBM Finance Inc is a **Delaware** corporation.

For information on translations, please e-mail booktranslations@springernature.com; for reprint, paperback, or audio rights, please e-mail bookpermissions@springernature.com.

Apress titles may be purchased in bulk for academic, corporate, or promotional use. eBook versions and licenses are also available for most titles. For more information, reference our Print and eBook Bulk Sales web page at www.apress.com/bulk-sales.

Any source code or other supplementary material referenced by the author in this book can be found here: www.apress.com/gp/services/source-code.

If disposing of this product, please recycle the paper

This work is dedicated to two exceptional individuals who have played a significant role in shaping my journey with PostgreSQL and inspiring the creation of this book.

To Dr. Michael Stonebraker, your contributions to the field of database technology have been truly exceptional with the creation of PostgreSQL. Your pioneering work and visionary ideas have been a constant source of inspiration throughout my career. I am grateful for the impact you have had on the industry and for the opportunities your contributions have provided.

To Professor P.S. Sarma, as an esteemed electronics professor, your guidance and mentorship have been pivotal in shaping my journey in the field. While your expertise lies in electronics, your unwavering support and belief in my abilities have been instrumental in me embarking on this book-writing endeavor focused on PostgreSQL. Thank you, Prof. P.S. Sarma, for being an outstanding professor and for your unwavering support. Your guidance has had a lasting impact on my journey.

Table of Contents

About the Author xxv

About the Technical Reviewer xxvii

Acknowledgments xxix

Preface xxxi

Chapter 1: Introduction to PostgreSQL Database Management............1

1.1 Abstract..1

1.2 Objective of Learning 2

1.3 Introduction..2

    1.3.1 PostgreSQL Cluster Origin 3

    1.3.2 PostgreSQL Server Operating System Resources 7

    1.3.3 Major Features of PostgreSQL...9

    1.3.4 Major Contributors to PostgreSQL Open-Source Software ...10

    1.3.5 Introduction to Database Management System 12

    1.3.6 Relational Data Model 19

    1.3.7 Star Schema 21

    1.3.8 Object Relational Model..23

    1.3.9 Install PostgreSQL Cluster on MAC 26

    1.3.10 PostgreSQL Cluster Install on a Windows PC......................30

    1.3.11 PostgreSQL Commercial Products.......................................33

    1.3.12 Version Changes 36

TABLE OF CONTENTS

    1.4 PostgreSQL Learning Approach 37

        1.4.1 Keywords 37

        1.4.2 Summary of Learning 38

    1.5 Practice Chapter 1 38

        1.5.1 Questions Chapter 1 39

    References 39

Chapter 2: Capacity Planning 41

    2.1 Abstract 41

    2.2 Objective of Learning 42

    2.3 Introduction 42

        2.3.1 Cloud Services 42

        2.3.2 AWS Web Services 44

        2.3.3 Microsoft Azure Web Service 47

        2.3.4 Operating System Selection 51

        2.3.5 AWS Hardware Configuration 51

        2.3.6 Azure Hardware Configuration 53

        2.3.7 Disk Space Estimation 54

        2.3.8 Data Management Policies 57

        2.3.9 PostgreSQL Cluster Provisioning Methods 59

        2.3.10 Database Limits 61

        2.3.11 Cloud Storage 61

    2.4 Keywords 70

        2.4.1 Practice Chapter 2 70

        2.4.2 Questions Chapter 2 70

        2.4.3 Summary of Learning 71

    References 72

TABLE OF CONTENTS

Chapter 3: Amazon EC2/Azure VM Linux Install Tasks 75

    3.1 Abstract 75

    3.2 Objectives of Learning 75

    3.3 Introduction 76

    3.4 Introduction to the Linux Operating System 76

        3.4.1 Major Features of Linux 77

        3.4.2 Cloud VM Creation 84

        3.4.3 Install Linux Azure VM 100

        3.4.4 Linux Tasks on Amazon ec2/Azure VM 105

        3.4.5 Linux Huge Pages 111

        3.4.6 Create a Billing Alert 112

        3.4.7 Volume Group Creation 114

        3.4.8 AWS OS Storage Allocation Procedure 117

        3.4.9 EC2/Azure VM Management Commands 121

        3.4.10 Azure CLI 122

        3.4.11 Keywords 122

        3.4.12 Summary of Learning 123

        3.4.13 Practice Chapter 3 123

        3.4.14 Questions Chapter 3 124

    References 125

Chapter 4: PostgreSQL Software Installation on Amazon EC2/Azure VM Linux 127

    4.1 Abstract 127

    4.2 Objectives of Learning 128

    4.3 Installation of PostgreSQL Software on Linux 128

        4.3.1 Download PostgreSQL Cluster Software 130

        4.3.2 PostgreSQL Software for Installation on Linux 130

TABLE OF CONTENTS

    4.3.3 PostgreSQL Server Software Installation 131

    4.3.4 Download Direct RPM Packages 134

    4.3.5 PostgreSQL RPM Packages on Azure 135

    4.3.6 Install PostgreSQL Software on Azure VM 135

    4.3.7 Install PostgreSQL with the Configuration Option 136

    4.3.8 PostgreSQL Cluster Install Directories and Files 139

4.4 Initialize PostgreSQL Cluster 141

    4.4.1 Set Up the Linux Environment 141

    4.4.2 Check Linux OS Disk Space 142

    4.4.3 Initialize PostgreSQL Cluster 143

    4.4.4 Connect to a Postgres Database 145

    4.4.5 Postgres Data Dictionary 145

    4.4.6 Postgres Configuration Files 146

4.5 Postgres Operating System Configuration 151

    4.5.1 Check Memory Size 151

    4.5.2 Check Huge Pages in the System 151

    4.5.3 Check Huge Page Size 152

    4.5.4 Check Huge Pages After Start of Cluster 152

4.6 Parameter Settings 152

    4.6.1 Expand Shared Buffers Memory 152

    4.6.2 Modify Parameters in the postgresql.conf File 153

    4.6.3 Modify Parameters with the Alter System 154

    4.6.4 New Parameters Between Versions 14-16 154

4.7 Create Extensions 155

4.8 Postgres Operating System Process Details 159

    4.8.1 Process Memory Details 160

4.9 Multiple Instances of PostgreSQL 160

4.10 Create a Non-Default Security Group 162

TABLE OF CONTENTS

    4.10.1 Create a Security Group From AWS 162

    4.10.2 Azure Security Group 163

  4.11 Post Installation Tasks 164

    4.11.1 Create a Database 164

    4.11.2 Validate Access from a Remote Client 165

    4.11.3 Validate WAL Archiving 166

    4.11.4 Validate Non-Default Block Size 167

    4.11.5 Client Connection Details 167

    4.11.6 Control Data 169

  4.12 Uninstall Postgres from a Linux Host 169

  4.13 Keywords 170

  4.14 Summary of Learning 170

  4.15 Practice Chapter 4 170

  4.16 Questions Chapter 4 171

  References 171

Chapter 5: Client Tools 173

  5.1 Abstract 173

  5.2 Objectives of Learning 173

  5.3 Introduction 174

  5.4 pgAdmin 175

    5.4.1 Create a New Server 176

    5.4.2 Provide the Host IP Address and User Connection Details 177

    5.4.3 Query Tool 177

    5.4.4 PSQL 178

  5.5 psql Client on Windows 179

    5.5.1 PostgreSQL Executable 179

ix

TABLE OF CONTENTS

 5.6 SQLJ Workbench 180

  5.6.1 Download Software 181

  5.6.2 Manage JDBC Drivers...181

  5.6.3 Statement Tab..183

 5.7 AWS CLI on Windows..185

  5.7.1 Create an IAM User Account 186

  5.7.2 Download AWS CLI..186

  5.7.3 Configure AWS CLI 187

  5.7.4 AWS CLI on a Mac..188

  5.7.5 AWS CLI Install on Linux 188

 5.8 Windows Git Bash 189

  5.8.1 Download Software 189

  5.8.2 Start EC2 from Windows Git Bash Shell 190

  5.8.3 Query S3..191

 5.9 ODBC..191

  5.9.1 Configuration of ODBC on Linux 192

  5.9.2 Configuration of ODBC on a Windows Client................................193

  5.9.3 ODBC with Configuration Option..196

 5.10 Install PostgreSQL Client on Linux 197

 5.11 Azure Client...199

  5.11.1 Azure CLI...199

 5.12 Keywords 200

 5.13 Summary of Learning 200

 5.14 Practice Chapter 5 200

 5.15 Questions Chapter 5..201

TABLE OF CONTENTS

Chapter 6: PostgreSQL on AWS RDS/Azure SQL Database 203
6.1 Abstract 203
6.2 Objective of Learning 204
6.3 Introduction 204
6.4 AWS RDS 205
6.4.1 Database as a Service Architecture 205
6.4.2 RDS PostgreSQL Creation Methods 207
6.4.3 PostgreSQL RDS Creation Procedure from the Console 208
6.4.4 Create RDS from the Command Line 210
6.4.5 Modification to RDS 219
6.4.6 RDS PostgreSQL Logs View 223
6.4.7 RDS Performance Monitoring 224
6.4.8 AWS Performance Insights 224
6.4.9 Dimensions Menu 226
6.4.10 PostgreSQL Dynamic View for Metrics 226
6.4.11 Performance Monitoring with the AWS CLI 227
6.4.12 AWS CLI JSON Metrics Monitoring 228
6.4.13 AWS CLI API 231
6.4.14 Script for Metric Data 231
6.4.15 RDS Extensions 232
6.5 Azure SQL Database 232
6.5.1 Azure SQL Database for PostgreSQL 233
6.5.2 Azure PostgreSQL Creation Steps 234
6.5.3 psql Connection From a Windows Laptop 235
6.5.4 Azure PostgreSQL CLI 236
6.5.5 Create a PostgreSQL Single Server 236
6.5.6 Create PostgreSQL Flexible Server Azure CLI 237
6.5.7 Create PostgreSQL Flexible Server with a Template 237

TABLE OF CONTENTS

    6.5.8 Enable PostgreSQL Parameter for Logging 242

    6.5.9 Enable Azure Database Logging 242

    6.5.10 Create Analytics Workspace 243

    6.5.11 Enable Diagnostic Setting 244

    6.5.12 Run KQL 245

  6.6 Keywords 245

  6.7 Summary of Learning 246

  6.8 Practice Chapter 6 246

  6.9 Questions Chapter 6 246

Chapter 7: PostgreSQL on Docker 249

  7.1 Abstract 249

  7.2 Objective of Learning 249

  7.3 Introduction 250

  7.4 Installation 251

  7.5 Docker Platform 251

    7.5.1 Docker Info 252

    7.5.2 Docker pull 253

    7.5.3 Docker Registry 253

    7.5.4 Create a PostgreSQL cluster in Docker 254

    7.5.5 Docker Compose 257

    7.5.6 Docker Process 260

    7.5.7 psql Connection to a Docker Local Host 261

    7.5.8 psql Connection from a Remote Laptop 262

    7.5.9 Docker Utility 262

  7.6 Backup and Recovery of Docker 263

    7.6.1 Back Up Docker 263

    7.6.2 Recover Docker 263

    7.6.3 Docker Restore on a Local Host 264

TABLE OF CONTENTS

7.7 Orchestration Framework 266

    7.7.1 Remove Docker 266

    7.7.2 Kubernetes 266

    7.7.3 Kubernetes Cluster Infrastructure 268

    7.7.4 Kubernetes Application Access 269

    7.7.5 Kubernetes Postgres Creation YAML 270

7.8 OpenShift 271

7.9 Amazon EKS 272

7.10 Docker Desktop 273

    7.10.1 Docker Export from a Mac and Import to Linux 276

7.11 Summary of Learning 278

    7.11.1 Keywords 278

7.12 Practice chapter 7 279

7.13 Questions Chapter 7 279

References 281

Chapter 8: Postgres Cluster and Database Backup 283

8.1 Abstract 283

8.2 Objectives of Learning 283

8.3 Introduction 284

8.4 pg_dump 286

    8.4.1 Back Up a Database 288

    8.4.2 Back Up a Database to S3 288

    8.4.3 Back Up One or Many Tables 289

    8.4.4 Back Up a Database for Table Restore 289

    8.4.5 Back Up DDL 290

    8.4.6 Parallel Backup Configuration 290

    8.4.7 Parallel Backup Script 291

xiii

TABLE OF CONTENTS

8.5 pg_dumpall 294
    8.5.1 pg_dumpall Shell Script for S3...295
    8.5.2 pg_dumpall Shell Script for Azure..297
    8.5.3 pg_dumpall Shell Script for Disk Copy....................................298

8.6 pg_basebackup...299
    8.6.1 pg_basebackup Script...301
    8.6.2 Backup Manifest File Details..301
    8.6.3 Incremental Backup..302

8.7 RDS Backup 303
    8.7.1 RDS Backup from the AWS Console 304
    8.7.2 RDS Backup from AWS CLI 305
    8.7.3 Backup from Azure Linux Host 305
    8.7.4 Back Up a Database from Azure DS to Azure Blob 306
    8.7.5 Azure Snapshot Backup..308
    8.7.6 Backup Tool 308
    8.7.7 Keywords..309

8.8 Summary of Learning 309

8.9 Practice Chapter 8 310

8.10 Questions Chapter 8..310

References..312

Chapter 9: PostgreSQL on Windows Server in Cloud 313

9.1 Abstract..313

9.2 Objective of the Chapter 314

9.3 Postgres on the Windows Operating System 314
    9.3.1 Install Windows on AWS 316
    9.3.2 JSON Template File...317
    9.3.3 RDP Download from AWS Console..319
    9.3.4 AWS Details for Windows OS 319

    9.3.5 Download the RDP Client 320

    9.3.6 Windows Admin Password 320

    9.3.7 Download RDP from the Apple Site 322

    9.3.8 Connect to Windows Server 322

9.4 Postgres Configuration on Windows 323

    9.4.1 psql Shell 324

    9.4.2 PostgreSQL Configuration Files 324

    9.4.3 Stop/Start Windows Server 324

    9.4.4 Initialize the Postgres Cluster 325

    9.4.5 Start and Stop of Postgres Cluster 325

    9.4.6 PowerShell Commands to Manage a Postgres Cluster 327

    9.4.7 Power Shell Execution 329

    9.4.8 Postgres Data Directory Files 329

    9.4.9 Registry Entry 330

    9.4.10 The forfiles Command 332

    9.4.11 Delete Large Files 333

    9.4.12 Identify Postgres Process 333

    9.4.13 Terminate Postgres Process 334

    9.4.14 Tail the Log File 334

    9.4.15 Windows PostgreSQL Service 335

9.5 Keywords 336

9.6 Summary of Learning 336

9.7 Chapter 9 Practice 336

9.8 Chapter 9 Questions 337

Chapter 10: PostgreSQL Post-Installation Tasks 339

10.1 Abstract 339

10.2 Objectives of Learning 339

10.3 Introduction 340

TABLE OF CONTENTS

10.4 psql 340
- 10.4.1 psql Connection from a Host 343
- 10.4.2 psql –help 343
- 10.4.3 psql Meta-Commands 346
- 10.4.4 psql Command Prompts 347
- 10.4.5 psql Background Job 348

10.5 Postgres Schemas 349
- 10.5.1 Schema Definition 350
- 10.5.2 Create a Read-Only User 352
- 10.5.3 Schema Search Path 352
- 10.5.4 Set Search Path to Schema 353
- 10.5.5 PostgreSQL Database Onboarding Process Summary 354

10.6 Schema Data Move Procedure..358
- 10.6.1 Postgres Schema Clone Procedure 358
- 10.6.2 Table Copy to a Different Schema.....................................359

10.7 Dynamic psql 360
- 10.7.1 Dynamic SQL script1 360
- 10.7.2 Dynamic SQL script2 362
- 10.7.3 Dynamic SQL script3 363
- 10.7.4 Table Row Count Dynamic Script.......................................365
- 10.7.5 Dynamic SQL Variable 366
- 10.7.6 Table Rename Script..368
- 10.7.7 Session Termination Script...369

10.8 Data Copy and Load 370
- 10.8.1 Table Copy to OS 370
- 10.8.2 Truncate Table...371
- 10.8.3 Table Copy from the OS 371

TABLE OF CONTENTS

10.9 Large Objects 371

10.10 SQL Overload Function 372

10.11 Postgres System Functions 375

10.12 Keywords 376

10.13 Summary of Learning 376

10.14 Practice Chapter 10 376

10.15 Questions Chapter 10 377

Chapter 11: Sequences 379

11.1 Abstract 379

11.2 Objectives of Learning 379

11.3 Introduction 380

11.4 Sequence Management Procedures 380

    11.4.1 Serial Data Type Sequence Creation and Grants 382

    11.4.2 Sequence with Identity column definition 390

    11.4.3 Manual Sequence Creation 391

    11.4.4 Manual Sequence Increment 392

    11.4.5 Data Insertion with Sequences 394

    11.4.6 Data Copy Procedures and Sequence Maintenance 398

    11.4.7 Data Copy without a Primary Key 402

    11.4.8 Sequences with an Empty Table for Data Copy 404

    11.4.9 Sequence Truncate Approach 406

    11.4.10 Sequence Cache 409

11.5 Keywords 410

11.6 Summary of Learning 410

11.7 Practice Chapter 11 410

11.8 Questions Chapter 11 411

References 412

TABLE OF CONTENTS

Chapter 12: Postgres Cluster Upgrade 413

12.1 Abstract 413

12.2 Objectives of Learning 414

12.3 Introduction 414

12.4 pg_upgrade Method 415

12.5 pg_dumpall Upgrade Method 421

    12.5.1 pg_dumpall Procedure 423

    12.5.2 Backup a Database with the pg_dumpall Backup Utility 424

    12.5.3 Restore a database with pg_dumpall 424

    12.5.4 Restore a Database with psql 425

12.6 Postgres Upgrade on RDS 425

    12.6.1 aws describe db Engine 426

    12.6.2 RDS Upgrade Check 427

    12.6.3 Upgrade Compatibility Matrix 428

    12.6.4 RDS Upgrade 428

12.7 Upgrade an AWS Instance by AWS CLI 429

    12.7.1 Upgrade RDS with the Command Line 430

    12.7.2 RDS Upgrade Log 431

    12.7.3 RDS Logs View 432

    12.7.4 Analyze Databases 433

12.8 Logical Upgrade Method 433

    12.8.1 Logical Replication Procedure 435

    12.8.2 Replication Configuration 435

    12.8.3 Replication Slot 437

    12.8.4 Postgres Log 438

    12.8.5 Remote Database Subscription Details 439

12.9 Azure Postgres Database Upgrade 440

    12.9.1 Database Upgrade from Azure Command Line 440

TABLE OF CONTENTS

  12.9.2 Upgrade Command 441

  12.9.3 psql Connection 442

 12.10 Upgrade Extensions 443

 12.11 Keywords 443

 12.12 Summary of Learning 443

 12.13 Practice Chapter 12 444

 12.14 Questions Chapter 12 444

 References 445

Chapter 13: PostgreSQL Recovery 447

 13.1 Abstract 447

 13.2 Learning Objectives 447

 13.3 Postgres Cluster Recovery 448

  13.3.1 Restore Procedure for Postgres Versions 11 and Below 449

  13.3.2 Point-in-Time Recovery 450

  13.3.3 Backup Metadata File 452

  13.3.4 Recovery Target Methods 454

  13.3.5 Recovery Parameters 457

  13.3.6 Recovery Until Backup Time 458

  13.3.7 Log Sequence Recovery 459

  13.3.8 Transaction ID Recovery 460

  13.3.9 Time-Based Recovery 461

  13.3.10 Recovery to Latest 462

  13.3.11 Reset Logs 464

  13.3.12 The pg_dumpall and recovery 465

  13.3.13 Remap Schema 469

  13.3.14 Restore from an RDS Backup from the Console 472

  13.3.15 Restore from an Azure SQL Database 476

xix

TABLE OF CONTENTS

    13.4 Keywords 477

        13.4.1 Summary of Learning 477

        13.4.2 Questions Chapter 13 478

        13.4.3 Practice 479

    References 479

Chapter 14: PostgreSQL High Availability 481

    14.1 Abstract 481

    14.2 Learning Objectives 482

    14.3 Introduction 482

    14.4 Set Up Replication Configuration 485

        14.4.1 Primary pg_hba.conf 485

        14.4.2 Standby pg_hba.conf 487

        14.4.3 Validate Primary Site Replication Access 487

        14.4.4 Perform Backup From the Standby Site 488

        14.4.5 Set Up Replication 489

        14.4.6 Validate Replication 489

        14.4.7 Replication Configuration Script 490

        14.4.8 Replication Status Check Script 495

        14.4.9 Replication Status Script Execution 497

        14.4.10 Replication Slot 498

        14.4.11 Promote Standby to Standalone Role 499

    14.5 RDS Read Replica 499

        14.5.1 Read Replica Diagram 500

        14.5.2 Create a Read Replica from AWS CLI 500

        14.5.3 Standby Recovery Log 501

        14.5.4 Standby Clone AWS Console View 501

        14.5.5 RDS Replica Clone Completed View 501

TABLE OF CONTENTS

14.5.6 Connect to a Replica from a Linux Host 502

14.5.7 Promote a Replica to a Standalone Cluster 502

14.5.8 Connect to Promoted Standby Clone 503

14.6 Azure Read Replica 503

14.6.1 Replication from Azure CLI 504

14.6.2 Validate Read Replica 505

14.6.3 Connection to Read Replica 505

14.6.4 Read Replica View from the Primary Database 506

14.6.5 Promote Read Replica 507

14.7 Keywords 508

14.8 Summary of Learning 509

14.9 Practice Chapter 14 509

14.10 Questions Chapter 14 509

References 510

Chapter 15: Table Partitions 511

15.1 Abstract 511

15.2 Objectives of Learning 512

15.3 Introduction 512

15.4 Partition Table Methods 513

15.4.1 Table Partition Creation Options 514

15.4.2 Partition Table Structure 514

15.4.3 Partition DDL Scripts 515

15.4.4 PostgreSQL Extension pg_partman 517

15.4.5 Partition a Non-Partitioned Table 518

15.4.6 Non-Partitioned to Partitioned Table with Sequences 520

15.4.7 Partition Indexes 521

15.4.8 List with Range Subpartition 522

xxi

TABLE OF CONTENTS

    15.4.9 Range with Hash Subpartition 523

    15.4.10 Range with List and Hash Partition 524

    15.4.11 List Partition with Range and Hash Subpartition 525

    15.4.12 Partitions with Inheritance 527

  15.5 PostgreSQL Partition Copy to Cloud Storage 529

    15.5.1 PostgreSQL Partition Shell Script to S3 Copy 530

    15.5.2 Partition Catalog Metadata Views 530

  15.6 Keywords 531

  15.7 Summary of Learning 532

  15.8 Practice Chapter 15 532

  15.9 Question Chapter 15 532

  References 533

Chapter 16: Postgres Tablespaces 535

  16.1 Abstract 535

  16.2 Objectives of Learning 535

  16.3 Introduction 536

  16.4 Tablespace Creation Procedures 537

    16.4.1 Create an Operating System Directory 537

    16.4.2 Create a Tablespace 537

    16.4.3 Create Tables in a Tablespace 537

    16.4.4 Create a Table in a Tablespace with the set Command 538

    16.4.5 Create a Table in a Default Tablespace 538

    16.4.6 Load Sample Data 539

    16.4.7 Query the Location of a Table in a Tablespace 539

    16.4.8 Non-Default Tablespaces Creation Summary 540

    16.4.9 pg_basebackup 543

16.5 Keywords	543
16.6 Summary of Learning	543
16.7 Practice Chapter 16	544
16.8 Questions Chapter 16	544
Reference	545

Chapter 17: MVCC 547

17.1 Abstract	547
17.2 Objectives of Learning	548
17.3 Multi-Version Concurrency Control	548
17.3.1 ANSI SQL Isolation Levels	548
17.3.2 Read Anomaly	549
17.3.3 Read Commit Isolation Level	550
17.3.4 Repeatable Read Isolation Level	551
17.3.5 Serializable Isolation Level	551
17.4 MVCC and Database Blocks	552
17.5 Linux and Database Concurrency	552
17.6 DBA Tasks	553
17.7 Serializable Isolation Configuration	556
17.8 MVCC and Implicit Locks	556
17.9 MVCC and Explicit Locks	556
17.10 Understanding MVCC Scenarios in the Real World	557
17.11 Serializable Concurrent Transaction Issue	559
17.12 Keywords	560
17.13 Summary of Learning	560
17.14 Questions Chapter 17	561
References	561

TABLE OF CONTENTS

Correction to: PostgreSQL Software Installation on Amazon EC2/Azure VM Linux C1

Appendix A: Project Work: Amazon AMI 563

Appendix B: DBA Tool in AMI 565

Appendix C: RDS Proxy 569

Appendix D: Postgres with Apache/PHP 577

Appendix E: pgBouncer 589

Appendix F: Red Hat Pacemaker HA 591

Appendix G: Python with PostgreSQL 593

Appendix H1: Incremental Backup 597

Appendix H2: Incremental Backup Restore 599

Appendix I: Answers to Chapter Questions 603

Index 605

About the Author

Venkat Vadlamani is an experienced database professional with a career spanning over 30 years as a database administrator and system administrator. He has provided solutions for high availability, distributed databases, and real-time data synchronization requirements for Fortune corporations in Singapore, Australia, and the United States. Venkat holds certifications as a Solaris Certified System Administrator, an Oracle Certified DBA, and an AWS Certified Solution Architect. In addition, he holds an MBA degree in Information Technology.

Currently, Venkat serves as a Senior Oracle and PostgreSQL Consultant, where he focuses on implementing PostgreSQL projects on the AWS cloud and Red Hat OpenShift environments in Southern California. The ideas, scripts, and exhibits presented in this book are derived from Venkat's extensive experience, utilizing his personal AWS account on EC2 and RDS.

About the Technical Reviewer

Deepak Vohra is an Oracle Certified Java Programmer, Oracle Certified Professional MySQL 8.0 Database Administrator, and MySQL 8.0 Database Developer Oracle Certified Professional. Deepak is the author of twenty books, six of which are for Apress.

Acknowledgments

I am deeply grateful to the numerous individuals who have supported me throughout my career and the creation of this book. I would like to express my heartfelt appreciation to the following individuals: Dr. Bhatt Vadlamani, Dr. Gopal Pingali, Gummadidala Ranga Rao, E.E. Prasad, Kodavalla Hanuma, Dr. Prabhu Ayyagari, Jay Raju, Manor Sutar, and Verlynn Mitchel.

Preface

Through my more than 20 years of experience working with PostgreSQL, I have implemented numerous projects for Fortune clients in Australia, Singapore, and the USA. Drawing on this expertise, I have developed a training method that covers day-to-day administration components of PostgreSQL. The content is based on real-life database events, maintenance tasks, and the implementation of PostgreSQL clusters ranging from several GB to multi-terabyte databases on on-premises infrastructure and in AWS and Azure cloud environments.

This is a two-part series to manage PostgreSQL databases on cloud: 1) Beginners Study Guide and 2) Advanced Study Guide. The Beginners Study Guide provides a basic introduction to Postgres database management on the cloud, whereas the Advanced Study Guide is for advanced users.

The Objective of This Book

This book serves as a handy reference for beginners and DBAs supporting Postgres in cloud environments. It covers basic Postgres database administration concepts from sources such as Postgres itself, Amazon Web Services, Azure Web Services, and Red Hat OS vendors.

PREFACE

Target Readers for This Book

This book is aimed at beginners in Postgres database administration, system administrators working on Postgres database administration tasks, and IT consulting DBA staff working on L1 and L2 support of Postgres administration in the cloud as well as general enthusiasts.

Benefits of Reading the Book

It aims to equip DBAs with the knowledge and skills necessary to confidently manage PostgreSQL databases in cloud environments.

This book aims to prepare or enhance your Postgres database administration skills in the ever-changing cloud landscape within Amazon and Azure environments. Whereas the official documentation for Postgres, Amazon Web Services, Azure Web Services, and the Red Hat OS encompasses several thousand pages, this book condenses all of the fundamental and essential concepts needed to manage a Postgres cluster in the cloud.

Each chapter of the book adheres to a structured approach, providing historical context and documenting version changes of the PostgreSQL cluster, elucidating practical "how-to" methods, accompanied by illustrations and keyword definitions, practices for application, a summary of key learnings, and questions to reinforce understanding.

With the comprehensive content and practical approach of this book, you will gain the confidence to manage all aspects of a PostgreSQL cluster in critical production environments. It will endow you with the necessary skills to successfully handle PostgreSQL administration tasks and support your organization's database infrastructure in both cloud and container environments.

How Is This Book Different?

- It provides a comprehensive approach to manage a Postgres Database on Amazon Web Services and Microsoft Azure Web Services in the cloud, as well as in Docker and container environments on the Red Hat OS.

- It includes ample references to scripting solutions and access to database management tools for working with Postgres, Redshift (based on Postgres 8.2), and Docker.

- It prepares DBAs to create Amazon Machine Images (AMI) and Azure Images for managing a fleet of Postgres clusters in the cloud.

- It outlines a clear study objective with a weekly learning schedule for readers.

- It guides users from simple concepts, such as how to choose the correct instance type, to creating complex machine images.

Chapter Overview

Chapter 1: Overview of the evolution of the Postgres database management system, version changes, and a list of major contributors and commercial vendors.

   Chapter 2: Deals with the selection of computer hardware, database software, storage capacity, planning roles and responsibilities, data archival, data retention, encryption, and data masking procedures on-premises as well as in the cloud infrastructure.

PREFACE

Chapter 3: Covers installation of a Postgres cluster on most popular Red Hat Linux environments, such as Amazon Elastic Cloud Computing (EC2) and Azure VM, plus Linux tasks.

Chapter 4: Presents detailed installation and configuration of Postgres cluster software with Red Hat Package Manger (RPM) procedures, as well as setup and configuration of a Postgres cluster database.

Chapter 5: Deals with the download, installation, and configuration of open-source Postgres client software.

Chapter 6: Installation of RDS and Azure from the console method.

Chapter 7: Installation, setup, and configuration of Docker.

Chapter 8: Offers scripting solutions to set up and configure Postgres cluster database backups. Different backup methods are discussed for backup on-premises and in cloud.

Chapter 9: A detailed account of a Postgres cluster in a Windows environment.

Chapter 10: Provides an overview of PSQL, schemas, and Dynamic SQL.

Chapter 11: Provides the basics about sequences and database administration tasks.

Chapter 12: Provides a detailed account of different Postgres cluster upgrade methods on EC2, RDS and Azure Data Service environments, complemented with scripting solutions.

Chapter 13: Covers Postgres cluster recovery procedures. All recovery methods provided by open-source Postgres software are described in detail with scripting solutions.

Chapter 14: Provides the configuration and setup of PostgreSQL cluster high availability procedures on EC2 as well as on RDS environments. You can utilize the scripts provided for a quick setup of replication procedures.

Chapter 15: Deals with basic and advanced table partition methods, procedures, and scripts, which are valid on EC2, Azure VM, and RDS.

Chapter 16: Deals with Postgres tablespaces creation and maintenance.

Chapter 17: Deals with MVCC and isolation levels.

Chapter Dependency

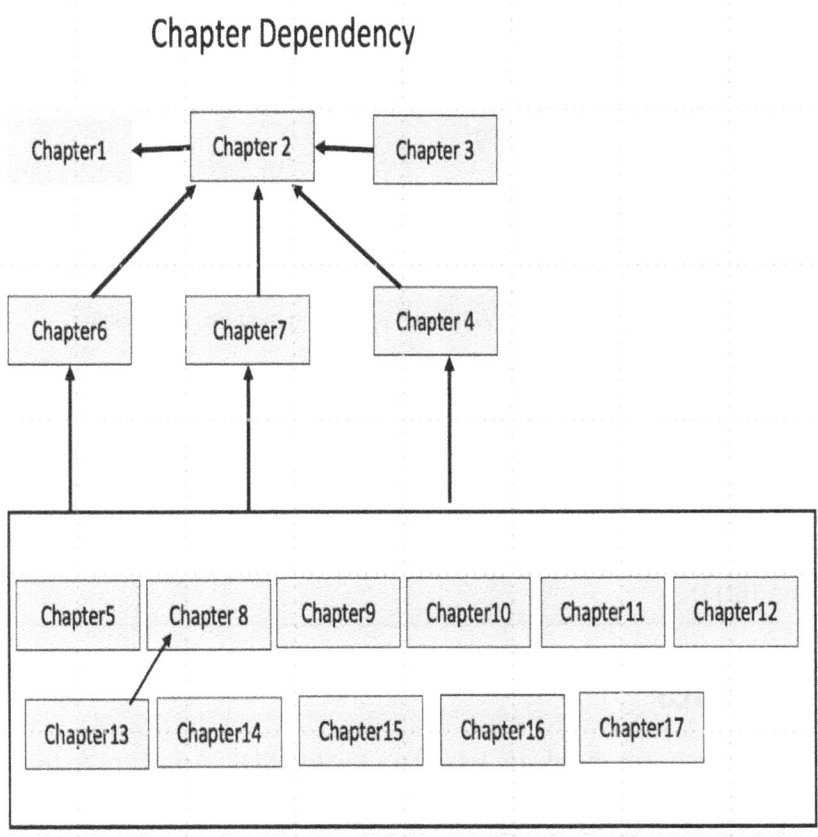

Study Objective

This book is designed as a six-week course in learning Postgres databases management in the Amazon cloud.

Table 1 shows the weekly learning objectives.

PREFACE

Table 1. *Weekly Learning Objectives*

Week 1 (Chapters 1/2)	Relational and object-oriented database concepts, PostgreSQL data types, index types, version changes. CPU, memory, storage, capacity planning, data retention, data archival, data encryption, and data masking
Week 2 (Chapters 3/4/5)	Postgres pre-install tasks, installation and configuration of Postgres Cluster with Red Hat RPM method
Week 3 (Chapters 6/7/8/9)	Relational database management configuration and setup, Windows operating system, and Docker
Week 4 (Chapters 10/11/12)	Postgres schemas, partitioning, data copy procedures and sequences
Week 5 (Chapters 13/14/15)	Backup and recovery, database upgrade and replication setup
Week 6 (Chapters 16/17)	Tablespaces, MVCC, and LAB

Disclaimer

The references in this book are based on PostgreSQL, Amazon, Azure, and Red Hat software, which is developed by several thousand people. Please refer to vendor documentation for the correct syntax for each release. I have tested all scripts in my personal AWS and Azure account for PostgreSQL versions 11-16. You can practice all database tasks and scenarios on your personal cloud with AMI for your personal learning and understanding. Thoroughly test all scripts before deploying in your environment.

CHAPTER 1

Introduction to PostgreSQL Database Management

1.1 Abstract

PostgreSQL is an open-source database that was originally created by academicians and has been subsequently enhanced by contributions from individuals and institutions, which provide cost-effective solutions for its software maintenance. PostgreSQL is an object-relational database system that was built to support simple to complex data types, and it is a preferred choice on the cloud for its portability and scalability. The PostgreSQL database can be installed on personal computers as well as large scale computers. The open-source PostgreSQL database has no official support from the development community. Corporations lean on several commercial products that provide additional wrapper components for high availability, distributed computing, and backup and recovery, among other extended features.

The original version of the chapter has been revised. A correction to this chapter can be found at https://doi.org/10.1007/979-8-8688-0817-3_18

CHAPTER 1 INTRODUCTION TO POSTGRESQL DATABASE MANAGEMENT

1.2 Objective of Learning

- History of PostgreSQL
- Introduction to relational/object database management
- Major contributors
- PostgreSQL installation on Mac/Windows
- Commercial PostgreSQL products
- Version history

1.3 Introduction

To efficiently manage, keep, and organize the data on computer disks, the relational database management system (RDBMS) plays a crucial role in managing valuable assets of the organization. Using the Structured Query Language (SQL) originally developed by IBM in the early 1970s, later by the Postgres query language (PGSQL), the RDBMS allows for effective data retrieval mechanisms with its robust techniques and methods. SQL follows a set of standards that every database vendor has implemented to develop procedures for security, data access, data insertion, and retrieval mechanisms. SQL is a standard programming language for storing and processing information in a relational database. It is supported by a set of standards (ANSI and ISO).

The PostgreSQL database management software was created by a research team at the University of California, Berkeley, led by Michael Stonebraker during 1986-1994. It has been open sourced for development by the global community. Michael Stonebraker initially developed the QUEL language for the Ingres database, adhering to SQL language functionalities, and later he developed PostgreSQL, which is influenced by the POSTQUEL query language. Subsequently, two Berkely graduate students named Jolly Chen and Andrew Yu added SQL capabilities to PostgreSQL [1]. Andrew Yu and Jolly Chen replaced the POSTQUEL query language interpreter with one for the SQL query language, creating Postgres95.

PostgreSQL is known for its reliability, stability, and scalability. It has gained immense popularity for individual and institutional usage because of its object-relational database model. PostgreSQL is a widely used database in the cloud infrastructure due to its scalability and portability. PostgreSQL continues to be in the realm of the open-source community. The PostgreSQL Global Development Group remains committed to making PostgreSQL available as a free and open-source software in perpetuity. There are no plans to change the PostgreSQL license or release PostgreSQL under a different license.[2].

The latest version 17, of the PostgreSQL cluster caught up with all the major features of commercial databases. It's an alternative to commercial paid subscription databases with "one size that fits all" capabilities. PostgreSQL was the DBMS of the Year 2023[3].

The product has gone through several revisions from Version 0 to Version 17, as of 2024. PostgreSQL 18 is the future development version of PostgreSQL, likely to be released in late 2025. The earliest official supported version is 12; version 11 and earlier are at the end of life.

1.3.1 PostgreSQL Cluster Origin

The PostgreSQL database code was originally written in the C language on the Unix operating system. Later it was written in the world's most open-source operating system, Linux. Figure 1-1 exhibits the outline of the evolution of PostgreSQL database.

CHAPTER 1   INTRODUCTION TO POSTGRESQL DATABASE MANAGEMENT

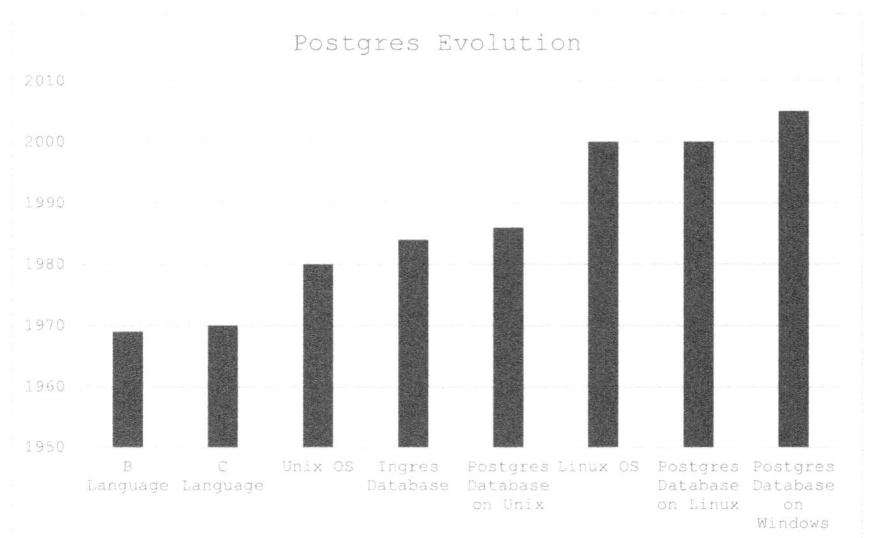

Figure 1-1. *Evolution of PostgreSQL in the Linux environment*

There are several milestones in the evolution of the PostgreSQL cluster. The major milestones are as follows:

1. Creation of PostgreSQL Cluster on Unix in 1985
2. Creation of PostgreSQL Cluster on Linux in 2000
3. Creation of PostgreSQL on Windows in 2005

PostgreSQL complies to the Atomic, Consistency, Isolation and Durability (ACID) properties of the database management system to support multiple version concurrency (MVCC) procedures which are managed by the Postmaster process.

With each release, several bugs were fixed. PostgreSQL conforms to the SQL standard ISO/IEC 9075. As of version 16 (released in September 2023), PostgreSQL conforms to at least 170 of the 179 mandatory features for SQL:2023 Core conformance. As of this writing, no relational database meets full conformance with this standard [4]. PostgreSQL is a client-server architecture where clients send requests to the server.

CHAPTER 1 INTRODUCTION TO POSTGRESQL DATABASE MANAGEMENT

The details of the user request and response details are conceptually illustrated in Figure 1-2. After the background process receives the request from the user processes, the first task is to parse the query to confirm to SQL standards, followed by validating the database tables and column access, which creates an optimal plan to access the data. If the requested data is present in the shared buffers, data is returned to the user process for the select request. For update, delete or insert requests, the committed data is updated in the shared buffer, which generates entries in the log buffer, which are written to the disk by the log write process. At frequent intervals, the checkpoint process writes the modified data in the shared buffer to disk by the db writer process. You have to configure database parameters to optimize the checkpoint process and background process, which are covered in subsequent chapters. The client PostgreSQL library libpq communicates with the PostgreSQL cluster to manage connectivity, SQL command execution, and error handling procedures. The major protocols of libpq are as follows:

1. Establishing connections

2. Submitting SQL statements

3. Retrieving the data from the PostgreSQL server

4. Error handling

5. Transaction management

CHAPTER 1 INTRODUCTION TO POSTGRESQL DATABASE MANAGEMENT

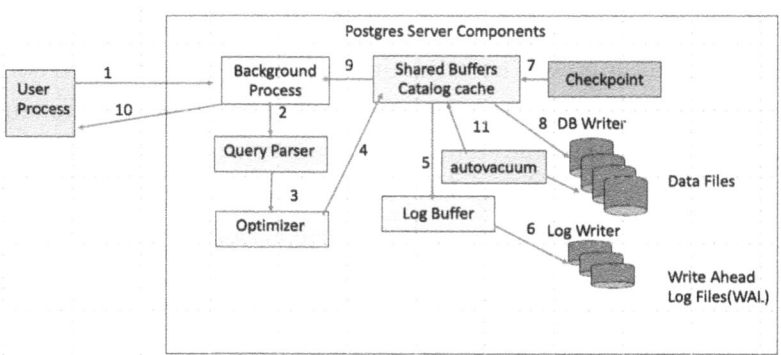

Figure 1-2. *PostgreSQL server architecture*

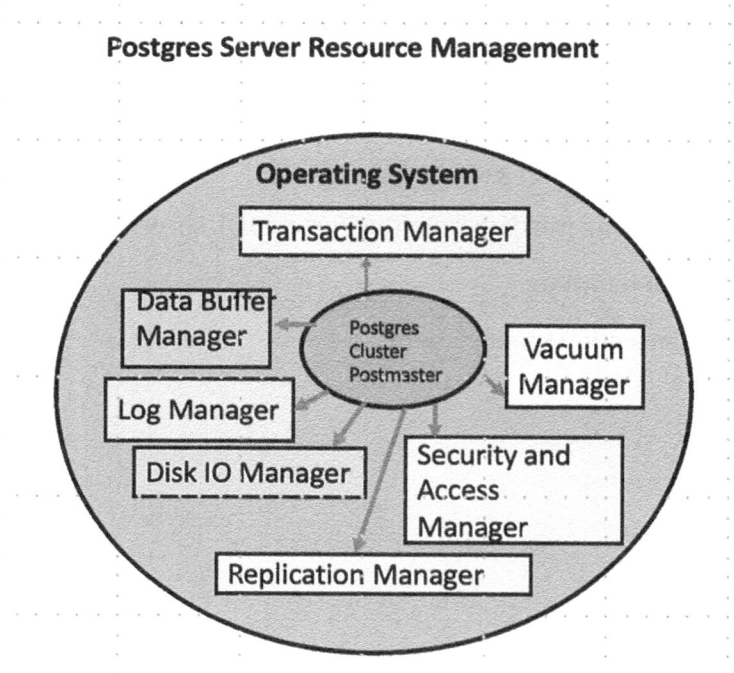

Figure 1-3. *PostgreSQL Cluster resource managers*

All the database background tasks are performed by the PostgreSQL Postmaster process.

The PostgreSQL server background tasks are: security and access manager, transaction processing manager, locking manager, query processing manager, I/O storage manager, write ahead log (WAL) manager, vacuum, and free space manager. See Figure 1-3.

The security of the database is performed in two steps: authentication, where user credentials are validated, and authorization, where user grants and access on the database objects such as tables are validated. The transaction manager confirms ACID properties. These are explained as follows: atomic (every transaction is either committed or aborted), consistent (the state of the database is consistent between transitions), isolation (each transaction is isolated from other sessions), and durability (all committed transactions are recovered). The MVCC (multi-version concurrency control) ensure the data consistency during the transactions. There is a dedicated chapter in the book dedicated to MVCC.

With shared locks, row level locks, and exclusive locks, PostgreSQL ensures concurrent user access to the database. PostgreSQL keeps data in the shared buffers to cache the data read from the disk using Least Recently Used (LRU). The cache reduces the disk access for the SQL requests. Vacuum is an important process to reclaim the space after a delete or update to the data. You will learn the vacuum simulation process in a subsequent chapter.

1.3.2 PostgreSQL Server Operating System Resources

The PostgreSQL server manages the operating system allocation of memory for the database, which includes shared buffers, temporary buffers, WAL buffers, work memory buffers, database cache size, and auto vacuum memory. To manage different database tasks, multiple processes

CHAPTER 1 INTRODUCTION TO POSTGRESQL DATABASE MANAGEMENT

are spawned for writing data to disk after a checkpoint which makes permanent changes, logs writer data to disk for committed transactions, and auto vacuums for garbage collection of dead tuples. PostgreSQL creates a data directory to store all database files including configuration files. The base directory stores database data files for all tables.

As shown in Figure 1-4, the PostgreSQL server is made up of a data directory to store database data, OS processes to perform database backend tasks, and OS memory to retrieve the query results to user sessions. The PostgreSQL database content is stored in the /base directory.

Database data can be logically separated by tablespaces for data and an index to store data on different storage layers for increased throughput.

Postgres Cluster Linux Operating System Resources

Database Memory	OS Process	data directory	
		/base	/pg_tblsp
Auto Vacuum Memory	auto Vacuum Launcher	current_logfiles	/pg_twophase
Effective Cache Size	background writer	/log	/ PG_VERSION
Maintenance Work Mem	checkpointer	/global	/pg_wal
Shared Buffers	logical replication launcher	/log	/pg_xact
Temp Buffers	logger	/pg_commit_ts	/postgresql.auto.conf
WAL Buffers	stats collector	/pg_dyn_shm	/postgres.conf
Work Memory	WAL writer	pg_hba.conf	/postmaster.opts
		pg_ident.conf	/postmaster.pid
		/pg_logical	
		/pg_multixact	
		/pg_notify	
		/pg_replslot	
		/pg_serial	
		/pg_snapshots	
		/pg_stat	
		/ pg_stat_tmp	
		/pg_subtran	

Figure 1-4. Postgres cluster operating system resources

Postgres Tablespaces

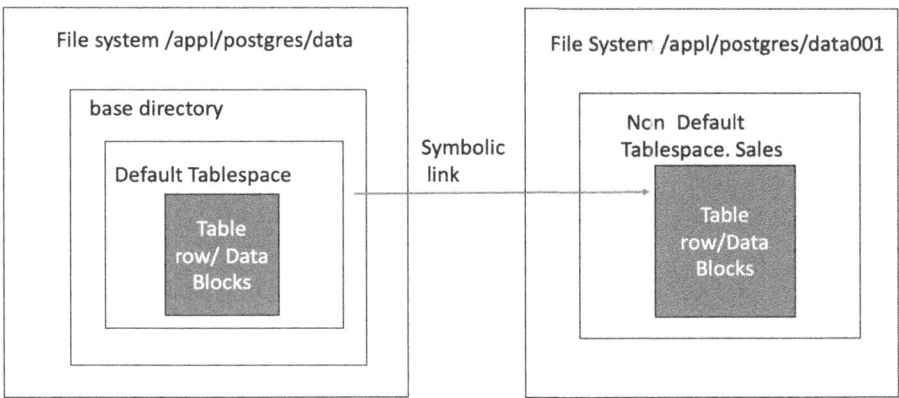

Figure 1-5. *PostgreSQL default and non default data tablespaces*

The database table data resides in the data directory, in default and non-default locations. For non-default tablespace, a symbolic link is created, which is used during creation of the tablespace. The details are illustrated in Figure 1-5.

1.3.3 Major Features of PostgreSQL

- It's an object relational database with support for many data types. It enforces data integrity constraints and offers in-built security with robust authentication methods.

- It's ACID compliant with MVCC, transactions, nested transactions (via save points), along with write-ahead logging (WAL) for point-in-time recovery.

CHAPTER 1   INTRODUCTION TO POSTGRESQL DATABASE MANAGEMENT

- It offers extensibility with stored procedures and functions. It offers support of procedural languages such as PL/pgSQL, Perl, Python, and Tcl. It supports Java, JavaScript (V8), R, Lua, and Rust with extensions.

- It offers rich index features such as B-tree, multicolumn, expressions, partial indexes, GiST, SP-Gist, KNN Gist, GIN, BRIN, covering indexes, bloom filters, and table partitioning with Hash, Range and List methods with sub partitions. It offers remote database and table access with functions and utilities. It provides a rich set of utilities for data masking and data encryption methods.

- It offers parallel processing with advanced optimization features.

1.3.4 Major Contributors to PostgreSQL Open-Source Software

Table 1-1 lists the major contributors of PostgreSQL until 2010. Subsequent development until 2023 was contributed by additional developers.

CHAPTER 1   INTRODUCTION TO POSTGRESQL DATABASE MANAGEMENT

Table 1-1. *Major Contributors to PostgreSQL*

Contributor	Date	Name	Notes
Michael Stonebreaker (US)	1977-1985	INGRES	First commercially successful relational database servers by Ingress Corp.
Michael Stonebreaker (US)	1986-1994	PostgreSQL1.0	Initial release of Postgres
Andrew Yu, Jolly Chen (US)	1995	Postgres 95	First release 0.01
Andrew Yu, Jolly Chen (US)	1995	PostgreSQL	1.0
Andrew Yu, Jolly Chen (US)	1997	PostgreSQL	Posgres95 renamed to PostgreSQL
J.M. D'Arcy (Canada)	1996-2000	PostgreSQL	TCL interface, PyGreSQL and the INET type
Jan Wieck	1996-2000	PostgreSQL	PL/Tcl, TOAST, NUMERIC data type
Massimo Dal Zotto (Italy)	1998-2000	PostgreSQL	Locking code
Peter Eisentraunt (Sweden)	1998-2000	PostgreSQL	Major contributor to psql
Oliver Elphick (UK)	1998-2000	PostgreSQL	PostgreSQL for Debian Linux
Daniel Horak (Czechoslovakia)	1998-2000	PostgreSQL	WinNT post or PostgreSQL
Inoue Hiroshi (Japan)	1998-2000	PostgreSQL	Improved Btree index access
Dr. Andrew Martin (UK)	1998-2000	PostgreSQL	Linux support
Peter Mount (UK)	1998-2000	PostgreSQL	Java, JDBC interface
Byron Nikolaidis (US)	1998-2000	PostgreSQL	ODBC interface for windows
Laman Owen (US)	1998-2000	PostgreSQL	RPM Package
Goran Thyni (Sweden)	1998-2000	PostgreSQL	Unix Socket code
Jan Wieck	2000-2010	PostgreSQL	Core team member

CHAPTER 1   INTRODUCTION TO POSTGRESQL DATABASE MANAGEMENT

Steering Committee: Bruce Momjian (US) from 1998-till now. He currently works for Enterprise Database (EDB).

1.3.5 Introduction to Database Management System

IBM researcher E. F. Codd in 1970 proposed the relational database system concept, using set theory examples to illustrate the relations between entities or things of interest to business that are related to each other. The entities have attributes such as customer `first name`, `last name`, and `date of birth`. The entities such as `customer` and `order` are related or linked by a customer placing one or many orders. The RDBMS is all about joining data among tables that are related to one another. The entities are logical names that are translated into tables and attributes into columns or fields in the database, where business transaction-related data is stored as a row or record in the table in the form of columns or fields. The user data is stored in the computer as a file or part of a file in the computer disk, logically organized as a record in the table. Each record is uniquely identified by a primary key, which serves as a foreign key in the child table if there is a join between two tables. A foreign key column in a child table points to the primary key column in the parent table. Chen incorporated a diagrammatic representation of the relations between tables with the entity relationship diagram (ERD) concept. With ERD, you can visualize the relationship between hundreds of entities or tables in the database.

SQL is a standardized language for interacting with relational databases. PostgreSQL supports a variant of SQL relational object-oriented database methods.

The SQL language provides three methods to work with databases:

1. a data definition language (DDL) which provides the syntax to create database objects such as tables, indexes, and views,

2. a data manipulation language (DML) which provides syntax to select, insert, update, and delete the data, and

3. a data control language (DCL) where grants on the database objects are granted.

The database objects are tables, indexes, and procedures. PostgreSQL implements SQL with psql and PL/pgSQL for procedural language, with which you can create reusable programs with variable interfaces. Like a spreadsheet, the table has rows and columns, where one row is translated into a record in the database. You have to define a data type when designing a table for its columns, to store specific type of data. PostgreSQL provides several data types. The most used ones are varchar to store string values plus date and timestamp to store data values and integer to store numeric values. Defining a new table is the fundamental aspect of database management as the table definition dictates how data is stored and organized in the database.

You can obtain the table create syntax from the psql help program as well as from the official documentation. Listing 1-1 shows the code to create a table.

Listing 1-1. Create Table DDL

```
# \help create table
Command:     CREATE TABLE
Description: define a new table
Syntax:
CREATE [ [ GLOBAL | LOCAL ] { TEMPORARY | TEMP } | UNLOGGED ]
TABLE [ IF NOT EXISTS ] table_name ( [
  { column_name data_type [ COMPRESSION compression_method ]
  [ COLLATE collation ] [ column_constraint [ ... ] ]
    | table_constraint
```

| LIKE source_table [like_option ...] }
    [, ...]
])
URL: https://www.PostgreSQL.org/docs/14/sql-createtable.html

Databases employ constraints to enforce data quality. The constraints are not null, null, unique check and referential integrity. The primary key is always defined as a not null constraint. In the null constraint, if data is not available at the time of insert, it will be updated when correct data is available. For instance, you may update the email address of a customer when it is available in the column defined with a null constraint. The unique constraint enforces distinct values; however, it allows only one null constraint. The check constraint enforces a specific value in a column. See Listing 1-2.

Listing 1-2. Data Insertion Statement

```
postgres=# create table t1(id integer not null, name
varchar(30) unique,address varchar(30));
CREATE TABLE
postgres=# insert into t1 values(1,'john','LA');
INSERT 0 1
postgres=# insert into t1 values(2,'','LA');
INSERT 0 1
postgres=# insert into t1 values(3,'','');
ERROR:  duplicate key value violates unique constraint "t1_name_key"
DETAIL:  Key (name)=() already exists.
```

In Listing 1-2, a table is created along with columns with data types and the data is inserted into the first two rows as per constraint rules, whereas the third row throws an error as you can't have more than one null value for a unique constraint.

The data is stored optimally on the disk with a database modeling technique called *normalization*. Normalization is a database design principle that optimizes the data consistency and data redundancy which facilitate the efficient data storage in the database.

The normalization defines the data storage based on the first normal form (1NF), second normal form (2NF), third normal form (3NF), BCNF, fourth normal form (4NF), and fifth normal form (5NF).

First Normal Form

In the 1NF, data is organized efficiently in the table such that there are no multiple values for columns or repeating groups where the column value is atomic, which is indivisible. The concept of atomic is fundamental for database design, in which the data in the column can't be further divided into multiple parts. For instance, the column of the telephone number can have only one value. Similarly, the column of date of birth or death should have only one value. If you have multiple values for one column, it violates the design principle for 1NF.

Considering the following example of data, the DOB values violate the 1NF due repeating groups as you can't have multiple dates of births for the same person:

```
CustId   FirstName   LastName   DOB
1.       John        Bogus.     01/30/1980,01/31/1980,01/31/1981
```

Figure 1-6 shows the example of data stored in first normal form, where data is organized into rows and columns.

CustId	FirstName	LastName	DOB	SSN	VehID	VIN	Model	AddId	Line1	Line2	city	State	Zip code
1	John	Bogus	10/10/1972	435-230-6512	1	1GMDX03E8VD266902	Acura	1	2121 Torrance Blvd #298		Torrance	CA	90054

Figure 1-6. *First normal form*

CHAPTER 1   INTRODUCTION TO POSTGRESQL DATABASE MANAGEMENT

The first normal form has insert, update, and delete irregularities, which are called anomalies. If a customer buys another vehicle, you have duplicate entries for address and customer details. If you update customer address, you have duplicate entries in vehicle and address details. If you delete a particular customer, the vehicle data along with the address is gone from the database.

Note XML and JSON documents do not violate 1NF as the value is considered atomic.

Second Normal Form

In the second normal form data design, the data is already in 1NF without any repeating groups, and each row is identified by a primary key, which uniquely identifies the data in the row. In the 2NF, not all columns depend on the primary key alone. Some of the column values are derived other than the primary key. In Figure 1-7, the value of address is derived from address id, rather than from the primary key.

Figure 1-7 shows data stored in 2NF where CustID is the primary key for the customer address and customer vehicle tables.

CustId	FirstName	LastName	DOB	SSN	AddId	Line1	Line2	City	State	Zip Code
1	John	Bogus	10/10/1972	435-230-6512	1	#298	2121 Torrance Blvd	Torrance	CA	90054

Figure 1-7. *Customer address table*

CustId	FirstName	LastName	DOB	SSN	VehiID	VIN	Make	Model
1	John	Bogus	10/10/1972	435-230-6512	1	1GMDX03E8VD266902	Honda	Acura

Figure 1-8. *Customer vehicle table*

In Figure 1-8, the values of VIN, Make, and Model are derived from the vehicle id and not from the customer id, although it is a primary key. It is worth noting the concept of functional dependency in the context of 2NF. The first name, last name, and date of birth are functionally dependent on the customer id, whereas the VIN, make, and model are functionally dependent on the vehicle id. The database design does not allow multiple functional dependencies in a single record. The second normal form also suffers from insert, update, and delete anomalies. If you insert or update the customer table, you have to insert null or empty values for the vehicle. If you delete the customer, the vehicle information is gone, and if you delete vehicle information, the customer information is gone.

Third Normal Form

The table in 3NF already confirms 1NF and 2NF, where all functionally dependent relations are resolved. In the third normal form, customer, vehicle and address are separate tables, as dependencies are resolved among the columns. In the third normal form, "all columns or non-key attributes are non-transitively dependent on the primary key, where transitive dependency is resolved between columns." It is worth noticing the transitive dependency definition in the context of 3NF. For instance, if A -> B and B -> C, then A -> C, so there is transitive dependency between A and C, which is not allowed in the 3NF design. Thus, the value of the table is based on one and only primary key, without any dependencies between columns In 3NF, each row is uniquely identified by primary key. Figure 1-9 is an example of a transitive relationships, where some of the non-key attributes are dependent on another non-key attribute.

CHAPTER 1   INTRODUCTION TO POSTGRESQL DATABASE MANAGEMENT

Transitive Dependency

User Id -> Veh Id -> Vin   **Vehicle Dependence on Non-Key**

Key	Non Key	Non Key	Non Key	Non Key	Non Key	Non Key	Non Key	Non Key
User Id PK	First Name	Last Name	DOB	Email	Veh ID	VIN	Make	Model
1	John	Bogus	12-12-1980	user@abc	1	J8977	Toyota	Prius

Figure 1-9. Transitive dependency example

The following are the resolved tables from 2NF into 3NF.
Customer entity (Figure 1-10)

CustId	FirstName	LastName	DOB	SSN
1	John	Bogus	10/10/1972	435-230-6512

Figure 1-10. Third normal form

Vehicle entity (Figure 1-11)

VehID	VIN	Make	Model
1	1GMDX03E8VD266902	Honda	Acura

Figure 1-11. Third normal form

Address entity (Figure 1-12)

AddId	Street1	Street2	city	State	Zip code
1	2121 Torrance Blvd	#298	Torrance	CA	90054

Figure 1-12. Third normal form

> **Note** It is only of academic interest to design a database beyond the third normal form. Higher normal forms require too many tables and relations between and the benefit of normalization is lessened overall.

1.3.6 Relational Data Model

Chen's diagrammatic representation of relationships between entities, which are things of interest to a business, simplifies the organization of data flow between participating entities, allowing for querying complex SQL statements to join data between tables. Business rules such as one-to-one and one-to-many relationships organize data efficiently in the database for effective query retrieval. Some relationships are mandatory; for instance, in a customer order, the customer's name is mandatory along with the product name. Efficient database design allows for effective data retrieval, preventing issues with self-joins or recursive relationships. You can place subject area details logically in the data model for clarity of data flow. See Figure 1-13.

CHAPTER 1 INTRODUCTION TO POSTGRESQL DATABASE MANAGEMENT

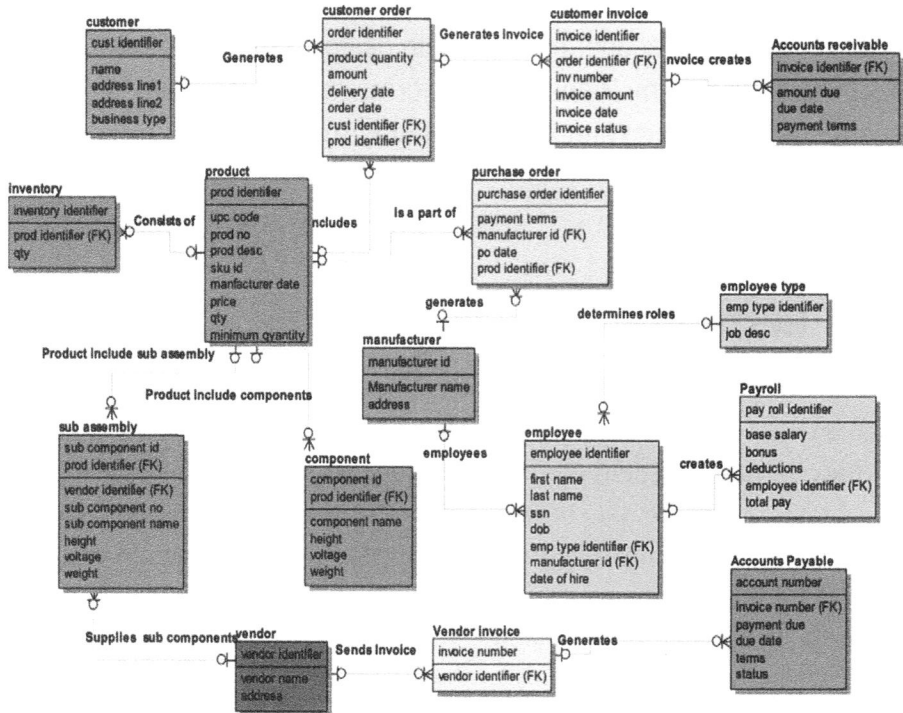

Figure 1-13. *Relational data model*

The above data model is enforced by the following business rules:

1. Customers can place one or many orders.

2. The order consists of one or many products, and this generates an invoice.

3. The product is based on inventory, sub assembly, part components, and part of a purchase order.

4. The manufacturer generates purchase orders managed by employees. The customer is the primary key, which is a foreign key in a customer order entity.

Ralph Kimble, a student from Stanford University, proposed the star schema as a design approach for database tables in summary management, specifically for the purpose of business reporting.

1.3.7 Star Schema

The star schema derives its name from the fact that the table is in the center, surrounded by dimensions like radiating stars. In dimensional modeling, dimensions are considered as parent entities, and facts are child entities derived from the values of dimensions. The star schema is designed based on the granularity of the fact table, which determines the level of data in the table, such as daily, weekly, monthly, or quarterly. This granularity allows for roll-up and drill-down reporting purposes. Dimensions in the star schema can have hierarchies, such as territory, region, and country. The fact table typically includes a date dimension, allowing for slicing and dicing of data based on the date dimension.

The star schema is based on facts and dimensions, where dimensions are referred to as descriptions of business events such as when, who, where, and how sales took place. The star schema represents an aggregation of data, which provides an efficient way to store and retrieve information for obtaining summary information.

The data warehousing concept is implemented by a PostgreSQL database by partitioning of data by date range, with indexing methods such as B-tree, hash, and Generalized Inverted Index (GIN), summary data with materialized views, and several analytical functions, with parallel query capabilities. With these features, PostgreSQL effectively manages large data sets in ranges of multi-terabytes in volumes.

CHAPTER 1   INTRODUCTION TO POSTGRESQL DATABASE MANAGEMENT

Star Schema Model

The product inventory details are illustrated by the star schema in Figure 1-14. It is called the star schema because of the star shape of the model with facts and dimensions. As facts are related to historical information, the past details about available quantity of product by date, purchase by customer business type, customer demographics, and vendor type are recorded in the fact table.

If you examine the diagram of the star schema in Figure 1-14, the primary key of the fact table, which is made up of foreign keys of dimensions. Facts are based on dimensions, which are parent to the fact table.

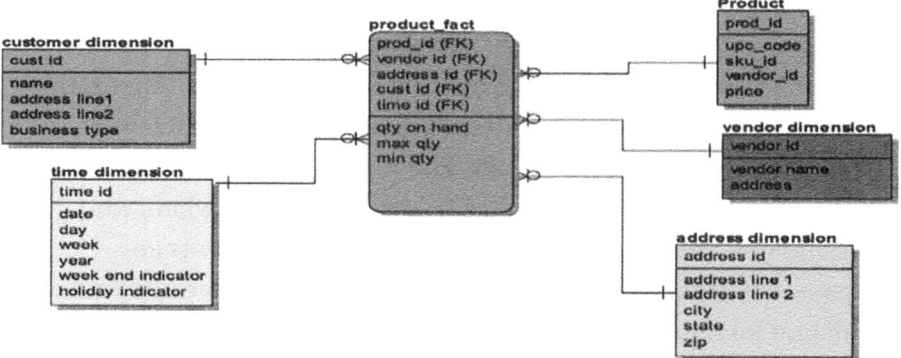

Figure 1-14. Star schema

When loading data into the fact table, the first step is to load data into dimension tables, followed by loading into the fact table. Ralph Kimball introduced the concept of slowly changing dimensions (SCD), which manages the changes to the dimension. For instance, if a customer moved from New York to California, the slowly changing dimensions records the customer's old and new address. There are five types of slowly changing dimensions:

Type 1: In this type, the old data is overwritten.

Type 2: In this type, both the new and old records are kept.

Type 3: In this type, a new column is added to the row.

Type 4: In this type, a new table is created to capture new records using a database trigger or snapshot mechanism.

Type 5: This type includes both type 1 and type 2, where the old record is overwritten along with tracking historical data by creating new tables.

1.3.8 Object Relational Model

Since you now understand the RDMS in general, you are ready to understand the object relational model of PostgreSQL. Figure 1-15 shows the object-oriented model of PostgreSQL.

CHAPTER 1 INTRODUCTION TO POSTGRESQL DATABASE MANAGEMENT

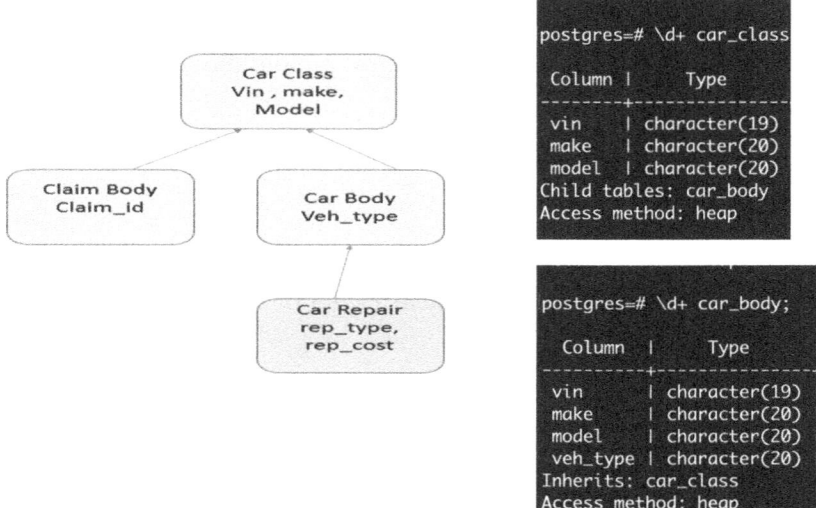

Figure 1-15. Object-relational model

In the given example, car_class is a parent class, and claim, body, and repair are child classes that inherit from car_class. This means that the child classes inherit the attributes and behaviors defined in the parent class. With the \d+ command on the table, you can identify the parent child class definitions to confirm the object-oriented methodology of PostgreSQL.

Database. Object relational DDL:

```
create table car_class (vin char(19), make char(20), model char(20));
create table car_body (veh_type char(20)) INHERITS (car_class);
```

Object-relational DML:

```
insert into car_class values ('1GMDX03E8VD266902', 'Honda', 'Accord');
```

CHAPTER 1 INTRODUCTION TO POSTGRESQL DATABASE MANAGEMENT

This command inserts a row into the car_class table with specific values for the vin, make, and model columns.

```
insert into car_body values ('1 KMHD25LE1DU04202', 'Honda', 'Accord', 'Compact');
```

This command inserts a row into the car_body table, which inherits the columns from the car_class table and adds the veh_type column specific to the car_body table.

Listing 1-3 shows the SQL execution details.

Listing 1-3. Data Insertion to Object Relational Tables

```
postgres=# create table car_class (vin char(19), make char(20), model char(20));
create table car_body (veh_type char(20)) INHERITS (car_class);
CREATE TABLE
CREATE TABLE
postgres=# insert into car_class values ('1GMDX03E8VD266902', 'Honda', 'Accord');
INSERT 0 1
postgres=# insert into car_body values ('1 KMHD25LE1DU04202', 'Honda', 'Accord', 'Compact');
INSERT 0 1
postgres=# select * from car_class;
        vin         |         make         |     model
--------------------+----------------------+-------------
 1GMDX03E8VD266902  | Honda                | Accord
 1 KMHD25LE1DU04202 | Honda                | Accord
(2 rows)
```

If you examine the above listing, the class call has values from car_body, without any join between these two tables, due to the properties of inheritance.

1.3.9 Install PostgreSQL Cluster on MAC

As Macs are based on Unix, you can work with the development environment on a local personal PC to work with command line tools for scripting and code development, which makes it easier to manage cloud-based PostgreSQL. Furthermore, it is easy and simple to connect to a Linux host with the ssh command.

To install a PostgreSQL cluster on a Mac, follow two steps:

1. Install the brew Mac OS package installer.
2. Install the PostgreSQL cluster.

Install brew on a Mac

If not already installed, install brew package manager on a Mac. curl is a program to download data from the Internet. Run the following command to install brew:

```
/bin/bash -c "$(curl -fsSL https://raw.githubusercontent.com/Homebrew/install/HEAD/install.sh)".
```

Install PostgreSQL Software

The brew executables are installed in the directory /opt/homebrew/bin. Set the environment with the following command and validate the brew with the command which brew:

```
$echo "export PATH=$PATH:/opt/homebrew/bin" >> .bashrc
$source .bashrc
$which brew
/opt/homebrew/bin/brew
```

After validating the brew program, install latest version of PostgreSQL with the command

`brew install postgresql@16.`

The PostgreSQL binaries are installed in the path /opt/homebrew/opt/postgresql@16/bin. Set the path of PostgreSQL with the command

`echo "export PATH=$PATH:/opt/homebrew/opt/postgresql@16/bin" >> .bashrc`

source .bashrc . Validate the psql program with the which command:

```
which psql
/opt/homebrew/opt/postgresql@16/bin/psql
```

The final step is to start the PostgreSQL with the command `brew services start postgresql@16.`

Download the script to install PostgreSQL Cluster on a Mac, which runs on the Linux OS from

https://docs.google.com/document/d/1aH6K2FP_1ANQdeW492tja2JLgoJhcna1/edit?usp=sharing&ouid=117618855868897795502&rtpof=true&sd=true.

The video reference for installing PostgreSQL on MAC is at

https://us02web.zoom.us/rec/share/kRxi9NJP84q9qP3uWwUo8BmQ5aA6Ln4NC8EYfmC9mCOioJ1bXlox01T5OJH3mDkw.KAdN_dfOdUN4BcCO.

Connect to a PostgreSQL Database

PostgreSQL uses a client server architecture where client computers request data from the server computer. psql is a client program that requests data from the server either from local computers or from remote computers. You can also connect to PostgreSQL with several tools, which are covered in Chapter 5. The psql program has -h for host and -d for

CHAPTER 1 INTRODUCTION TO POSTGRESQL DATABASE MANAGEMENT

database and -U as username as arguments; you can connect to a local or remote host. See Listing 1-4.

Listing 1-4. psql Connection to a Mac Local Host

```
$psql -d postgres
psql (14.11 (Homebrew))
Type "help" for help.
postgres=#
```

When you connect to PostgreSQL as database root user, you will get the # prompt at the command line. When you connect as a non-Administrator user, you get the $ prompt.

The database is a subject area of business to create database objects in the PostgreSQL cluster.

DDL and DML Scripts

As a DBA, after the installation of the PostgreSQL cluster, the next task is to create a database(s) and deploy scripts provided by the Application Team.

Create a Database

`create database` is a simple command which takes the database as an argument. The following is the syntax to create the database named `sales`:

```
postgres=# create database sales;
postgres=# \c sales
You are now connected to database "sales" as user "venkat"
```

Deploy Scripts

You can deploy scripts in three methods:

1. Use the psql program from OS with the -c command to execute the script.

28

CHAPTER 1 INTRODUCTION TO POSTGRESQL DATABASE MANAGEMENT

2. Connect to psql and execute the script.

3. Run the DDL command from psql.

Refer to Chapter 10 for detailed notes on the usage of the psql program.

Create a file called cr.sql and add the create table DDL details in the contents. Download cr.sql from the link provided and execute the script.

```
1. psql -d sales -c "\i cr.sql" .
2. psql -d sales
 sales=# \i cr.sql
3. psql -d sales
sales=#
CREATE TABLE customer (
        cust_id                 serial NOT NULL,
        name                    VARCHAR(20) NULL,
        address_line1           VARCHAR(20) NULL,
        address_line2           CHAR(18) NULL,
        business_type           VARCHAR(20) NULL,
        username                varchar(30) default user
);
ALTER TABLE customer ADD CONSTRAINT cust_id  PRIMARY KEY
(cust_id) ;
CREATE TABLE customer_order (
        ord_id                  serial NOT NULL,
        prod_qty                INTEGER NULL,
        amount                  INTEGER NULL,
        delivery_date           DATE NULL,
        order_date              DATE NULL,
        cust_id                 INTEGER NULL,
        prod_id                 INTEGER NULL,
        upc_code                INTEGER NULL
);
```

```
ALTER TABLE customer_order ADD CONSTRAINT pk_cust_ord_id
PRIMARY KEY (ord_id) ;
ALTER TABLE customer_order ADD CONSTRAINT fk_customer_order_
customer
FOREIGN KEY (cust_id)
REFERENCES customer (cust_id);
```

You can download the cr.sql script from https://docs.google.com/document/d/1iixvz_OSigmIHFCtO29STYj1lsD14OBC/edit?usp=sharing&ouid=117618855868897795502&rtpof=true&sd=true.

After the completion of the requirement analysis, the final phase is to deploy the business requirements into database objects. The database objects are tables, indexes, triggers, and constraints.

After completion of testing, you can stop the PostgreSQL Services on a Mac with the command `brew services stop postgresql`.

Task 2: Deploy the above script.

1.3.10 PostgreSQL Cluster Install on a Windows PC

To install a PostgreSQL cluster on Windows, download the software from the edb site, extract the software, and run the installer in unattended mode for the default installation.

Download Software

Download the software from www.enterprisedb.com/downloads/PostgreSQL-PostgreSQL-downloads.

Execute Binaries

Download Windows x86-64 and execute the binaries to begin installing PostgreSQL on a Windows PC. See Figure 1-16.

CHAPTER 1   INTRODUCTION TO POSTGRESQL DATABASE MANAGEMENT

PostgreSQL Version	Linux x86-64	Linux x86-32	Mac OS X	Windows x86-64
16.2	postgresql.org	postgresql.org	⬇	⬇

Figure 1-16. PostgreSQL Windows software

Install PostgreSQL Software

For enterprise-level installations of the PostgreSQL client on multiple Windows machines, using unattended mode with a batch file is the preferred method for mass deployments. This approach automates the installation process, ensuring consistency and reducing manual effort across multiple systems, which can be a part of Windows image.

Figure 1-17 shows the following command:

```
c:\Users\pvadl\Downloads\PostgreSQL-16.2-1-windows-x64.exe
--mode unattended  --superpassword MyStrongP8
```

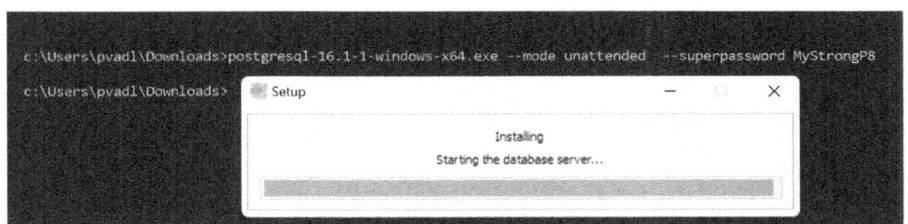

Figure 1-17. PostgreSQL install on Windows

The default installation installs PostgreSQL Server, pgAdmin, Stack Builder, and command line tools. You will learn pgAdmin in a later chapter.

CHAPTER 1   INTRODUCTION TO POSTGRESQL DATABASE MANAGEMENT

Set PATH in Windows

The installer will not set the PATH environment variable for the psql program. After install, set the PATH permanently in Windows OS with the `setx` command. With the `where` command you can check the path of the psql program. See Figure 1-18.

```
c:\>setx PATH "%PATH%;C:\Program Files\PostgreSQL\16\bin" /M

SUCCESS: Specified value was saved.

c:\>where psql
C:\Program Files\PostgreSQL\16\bin\psql.exe

c:\>
```

Figure 1-18. *Setting PATH for PostgreSQL executables*

SetX has three ways of working:

Syntax 1:

SETX [/S system [/U [domain\]user [/P [password]]]] var value [/M]

Syntax 2:

SETX [/S system [/U [domain\]user [/P [password]]]] var /K regpath [/M]

Syntax 3:

SETX [/S system [/U [domain\]user [/P [password]]]]
/F file {var {/A x,y | /R x,y string}[/M] | /X} [/D delimiters]

After install, connect to the PostgreSQL cluster by providing a database root user postgres password.

```
psql -U postgres
Password for user postgres:
postgres=#
```

You may also refer to absolute PATH of the psql program with the command C:\Program Files\PostgreSQL\16\bin\psql.

1.3.11 PostgreSQL Commercial Products

Within corporations, applications are classified into three tiers: Tier 1, Tier 2, and Tier 3. Tier 1 applications are of critical importance to the business, to the extent that the disruption or failure of the PostgreSQL database supporting these applications could lead to a grinding halt or significant impact on production assembly lines. Due to this criticality of database availability, the following are the major commercial vendors providing support for PostgreSQL software on a 7/24 support model.

The Major PostgreSQL Commercial Product Vendors

Enterprise Database (EDB): EDB has provided additional tools that extend PostgreSQL for enterprise workloads since 2004. It is responsible for managing documentation and the PostgreSQL open-source software repository; it also developed installers for installation of PostgreSQL software. EDB serves more than 1,500 customers, including leading financial services, government, media, and communications and information technology organizations. The URL source is https://en.wikipedia.org/wiki/EnterpriseDB.

Amazon Redshift: Amazon Redshift Database is created on version 8.0.2 of PostgreSQL database in Amazon Web Services. Redshift is a columnar database, which adds several additional features and functionality to PostgreSQL software. Amazon Redshift is based on PostgreSQL. "Amazon Redshift and PostgreSQL have several especially important differences that you must be aware of as you design and develop your data warehouse applications;" see `https://docs.aws.amazon.com/redshift/latest/dg/c_redshift-and-PostgreSQL-sql.html`.

Heroku PostgreSQL: Heroku PostgreSQL is a managed database service provider used in Salesforce applications. Heroku PostgreSQL delivers the world's most advanced open-source database as a trusted, secure, and scalable service that is optimized for developers. Go to `www.heroku.com/PostgreSQL` for more information.

Crunchy Data: Crunchy Data has several extensions to PostgreSQL with its operator feature for HA, backup and recovery, performance tuning, connection pooling, and DR in Kubernetes and Container environments. You can get a full-service scripted solution for deploying production PostgreSQL including backups, high availability, monitoring, disaster recovery, connection scaling, and more from the experts at Crunchy Data; see `www.crunchydata.com/`.

Amazon Aurora: Amazon Aurora provides compatibility with PostgreSQL or MySQL. It provides built-in security, continuous backups, serverless computer, up to 15 read replicas, and automated multi-region replication and integrations with other AWS services. Go to `https://aws.amazon.com/rds/aurora/` for more information.

Microsoft: Microsoft Azure Web Services provides PostgreSQL with Flexible Server Architecture with enhanced performance tuning optimization features, extending the core server capabilities. With Cosmos DB for PostgreSQL, Microsoft added high availability and distributed computing for PostgreSQL databases. The additional features are: high availability across Availability Zones (AZ), scaling up/down CPU and storage resources, encryption at rest and private endpoints; see `https://azure.microsoft.com/en-us/products/cosmos-db`.

CHAPTER 1   INTRODUCTION TO POSTGRESQL DATABASE MANAGEMENT

Percona: Percona offers support, consulting, training, and help to host managed services on the cloud for PostgreSQL open-source databases. The Percona support extends to Tier 1, Tier 2, and Tier 3 application service level agreements. Performance tuning and query optimization is its core competency for managing a fleet of PostgreSQL servers on the cloud. Go to www.percona.com/PostgreSQL/support-and-services.

The open-source PostgreSQL software does have some limitations:

> **Incremental database backup and point-in-time recovery**: While PostgreSQL provides full backups, there is no built-in support for incremental backups, which take longer till version 16. Version 17 introduced native support for incremental backups. Furthermore, in PostgreSQL, there is no provision to back up and restore a database with point-in-time capability.
>
> **Official support**: Although the community provides frequent updates and patches, due to lack of official support for patching and bug fixing, organizations are leaning towards managed support with cloud vendors such as AWS or Azure.

One of the key advantages of PostgreSQL is its extensibility to cluster software These extensions are additional modules beyond the core functionality of PostgreSQL.

CHAPTER 1   INTRODUCTION TO POSTGRESQL DATABASE MANAGEMENT

1.3.12 Version Changes

Table 1-2. *PostgreSQL Versions*

PostgreSQL Version	Release Date	Release Notes
6	1997	Vacuum, explain plan, unique index, order by
6.5	1999	Multi version concurrency control, hot backup of pg_dump, temporary tables
7	2000	Foreign keys, SQL92 join, write-ahead log (WAL), schemas, cursors
8	2005	Microsoft Windows Native Server, two-phase commit, full text search
9	2011-2016	Synchronous replication, foreign tables, foreign tables, PL/Python server-side
10	2017	Logical replication using publish/subscribe, declarative table partitioning
11	2018	Primary key, foreign key, indexes, and triggers on partitioned tables
12	2019	Partitioning performance enhancements, multi-factor authentication, reindex online
13	2020	De-duplication of B-tree index entries, parallelized vacuuming of indexes
14	2021	Stored procedures can now return data via OUT parameters, parallel queries
15	2022	Partitions, parallelism, index and vacuum enhancements, WAL inspect
16	2023	Bidirectional replication, bulk loading, and enhanced security

(continued)

Table 1-2. *(continued)*

PostgreSQL Version	Release Date	Release Notes
17	2024	Incremental backup, improved Query Planning and performance. Expanded SQL/JSON support and Logical Replication Enhancements

https://docs.google.com/document/d/1nSlogN96hTgD2OtZRuOohybdY07tT8RN/edit?usp=sharing&ouid=117618855868897795502&rtpof=true&sd=true

1.4 PostgreSQL Learning Approach

The learning approach of the book is based on hands-on questions on hardware and software cloud self-service providers Amazon Web Services and Microsoft Azure. All the exhibits, examples, and code are based on tested scripts in AWS and Azure Cloud. AWS provides 750 hours of free time to use its products, whereas Azure gives $200 credit towards usage of web services. With these free credits, you should be able to learn PostgreSQL on the cloud with the scripts, examples, and exhibits referenced in this book. In the Appendix of the book, references are provided for commercial paid products.

1.4.1 Keywords

PostgreSQL, contributors, database management, first normal form, second normal form, third normal form, relational data model, star schema, object relational model, commercial products, version changes.

1.4.2 Summary of Learning

In this chapter, you learned about the history of PostgreSQL, major contributors, version changes, server architecture, and data directory details. You got an overview of database management, focusing on important concepts such as normalization and the star schema. You identified methods to normalize data to reduce redundancy, identified facts and dimensions, and reviewed slowly changing dimension details. You worked on the steps to install and configure PostgreSQL in Mac and Windows environments, deployed scripts, and explored object relational database design and data insertion. Additionally, you reviewed the commercial PostgreSQL products in the cloud market such as Amazon Web Services and Azure Web Services.

1.5 Practice Chapter 1

1. Install and configure the brew package on a Mac. Download the script from:
2. Install PostgreSQL cluster software on a Mac.
3. Start PostgreSQL service on a Mac.
4. Configure the shell profile to include PostgreSQL executables.
5. Execute DDL and DML scripts from a psql program.
6. Stop PostgreSQL service on a Mac.
7. Install PostgreSQL on Windows.
8. Deploy scripts from Windows PostgreSQL.
9. Generate DDL statements from the data model defined in section 1.4.

CHAPTER 1 INTRODUCTION TO POSTGRESQL DATABASE MANAGEMENT

1.5.1 Questions Chapter 1

1. What are the commercial versions of PostgreSQL?
2. Who are the major developers of PostgreSQL?
3. What is the latest version of PostgreSQL?
4. Which version of PostgreSQL introduced multi-version concurrency?
5. How do you distinguish between open-source and commercial versions of PostgreSQL?
6. How do you create a table with multiple inheritances in PostgreSQL?
7. In which version was support for Microsoft added?
8. What are the main OS processes for PostgreSQL?
9. What are the contents for the base directory in the PostgreSQL?
10. In which version were foreign keys added?

Answers:

DDL scripts for practice question 9:
https://docs.google.com/document/d/1NCOMZlSQuaKUGIzxx-k-hzjJYK-WiGsl/edit?usp=drive_link&ouid=117618855868897795502&rtpof=true&sd=true

References

1. Momjian, Bruce. *PostgreSQL Introduction and Concepts*. Addison-Wesley, 2001, p. 1.
2. PostgreSQL. "License." www.PostgreSQL.org/about/licence/
3. https://db-engines.com/en/blog_post/106
4. PostgreSQL. "About PostgreSQL." www.PostgreSQL.org/about.

CHAPTER 2

Capacity Planning

2.1 Abstract

DBAs are responsible for recommending the right sizing of PostgreSQL cluster hardware resources, which remains consistent for both virtual machines and physical ones in the cloud database service offerings. The capacity planning initiative involves choosing storage size, CPU, and memory resources. The instance type in the cloud determines the required capacity to stage a PostgreSQL cluster. The number of concurrent connected users, ranging between 50 to 5000 or more, determines the instance type in the cloud. Once storage is allocated, downsizing it is neither easy nor a simple process, as it involves taking a backup, creating a new instance with the desired capacity, and restoring the data, causing an outage to the availability of the critical production environment. Additionally, DBAs are responsible for designing solutions for long-term storage, short-term storage, data archival, and data retention in S3 or in Azure Data Blob storage areas for SOX and legal requirements. Thus, efficient capacity planning is a good practice for the installation of a PostgreSQL cluster on the cloud environment to optimize excessive or insufficient storage.

The original version of the chapter has been revised. A correction to this chapter can be found at https://doi.org/10.1007/979-8-8688-0817-3_18

CHAPTER 2   CAPACITY PLANNING

2.2 Objective of Learning

- Identify suitable computer hardware resources and estimate the required storage for capacity planning
- PostgreSQL on the Amazon/Azure cloud services
- Different PostgreSQL cluster provisioning methods
- PostgreSQL cluster configuration checklist
- Azure S3 and Azure Data Blob

As a PostgreSQL DBA, you will be required to provide computer hardware capacity planning for the installation of PostgreSQL cluster software on EC2 and provisioning RDS or Azure SQL databases. This chapter will prepare you for the above tasks.

2.3 Introduction

As you know, open-source software is the emerging winner in database software usage across the globe. The scope of the book is to provide examples and exhibits from PostgreSQL open-source software installed on the Red Hat Linux OS. After your business has decided to go with Amazon Web Services (AWS) or Azure to stage the PostgreSQL cluster, the next task is to identify the operating system, the computer hardware resources, and the estimated storage capacity.

2.3.1 Cloud Services

Amazon Web Services and Microsoft Azure (Azure) are the leading providers of cloud services with the shared responsibility model. See Figure 2-1. The scope of the book is limited to AWS and Azure offerings of PostgreSQL on the cloud.

CHAPTER 2 CAPACITY PLANNING

PostgreSQL can be provisioned using four cloud services: Infrastructure as a Service (IaaS), Database as a Service (DBaaS), Container as a Service (CaaS), and Platform as a Service (PaaS). With IaaS, you can provision AWS Elastic Cloud Computing (EC2)/Azure VM instances that are fully managed with the ability to dynamically expand hardware resources such as CPU capacity and memory with snapshots for backup and recovery. EC2/Azure VM instances come with pre-built operating systems, such as Red Hat. With DBaaS, you can provision AWS Relational Database Service (RDS)/Azure SQL Database Services, which includes hardware and database software, including installation, support, upgrades, and patching, all performed by cloud vendors. With CaaS, you can provide PostgreSQL databases in a containerized environment, which has a dependency on IaaS. It is worth noting that with IaaS the PostgreSQL Server is deployed in a single availability zone, whereas with DBaaS you can deploy a PostgreSQL server in multiple availability zones, which isolates a single point of failure and ensures continued database availability.

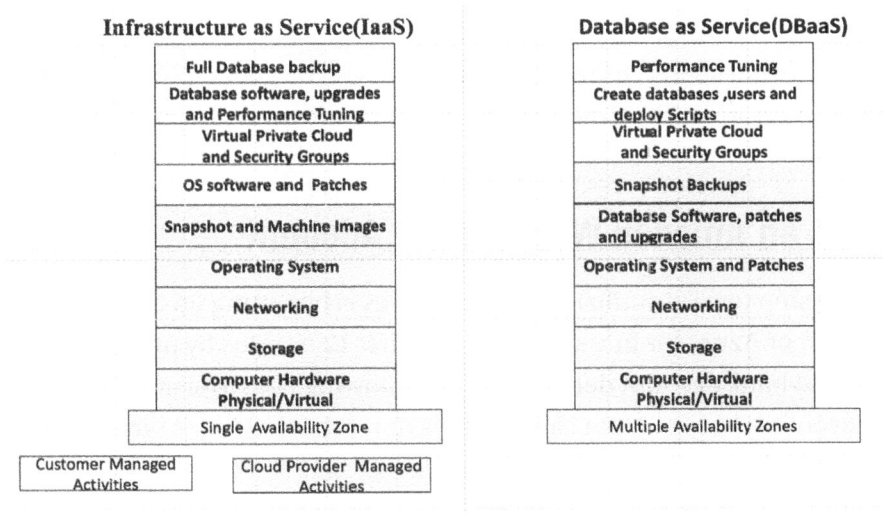

Figure 2-1. *IaaS and DBaaS shared responsibility model*

2.3.2 AWS Web Services

AWS has created a paradigm shift in the computer industry where users no longer need to invest heavily in infrastructure resources ahead of time; instead they can pay for the actual resource usage in the cloud. AWS offers a pay-as-you-go approach to pricing for over 70 cloud services. With AWS, you only pay for the individual services you need, for as long as you use them, without the need for long-term contracts or complex licensing. [1]. In Figure 2-1, notice the two service models to provision PostgreSQL server on the cloud.

For further details of shared service responsibilities, for AWS, go to https://aws.amazon.com/compliance/shared-responsibility-model/ and for Azure, go to https://learn.microsoft.com/en-us/azure/security/fundamentals/shared-responsibility.

AWS is a self-service option on the cloud, where the roles and responsibilities of system, network, storage, and database administrators are redefined. Amazon has installed thousands of computers in its data centers, which are located in several regions across the world. The data centers are highly secure buildings located in three locations of a region. The AWS cloud spans 105 availability zones with 33 geographic regions around the world. [2]. Dedicated VM instances are provided by both Azure and AWS.

Set Up an Amazon Web Service Account

The first step towards utilizing cloud services is by setting up an account with AWS or Azure for free service for the first 12 months by providing email and bank account details. Use the following URL to sign up for an AWS account: https://portal.aws.amazon.com/billing/signup#/start/email.

CHAPTER 2   CAPACITY PLANNING

Capacity Estimation for AWS Configurations

With AWS Cloud Shell, you can query all the available EC2 instance types to gain a comprehensive understanding about instance configurations such as allocated memory, CPU, and hard disk capacity.

After connecting to the AWS console, enter Cloud Shell in the search box to start the service. You can launch Cloud Shell from the Bash shell, Powershell, or zshell. Choose the Bash shell to work on Linux. See Figure 2-2.

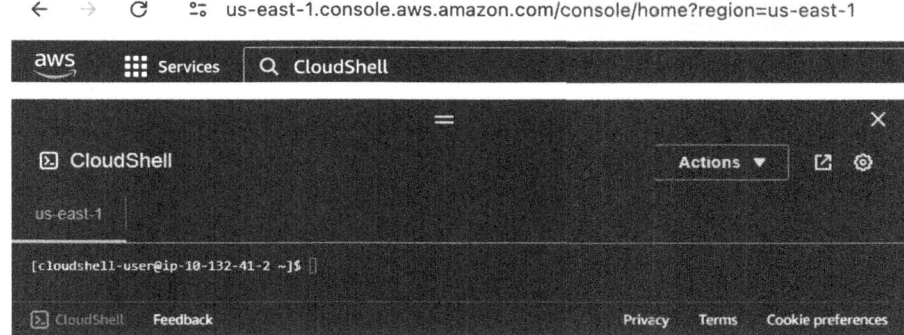

Figure 2-2. *Amazon Cloud Shell*

After connecting to Cloud Shell, you get the prompt [`cloudshell-user@ip-`]$.

AWS Cloud Shell is a fully managed, browser-based service accessible from the AWS console. You can perform all administrative tasks with Cloud Shell to manage a fleet of EC2 or RDS instances. AWS provides several commands to manage EC2 instances. One such command is `aws ec2 describe` to get an overview of the profile of the instance. With four basic commands, you get detailed information about AWS computers used both for provisioning PostgreSQL on EC2 or RDS. With AWS commands, you have the ability to obtain details about allocated versus usage details about all instances in your environment.

With AWS commands, you can pass values to variables that are used to store or display instance details. You can query all your instance attributes with the `aws ec2 describe` command. For instance, in each region, you can display the available AWS EC2 instance types with commands, although the generic instance details are available from the web site.

```
aws ec2 describe-regions --query 'Regions[].RegionName'
--output text
ap-south-1       eu-north-1       eu-west-3       eu-west-2
eu-west-1        ap-northeast-3   ap-northeast-2  ap-northeast-1
       ca-central-1    sa-east-1        ap-southeast-1
ap-southeast-2   eu-central-1     us-east-1       us-east-2
us-west-1        us-west-2
Set region with command  export AWS_REGION=eu-west-3 to obtain
instances in Europe West3.
aws ec2 describe-instance-type-offerings --query
'InstanceTypeOfferings[*].[Location, InstanceType]' --output
table| sort -u
```

The above command returns 388 instance types. You have to choose the correct instance for your requirements. For instance, you can query CPUs and allocated memory for the instance

```
eu-west-3   c5.12xlarge with below command "aws ec2 describe-
instance-type"
 aws ec2 describe-instance-types --instance-types c5.12xlarge |
egrep "DefaultVCpus|SizeInMiB"
            "DefaultVCpus": 48,
            "SizeInMiB": 98304
```

Create a file in your CloudShell and execute the commands shown in Listing 2-1 to obtain instance details.

Listing 2-1. AWS Instance Capacity Estimate

```
/path/aws_capacity.sh
aws ec2 describe-regions --query 'Regions[].RegionName'
--output text
export AWS_REGION=eu-west-3
aws ec2 describe-instance-type-offerings --query
'InstanceTypeOfferings[*].[Location, InstanceType]' --output
table| sort -u
echo " Instance CPU and Memory for c5.12xlarge "
aws ec2 describe-instance-types --instance-types c5.12xlarge |
egrep "DefaultVCpus|SizeInMiB"
```

Here is the download file link: https://drive.google.com/file/d/12 mCwCXQ4AHvLnESBlMLQHlbF5JGb8Vk2/view?usp=sharing

2.3.3 Microsoft Azure Web Service

With Azure, you can spawn all the hardware and software components required to support the database requirements in several high availability zones across the world. The availability zones ensure the continuous availability of your data. You can choose the availability zones closer to your region to work with virtual machines. Azure supports all computing models such as IaaS, DBaaS, CaaS, and PaaS for PostgreSQL databases on the cloud.

Azure provides the most extensive global footprint of any cloud provider and is rapidly opening new regions and availability zones. Azure has availability zones in every country/region where Azure operates a datacenter region [3].

Sign up with a Microsoft account at https://login.microsoftonline.com/.

CHAPTER 2   CAPACITY PLANNING

Azure Cloud Shell

After connecting to the Azure portal, click the Cloud Shell icon. You will be prompted to select a shell type, Bash or Powershell. If you are comfortable with Linux, choose the Bash shell, which will request you to create a storage account. As most of the examples in this book are based on Linux on Red Hat, the Bash shell is the way to go to work with databases. See Figures 2-3 and 2-4. If you manage databases on Windows and are familiar with Powershell scripting, choose this option.

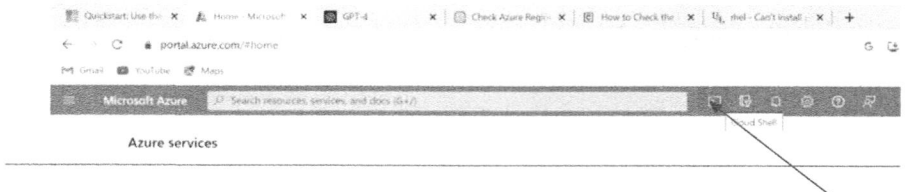

Figure 2-3.   Connect to Azure Cloud Shell

Welcome to Azure Cloud Shell

Select Bash or PowerShell. You can change shells any time via the environment selector in the Cloud Shell toolbar. The most recently used environment will be the default for your next session.

Bash   PowerShell

Figure 2-4.   Azure Cloud Shell storage

Upon completion of the storage account, you can access Cloud Shell. Cloud Shell is a private dedicated VM to work on the Bash shell. Similar to AWS CLI, the Azure command line interface is called AZ, which provides several API calls to work with tasks on the cloud. See Figure 2-5.

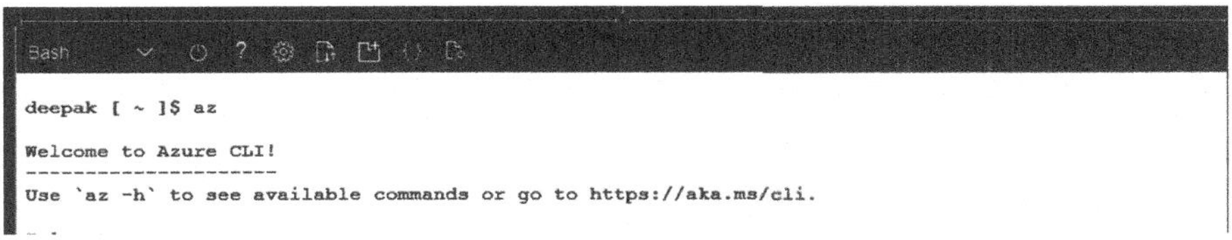

```
Bash              ? ⚙ ▯ ▯ {} ▯
deepak [ ~ ]$ az

Welcome to Azure CLI!
---------------------
Use `az -h` to see available commands or go to https://aka.ms/cli.
```

Figure 2-5. *Azure command line interface*

With commands and scripting, you can perform all administrative tasks for PostgreSQL administration in the cloud to manage a fleet of servers. The command is az.

The az command is useful to pass the values to shell variables to query or store Azure virtual or dedicated hosts, although you can get the details from the Azure website.

Azure Commands for Virtual Machine Metadata

1. Available regions command:

   With the list-locations command, you can identify all the regions of Azure cloud services.

   ```
   az account list-locations | grep -i
   regionaldisplayname | wc -l
   90
   ```

   Azure provides 90 regions across the globe. Furthermore, you can identify the specific region with a query.

   ```
   az account list-locations --query
   "[?contains(displayName, ' US')].{Region:name}"
   --output table
   eastus
   eastus2
   ```

CHAPTER 2   CAPACITY PLANNING

```
southcentralus
westus2
::: output truncated
```

2. Dedicated hosts provide physical servers, which are dedicated to the organization.

   The `list-sku` command with a filter on the `hostGroup` command displays dedicated hosts.

   ```
   az vm list-skus --location eastus --output table
   | grep -i hostGroups | awk '{print $3,$4}'
   DADSv5-Type1 1,2,3
   DASv4-Type1 1,2,3
   DASv4-Type2 1,2,3
   :::: Output truncated
   ```

3. Virtual machine inventory command:

   With a filter on virtual machines, you can obtain the virtual machines available in Azure. This is the command:

   ```
   az vm list-skus --location eastus --output table |
   grep -i virtualMachines| awk '{print $3,$4}'
   Standard_A1_v2 1,2,3
   Standard_A2m_v2 1,2,3
   Standard_A2_v2 1,2,3
   ```

4. Instance type configuration command:

   With the following command, you can list the CPU and memory allocated to an instance:

```
az vm list-sizes --location eastus --output table
| awk 'BEGIN {print "Memory(MB) Instance_Type CPU"}
{print $2 " " $3 " " $4}'
Memory(MB) Instance_Type CPU
MemoryInMB  Name               NumberOfCores
----------- ------------------ ---------------
65536   Standard_L8as_v3   8
131072  Standard_L16as_v3  16
262144  Standard_L32as_v3  32
393216  Standard_L48as_v3  48
::: output truncated
```

2.3.4 Operating System Selection

Red Hat has been managing Linux open-source software since as early as 2000, making it the outstanding player in the industry to support open-source initiatives. The company curates, secures, and supports a Linux distribution, which is now known as Red Hat Enterprise Linux, following a merger with the Fedora Linux Project in 2003 [4]. Red Hat Enterprise Linux has become a default operating system for many cloud providers, including those using PostgreSQL clusters, due to its popularity, usage, and robust support.

2.3.5 AWS Hardware Configuration

AWS provides a wide array of computer models called instance types. The M5 model is ideally suitable for databases. **db.m5** is a general-purpose DB instance class that provide a balance of compute, memory, and network resources and is a good choice for many applications [5]. The db.m5 is ideally suitable for EC2 and RDS environments.

CHAPTER 2   CAPACITY PLANNING

Table 2-1 shows an M5 instance class computer hardware for a PostgreSQL cluster.

Table 2-1. Suggested AWS Instance Types for PostgreSQL [5]

Database Profile	Amazon Instance Class	CPU	Memory (GB)	Disk Space (GB)	Maximum User Connections
Small	db.m5.large	vcpu 4	16	General purpose SSD (gp2) 100GB	1802
Medium	db.m5.2xlarge	vcpu 8	32	General purpose SSD (gp2) 200GB	3604
Large	db.m5.4xlarge	vcpu 16	64	General purpose SSD (gp2) 1TB	5000
Extra Large	m5.16xlarge	vcpu 64	256	General purpose SSD (gp2) 4TB	5000

For proof-of-concept (POC) and test environments, you can consider db.t3.xlarge with vCPU4, 16GB memory, and 200GB of diskspace.

The maximum number of user connections for a database instance is typically based on the available OS memory. For example, an m5.large instance type with 16GB RAM can typically support a maximum of 1802. In contrast, an M5.4xlarge instance type with 64GB RAM can typically support up to 5000 allowed user connections. The maximum number of user connections will vary depending on several factors, including the specific instance type, the amount of available memory, and the workload demands placed on the database [6]. To avoid the overhead of virtual machine software, the nitro model provides physical servers for highly scalable environments. The nitro system provides bare metal capabilities that eliminate virtualization overhead and support workloads that require full access to host hardware [7]. The `max_connections` parameter sets the maximum number of concurrent connections for your PostgreSQL [8]. The min and maximum connection ranges from 6 to 8,388,607 [9]. You can use the query `Select * From pg_setting where name='max_connections'` to get details about the maximum connections defined for an instance.

2.3.6 Azure Hardware Configuration

Azure provides a wide array of computers called VMs (virtual machines). The Standard D class is suitable for most PostgreSQL computing requirements. It is a typical question or enquiry from management to suggest the proposed hardware configuration when considering the PostgreSQL cluster server. The hardware profile is based on the number of user connection limits. You request them for maximum user connections; based on the connection limit, you propose the following hardware profiles shown in Table 2-2.

Table 2-2. Suggested Azure Instance Types for PostgreSQL [10]

Database Profile	Azure Instance Class	CPU	Memory (GB)	Disk Space (GB)	Maximum User Connections
Small	Standard_D4s_v3	vcpu 4	16	SSD 32GB	1719
Medium	Standard_D8s_v3	vcpu 8	32	SSD 64GB	3438
Large	Standard_D16s_v3	vcpu 16	64	SSD 128 GB	5000
Extra Large	Standard_D64s_v3	vcpu 64	256	SSD 512 GB	5000

CHAPTER 2   CAPACITY PLANNING

Note It is not common to have more than 5000 concurrent user sessions accessing the PostgreSQL database. To optimize the connection pooling and load balancing to connected sessions exceeding 5000 in count, you have to use pg_bouncer open-source software or Proxy for RDS on AWS or Data Service on Azure. This topic is covered in a subsequent chapter in the book.

2.3.7 Disk Space Estimation

Estimating the required disk capacity depends on several factors, including the number of tables and the size of each column. For text data, a simple formula can be used: [rows] x [columns] x [size of the column], which refers to the number of records and fields in each table. For image and multimedia storage, the actual capacity required will depend on a variety of factors, including the size and format of the files, as well as any compression or optimization techniques used.

Based on the provided table information, the estimated disk capacity required for each table can be calculated using the formula [rows] x [columns] x [size of column] / (1024^2) to convert the result from bytes to megabytes.

Table A: 10,000 x 50 x 100 bytes = 48.828125MB

Table B: 100,000 x 120 x 60 bytes = 687.890625MB

Table C: 1,000,000 x 100 x 80 bytes = 7,629.39453125MB

Adding the disk capacity required for each table, the total disk capacity required can be calculated as total disk capacity = 48.828125 + 687.890625 + 7,629.39453125 = 8,366.11328125MB

Rounding up to the nearest whole number, the total disk capacity required for these three tables is 8,367MB or approximately 8.2GB. See Table 2-3.

CHAPTER 2   CAPACITY PLANNING

Table 2-3. *Capacity Estimate*

Year	Initial	Growth
Q1-Year1	8GB	10%
Q2-Year1	8.1GB	10%
Q3-Year1		
Q4-Year1		
Q1-Year2		
Q2-Year2		

The average number of tables in a typical database is around 150. Using the formula [rows] x [columns] x [size of the column] for text data, you can estimate that for a database with three tables, the required hard disk capacity is around 8.3GB. However, it's important to note that this is a rough estimate and the actual capacity required may vary depending on many factors.

To accommodate future growth, it's also important to consider annual capacity growth. Assuming a 20% annual growth rate, the required storage capacity would increase to around 15GB.

Although you can expand storage capacity dynamically in AWS or Azure, there is no option to resize the storage capacity with a lower value. For example, if you expand the storage capacity by 4TB, you cannot reduce the capacity to 1TB later. You must create a new instance, followed by a restore to reclaim the excess allocated data, which is not easy with a critical production system, as this would involve downtime. In AWS, you can only increase the allocated storage. You can't reduce the allocated storage [11]. In Azure, after you increase the storage size, you can't reduce the size. Storage can only be scaled up, not down [12].

CHAPTER 2 CAPACITY PLANNING

RDS comes to a grinding halt when the allocated space exceeds 95% in the capacity, which places the database in a read-only mode, preventing future transactions and leading to a severity 1 outage to the business. The server is automatically switched to read-only mode when the storage usage reaches 95 percent or when the available capacity is less than 5GiB [13].

With pg_size_function you can estimate the allocated storage to the PostgreSQL database, table, and indexes. The details of the pg_size_function is illustrated in Chapter 15.

Disk Space Optimization

Wasted disk space, caused by deletions, frequent inserts, and updates to table rows or tuples, is referred to as bloat. Bloat can also occur in index space due to table data deletions and associated index space. The vacuum process optimizes space utilization by reclaiming free space for database usage.

As you can see in Figure 2-6, deleted rows have hot spots and data fragmentation, which can be optimized by the vacuum process, based on 30 database parameter settings. Until the vacuum process completes, the application will have performance issues while accessing data in hotspot area.

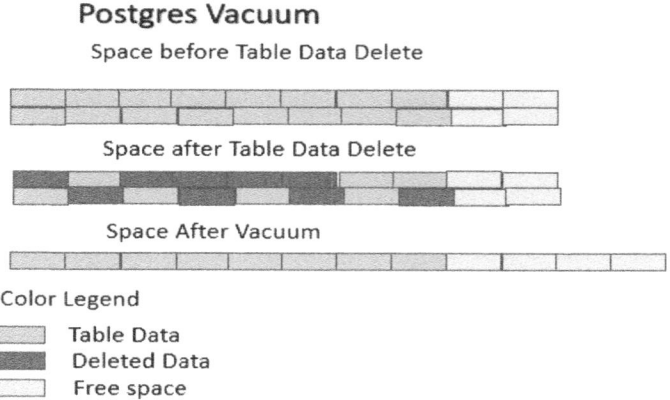

Figure 2-6. PostgreSQL vacuum

As a DBA, it is your responsibility to manage table bloat. This can be achieved through reorganizing the table data, partitioning, moving older partitions to S3 or Azure storage, and reindexing the table to ensure efficient query performance.

2.3.8 Data Management Policies

As a DBA, you have to work on or familiarize yourself with the following data management policies and procedures.

Data Retention Policies

The data retention policies determine the storage capacity for your PostgreSQL database. You have to work with the business team to have a clear understanding of your organization's data retention policies and legal compliance requirements when designing backup and recovery policies. Manufacturing and medical fields, along with several other industries, require up to 12 years of data retention to support legal and regulatory compliances.

The preferred approach for long-term retention is to archive older database partitions to AWS S3 Glacier or Azure Blob storage systems, which are low-cost, secure, and durable storage services designed for data archiving and long-term backup. You have to understand the data retrieval time from S3 or Azure when working with long-term archival and retention requirements and design your storage capacity accordingly.

Read-Only Historical Data

Historical data is typically kept for reporting, analysis, and reference purposes. Since it is rarely updated or modified, it can be stored in read-only format in the database. This helps to reduce the amount of disk space required and improve database performance by minimizing read-write operations. It also ensures that the historical data remains accurate and consistent over time.

Data Encryption Policies

As a DBA, you are responsible for protecting the data from external and internal threats. There are several ways to implement encryption in PostgreSQL:

1. Transparent data encryption (TDE)
2. Column-level encryption
3. Application-level encryption
4. SSL/TLS encryption

Data encryption is a crucial method to ensure data security both at rest and in transit. At rest, data can be encrypted on local hard disks and on backup media to prevent unauthorized access if these devices are lost or stolen. In transit, data can be encrypted to protect it from interception by hackers or other unauthorized parties. As a DBA, you are responsible for providing solutions to data encryption solutions whether to encrypt the data in the database with its native procedures or encrypt the data with third-party providers. From the capacity planning perspective, plan for additional 1 or 2% to the existing storage.

Data Masking

As a DBA, you are responsible for masking the data in non-prod environments in order to comply with Sarbanes-Oxley (SOX) Act guidelines. Data masking involves creating a copy of the production database and masking sensitive data such as Social Security numbers, credit card numbers, and other personally identifiable information (PII) before transferring it to non-production environments like development or QA. This process ensures that the sensitive data is not accessible to unauthorized personnel during development or testing. However, data masking requires additional storage space to store the masked data, which must be accounted for in the database capacity planning process. Data masking changes the content of the original data, which is irreversible. Figure 2-7 shows an example of data masking.

Original Data	Masked Data
2020 Torrance Blvd, Torrance CA 90005	1678 Western Avenue, Los Angeles CA 90010
1247 Western Ave, Torrance CA 90002	7862 Torrance Blvd, Torrance CA 90004

Figure 2-7. *Data masking example*

AWS RDS has inbuilt data masking capability, whereas with Azure you have to use dynamic data masking with Azure API management

---

Note Data masking involves additional capacity planning as you have to create a new instance for data masking.

2.3.9 PostgreSQL Cluster Provisioning Methods

The PostgreSQL cluster is provisioned by several methods. You can install PostgreSQL on Windows, Linux, and Mac operating systems. For downward compatibility, you can install PostgreSQL on Unix operating systems such as AIX, HP, and Solaris. You can install PostgreSQL on premises in a local data center or on Amazon Cloud EC2 or provision an AWS-managed RDS. Several installation methods include Red Hat Package Manager (RPM) and configuration on EC2/Azure VM. There are several provisioning methods of PostgreSQL on Amazon RDS and Azure. PostgreSQL can be installed by any unprivileged user; no superuser (root) access is required [14]. Figure 2-8 exhibits all possible PostgreSQL installation methods.

CHAPTER 2   CAPACITY PLANNING

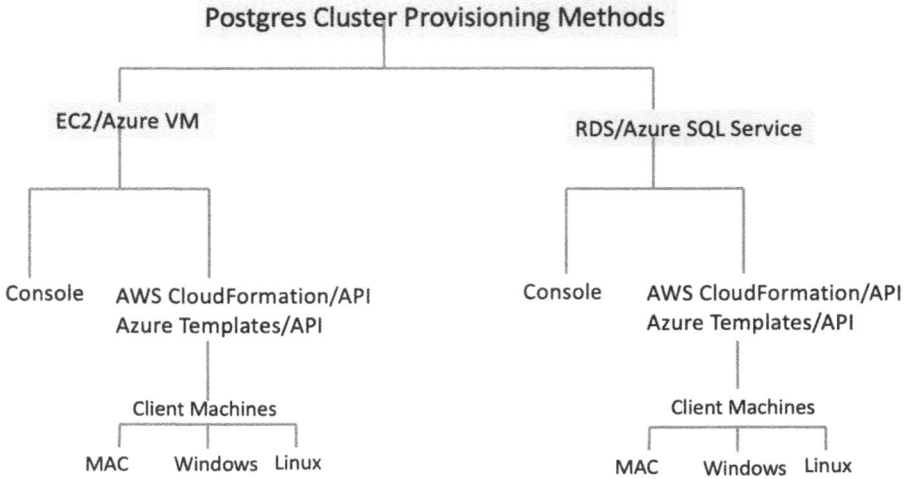

Figure 2-8. *PostgreSQL cluster provisioning methods*

Checklist for Provisioning and Configuration

Table 2-4 shows the main tasks when provisioning a PostgreSQL cluster on EC2/Container/Azure.

Table 2-4. *Checklist for Installation*

Task Id	Task Name
1	Set up AWS/Azure account
2	Identify AWS instance types
3	Identity Azure instance types
4	Complete capacity planning
5	Identify data masking requirements
6	Identify PostgreSQL cluster install methods
7	Access S3 and Azure Blob

2.3.10 Database Limits

While designing the database, you must check the database limits defined at the PostgreSQL cluster. The database size is unlimited, the number of databases size is unlimited, the number of databases caps at 4,294,950,911, the number of tables caps at 1,431,650,303, the relation size is 32TB, the rows per table caps at 4,294,967,295, the columns per table caps at 1600, the columns in a result set stop at 1664, and the indexes per table are unlimited [15].

2.3.11 Cloud Storage

Amazon and Azure provision similar storage solutions on the cloud. S3 or Azure Blob serves as a staging area to load data to PostgreSQL from other databases. It also serves as a long-term archive to copy historical data from a database. The cloud storage is categorized into types: store static data, provision storage for a database file system, or a network or shared file system. See Figure 2-9.

AWS	Azure	Description
S3: Simple Storage Service	Azure Blob Storage	Store documents, images, static web site content etc.
Elastic Block Storage (EBS)	Azure Disk Storage	Database file system usage AWS gp2(general purpose SSD) Azure premium/standard SDD
Elastic File System (EFS)	Azure File Storage	Network file share AWS Elastic File System(efx) Azure files
Glacier and Deep Glacier	Azure Archive Storage	Long Term Archival

Figure 2-9. S3 and Azure storage

Amazon S3

S3 is a global service that can be accessed from any region, where you can store files with cost effective solutions and where you can store petabytes of data in S3. Based on the access pattern, you can move files to low tiers for cost optimization. The tiers are as follows:

1. Standard is the default tier and it provides durability, availability, and scalability for all applications.
2. Standard Infrequent Access for least used files
3. One Zone Infrequently Accessed for access from only one zone
4. Intelligent Tiering where S3 will move the contents to different tiers to optimize storage costs
5. S3 Glacier and S3 Glacier Deep Archival for lastly used objects such as videos and photos [16]

You can back up all files to S3 and restore in the same or another region You can load data into PostgreSQL from files located in S3. You can add files to S3 with the AWS console or from AWS API calls. The directories in the S3 are called buckets, which is like a directory or folder hierarchy structure with version control mechanisms. The retrial time of files are different between all tiers. All S3 files are data protected by accidental deletes and are version controlled as well as encrypted.

Note S3 is not suitable to stage PostgreSQL database files.

File Copy to S3

As a DBA, you are responsible for copying and restoring files from S3.

CHAPTER 2 CAPACITY PLANNING

Here are the steps to create buckets in S3:

1. Connect to https://us-east-console.aws.amazon.com/cloudshell.

2. Create a bucket with the command aws s3 mb s3://palossales1 --region us-east-2.

3. Copy a file to the bucket like so: aws s3 cp testfile.txt s3://palossales1.

4. List the bucket content like so: aws s3 ls s3://palossales1

   2024-03-17 00:36:07 5 testfile.txt

5. Restore a file from s3 like so: aws s3 cp s3://palossales1/testfile.txt . (local directory)

You can estimate bucket size with this script:

```
for buck in $(aws s3 ls s3:// | awk '{print $3}')
do
echo " size of Bucket $buck"
ret=$(aws s3api list-objects --bucket $buck --output json --query "[sum(Contents[].Size), length(Contents[])]")
echo $ret
done
./file.sh
size of Bucket palos123
[ 0, 1 ]
 size of Bucket palos123bk
[ 39008273, 4 ]
```

Note The above script does not work with empty buckets.

Here is the script download link:

https://docs.google.com/document/d/1UsL4ZOumy4LKbYmciulGpCe5BooFXZ5V/edit?usp=sharing&ouid=117618855868897795502&rtpof=true&sd=true

AWS S3 Console

You can use the AWS console to create S3 folders and upload files. See Figure 2-10. The URL is https://s3.console.aws.amazon.com/s3.

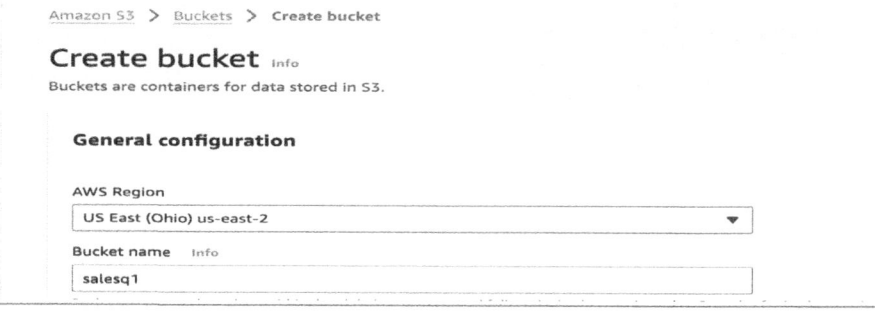

Figure 2-10. *AWS S3 Create bucket page*

Azure Data Blob

With Azure Blob, you can store all files, which can be accessible from any region, with cost effective solutions and four different access tiers:

1. Hot Access Tier for frequently accessed data

2. Cool Access Tier for infrequent access data

3. Archive Access Tier to storage infrequently accessed data for a low access pattern

4. Premium blob storage for rarely accessed data with deep discounted storage price

CHAPTER 2 CAPACITY PLANNING

All Azure Blob files are data protected by accidental deletes and are version controlled as well as encrypted.

The first task in Azure is to create a resource group where all subsequent resources are tied to the resource group. For instance, you have created 10 resources and with termination of the resource group, all services will be terminated.

It is a three-step process to upload the files to Azure Blob. See Figure 2-11.

Figure 2-11. *Azure storage container creation process*

Connect to Cloud Shell to perform the storage activities on Azure. See Figure 2-12. If you prefer to work with the console, go to https://portal.azure.com/#create/Microsoft.StorageAccount-ARM.

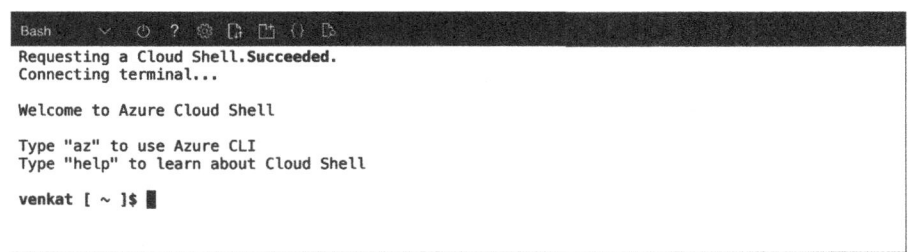

Figure 2-12. *Azure CloudShell*

The first step is to create a storage account with a simple Azure command which takes the storage account and resource group name and creates a storage account in your default region. See Listing 2-2.

65

Listing 2-2. Azure Storage Account Creation

```
 az storage account create \
    --name palos123 \
    --resource-group PostRG
```

Partial output:

```
{
  "accessTier": "Hot",
  "accountMigrationInProgress": null,
::: Lines omitted
"table": "https://palos123-secondary.table.core.windows.net/",
::: Lines omitted
  "type": "Microsoft.Storage/storageAccounts"
}
```

The next task is to create a storage container to store your files, which takes the storage account name, name of the container, and the account key, which you get by providing the resource group name and account name to the command az storage account key list.

```
storagekey=$(az storage account keys list --resource-group PostRG --account-name palos123 --query '[0].value' --output tsv)
 az storage container create \
    --account-name palos123 \
    --name palosdata \
    --account-key $storagekey
```

Output:

```
WARNING: [Warning] This output may compromise security by
showing secrets. Learn more at: https://go.microsoft.com/
fwlink/?linkid=2258669
{
  "created": false
}
```

> **Note** Make sure the storage is secure.

Congratulations, you have created a storage account and container with Azure commands. The next task is to load files to Azure Container (Data Blob).

Load Data to Azure Programmatically

After logging into the Azure portal to identify the subscription id as well as the account key, based on these details you can store files in Azure Blob. You created a resource group, storage account, and container in the previous section.

The following are the steps to create a Data Blob folder and upload a test file. The az is a program that takes several arguments to manage the Data Blob service [17]:

1. az account set,
2. az storage account create -name,
3. az storage container create --account-name,
4. az storage blob upload --container-name [name] -file[path of the file],
5. az storage blob list --container-name

CHAPTER 2 CAPACITY PLANNING

With scripting, you can load several thousand files to be uploaded to Azure Blob. It is not feasible to use the console to load files and it is not a recommended practice. The following shell script takes three arguments to load files into blob storage (the resource group name, the storage account name, and the container name and file path):

```
echo "Enter Resource Group Name"
read rg
acctid=$(az account show --query id -o tsv)
az group create --name $rg --location eastus
echo "Enter Storage account name"
read sact
az storage account create --name $sact --resource-group $rg
--location eastus --sku Standard_LRS
skey=$(az storage account keys list --account-name
$sact --resource-group $rg --output table | tail -1 | awk
'{print $4}')
echo "Enter Container name"
read cont
az storage container create --account-name $sact --name $cont
--account-key $skey
for file in $(ls  test*)
do
   az storage blob upload --container-name $cont --file /home/
   venkat/$file --account-name $sact
   az storage blob list --container-name $cont --account-name
   $sact --output table
done
```

In Figure 2-13, you enter the resource group name.

CHAPTER 2 CAPACITY PLANNING

```
venkat [ ~ ]$ ./load.sh
Enter Resource Group Name
demostorage
{
  "id": "/subscriptions/68224f32-8283-4919-923d-401dd223c603/resourceGroups/demostorage",
  "location": "eastus",
  "managedBy": null,
  "name": "demostorage",
  "properties": {
    "provisioningState": "Succeeded"
  },
  "tags": null,
  "type": "Microsoft.Resources/resourceGroups"
}
```

Figure 2-13. *Enter the resource name*

In Figure 2-14, you enter the storage account name.

```
Enter Storage account name
palosdevstorage
{
  "accessTier": "Hot",
  "accountMigrationInProgress": null,
  "allowBlobPublicAccess": false,
  "allowCrossTenantReplication": false,
```

Figure 2-14. *Enter the storage account name*

In Figure 2-15, you enter the container name.

```
Enter Container name
palosdemodata
{
  "created": true
}
```

Figure 2-15. *You enter the container name*

Here is the result of the shell script loading data to Azure Blob Storage:

```
Name        Blob Type     Blob Tier    Length     Content
Type                   Last Modified              Snapshot
---------   -----------   -----------   --------   ----------------
---------   ------------------------    ----------
testfile    BlockBlob     Hot           5          application/
octet-stream  2024-03-18T03:49:53+00:00
testfile1   BlockBlob     Hot           5          application/
octet-stream  2024-03-18T03:49:58+00:00
testfile2   BlockBlob     Hot           5          application/
octet-stream  2024-03-18T03:50:02+00:00
testfile3   BlockBlob     Hot           5          application/
octet-stream  2024-03-18T03:50:07+00:00
```

Here's the link to download the Azure Blob data load script:
https://docs.google.com/document/d/1KJ13kYRlsCy-LJSjIAzkr6z8SvFC9jKK/edit?usp=sharing&ouid=117618855868897795502&rtpof=true&sd=true.

2.4 Keywords

aws s3api, aws s3, aws ec2 describe-regions, az vm list-skus, AWS, AWS instance types, Azure instance types, data masking, vacuum, PostgreSQL cluster provisioning methods, AWS S3, and Azure Blob.

2.4.1 Practice Chapter 2

1. How do you check the CPU and memory configuration of the m7gd.12xlarge instance type in AWS?
2. Create an S3 bucket and upload a test file.
3. Create a Data Blob folder and upload a test file.
4. Load 10 files programmatically from AWS and Azure Cloud Shell.
5. Change the lifecycle of test files into deep archival in AWS and Azure storage.

2.4.2 Questions Chapter 2

1. How do you determine the capacity planning for PostgreSQL storage?
2. Identify all AWS instance types.

CHAPTER 2   CAPACITY PLANNING

3. Identify all Azure instance types.

4. How do you estimate capacity planning for three years of database storage?

5. Identify all methods by which you can install PostgreSQL cluster.

6. How do you determine the hardware configuration for a PostgreSQL cluster? What are the minimum required configurations?

7. What configuration do you propose for 4,000 concurrent users access to the PostgreSQL cluster?

8. How do you determine the approach for storing historical and archival data? How do you store the data in the database?

9. How do you copy data to AWS S3 folders?

10. How do you copy data to Azure Data Blob?

2.4.3 Summary of Learning

You've covered topics such as identifying the correct instance types for your PostgreSQL AWS and Azure deployment, estimating the required storage capacity, and the different methods of installing a PostgreSQL cluster on various operating systems including Windows, Linux, and macOS. Additionally, you also learned PostgreSQL installation methods on Amazon/AZURE and the importance of data encryption and data masking for sensitive information as well as the data storage approach in AWS S3 and Azure Blob.

References

1. https://aws.amazon.com/pricing/?aws-products-pricing.sort-by=item.additionalFields.productNameLowercase&aws-products-pricing.sort-order=asc&awsf.Free%20Tier%20Type=*all&awsf.tech-category=*all
2. https://aws.amazon.com/about-aws/global-infrastructure/?p=ngi&loc=1
3. https://learn.microsoft.com/en-us/azure/reliability/availability-zones-service-support
4. www.redhat.com/en/topics/linux
5. https://docs.aws.amazon.com/AmazonRDS/latest/UserGuide/Concepts.DBInstanceClass.html
6. https://docs.aws.amazon.com/AmazonRDS/latest/UserGuide/CHAP_Limits.html
7. https://docs.aws.amazon.com/AWSEC2/latest/UserGuide/instance-types.html#instance-type-names%20nitro
8. The max_connections parameter sets the maximum number of concurrent connections for your PostgreSQL.
9. https://docs.aws.amazon.com/AmazonRDS/latest/UserGuide/CHAP_Limits.html#RDS_Limits.MaxConnections
10. https://learn.microsoft.com/en-us/azure/PostgreSQL/flexible-server/concepts-limits
11. https://docs.aws.amazon.com/AmazonRDS/latest/UserGuide/Overview.DBInstance.Modifying.html
12. https://learn.microsoft.com/en-us/azure/PostgreSQL/flexible-server/concepts-compute-storage
13. https://learn.microsoft.com/en-us/azure/PostgreSQL/flexible-server/concepts-compute-storage
14. www.PostgreSQL.org/docs/current/tutorial-install.html

15. www.PostgreSQL.org/docs/current/limits.html
16. https://aws.amazon.com/s3/storage-classes/
17. https://learn.microsoft.com/en-US/cli/azure/storage/container?view=azure-cli-latest#code-try-1

CHAPTER 3

Amazon EC2/Azure VM Linux Install Tasks

3.1 Abstract

The durability, scalability, stability, and sustainability of a PostgreSQL database heavily relies on the selection of computer hardware resources. To ensure a robust database management system, administrators need to perform several preparatory steps on Amazon EC2/Azure VM instances to facilitate the installation of PostgreSQL on the Linux OS. These steps include capacity planning for PostgreSQL storage, choosing the appropriate environment for EC2/Azure VM, determining the hardware configuration for the PostgreSQL cluster, and proposing the best EC2/Azure VM configuration for a certain number of concurrent users. By following these steps, administrators can ensure the optimal performance and reliability of PostgreSQL database services.

3.2 Objectives of Learning

- Introduction to the Linux OS
- Introduction to shell scripts

- Installation and configuration of Amazon EC2/Azure VM
- Creation of Linux volume groups and logical volumes
- Amazon command line utility
- Azure command line utility

The tasks in this chapter are shown in Figure 3-1.

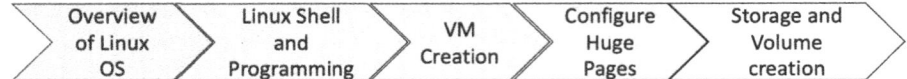

Figure 3-1. *Chapter overview*

3.3 Introduction

In this chapter, you will learn about the AWS EC2 and Azure VM, configuration of OS parameters and the allocation of storage volumes, which is a prerequisite to install a PostgreSQL cluster on Linux. You have the full control of managing all aspects of PostgreSQL administration on Linux, which includes installation and configuration plus setting up backup and recovery procedures and upgrade methods. You can manage a fleet of Linux computers in the cloud environment with AWS CloudFormation and Azure Templates scripting solutions.

3.4 Introduction to the Linux Operating System

Ken Thompson and Dennis Ritchie developed the Unix operating system at AT&T Bell Labs in 1969, and it was later refined at University of Berkeley, California. Unix is a highly scalable operating system that is suitable for work on small to large computers due to its portability and multi-user and multi-tasking capabilities. Unix, although created 50 years ago, wasinitially used by the academic community. It later gained prominence and adoption by small to large corporations for the database management systems.

In 1991, Linus Torvalds created a Unix-like operating system called Linux. Linus was inspired by Unix operating features and functionalities. It was designed to be a free and open-source alternative for deployment on small computers. Linus Torvalds released the initial version of the Linux kernel and invited the global community to contribute and improve it.

The fundamental feature of the Linux operating system is to create files to store user data, offer access data from remote computers, provide security, provision access control mechanism for concurrent access to the files, and provision the inter-process communication for shared system resources. As PostgreSQL cluster data resides on the Linux file system, understanding file system basics, memory allocation basics, and CPU resource allocation basics is essential from a support and administration perspective.

3.4.1 Major Features of Linux

The Linux kernel is the core of the operating system, acting as an interface between computer software and hardware. It interacts with memory, CPU, and device drivers, providing essential utilities for managing multiple user tasks. In Linux, a process is a fundamental aspect of the operating system. It is created when a program is loaded into memory for execution. Processes in Linux communicate and share resources through inter-process communication, such as shared access to computer memory. Features such as SHMMAX (maximum size of shared memory segment bytes) and SHMALL (total amount of shared memory available bytes or pages) limit the usage of memory resources, although it is common to run PostgreSQL with unlimited resource governance. However, a good starting point is to allocate 25-40% memory to PostgreSQL database memory.

Linux, due to its efficiency, performance, portability, access control, and scalability, is the default operating system for Android devices, with millions of installations across the globe. Linux has no software license cost. There are several products and services offered by Red Hat OS, which require a license cost.

Detailed information about the Linux operating system goes beyond the scope of this book. However, it is important to understand basic 40 to 50 commands to support and work with the PostgreSQL cluster on an AWS EC2/Azure VM instances running on Linux.

Introduction to Linux Shell

The Linux shell is a command-line program that interacts with the operating system, enabling users to perform various tasks. There are several variants of shell in Linux: Bourne shell (sh), Bourne Again Shell (bash), Korn shell (ksh), and cshell. The most popular shell on Linux is bash. Bash is largely compatible with sh and incorporates useful features from the Korn shell ksh and the C shell csh (www.gnu.org/software/bash/manual/html_node/What-is-Bash_003f.html). The shell tasks include creating files, searching the contents of files, editing file contents, managing user accounts, creating and storing data in the file system, checking storage space, monitoring process status, and utilizing programmatic logic with for loops, while loops, and if-then-else statements, along with working with variables. The shell executes all the tasks requested by the user from the computer. It instructs the core of the OS kernel to execute the commands. The most notable command is `pipe`.

The `pipe` command, represented by the vertical bar symbol |, is a brilliant feature in Linux. It allows you to connect the output of one command as the input to another command, enabling the seamless chaining of multiple commands together. Other shell commands to manage PostgreSQL on Linux are `cat, grep, sed, ps, awk, mkdir, pwd, cd, touch, cp, mv, list, chown, find, tail, compress, tar,` mount, dd, head, tail, diff, du and df. Refer to the following link for shell command examples: https://docs.google.com/document/d/1vkw9HaHcpSQ8npog3zOyLALXhujLrim9/edit?usp=sharing&ouid=117618855868897795502&rtpof=true&sd=true.

For comprehensive details, go to www.man7.org/linux/man-pages/man1/bash.1.html.

Shell Programming

The main feature of the shell is its ability to provide a framework for programming logic. The main programming language constructs are if-then-else, for-loops, while, and case. The following sections cover examples of shell scripts in the context of managing a PostgreSQL cluster. The comment is # in the shell program.

If Statement

The most used programming logic is the if-then-else construct, which evaluates to true or false during the execution of a code block. This is fundamental to the shell programming language. For instance, if the database is up and running, it displays the message "up;" otherwise, it displays the message "down." You have already installed PostgreSQL on a Mac. Create a file named check.sh and add the content in Listing 3-1. Execute the script with the command sh check.sh.

Listing 3-1. If-then-else Condition Check

```
#!/bin/sh
# pg_isready check for status of PostgreSQL server
# If return status is not equal to 0 then raise error
# set the PGHOME to PostgreSQL Binary directory
export PGHOME=/opt/homebrew/bin   # Change it to your version
$PGHOME/pg_isready # PostgreSQL program checks for running instance
```

```
  if [ $? -eq 0 ]; then     # The successful execution of program returns 0
      echo "PostgreSQL is UP"
  else
          echo "PostgreSQL is down: Check with DBA."
  fi
execute the script

sh check.sh
/tmp:5432 - accepting connections
PostgreSQL is UP
```

This script is a basic shell script that uses the `pg_isready` command to check the status of the PostgreSQL server. After setting the path, the script captures the return status. The shell returns 0 for the successful execution of the command. If the status is not equal to 0. it sends a warning message.

for Loop

The for loop iterates over a result set until it processes all the items in the list. Mostly it is used in assigning the results to a variable from the database. It loops until the items in the result set are complete. Listing 3-2 is a simple for a loop statement to display the databases in the cluster connected as postgres user. Create a file named for_loop.sh and execute as sh for_loop.sh.

Listing 3-2. for Loop Example

```
#!/bin/sh
export PGHOME=/opt/homebrew/bin   # set your own path of PostgreSQL binaries home
# for_loop.sh
# This script retrieves the list of PostgreSQL databases using psql utility, the result is stored in #variable "db", ignore template database.
```

CHAPTER 3 AMAZON EC2/AZURE VM LINUX INSTALL TASKS

```
for db in $(psql -d postgres -t -c "SELECT datname FROM
pg_database where datistemplate=false;")
do
echo $db
done
# execute the script with command sh [*.sh ]
sh for_loop.sh
postgres
demo
```

This script demonstrates a for loop in sh to iterate over the list of database names returned by the psql command, by querying the pg_database system catalog. The -t options remove the header and footer of the query. You can use similar logic to work with database data to script DBA tasks.

while Loop

A while loop executes a block of code if the condition is true. Like an if statement, you can check the status of a PostgreSQL cluster with the while loop syntax. Create a file named while.sh and run it with sh. Listing 3-3 is a shell script to check the while loop syntax.

Listing 3-3. PostgreSQL Server Status

```
#!/bin/sh
export PGHOME=/opt/homebrew/bin  # change to to your home
while true; do
    # Wait for 10 seconds before each check
    sleep 10
    # Execute the pg_isready command and check its exit status
    $PGHOME/pg_isready
    ret_status=$(echo $?)
```

```
    # Print the return status of the database
    echo "Return Status of database: $ret_status"
    if [ $ret_status -ne 0 ]; then
        echo "postgres is Down: Check with DBA"
    else
        echo "postgres  is running"
    fi
done
# execute the shell script
sh while.sh
/tmp:5432 - accepting connections
Return Status of database: 0
postgres  is running
/tmp:5432 - accepting connections
Return Status of database: 0
postgres  is running
```

The case Statement

The case statement is a contraflow statement which executes a program based on the value of the variable. The case statement is based on the search of value in a variable.

The main usage is with the result set with unknown status equate with the *. See Listing 3-4.

Listing 3-4. Case Statement

```
#!/bin/sh
#Execute the program pg_isready
export PGHOME=/opt/homebrew/bin
$PGHOME/pg_isready
ret_status=$?
echo "Return Status : $ret_status"
```

```
case $ret_status in
    0)
        # If the exit status is 0, then PostgreSQL is up and
        running.
        echo "PostgreSQL cluster is Running"
        ;;
    2)
        # If the exit status is 2, then PostgreSQL is down.
        echo "PostgreSQL cluster is in  down state,
        contact DBA."
        ;;
    *)
        # For any other errors .
        echo "Cluster Error : Check with DBA "
        ;;
esac
```

Output:

```
sh case.sh
/run/postgresql:5432 - accepting connections
Return Status : 0
PostgreSQL cluster is Running
After stopping the PostgreSQL if you execute the script you
would receive error with status code 2
sh case.sh
/run/postgresql:5432 - no response
Return Status : 2
PostgreSQL cluster is in  down state, contact DBA.
Reference shell script:
https://drive.google.com/file/d/1psMwaMeH1_Qu9-
ia28AcjvAyWp5bHunC/view?usp=sharing
```

3.4.2 Cloud VM Creation

This section covers the EC2/Azure VM installation. As you reviewed in Chapter 1, the cloud region spans several availability zones (which are physical buildings hosting infrastructure hardware and software resources in a virtual private network dedicated to each customer) where EC2 or Azure VM is created with its local storage. See Figure 3-2.

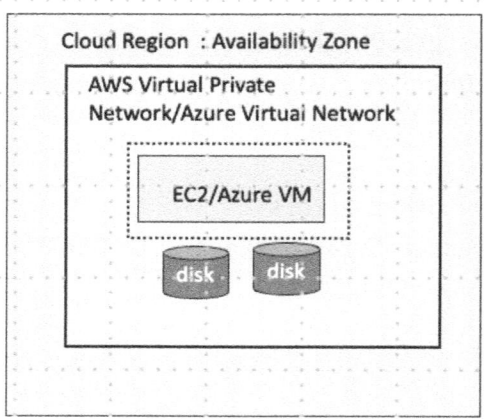

Figure 3-2. *Cloud region*

With a few clicks of the mouse, after signing on to the AWS/Azure console, you can create a Red Hat Linux operating system. The installation of virtual machines along with the Red Hat operating system software is performed by AWS/Azure in the background, as this is a managed service. The EC2/Azure VM is installed in a region that has a dedicated network.

EC2/Azure VM Installation Methods

You can install EC2/Azure VM with the console, CloudShell, or a client command line interface. See Figure 3-3.

CHAPTER 3 AMAZON EC2/AZURE VM LINUX INSTALL TASKS

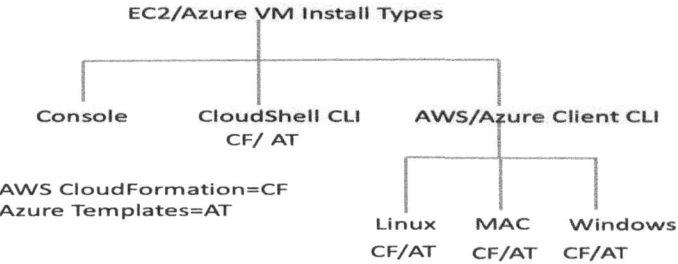

Figure 3-3. VM install types

As you can see in Figure 3-3, you can install from different methods, although the preferred method to install is by CloudShell.

AWS Instance Creation

The major tasks of VM creation are shown in Figure 3-4.

Figure 3-4. VM creation tasks

To create an EC2 instance with the Red Hat operating system, you need to create an account on the AWS console. You can use the following URL to sign into the AWS console: https://aws.amazon.com/console/. The first task after signing on to the console is to create a new keypair, which is downloaded to your laptop and is used to authenticate your access to AWS instances from remote machines.

Once you have an account, you can provision one or multiple EC2 virtual instances located in one or many availability zones (multi-AZ).

CHAPTER 3 AMAZON EC2/AZURE VM LINUX INSTALL TASKS

Launch EC2 Instances from the AWS Console

To perform administrative tasks on an EC2 instance, you need to connect to the AWS console as the root user or with a user that has been granted EC2 full control privileges. This will allow you to perform various administrative tasks, such as creating, modifying and terminating instances, and managing network settings, storage, and security groups.

Get the Launch Instances option by connecting into https://us-east-2.console.aws.amazon.com/ec2/home?region=us-east-2 and change it to your region. You identified several regions in Chapter 2. Choose the instance that is in close proximity to your region

Choose the Red Hat Option

After launching the Instance Creation menu, enter Red Hat in the Amazon Machine Image window, which will display the latest version of the image. See Figure 3-5.

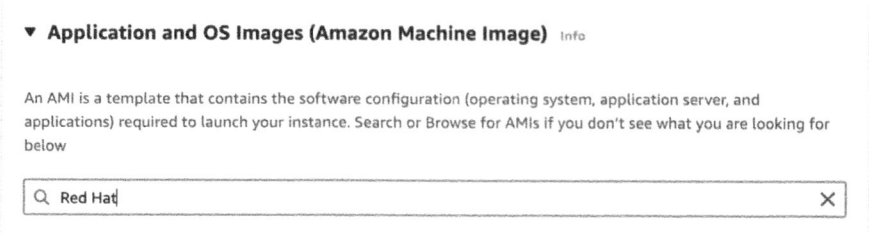

Figure 3-5. *Select the Red Hat option*

After choosing Red Hat, Figure 3-6 is displayed.

CHAPTER 3   AMAZON EC2/AZURE VM LINUX INSTALL TASKS

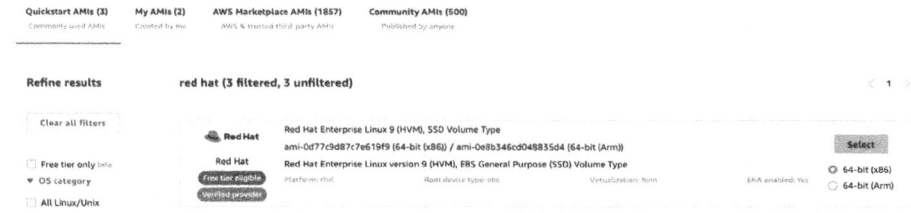

Figure 3-6. *Red Hat infotmation*

Choose the top one from the result and choose the latest version of Red Hat by clicking the Select icon.

You can also create Red Hat from My AMIs(2), which has PostgreSQL training modules.

Choose an Instance Type

The select icon displays the details shown in Figure 3-7. Verify the free tier eligibility.

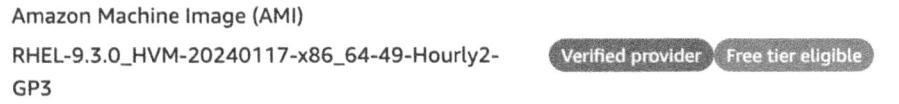

Figure 3-7. *AMI selection*

Choose t2.micro as this is a free tier eligible for 750 hours in the first 12 months of usage. See Figure 3-8.

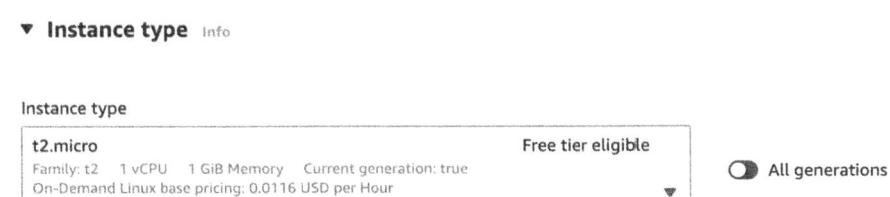

Figure 3-8. *Choose the instance type*

87

CHAPTER 3   AMAZON EC2/AZURE VM LINUX INSTALL TASKS

Create a New Key Pair

The key pair is now optional at large enterprises for security/rotation/management reasons.

After choosing the instance type, next you choose Create key pair, which will prompt to download. The key is used to connect to remote Linux hosts from client machine. See Figure 3-9.

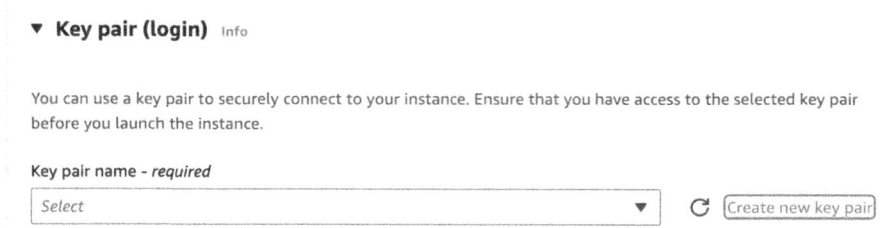

Figure 3-9.   Create a key pair

AWS Network Settings

Choose the default option, as AWS provides a default virtual private network (VPN) along with a default subnet. VPC has three subnets. You can assign a computer to a specific subnet in an AZ. See Listing 3-5. Figure 3-10 shows the default subnet assigned by AWS.

Listing 3-5.   Network Details

```
Network Info
vpc-nce7e5a4
Subnet Info
No preference (Default subnet in any availability zone)
```

Figure 3-10.   Network settings

CHAPTER 3 AMAZON EC2/AZURE VM LINUX INSTALL TASKS

If you wish to dedicate the computer to specific AZ, edit the network setting.

With the edit of network settings, you can assign a specific availability zone for the computer. Listing 3-6 shows the details of the IP address allocation in us-east-2a AZ.

Listing 3-6. VPC Details

```
VPC - required Info
vpc-nce7e5a4(default)
172.22.0.0/16
Subnet Info
Availability Zone: us-east-2a
```

Choose the defaults. After creating the instance, you have to add rules for PostgreSQL. See Figure 3-11.

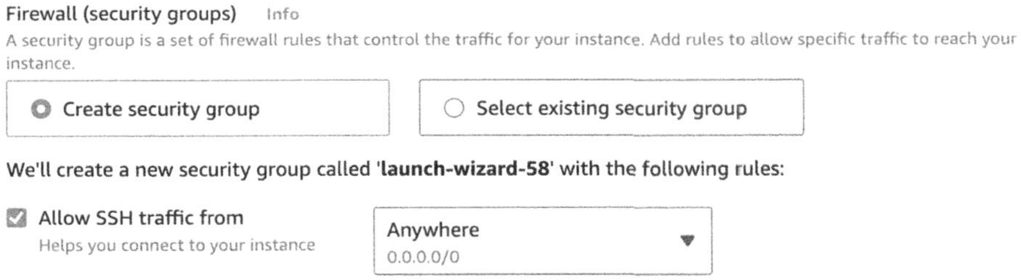

Figure 3-11. *SSH rules*

Choose Storage

In the Configure storage option, increase the storage from default 10GB to 20GB as 10GB is low. See Figure 3-12.

CHAPTER 3　AMAZON EC2/AZURE VM LINUX INSTALL TASKS

Figure 3-12. Storage expansion

After completing all the above steps, click "Launch instance," which will spawn the EC2 instance.

AWS Security Group Networking Configuration

The Transaction and Communication Protocol (TCP) enables transmission of data over the Internet in the form of packets between computers. PostgreSQL uses a message-based protocol for communication between frontends and backends (clients and servers). The protocol is supported over TCP/IP (www.postgresql.org/docs/current/protocol.html).

To differentiate multiple incoming requests from client machines, each service or request is associated with a port in the OS. The commonly used port numbers are 22 for Security Shell (SSH), 80 for HTTP, 443 HTTPS, and 5432 for PostgreSQL. AWS with Security Group allows the requests from clients to servers, which is a firewall in traditional nomenclature. There are two network protocols to assign IP addresses to computers: Internet Protocol Version 4 (IPV4), which is based on 32-bit address spaces for IP addresses, and Internet Protocol Version 6 (IPV6) for 128-bit address spacees. AWS will assign two IP addresses for the computer in the cloud: a public IP and a private IP. The public IP address is dynamic and is available during the instance availability state and a new IP is assigned after reboot. AWS provides a charged elastic IP service where the public IP is static during the life of the instance.

AWS creates a default virtual private cloud (VPC) for client accounts, which is a virtual network for the simplicity of network management, where IP addresses are allocated to a computers along with subnets

CHAPTER 3 AMAZON EC2/AZURE VM LINUX INSTALL TASKS

configured to partition networks in the regions for AZs, which is a fundamental benefit of cloud services with the isolation of the network configuration.

Security Groups filter IPV4 or IPV6 addresses based on the configuration of inbound and outbound rules. The client access to EC2 or RDS in the AWS cloud is governed by inbound and outbound rules which are defined in the security group.

With the inbound rules, you define which computers have access to EC2 or RDS instances. The outbound rules follow the same security as the inbound rules, although default in many cases; however, you can restrict outbound traffic for high security configurations. As databases reside in a private network, the IPV4 number range is sufficient. During installation, the SSH port 22 is open, and you have to add PostgreSQL in the AWS Security Group to enable clients to connect to PostgreSQL Server

The next step after creating EC2 is to assign firewall rules with Security Group assignment, where you allow users to connect to the PostgreSQL databases in the cloud. Choose the EC2 and Security Groups menu from the console to create the rules. From the AWS console, choose the Security group option and add PostgreSQL for inbound rules.

From the AWS console, choose EC2 > Security Group, provide a security group name, and add one rule for incoming traffic. PostgreSQL port 5432 and IP address range 0.0.0.0./0 are for training and testing purposes. Provide a security group name and choose default VPC. See Figure 3-13.

EC2 > Security Groups > **Create security group**

Create security group Info

Figure 3-13. Security group creation

Provide your IP address in the input rules source windows. Use 0.0.0.0/0 for testing purposes. See Figure 3-14.

CHAPTER 3 AMAZON EC2/AZURE VM LINUX INSTALL TASKS

Figure 3-14. Inbound rules definition

By default, all inbound traffic is allowed by outbound rules. Under rare incidents of hacker attacks, you can block incoming traffic. See Figure 3-15.

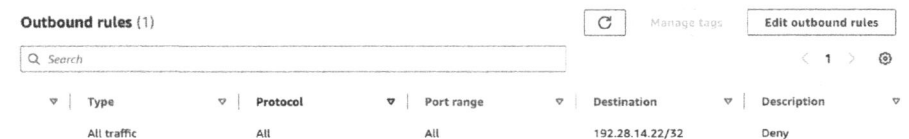

Figure 3-15. Outbound rules definition

After adding inbound and outbound rules for PostgreSQL port and IP address range, click the Save rules icon.

Congratulations. All tasks have been completed to install EC2 on Linux with the Red Hat OS towards installation of a PostgreSQL cluster.

Note   AWS EC2 resides on one subnet in an AZ.

Create EC2 from the Command Line

If you want to install a fleet of EC2 instances, the command line is the way to go. It is an established practice in corporations, where the command line script is customized and validated by all teams. The first step is to connect to the AWS console and choose the service AWS Cloud Shell.

The steps to create EC2 from command line are as follows:

1) Create a *.pem key.
2) Create a security group.
3) Authorize the security group.
4) Create an instance.

After creating the *.pem key, the next step is to create a security group, which is a firewall to the EC2 instance where you can restrict access to IP addresses that have the access. For demo servers, the 0.0.0.0.0/0 notation allows global access. From Cloud Shell, run the commands below, which will create a security group and EC2 instance.

Run the commands in Listing 3-7 from Cloud Shell, which will create an EC2 instance in minutes. The reference AMI may be different or not available. Choose an instance of your OS version.

Listing 3-7. AWS/EC2 create Script

```
aws ec2 describe-images --owners amazon --filters
"Name=name,Values=*RHEL*"| egrep 'ImageId|ImageLocation'
```

Output:

```
        "ImageId": "ami-0bce8a6275613e7ed",
        "ImageLocation":"amazon/RHEL_HA-9.3.0_HVM-20231207-
        x86_64-20-Hourly2-GP3",
         "ImageId": "ami-019b7ad7b8c9900f6",
        "ImageLocation": "amazon/RHEL-8.7.0_HVM-20221101-
        x86_64-0-Hourly2-GP2",
   ::: Lines omitted
aws ec2 create-key-pair --key-name devec2 --query 'devkey'
--output text > devec2.pem
aws ec2 create-security-group \
           --group-name PGSG \
              --description "Description of your
                security group"
```

```
aws ec2 authorize-security-group-ingress \
          --group-name PGSG \
            --protocol tcp \
              --port 22 \
                --cidr 0.0.0.0/0
aws ec2 authorize-security-group-ingress \
          --group-name PGSG\
            --protocol tcp \
              --port 5432 \
                --cidr 0.0.0.0/0
aws ec2 run-instances \
          --image-id ami-0bce8a6275613e7ed \
            --count 1 \
              --instance-type t2.micro \
                --key-name devec2\
                  --security-groups PGSG
```

https://docs.google.com/document/d/1wfItgoqNrBMhU-6epjR-E10q_fon4Jqz/edit?usp=sharing&ouid=117618855868897795502&rtpof=true&sd=true

EC2 Deployment with CloudFormation YAML File

You can provision infrastructure as code from the AWS CloudFormation (CF) program to manage a fleet of computers with templates in the cloud. You can efficiently manage complex environments with CF. The preferred method to install EC2 in corporations is with the Ain't Markup Language (YAML) template, which has two components: resources and parameters. You create parameters for networking, storage, security, instance type, AMI, IAM, and user data (to deploy custom scripts).

Listing 3-8 is the simple CF YAML template file with instance type, AMI, and Security Group details. Create a file named `ec2.yaml` with these details in the Cloud Shell home directory or a directory of your choice.

Listing 3-8. CloudFormation YAML Template to Create an EC2 Instance

```
AWSTemplateFormatVersion: '2010-09-09'
Resources:
  MyEC2Instance:
    Type: 'AWS::EC2::Instance'
    Properties:
      InstanceType: t3.micro
      ImageId: ami-0a04068a95e6a1cde # replace with your AMI ID
      KeyName: dev # replace with your key pair name
      SecurityGroups:
        - Ref: SSHAndPostgreSQLSecurityGroup

  SSHAndPostgreSQLSecurityGroup:
    Type: 'AWS::EC2::SecurityGroup'
    Properties:
      GroupDescription: Enable SSH and PostgreSQL access
      SecurityGroupIngress:
        - CidrIp: 0.0.0.0/0
          IpProtocol: tcp
          FromPort: 22
          ToPort: 22
        - CidrIp: 0.0.0.0/0
          IpProtocol: tcp
          FromPort: 5432
          ToPort: 5432
```

After creating a YAML file, the next step is to run the CF with the command `cloudformation`. There are over 138 commands to manage resources with CF. Listing 3-9 shows a partial description of the `aws cloudformation help` command.

Listing 3-9. CloudFormation Help

```
CLOUDFORMATION()                              CLOUDFORMATION()
NAME
       cloudformation -
DESCRIPTION
       CloudFormation allows you to create and manage Amazon
       Web Services infrastructure deployments predictably and
       repeatedly.
```

If you are creating for the first time in AWS, you have to use the aws cloudformation create-stack command. The --template-body argument must be specified as a file URI. Listing 3-10 is the example of the command and output.

Listing 3-10. CF YAML Deployment

```
aws cloudformation create-stack --stack-name MyFirstEc2
--template-body file:///Users/venkat/work1/work/myec2.yaml
{
    "StackId": "arn:aws:cloudformation:us-east-2:222103471238:
    stack/MyFirstEc2/79dfcda0-089e-11ef-8661-0a5fc6c787e5"
}
```

Upon successful completion, you can query the stack with the command in Listing 3-11.

Listing 3-11. CF describe stack

```
aws cloudformation describe-stacks | grep MyFirstEc2
            "StackId": "arn:aws:cloudformation:us-east-2:
            222103471238:stack/MyFirstEc2/79dfcda0-089e-11ef
            -8661-0a5fc6c787e5",
            "StackName": "MyFirstEc2",
 ::: Lines ommitted
```

After initial create stack command, you can provision ec2 with the CF deploy command.

$aws cloudformation deploy --template-file /home/cloudshell-user/ec2.yaml --stack-name devec201

Figure 3-16 shows the command and deployment details.

```
$aws cloudformation deploy --template-file /home/cloudshell-user/ec2.yaml --stack-name devec201
Waiting for changeset to be created..
Waiting for stack create/update to complete
Successfully created/updated stack - devec201
```

Figure 3-16. *CloudFormation deployment of an EC2 instance with a YAML file*

https://docs.google.com/document/d/1wTPap6ZiKV3r2Oeu8X1lT39Z9I5OBl7K/edit?usp=sharing&ouid=117618855868897795502&rtpof=true&sd=true

AWS CloudFormation Deployment from JSON

Like the YAML template, JSON has two components: resources and parameters. You create parameters for networking, storage, security, instance type, AMI, IAM, and userdata (to deploy custom scripts). Listing 3-12 the sample JSON file to create an EC2 instance where a default VPC is used.

Listing 3-12. CF with JSON

```
{
  "AWSTemplateFormatVersion": "2010-09-09",
  "Resources": {
    "MySecurityGroup": {
      "Type": "AWS::EC2::SecurityGroup",
      "Properties": {
        "GroupDescription": "My Security Group",
```

```json
      "SecurityGroupIngress": [
        {
          "IpProtocol": "tcp",
          "FromPort": 22,
          "ToPort": 22,
          "CidrIp": "0.0.0.0/0"
        },
        {
          "IpProtocol": "tcp",
          "FromPort": 5432,
          "ToPort": 5432,
          "CidrIp": "0.0.0.0/0"
        },
        {
          "IpProtocol": "tcp",
          "FromPort": 80,
          "ToPort": 80,
          "CidrIp": "0.0.0.0/0"
        }
      ]
    }
  },
  "MyEC2Instance": {
    "Type": "AWS::EC2::Instance",
    "Properties": {
      "ImageId": "ami-02b8534ff4b424939",
      "InstanceType": "t2.micro",
      "KeyName": "dev",
      "SecurityGroups": [
        {
          "Ref": "MySecurityGroup"
        }
```

```
    ],
    "UserData": {
      "Fn::Base64": {
        "Fn::Join": [
          "",
          [
            "#!/bin/bash\n",
            yum update -y    # You can all commands in
            this section
          ]
        ]
      }
    }
  }
 }
}
```

```
aws cloudformation deploy --template-file /home/cloudshell-
user/ec2.json --stack-name devec201
```

```
$aws cloudformation deploy --template-file /home/cloudshell-user/ec2.json --stack-name devece02
Waiting for changeset to be created..
Waiting for stack create/update to complete
Successfully created/updated stack - devece02
```

Figure 3-17. *CloudFormation deployment of an EC2 instance JSON file*

See Figure 3-17. The JSON template files to create EC2 instances are provided in the link below. Download the file and deploy it from Cloud Shell.

https://docs.google.com/document/d/1odcEQjDRdlN8t6Y2pdFURL ZcecM5km50/edit?usp=sharing&ouid=117618855868897795502&rtpof=tr ue&sd=true

3.4.3 Install Linux Azure VM

The major tasks are shown in Figure 3-18.

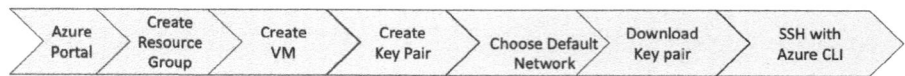

Figure 3-18. *Azure VM tasks*

This section covers the preparation required for the installation of PostgreSQL cluster software on Azure VM instances. The installation of the virtual machine along with the Red Hat OS software is performed by Azure in the background, as this is a managed service.

Connect to Azure Portal

After you connect to Azure Portal, choose to create a virtual machine, enter the virtual machine name and Red Hat Enterprise 8.7, or choose your version of choice, and click Review+create to create a basic VM. See Figures 3-19 and 3-20.

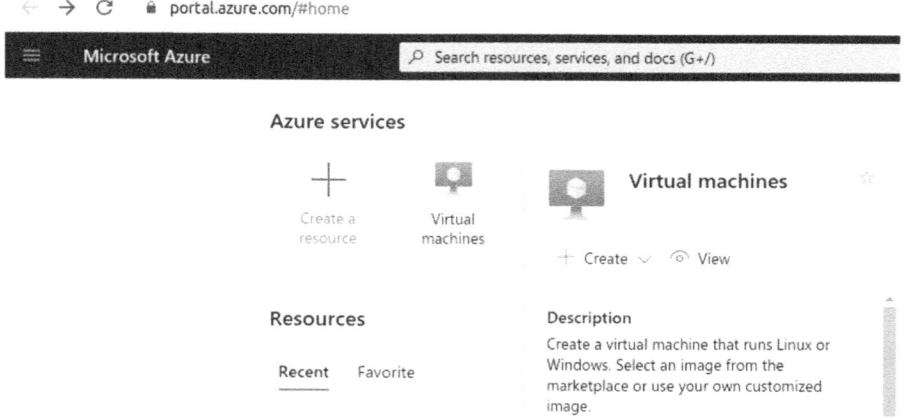

Figure 3-19. *Review and create*

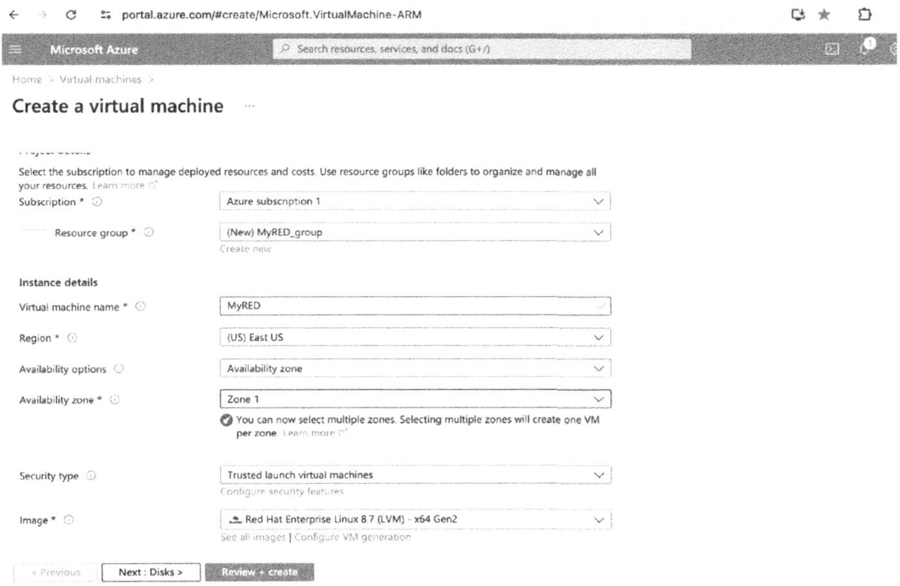

CHAPTER 3   AMAZON EC2/AZURE VM LINUX INSTALL TASKS

Figure 3-20. Azure VM create

Upon completion of the basic validation checks, click the Create icon.

To create the Red Hat OS, proceed with the default values for the Disks, Networking, Management and Advanced options. See Figure 3-21.

CHAPTER 3 AMAZON EC2/AZURE VM LINUX INSTALL TASKS

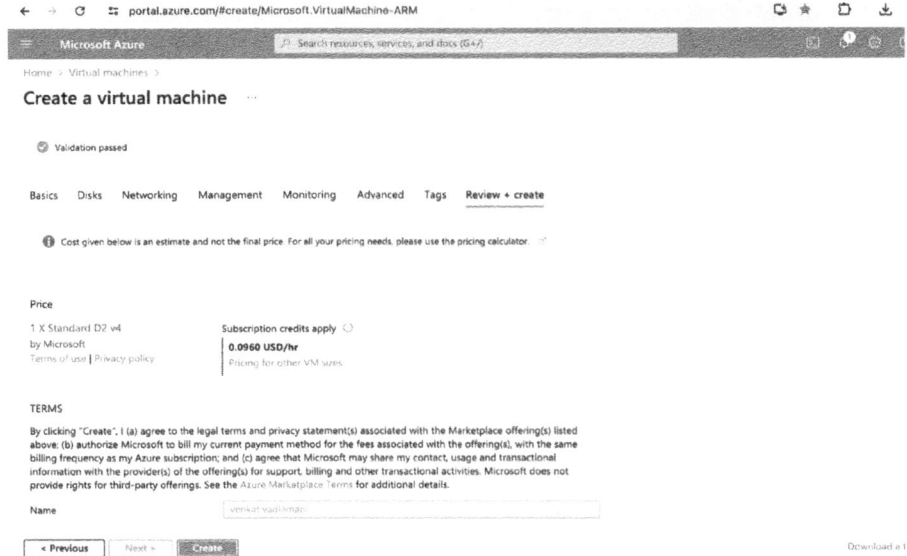

Figure 3-21. *Azure VM create*

Next, download the keys. After clicking the Create button, you will be prompted to download the *.pem, which is used to connect to Azure VM.

Next, validate the completion of Red Hat VM. After deploying is completed, choose the Go to resource icon, which will take you to the Red Hat Azure VM console. See Figure 3-22.

CHAPTER 3 AMAZON EC2/AZURE VM LINUX INSTALL TASKS

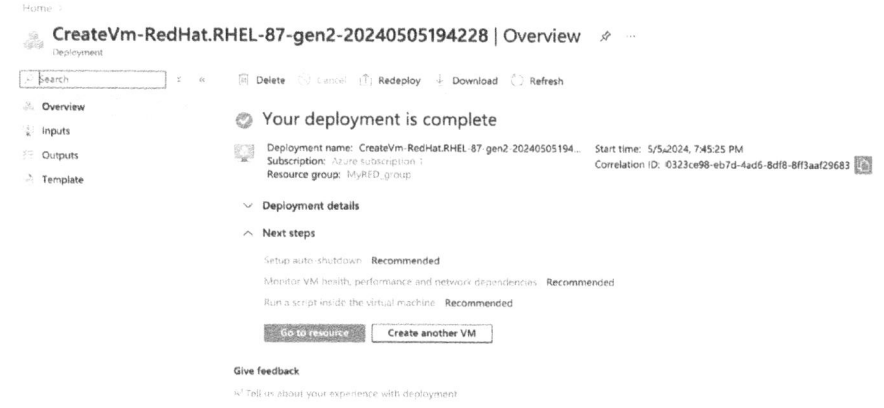

Figure 3-22. Azure VM completion

Next, connect to Red Hat VM. After connecting to the VM home screen, choose the connect icon, which will enable access to VM with a Secure Shell Connection (SSH), as shown in Figure 3-23.

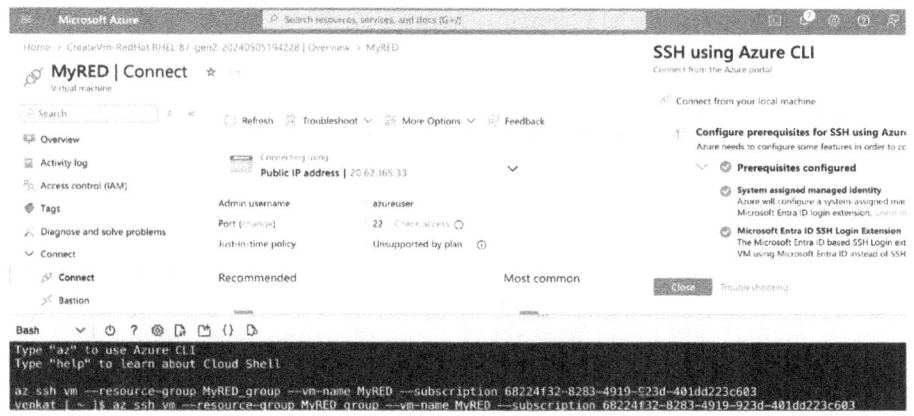

Figure 3-23. Connect to Azure VM

103

CHAPTER 3   AMAZON EC2/AZURE VM LINUX INSTALL TASKS

Create Azure VM from the Command Line

With an Azure Resource Group, you can deploy and manage all services as a single unit. It is a top-level container for managing related Azure resources collectively. To create an Azure VM, you must first create a Resource Group and then create the VM using the az vm create command. You can customize the script with your username and resource group.

After connecting from Cloud Shell, run the following commands to create Azure VM for Red hat:

```
az group create --location eastus --resource-group PostRG
az vm create   --resource-group PostRG   --name REDHAT
--image RHELRaw8LVMGen2   --admin-username azureuser
--generate-ssh-keys   --public-ip-sku Standard
```

Listing 3-13 shows a partial output of the command.

Listing 3-13. Azure VM Creation from a CLI

```
$ az group create --location eastus --resource-group PostRG
{
  "id": "/subscriptions/ /resourceGroups/PostRG",
  "location": "eastus",
  "managedBy": null,
$ az vm create   --resource-group PostRG   --name REDHAT
--image RedHat:RHEL:9-LVM:latest   --admin-username azureuser
--generate-ssh-keys   --public-ip-sku Standard
{
  "fqdns": "",
  "publicIpAddress": "20.185.45.10",
  "resourceGroup": "PostRG",
  "zones": ""
}
```

https://docs.google.com/document/d/15V00-yYo5tgjpeZmxDYukg
IpFUWYnZxR/edit?usp=sharing&ouid=117618855868897795502&rtpof=tr
ue&sd=true

3.4.4 Linux Tasks on Amazon ec2/Azure VM

After installing Linux OS, you have to work on several tasks. The following sections cover this in detail.

Connect to EC2/Azure VM

After installing the Red Hat operating system, AWS creates a default user called ec2-user and the AZURE user by Azure. There are four ways to connect to a Linux host from a client PC such as Mac or Windows or other Linux host. See Figure 3-24.

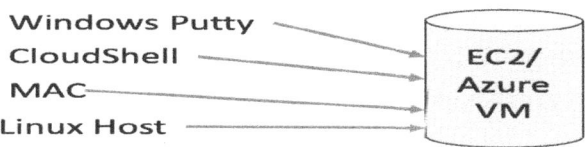

Figure 3-24. *Client programs to VM*

> **Note** These tasks are similar to tasks on Azure VM.

Connect to EC2 from Cloud Shell

You must upload the *.pem key to Cloud Shell in order for you to connect to any EC2 host. The connection to EC2 is from the `ssh` command. You can obtain the host name from the AWS console or from the AWS CLI describe option. Figure 3-25 shows the connection to a Linux host.

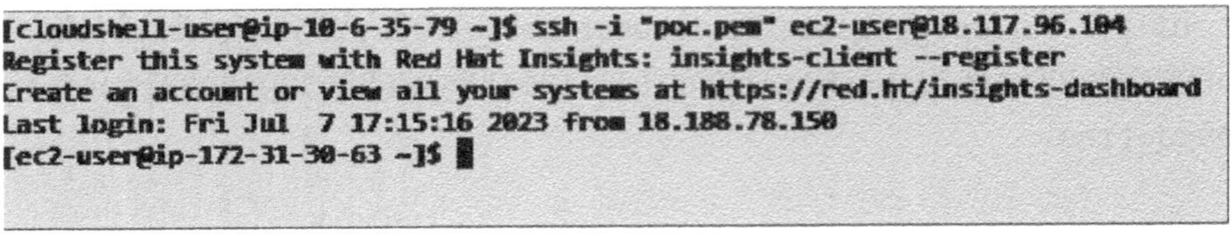

CHAPTER 3   AMAZON EC2/AZURE VM LINUX INSTALL TASKS

```
[cloudshell-user@ip-10-6-35-79 ~]$ ssh -i "poc.pem" ec2-user@18.117.96.104
Register this system with Red Hat Insights: insights-client --register
Create an account or view all your systems at https://red.ht/insights-dashboard
Last login: Fri Jul  7 17:15:16 2023 from 18.188.78.150
[ec2-user@ip-172-31-30-63 ~]$
```

Figure 3-25. ssh connection to Linux

Configuration of putty

The putty program is the most common utility to connect to Linux host from a Windows PC.

To securely connect to the Linux host from a Windows client, a common key is shared between the Linux host and the Windows client. Note that you already downloaded the *.pem key when creating the EC2 host. There are two steps to set up a connection to the Linux host from a Windows client using the downloaded *.pem key: generate a private key from the puttygen tool, and provide the hostname and *.ppk with the putty tool.

To work with putty, you must install two software packages: download Putty from putty.org and download puttygen from www.puttygen.com/download-putty. After extracting both software packages, type puttgen at the search bar. See Figure 3-26.

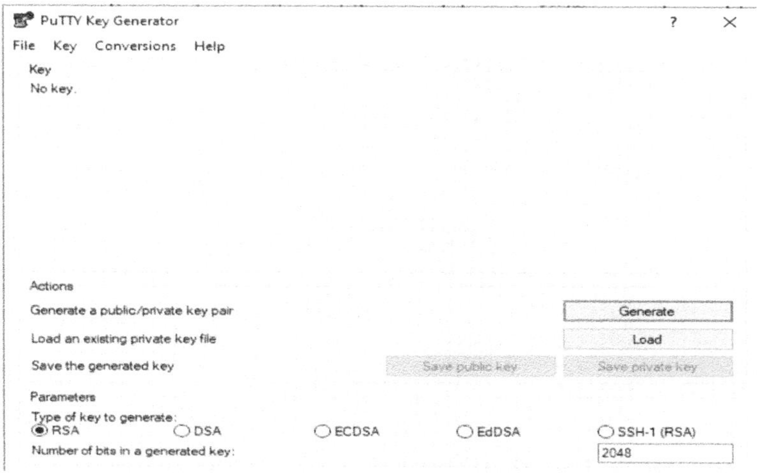

CHAPTER 3 AMAZON EC2/AZURE VM LINUX INSTALL TASKS

Figure 3-26. Putty key generator

Load the poc. pem key downloaded when creating the instance. See Figure 3-27.

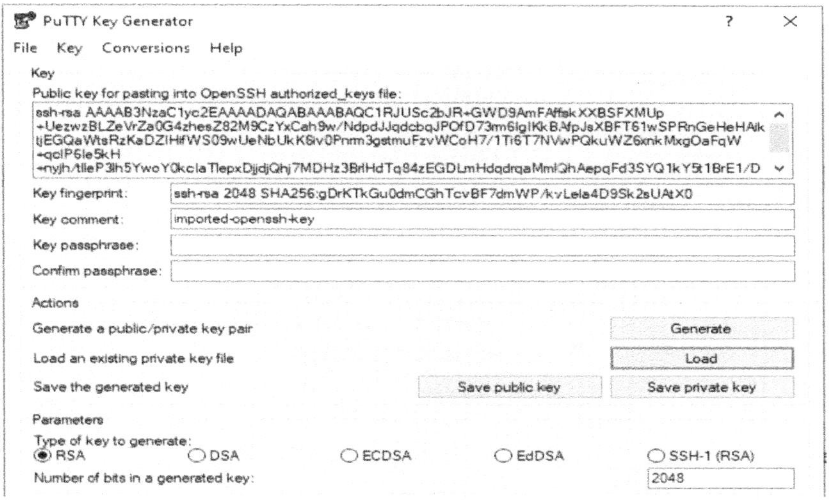

Figure 3-27. Private key

107

Choose the Save private key option to save the file as devpoc.ppk.

Click Yes to complete the configuration of the key generation. See Figure 3-28.

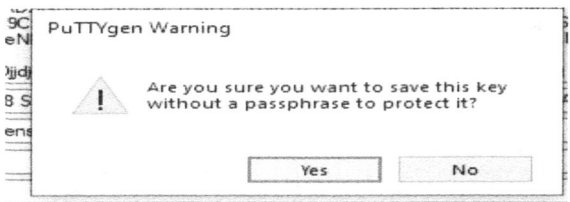

Figure 3-28. *Click yes*

After the ppk is created, the next step is to connect to the EC2 host by providing *.ppk in the Authentication option. Figures 3-29 and 3-30 show how to connect to the Linux host.

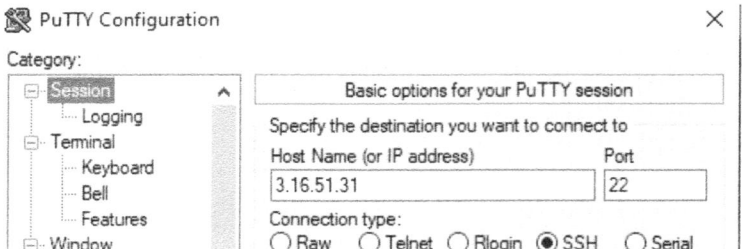

Figure 3-29. *putty connection to host*

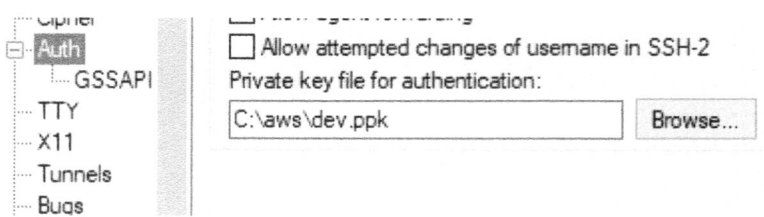

Figure 3-30. *Putty key selection*

CHAPTER 3   AMAZON EC2/AZURE VM LINUX INSTALL TASKS

If you provide the correct key, you will be authenticated to the Linux host on AWS. See Figure 3-31.

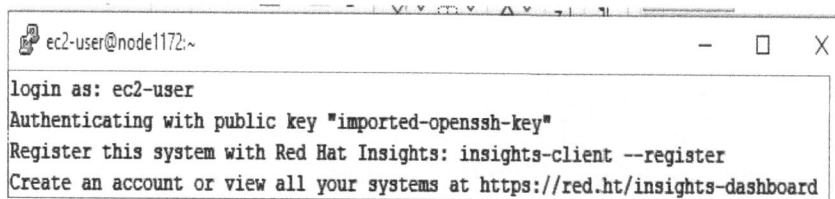

Figure 3-31. *ec2 connection*

In this screenshot, notice the authentication of the key from the Windows client in the Linux host.

For detailed putty configuration details, refer to the URL provided by AWS.

Congratulations, you have configured EC2 and established a connection to the Linux host.

Connect to EC2 from the Linux Host

In a typical organization, you log on to a secure Linux Server and then connect to the rest of the Linux servers from that host. By sharing the *.pem key, you can connect to a Linux host virtual host or machine

Connect to EC2 from MAC

During install you downloaded the *.pem key. Make sure you are in the directory where the key is installed and run the ssh command to connect to ec2.

```
ssh -i "secdb.pem" ec2-user@18.245.12.23
ec2-user@:~
```

109

Linux Environment

After successfully creating an EC2 instance, the next task is to understand the Linux OS configuration.

Check the OS Version

The first step after installing the OS is to validate the version. The cat is a program in Linux to display the contents of the file. With the cat program, you can check the OS version. Type the command cat /etc/redhat-release to display the installed version of Linux. See Listing 3-14.

Listing 3-14. Linux Version

```
$ cat /etc/redhat-release
Red Hat Enterprise Linux release 9.3 (Plow)
```

Linux Kernel

The kernel-related files are in the directory /proc/sys/kernel. The security limits are defined in the file /etc/security/limits.conf. The limits are unlimited unless limits are imposed based on the quota per process. All limits are based on the per process basis.

Check OS Memory Configuration

As mentioned, operating system memory is assigned to processes based on SHMMAX and SHMALL parameters. The values of these parameters are shared between the processes, which is why it's called Inter Process Communication (IPCS). By default, the memory allocation is unlimited, unless limited to specific processes by imposing limits or quota. Listing 3-15 shows commands to identify OS resources.

Listing 3-15. Red Hat Resource Query

```
cat /proc/sys/kernel/shmmax  #maximum size of shared memory
cat /proc/sys/kernel/shmall.   # semaphore details
 ipcs -m # memory usage details by process
cat /proc/meminfo # memory allocation and usage details
cat /proc/cpuifo # No of cpu's on the system
```

3.4.5 Linux Huge Pages

On Linux, the default memory allocation unit is the page size, which can be between 4KB to 64KB based on the hardware architecture and kernel configuration. The memory consumption of a PostgreSQL database can vary from several megabytes to multiple gigabytes or even terabytes, depending on the workload and configuration.

The configuration of huge pages enables a continuous area of memory reserved for a PostgreSQL database, used by PostgreSQL database shared memory [1]. Simply put, huge pages are blocks of memory that come in 2MB and 1GB sizes. The page tables used by the 2MB pages are suitable for formatting multiple gigabytes of memory, whereas the page tables of 1GB pages are best for scaling to terabytes of memory. [2]

Configuration of Huge Pages

The huge pages are configured in a two-step process: configure huge pages in Linux and enable huge pages in the database.

Configuration of Huge Pages in the Operating System

The default huge page size on Linux is typically set to 2048KB (or 2MB). When running a PostgreSQL database, it is common practice to reserve 70% of the operating system memory for huge pages. This means that if your system has 4GB of RAM, you reserve 3.2GB (or 3200MB) for huge pages. To accommodate the PostgreSQL database, you 1600 huge pages (3200MB/2MB).

The procedure to configure huge pages is to add vm.nr_hugepages=1600 in the /etc/sysctl.conf kernel file and then dynamically reload the kernel. Listing 3-16 shows the result of executing the huge pages configuration command.

Listing 3-16. Huge Pages

```
echo "vm.nr_hugepages = 1600" >> /etc/sysctl.conf
sysctl -p. # reboot the system
 cat /proc/meminfo | grep HugePages_# identify the changes
HugePages_Total:       1600
HugePages_Free:        1546
HugePages_Rsvd:          86
HugePages_Surp:           0
```

Around 1600 huge pages are reserved for PostgreSQL database memory. You may utilize 3.2GB huge pages for one PostgreSQL cluster or for multiple PostgreSQL clusters (for instance, 1GB for three clusters).

Congratulations, you have successfully configured huge pages in the Linux OS.

3.4.6 Create a Billing Alert

It is essential to create a billing alert to avoid surprise bills by month end. You can create a billing alert with two methods in AWS: AWS CLI and the AWS Billing console.

CHAPTER 3   AMAZON EC2/AZURE VM LINUX INSTALL TASKS

Billing Alert with AWS CLI

You can obtain details with the aws ce get-cost-and-usage command (shown in Figure 3-32).

```
aws ce get-cost-and-usage --time-period Start=$sdate,End=$edate
--granularity DAILY --metrics "BlendedCost" "UsageQuantity"
```

```
"Total": {
    "BlendedCost": {
        "Amount": "1.890114413"
        "Unit": "USD"

    "UsageQuantity": {
        "Amount": "43.48187244",
        "Unit": "N/A"
```

Figure 3-32.   AWS billing

Billing Alert with Azure CLI

For Azure, use the Azure console to get billing details (see Figure 3-33) with the following link: https://portal.azure.com/#view/Microsoft_Azure_GTM/ModernBillingMenuBlade/~/costManagementMenuItem.

Figure 3-33.   Azure billing cost analysis

3.4.7 Volume Group Creation

Using logical volumes allows for more flexibility and scalability in managing storage for PostgreSQL databases and tablespaces. It enables the expansion and resizing of file systems without requiring downtime. Creating volume groups (VG) combines multiple physical disks and provides logical partitions called logical volumes (LV). Each LV is then mounted as a file system, and the PostgreSQL user can create and manage their database files within this file system. To expand the file system, you have to expand the capacity to the VG by adding disks, followed by expanding the LV, which is mounted as PostgreSQL data or backup file system [3]. See Figure 3-34.

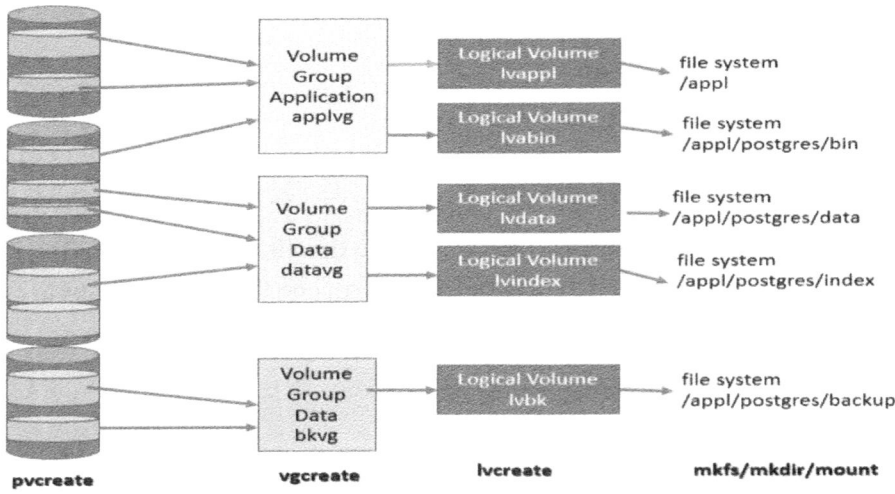

Figure 3-34. Red Hat logical volume groups

Logical Volume Setup Commands

Assuming there are two physical disks named /dev/xvdn and /dev/xvdr, the following is an example to create logical volumes in Red Hat:

```
sudo pvcreate /dev/xvdn /dev/xvdr
```

```
sudo vgcreate applvg  /dev/xvdn /dev/xvdr
sudo lvcreate -n pgdatalv -L 1G applvg
sudo mkfs.ext4 /dev/applvg/pgdatalv
mke2fs 1.46.5 (30-Dec-2021)
Creating filesystem with 262144 4k blocks and 65536 inodes
Filesystem UUID: 25e85087-0ecc-4fb5-96a2-7318fa8a908e
::::: Lines omitted
sudo mkdir /appls
sudo mount /dev/applvg/pgdatalv /appls
df -h /appls
Filesystem                      Size  Used Avail Use% Mounted on
/dev/mapper/applvg-pgdatalv     974M   24K  907M   1% /appls
Add  following entry in /etc/fstab for permanent mount
UUID=25e85087-0ecc-4fb5-96a2-7318fa8a908e /appls ext4
defaults 0 2
```

Screen Images of Logical Volume Creation

The pvcreate command is shown in Figure 3-35.

```
$sudo pvcreate /dev/xvdn /dev/xvdr
  Physical volume "/dev/xvdn" successfully created.
  Physical volume "/dev/xvdr" successfully created.
  Creating devices file /etc/lvm/devices/system.devices
```

Figure 3-35. *Physical volume create command and listing*

To create a volume group, logical volume, and make the file system, see Figures 3-36 and 3-37.

CHAPTER 3 AMAZON EC2/AZURE VM LINUX INSTALL TASKS

```
$sudo vgcreate applvg  /dev/xvdn /dev/xvdr
  Volume group "applvg" successfully created
$sudo lvcreate -n pgdatalv -L 1G applvg
  Logical volume "pgdatalv" created.
```

Figure 3-36. *Volume group and logical volume creation and listing*

```
$sudo mkfs.ext4 /dev/applvg/pgdatalv
mke2fs 1.46.5 (30-Dec-2021)
Creating filesystem with 262144 4k blocks and 65536 inodes
Filesystem UUID: 25e85087-0ecc-4fb5-96a2-7318fa8a908e
```

Figure 3-37. *Make file system*

Mount the file system to a directory as in Figure 3-38 and validate it as in Figure 3-39.

```
$sudo mount /dev/applvg/pgdatalv /appls
```

Figure 3-38. *Mount a file system*

```
$df -h /appls
Filesystem                   Size  Used Avail Use% Mounted on
/dev/mapper/applvg-pgdatalv  974M   24K  907M   1% /appls
```

Figure 3-39. *Validate the mount*

You must connect as a root user or use sudo from ec2-user to create PostgreSQL user credentials. When connected as root user, notice the # before the prompt of the user account. The following command adds a user and group in the host computer:

useradd -u 5435 -g postgres -G postgres -b /appl -c "PostgreSQL Server on-premises".

The usage of the useradd command is as follows:

CHAPTER 3 AMAZON EC2/AZURE VM LINUX INSTALL TASKS

```
Usage: useradd [options] LOGIN, useradd -D useradd -D
[options] -b -base-dir BASE_DIR base directory for the home
directory of the new account, -g, --gid GROUP name or ID of
the primary group of the new account, -G, --groups GROUPS list
of supplementary groups of the new account. For additional
commands, use the command man useradd.
```

3.4.8 AWS OS Storage Allocation Procedure

You can create multiple file systems to install several PostgreSQL instances, expand database storage, create non-default tablespaces, and for separate log file locations. Tablespaces allow for the separation of data based on business requirements. Non-default tablespaces can be created on different file systems on different storage types to optimize performance and manage storage more effectively. Figure 3-40 shows the tasks to expand storage on Red Hat OS on AWS.

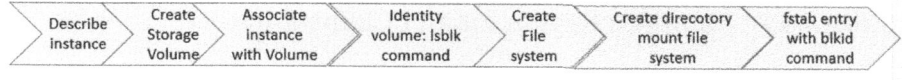

Figure 3-40. Allocate AWS storage

Allocate Storage from AWS CLI

If you would like to create additional storage for a PostgreSQL database backup or for additional tablespace, you provision AWS storage volumes
    The steps are as follows:

1. Describe the instance to obtain the AZ associated with it.
2. Create a volume.
3. Associate the volume with the instance.

CHAPTER 3 AMAZON EC2/AZURE VM LINUX INSTALL TASKS

4. Create a directory.

5. Create a file system.

6. Attach a file system to a directory.

7. Mount the file system.

8. Make an entry in /etc/fstab.

After you attach an Amazon EBS volume to your instance, it is exposed as a block device [4].

Identify Instance Availability Zones

You can query all the attributes of the EC2 instance with the command `aws ec2 describe-instances`, which takes instance id as an argument. With the query you obtain the location of the instance. With the command in Listing 3-17, you identify the instance availability zone of us-east-2b. Use your own instance id, as instance ids are different for different users.

Listing 3-17. Identify a Region for an EC2 Instance

```
$ aws ec2 describe-instances --instance-ids i-0a83b1b9403ac2ab2
--query 'Reservations[].Instances[].Placement.AvailabilityZone'
[
    "us-east-2b"
]
```

Create a Volume

The `aws create-volume` command creates a volume in an availability zone. The size is provisioned in GBs. You can create one or many volumes and attach to one or many instances. Listing 3-18 shows the command to create a volume which creates a volume ID.

Listing 3-18. Create a volume

```
aws ec2 create-volume --availability-zone us-east-2b --size 2
{
    "AvailabilityZone": "us-east-2b",
        }
```

Attach an Instance to a Volume

After creating a volume, the next step is to assign it to an instance for a device. The maximum number of Amazon EBS volumes that you can attach to an instance depends on the instance type and instance size [5]. The AWS block device naming convention is /dev/xvd*, where you can assign from a to z. A block device is a type of storage required to create a file system, where the operating system will write data into blocks. The command in Listing 3-19 attaches a volume to an instance on a device.

Listing 3-19. Attach a Volume to an Instance

```
$ aws ec2 attach-volume --volume-id vol-098e2142f62f38370
--instance-id i-0a83b1b9403ac2ab2 --device /dev/xvdf
{
    "AttachTime": "2023-07-25T21:25:08.824000+00:00",
    "Device": "/dev/xvdf",
    "InstanceId": "i-0a83b1b9403ac2ab2",
    "State": "attaching",
    "VolumeId": "vol-098e2142f62f38370"
}
```

mkfs and Mount the Volume

On a storage device you created earlier, such as /dev/xvdf, the file system is formatted with the mkfs command. The file system is used by the operating system to manage files in a hierarchical manner. After creating the file system on the device, you need to mount the device to a directory where you will assign data for the PostgreSQL database. Listing 3-20 shows the commands to create a directory, make the file system, and mount it on the directory.

Listing 3-20. mkfs and mount

```
cd /
sudo mkdir postdata
sudo mkfs -t ext4 /dev/xvdf
Writing superblocks and filesystem accounting information: done
sudo mount /dev/xvdf   /postdata
```

fstab Entry

By making the entry /etc/fstab, the file system will mount after reboot of the system. The steps are shown in Listing 3-21.

Listing 3-21. blkid Output

```
(1) use blkid command to identify the UUID of the storage
device. Use the blkid command to find the UUID of the device.
Make a note of the UUID of the device that you want to mount
after reboot[4]
# blkid
/dev/xvdg: UUID="baba989e-d4ec-4296-b356-e5c49ae7ad27" BLOCK_
SIZE="512" TYPE="xfs"
```

After backing up /etc/fstab, add the entry in Listing 3-22 to /etc/fstab for an auto mount of the file system.

Listing 3-22. fstab Entry

```
UUID=baba989e-d4ec-4296-b356-e5c49ae7ad27 /pgdata15
             xfs      defaults,nofail  0  2
```

The final command to mount `# mount -a`, reboot, and identify the mounted file systems.

Here is a video recording of adding storage: https://us02web.zoom.us/rec/share/X6hU36lu6FyFULVGdkdeeWYwmI1k35dn3IqvJrMijhe05Uxc8e9tEXAWFxbcjmpP.qpavNNi83SDjRoDs.

3.4.9 EC2/Azure VM Management Commands

You can manage a fleet of instances with the following commands.

aws cloudformation list-stacks

Displays all deployed configurations

aws ec2 describe-instances --query

Display all EC2 instances:

```
"Reservations[*].Instances[*].{ID:InstanceId,Type:InstanceType,State:State.Name}" --output table
```

aws ec2 start-instances

Start an EC2 instance with the instance id argument:

```
aws ec2 start-instances  --instance-id i-0e51b5e8ouu234189
```

aws ec2 stop-instances

Stop an instance with the instance id argument:

```
aws ec2 stop-instances  --instance-id i-0e51b5e8ouu234189
```

3.4.10 Azure CLI

With Azure CLI, you can perform all administrative tasks.

Azure Deployment Group List

With the `group list` command, all resources deployed under a resource group are displayed:

```
az deployment group list --resource-group demo # enter your resource group name
```

az vm start

Start a VM with the vmname and resource group name:

```
az vm start --name [your instance name]  --resource-group demo # enter your resource group name
```

az vm stop

Stop a VM with the vmname and resource group name:

```
az vm stop --name <YourVMName> --resource-group <YourResourceGroupName>
```

3.4.11 Keywords

AWS console, Cloud shell, create key pair, aws ec2 create-security-group, aws ec2 authorize-security-group-ingress, aws ec2 run-instances , aws ec2 start-instances, aws ec2 stop-instances, az vm, az vm start, az vm stop, Azure CloudShell, az group create, az vm list-skus, az vm create image, Linux shell, and huge pages.

3.4.12 Summary of Learning

In this chapter, you learned the basics of the Linux operating system, Linux shell commands, basic shell programming, and AWS/EC2 and Azure VM installation methods. You provisioned AWS/EC2 and Azure VM machines, set up an SSH configuration with putty, configured huge pages, set up firewall and security roles, expanded storage on Linux with Red Hat volume groups and AWS storage volumes, and reviewed basic cloud commands to manage virtual machines. This chapter completes all preparatory steps to install PostgreSQL on a Linux ASWEc2 and Azure VM environment.

3.4.13 Practice Chapter 3

1. Create an AWS account.
2. Create an Azure account.
3. From the AWS console, launch Cloud Shell.
4. Create a Red Hat OS (version 9 or latest) VM from AWS Cloud Shell.
5. Download an AWS key pair.
6. Connect to a Red Hat VM from AWS Cloud Shell.
7. From the Azure console, launch Cloud Shell.
8. Create a Red Hat OS (version 9 or latest) VM from Azure Cloud Shell.
9. Connect to a Red Hat VM from Azure Cloud Shell.

10. Execute, test, and practice shell commands from a Red Hat VM.

11. Configure huge pages on Linux.

12. Create a directory named /pgdata on AQWS and allocate 10GB of storage.

3.4.14 Questions Chapter 3

1. How many installation methods are available to install EC2/Azure VM on Linux?

2. How do you create EC2 with JSON and YAML templates?

3. How do you create an Azure VM with the command line?

4. What tasks can you do with the userdata section of an AWS CloudFormation template?

5. How can huge pages be configured when the system has 128GB of memory and what benefits does it provide for PostgreSQL cluster performance and efficiency?

6. What are the steps involved in increasing the volume size of a PostgreSQL cluster from 1GB to 2GB?

7. How does expanding the volume using volume groups impact the scalability and storage capacity of a PostgreSQL cluster?

8. How do you extract us-east-2c text from the below exhibit? Tip: use the grep, awk, and sed commands.

CHAPTER 3 AMAZON EC2/AZURE VM LINUX INSTALL TASKS

```
    Placement": {
    "AvailabilityZone": "us-east-2c",
    "GroupName": "",
    "Tenancy": "default"
}
```

References

1. https://access.redhat.com/documentation/en-us/red_hat_enterprise_linux/6/html/performance_tuning_guide/s-memory-transhuge
2. www.PostgreSQL.org/docs/9.0/kernel-resources.html
3. www.redhat.com/sysadmin/create-volume-group
4. https://docs.aws.amazon.com/AWSEC2/latest/UserGuide/ebs-using-volumes.html
5. https://docs.aws.amazon.com/AWSEC2/latest/UserGuide/volume_limits.html

CHAPTER 4

PostgreSQL Software Installation on Amazon EC2/Azure VM Linux

4.1 Abstract

On an Amazon EC2 or Azure VM Linux host, the PostgreSQL software is installed by the package manager provided by the Red Hat OS, which is based on the default configuration. For customization, you have to work with the configuration options. You can create multiple PostgreSQL clusters on Linux hosts to segregate business requirements for separate windows of maintenance, with different ports for access. You have to work on several configuration tasks after installing the PostgreSQL cluster software, such as initializing the PostgreSQL cluster database, configuring the database parameters to expand the default memory, installing and configuring extensions, setting up firewall and network rules, and creating user

---

The original version of the chapter has been revised. A correction to this chapter can be found at https://doi.org/10.1007/979-8-8688-0817-3_18

databases. As the default PostgreSQL port 5432 is not secure, you have to create a non-default port for database access to protect the database from internal and external threats and vulnerabilities.

4.2 Objectives of Learning

- Red Hat package manager (RPM) download
- Installation and configuration of PostgreSQL with Red Hat packages
- Installation and configuration of PostgreSQL with the configuration method
- Creation of a PostgreSQL cluster and database
- Identification of PostgreSQL server operating system resources (see Figure 4-1)
- After completion of this chapter, you should be able to install and configure PostgreSQL software, initialize the PostgreSQL cluster and work with configuration files.

4.3 Installation of PostgreSQL Software on Linux

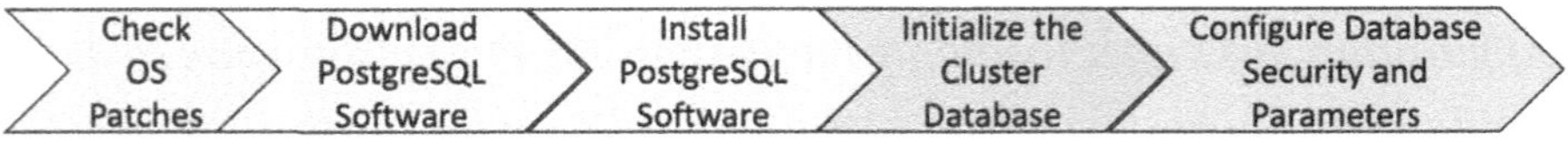

Check OS Patches → Download PostgreSQL Software → Install PostgreSQL Software → Initialize the Cluster Database → Configure Database Security and Parameters

Figure 4-1. *PostgreSQL software install and configuration on Linux*

CHAPTER 4   POSTGRESQL SOFTWARE INSTALLATION ON AMAZON EC2/AZURE VM LINUX

Yellowdog Updater Modified (yum) and Dandified YUM (dnf) are package managers for RPM-based distributions to install and upgrade software on the Red Hat OS. With RPM, users can install, update, verify, and remove software on the OS. The dnf is the default from Linux 8 onwards, whereas yum is used for Linux versions 7 and below.

The PostgreSQL software is installed as a root user in Linux or as a user with superuser do(sudo) to root privilege as am RPM. The PostgreSQL software is installed in the cloud by three methods:

1. The RPM method, which is a precompiled binary package built for Red Hat

2. The configuration method using make and make all

3. Pulling from Docker, which is covered in Chapter 7

The following are the software packages required to install PostgreSQL for version 16:

postgresql16-libs-16.2-1PGDG.rhel9.x86_64. # Libraries
postgresql16-16.2-1PGDG.rhel9.x86_64. # Client side tools and utilities
postgresql16-server-16.2-1PGDG.rhel9.x86_64 # PostgreSQL Server
postgresql16-contrib-16.2-1PGDG.rhel9.x86_64 # Contributory packages

The PostgreSQL cluster software is available for download from the official Postgres site.

After connecting to your AWS EC2/Azure VM instance, you must create an account to view all your systems at https://access.redhat.com/ for support with Red Hat Linux.

129

4.3.1 Download PostgreSQL Cluster Software

Download the official PostgreSQL software from www.postgresql.org/
download/linux/redhat/.

From the PostgreSQL Yum Repository, choose PostgreSQL version 16 and Red Hat version 9, which are the latest at the time of writing the book. Choose the Red Hat OS of your choice and choose the PostgreSQL version depending on your requirements and compatibility with the application. In this section, you will install the PostgreSQL software on Amazon EC2 or Azure VM. The package postgresql16-server handles all required packages to install PostgreSQL on a Linux host.

4.3.2 PostgreSQL Software for Installation on Linux

Listing 4-1 shows the PostgreSQL installation notes from the download page for the latest version 16.x.

Listing 4-1. PostgreSQL Server Software Command Line Instructions

```
# Download latest repositories from PostgreSQL Global Development Group
sudo dnf install -y https://download.postgresql.org/pub/repos/yum/reporpms/EL-8-x86_64/pgdg-redhat-repo-latest.noarch.rpm
sudo dnf -qy module disable postgresql # Disable existing psql on the host
sudo dnf install -y postgresql16-server #Install 3 packages.
sudo /usr/pgsql-16/bin/postgresql-16-setup initdb #Optionally initialize the database
sudo yum install -y postgresql16-contrib
sudo systemctl enable postgresql-16. # Enable auto start of Postgres Service
```

The installation log is at https://drive.google.com/file/d/16LJrsvPZjhsCy-WJI8zGPu6Pnev5crJn/view?usp=sharing.

You can run all commands in one go or run individual commands to understand the details. The first task is to install the latest repositories in Linux from the official PostgreSQL repository, which is a collection of software packages created by the Postgres Global Development team. The software `pgdg-redhat-repo-latest.noarch.rpm` downloads a file that contains the PostgreSQL configuration details. Listing 4-2 shows the commands to install the latest repositories from PostgreSQL's official site.

Listing 4-2. Updating the Latest Red Hat Repositories

```
$sudo su -
$sudo dnf install -y https://download.postgresql.org/pub/repos/yum/reporpms/EL-8-x86_64/pgdg-redhat-repo-latest.noarch.rpm
::::::::::::Lines omitted.
Dependencies resolved
```

After successfully resolving all dependencies, you should receive a message saying "Dependencies resolved."

4.3.3 PostgreSQL Server Software Installation

After all software dependencies are resolved, the next task is to install PostgreSQL server. which includes the three packages shown in Listing 4-3.

Listing 4-3. PostgreSQL Software Packages

postgresql16-server-16.2-1PGDG.rhel9.x86_64	PostgreSQL server package
postgresql16-16.2-1PGDG.rhel9.x86_64	Client-side tools and utilities
postgresql16-libs-16.2-1PGDG.rhel9.x86_64	Libraries

Listing 4-4 shows the command to install PostgreSQL and the output log.

Listing 4-4. PostgreSQL Install

```
$sudo dnf install -y postgresql16-server
Waiting for process with pid 1624 to finish..
Dependencies resolved.
Installing:
 postgresql16-server         x86_64         16.2-1PGDG.
rhel9          pgdg16        6.8 M
:::::::::::::: Lines omitted
Installed:
  postgresql16-16.2-1PGDG.rhel9.x86_64        postgresql16-
server-16.2-1PGDG.rhel9.x86_64
```

After successfully installing the PostgreSQL server software, you should notice the "Installed" message.

Now you must install the contributory packages. The contributory packages are additional extensions to Postgres server. You have to install the contributory (contrib) packages after installing the PostgreSQL server software. Around 50 additional features or options are added with the contributory packages. AWS and Azure have additional extensions that are open-source software provisioning. Listing 4-5 shows the commands to install the PostgreSQL contrib package.

Listing 4-5. Install Contributory Packages

```
$sudo yum install -y postgresql16-contrib
Dependencies resolved.
Installing:
 postgresql16-contrib          x86_64         16.2-1PGDG.rhel9
pgdg16         717
```

::::::::::::Lines omitted
Installed:
  postgresql16-contrib-16.2-1PGDG.rhel9.x86_64
Complete

After the PostgreSQL software is installed, you can check the installed packages with the rpm command. The basic rpm commands are -q to query, -V to verify, -i to install, -U to update, and -e to erase. Validate the installed PostgreSQL packages with the rpm -qa command. See Listing 4-6.

Listing 4-6. PostgreSQL Installed Packages

```
rpm -qa | grep -i post
postgresql16-libs-16.2-1PGDG.rhel9.x86_64. # Libraries
postgresql16-16.2-1PGDG.rhel9.x86_64. # Client side tools and
utilities
postgresql16-server-16.2-1PGDG.rhel9.x86_64 # PostgreSQL Server
postgresql16-contrib-16.2-1PGDG.rhel9.x86_64 # Contributory
packages
```

The PostgreSQL binaries are installed in the directory /usr/pgsql-16/bin.

After the PostgreSQL Server install, identify the binaries or programs you will be working with for PostgreSQL database administration. Figure 4-2 shows the PostgreSQL binaries or executables.

```
$ls /usr/pgsql-16/bin
clusterdb     pg_amcheck         pg_ctl              pg_restore        postgres
createdb      pg_archivecleanup  pg_dump             pg_rewind         postgresql-16-check-db-dir
createuser    pg_basebackup      pg_dumpall          pg_test_fsync     postgresql-16-setup
dropdb        pgbench            pg_isready          pg_test_timing    psql
dropuser      pg_checksums       pg_receivewal       pg_upgrade        reindexdb
initdb        pg_config          pg_recvlogical      pg_verifybackup   vacuumdb
oid2name      pg_controldata     pg_resetwal         pg_waldump        vacuumlo
```

Figure 4-2. *PostgreSQL binaries*

The most used commands while working with PostgreSQL Server are `psql`, `initdb`, `pg_dump`, `pg_ctl`, `pg_dumpall` and `vaccumdb`. In this chapter, you will use the `psql` and `initdb` commands.

4.3.4 Download Direct RPM Packages

In corporations, database servers do not have direct Internet connectivity to download the PostgreSQL software. As a result, you must download the software from an Internet-facing computer and distribute it to the database servers for software installation. The following is the link to download the Red Hat RPM: https://download.postgresql.org/pub/repos/yum/16/redhat/.

If you have access to the Internet, install the package with the commands shown in Listing 4-7.

Listing 4-7. Install PostgreSQL Packages from Red Hat Repositories

```
sudo dnf install --nobest --skip-broken -y https://download.
postgresql.org/pub/repos/yum/16/redhat/rhel-8-x86_64/
postgresql16-server-16.0-1PGDG.rhel8.x86_64.rpm
sudo dnf install --nobest --skip-broken -y https://download.
postgresql.org/pub/repos/yum/16/redhat/rhel-8-x86_64/
postgresql16-libs-16.0-1PGDG.rhel8.x86_64.rpm
sudo dnf install --nobest --skip-broken -y https://download.
postgresql.org/pub/repos/yum/16/redhat/rhel-8-x86_64/
postgresql16-server-16.0-1PGDG.rhel8.x86_64.rpm
sudo dnf install --nobest --skip-broken -y https://download.
postgresql.org/pub/repos/yum/16/redhat/rhel-8-x86_64/
postgresql16-contrib-16.0-1PGDG.rhel8.x86_64.rpm
```

CHAPTER 4　POSTGRESQL SOFTWARE INSTALLATION ON AMAZON EC2/AZURE VM LINUX

4.3.5　PostgreSQL RPM Packages on Azure

Note　You must resolve several dependencies while installing the RPM packages.

4.3.6　Install PostgreSQL Software on Azure VM

Sections 4.1.1 to 4.1.5 cover the installation of PostgreSQL software on Azure VM. Figure 4-3 shows the details of the Red Hat OS version and the installed PostgreSQL packages and versions.

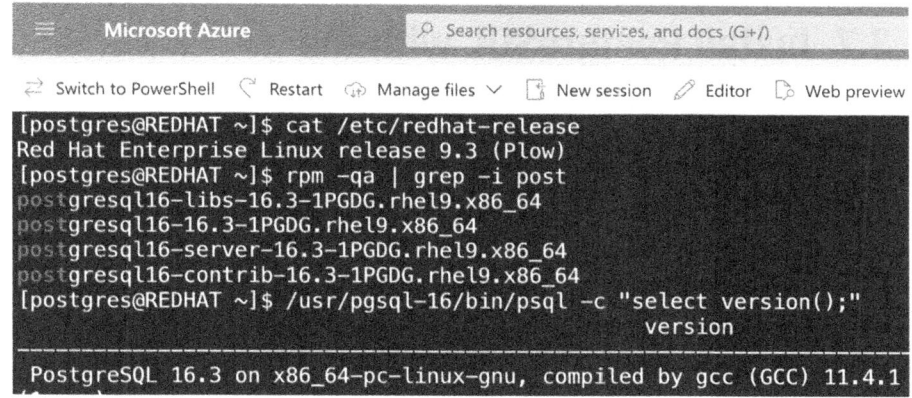

Figure 4-3. Red Hat on Azure

The installation source files for the RPM method are in the directory /usr/pgsql-[version], which is /usr/pgsql-16 for PostgreSQL Cluster version 16. The sub directories are bin, doc, lib, and share. See Figure 4-4. The PostgreSQL executables are in the bin directory.

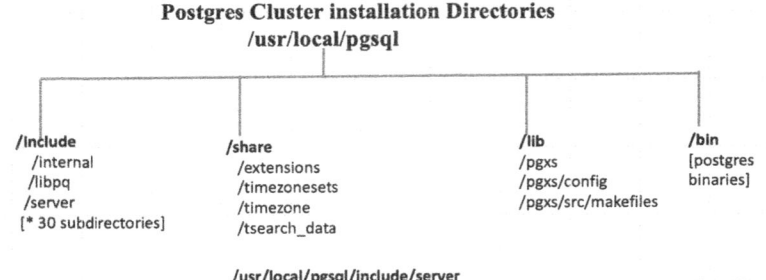

Figure 4-4. Directories

4.3.7 Install PostgreSQL with the Configuration Option

With the configuration option, PostgreSQL compiles the source code with the make file procedure. You can customize the software components to build a robust PostgreSQL server, depending on the specific requirements. Let's customize the software to increase the default database block size from 8k to 16k, and let's change the segment size to 2B. Similar to the RPM install, you have to connect as a root user or user with sudo to perform this task. You can perform a second installation on the same machine with the configuration option in a different directory of the filesystem.

To work with configuration options, you must download software from the EDB site. The following is the download image. The URL for the download is www.postgresql.org/ftp/source/v16.3/.

Download the following file:

postgresql-16.3.tar.gz

Copy Installation Software

Since database servers are not public-facing in corporations, you have to install it on jump server where you have Internet access and then copy the software to the database server. The next step, after downloading the software to your laptop, is to copy it to the ec2-user/Azure vm host. After downloading software to your laptop, open CloudShell and import the file and use the scp (secure file copy) procedure to the Linux host.

With the scp command, copy the file postgresql-16.1.tar.gz from your Mac to the Linux host. For Windows, use the winscp program, provide *.ppk, and copy the file to the Linux host.

The following is the scp command from the Mac, where you have to provide the *.pem file, software file, Linux host name, and directory:

```
$scp -i "dev.pem" postgresql-16.1.tar.gz admin@3.78.247.245:/tmp
```

Extract the Software

Use these commands to extract the software:

1. `$ mkdir post16install`
2. `$ cp /tmp/postgresql-16.1.tar.gz post16install # copy file from to install directory`
3. `$ cd post16install # change to this directory`
4. `$ tar -xvf postgresql-16.1.tar.gz`

After extracting the tar file, change directory to postgresql-16.1 and run the configure command.

The tar copies files or directories with the command `tar -cvf [filename].tar [directory name]`, where c refers to create, v for verbose, and f for file. With `tar -xvf` you can extract files from the tar backup.. You can obtain all the configurable values of PostgreSQL server with the `help` command.

Execute the Configure Command

You can obtain all the available configuration parameters for PostgreSQL with

`./configure --help command.`

Let's change the database and log block size to 16K from the default block size of 8k with the RPM install method. Increasing the block size to 16K has several benefits for large tables:

1. More data is read or written.
2. Better sequential read performance.
3. Increased cache efficiency.
4. Better index scans.

Here is the usage of the configuration command:

`Usage: ./configure [OPTION]... [VAR=VALUE]...`

```
[--with-blocksize=BLOCKSIZE] # set table block size in KB
[--with-segsize=SEGSIZE]   #set table segment size in GB
[--with-wal-blocksize=BLOCKSIZE] # set WAL block size in KB
```

Run the configuration command in Listing 4-8, which will configure PostgreSQL Server with 16k block size, without-readline indicates (ignore read line support), zlib compression library indicates (ignore zlib compression library), and without icu indicates (ignore International Unicode Support).

Listing 4-8. PostgreSQL Install with Configuration Option

```
$ ./configure --without-readline --without-zlib --with-segsize=2 -with-blocksize=16 --with-wal-blocksize=16 --without-icu
make
make all
```

https://drive.google.com/file/d/1r5wY-u8IGzNjPXBBNrrF2--xcRH8Z--K/view?usp=sharing

When you install PostgreSQL with the configuration method, the default directory is /usr/local/pgsql/bin for the binaries location. .For instance, if you wish to install PostgreSQL version 14 and 15 along with 16, you have to provide a different path for the bin directory. Listing 4-9 shows the example of configuring PostgreSQL with a block size of 16k and segment size of 2GB, along with non-default binary directory.

Listing 4-9. PostgreSQL Configuration Command with Non-Default Binary Directory

```
./configure --without-readline --without-zlib --with-segsize=2 -with-blocksize=16 --with-wal-blocksize=16 --without-icu --bindir=/usr/local/pgsql/16/bin
```

4.3.8 PostgreSQL Cluster Install Directories and Files

With the configuration default option, the PostgreSQL software is installed in the /usr/local/pgsql directory. The configuration-related files are in the include directory, which are used during the make and make install processes. All the PostgreSQL software development programs are written in the C language by the PostgreSQL Global Development

CHAPTER 4   POSTGRESQL SOFTWARE INSTALLATION ON AMAZON EC2/AZURE VM LINUX

team. As PostgreSQL is an open-source product, the source code is made available to all. Advanced uses may delve into these directories to get an understanding of PostgreSQL Server creation modules.

You learned the major Postmaster process in the first chapter. The file related to Postmaster is in the directory /usr/local/pgsql/include/server/postmaster and is required for PostgreSQL Server's postmaster tasks related to autovacuum, background workers, background writer, interrupt handler, Write Ahead Logger (WAL) writer, startup, and syslogger. It is worth noting the foundation of PostgreSQL client server computing protocols of the libpq reference in the libpq-events.h file with major events of PostgreSQL register, connection reset, connection destroy, results create, results copy, and results destroy. Further details of client server protocols are defined in the header file libpq-fe.h for front-end applications with references to connection status, polling status, copy in and out data, and error handling. Figure 4-5 displays the directory structure of PostgreSQL used for configuration and installation of software.

Figure 4-5. *PostgreSQL Security Access*

4.4 Initialize PostgreSQL Cluster

Connect to Amazon EC2 or Azure VM as the postgres user account to initialize the PostgreSQL cluster. Validate the connected user with the `id` command. The preferred user to create PostgreSQL software is postgres, which is created by an RPM procedure. See Listing 4-10.

You have already connected to the Linux host from Windows putty. For additional reference, go to https://docs.aws.amazon.com/AWSEC2/latest/UserGuide/putty.html.

Listing 4-10. id Command

```
$id
uid=26(postgres) gid=26(postgres) groups=26(postgres)
```

4.4.1 Set Up the Linux Environment

You have to set up a Linux environment for a PostgreSQL user account. PostgreSQL requires two Linux environmental variables, PGHOME and PGDATA, to configure a PostgreSQL cluster database. The Home directory is different as set by PGHOME. The configuration and data files used by a database cluster are stored together within the cluster's data directory, commonly referred to as PGDATA.

The variable PGHOME is set to the location of PostgreSQL executables and the PATH variable is set to the PostgreSQL executable location where the executable programs are located on the file system. Change to the home directory by the `cd` command and execute the commands shown in Listing 4-11 to set up the environment. With the `echo` command, you can programmatically insert text into a file without the help of the editor. Run the commands in Listing 4-11 to set the PostgreSQL user profile and validate the PostgreSQL executable program `initdb`.

Listing 4-11. Execute Shell Profile Command

```
echo "export PGHOME=/usr/pgsql-16/bin" > .bash_profile # clear old values
echo "export PATH=$PGHOME:$PATH" >> .bash_profile # add path
echo "export PGDATA=/var/lib/pgsql/16/data" >> .bash_profile # Adjust values to your location of data directory
cd
source .bash_profile
which initdb
# result of which command : /usr/pgsql-16/bin/initdb
```

https://drive.google.com/file/d/1_J2qcJJ8KVnSf441Xx3J_IzwtjUaokNs/view?usp=sharing

4.4.2 Check Linux OS Disk Space

You created a file system for the PostgreSQL database in Chapter 3. With the df -h command you can view the file system space allocation. For a test instance, 2GB of space is sufficient. Since you have identified the instance types in the Chapter 2, you can expand the additional space as per the notes in Chapter 3. Use df -h to check the file system space. As you created /postgres/pgdata, check it with the df -h | grep post command. See Listing 4-12.

Listing 4-12. df-h Command

```
$df -h | grep post
/dev/xvdg        2.0G    39M   1.8G   3% /postgres/pgdata
```

If the directory is not available run the command

a) sudo mkdir -p /postgres/pgdata

b) chown postgres:postgres /postgres/pgdata

After successful installation of the PostgreSQL cluster software, you are ready to initialize the PostgreSQL cluster, which creates a data directory, default database, and template database.

4.4.3 Initialize PostgreSQL Cluster

The PostgreSQL cluster database is created by the initdb command with the D argument for the data directory, with optional flags -A for password authentication method and -W for root password. The databases postgres, template, and template1 are created by the initdb process. There are two widely used character sets: ASCII and UTF8. While ASCII is the most used character set, UTF8 accommodates several languages across the world. The default character set is UTF8 for the PostgreSQL cluster install.

initdb initializes a PostgreSQL database cluster.

Commonly used input commands:

```
[-D or  --pgdata=DATADIR]   # Provide data directory path
[-E or --encoding=ENCODING] # Do not change default is UTF8
[-g or --allow-group-access] # optional default user is
postgres
[-U or --username=NAME] # optional default to postgres
[-W or  --pwprompt]   # optional you can set it after the
creation of the database.
[-A -or -auth=METHOD] #
```

Listing 4-13 shows the command and installation details of the initdb command execution.

Listing 4-13. Initialize PostgreSQL Cluster Command

```
$echo $PGDATA # validate the Data Directory location
/postgres/pgdata
$initdb -D $PGDATA
```

```
The files belonging to this database system will be owned by
user "postgres".
The database cluster will be initialized with locale "en_
US.UTF-8".
The default database encoding has accordingly been set
to "UTF8".
The default text search configuration will be set to "english".
:::::::::::::Lines omitted
initdb: warning: enabling "trust" authentication for local
connections
initdb: hint: You can change this by editing pg_hba.conf or
using the option -A, or --auth-local and --auth-host, the next
time you run initdb.
Success. You can now start the database server using:
    pg_ctl -D /postgres/pgdata -l logfile start
```

pg_ctl is a utility to initialize, start, stop, or control a PostgreSQL server. You will be working with this utility to manage PostgreSQL.

Commonly used commands:

```
pg_ctl start      [-D DATADIR] # Starts the Postgres Server
pg_ctl stop       [-D DATADIR] # Stops the Postgres Server
pg_ctl restart    [-D DATADIR] # Restart the Postgres Server
pg_ctl status     [-D DATADIR] # Status of  the Postgres Server
```

The state of a PostgreSQL cluster is down after the initialization. Start the PostgreSQL cluster and check the version with the program pg_ctl which will start, stop, and restart PostgreSQL.

Start the PostgreSQL server with the command in Listing 4-14.

Listing 4-14. pg_ctl Command

```
$pg_ctl  -D /postgres/pgdata -l logfile start or pg_ctl start -D $PGDATA
waiting for the server to start.... done
server started
```

4.4.4 Connect to a Postgres Database

After initializing and starting the PostgreSQL cluster, you can connect to the database using the psql program. The program psql is ideal for interactively entering SQL commands and for running automated scripts[1]. By default, PostgreSQL uses network port 5432. You can connect to the database on the default port using the `psql` command.

psql is a PostgreSQL client program that requests data from a server residing on a local or remote computer. You probably noticed the `psql -c` command earlier in this chapter. With the psql client program, you can connect to local as well as to remote PostgreSQL servers. The syntax is psql -h[hostname] -U[username] -p[port]. See Listing 4-15.

Listing 4-15. psql Command

```
$ psql -c "select version();"

 PostgreSQL 16.2 on x86_64-pc-linux-gnu, compiled by gcc (GCC)
11.4.1 20230605 (Red Hat 11.4.1-2), 64-
bit
```

4.4.5 Postgres Data Dictionary

You can find the data dictionary and database files in the base directory of the $PGDATA location. By default, Postgres stores all the user-created databases, tables, system database objects, and temporary space objects in the $PGDATA directory

You can create a table and identify the location of the database table with the `pg_relation_filepath` function. Listing 4-16 shows an example where the table `test` is created in the base directory.

Listing 4-16. Identification of PostgreSQL Table File Location

```
postgres=# create table test as select * From pg_database;
SELECT 3
postgres=# select pg_relation_filepath('test');
 pg_relation_filepath
----------------------
 base/5/16388
(1 row)
```

4.4.6 Postgres Configuration Files

After installation, you must configure and edit two files: `postgres.conf` and `hba.conf`, which are created by the PostgreSQL cluster installation program in the $PGDATA directory. With these files, you can secure access to the PostgreSQL database as well as assign database values to over 300 database parameters.

Configure postgresql.conf

The database parameters are defined in the `postgresql.conf` file. There are over 350 configurable parameters for the PostgreSQL database. The most fundamental way to set these parameters is to edit the file [2]. The parameters define the configuration of values for PostgreSQL. At a minimum, you have to add values for the following:

1. Database port (the default values is 5432)

2. Listener address to "*" values, which allow client access from any host

CHAPTER 4 POSTGRESQL SOFTWARE INSTALLATION ON AMAZON EC2/AZURE VM LINUX

3. `wal_level replica` for replication
4. `archive_mode` to copy log files to backup
5. `archive` for the destination of archived log files
6. Enable logging
7. `log directory`

Listing 4-17 shows the command to define the parameters in the postgresql.conf file. You have to reboot the PostgreSQL cluster to make the parameters effective. Run this command to make changes to the postgres.conf file. Advanced users may edit with vim or vi editors to add values for these parameters.

Listing 4-17. postgresq.conf Entry

```
# postgresql.conf entry
# make directory for continued archive log storage
mkdir -p $PGDATA/archive
echo "port = 5432" >>$PGDATA/postgresql.conf
# enable access from all hosts
echo "listen_addresses = '*'" >>$PGDATA/postgresql.conf
echo "wal_level = replica"  >>$PGDATA/postgresql.conf
# enables archiving on
echo "archive_mode =on" >>$PGDATA/postgresql.conf
# specify archive path
echo "archive_command = 'test ! -f $PGDATA/archive/%f && cp %p $PGDATA/archive/%f'" >> $PGDATA/postgresql.conf
# enable logging
echo "logging_collector = on"  >>$PGDATA/postgresql.conf
# log directory
echo "log_directory = 'log'"  >>$PGDATA/postgresql.conf
```

https://drive.google.com/file/d/1YNtuEwpisbp9Bengy9XwXVsUK JwmT409/view?usp=sharing

The firewall rules are enforced at three layers: cloud security, pg_hba.conf, and the listen_addresses parameter. With security groups, there are inbound and outbound rules. Inbound rules allow access to hosts, while outgoing traffic is allowed by outbound rules. Under rare circumstances such as a hacker attack, you can block outbound rules. In the pg_hba.conf file, you can allow access or restrict access to specific databases, users, and hosts. In the listen_addresses parameter, you can specify the network interfaces from which PostgreSQL will accept connections. See Figure 4-6.

TYPE	DATABASE	USER	ADDRRESS	METHOD	COMMENT
local : domain socket	all	all		peer	local host access without password for postgres user, and restricted access for all. who am I ec2-user $psql -U postgres psql: error: connection to server on socket "/run/postgresql/.s.PGSQL.5432" failed:
				trust	FATAL: Peer authentication failed for user "postgres" any local Linux user connect to postgres without password
IPV4: host	all	all	127.0.0.1/32	trust	IPV4 loop back local host. The 32 represents only 1 IP. Trust the local host connections without password authentication
IPV6: host	all	all	::1/128	trust	IPV6 loopback local host. The 128 signifies one IP. Trust the local host connections without password authentication
host	all	all	0.0.0.0/0	scram-sha-256	Remote connections to Postgres host. The IPV4 0.0.0.0/0 is for global access
replication: local	replication	all		trust	
host	replication	all	172.43.1.29/32	trust	Standby Remote host address

Figure 4-6. *Host based file access rules*

You configured database security access from the cloud in Chapter 3 and the listener address in the postgres.conf file.

After the `initdb` command, add following entry in the `pg_hba.conf` file:

```
echo "host all    all 0.0.0.0/0 scram-sha-256" >> $PGDATA/pg_hba.conf
```

The address 0.0.0.0/0 allows access from any IP and the password is validated by the Postgres server. To allow external users to access the PostgreSQL database, you have to add the line `host all all [IP/[port range] scram-sha-256` in the `pg_hba.conf` file.

The sections of the `pg_hba.conf` file are Type for host, Database, user, address, and method. The external users are connected to the host and address with a connection method. Make sure that the method is not "trust" as this will compromise the security of the PostgreSQL database. The peer authentication will allow only the postgres user to access the database in the local machine. The trust authentication will allow any user on a local machine to access the database where the address is 127.0.0.1 or ::1/128. The IP address with /32 suffix resolves to only one IP.

Figure 4-7 shows the authentication methods.

```
# TYPE  DATABASE        USER            ADDRESS                 METHOD
# "local" is for Unix domain socket connections only
local   all             all                                     trust
# IPv4 local connections:
host    all             all             127.0.0.1/32            trust
# IPv6 local connections:
host    all             all             ::1/128                 trust
# Allow replication connections from localhost, by a user with the
# replication privilege.
local   replication     all                                     trust
host    replication     all             127.0.0.1/32            trust
host    replication     all             ::1/128                 trust
host    all             all             0.0.0.0/0               scram-sha-256
```

Figure 4-7. *Host based file access*

Listing 4-18 is the sample ph_hba.conf file. Change the host address based on your client access to the PostgreSQL database.

Listing 4-18. pg_hba.conf File Example

```
# TYPE   DATABASE        USER            ADDRESS                 METHOD
# "local" is for Unix domain socket connections only
local    all             all                                     trust
# IPv4 local connections:
host     all             all             127.0.0.1/32            trust
# For dedicated database host
# IPv6 local connections:
host     all             all             ::1/128                 trust
# Allow replication connections from localhost, by a user with the
# replication privilege.
```

```
local       replication   all                            trust
host        replication   all     127.0.0.1/32           trust
host        replication   all     ::1/128                trust
host all    all 0.0.0.0/0 scram-sha-256
$
```

After making configuration changes, start the PostgreSQL cluster with the command pg_ctl start -D $PGDATA.

4.5 Postgres Operating System Configuration

In the above steps you configured the Postgres cluster with default options. You must configure memory options based on the available memory in the OS. The following are the steps to extend the database memory and OS huge pages.

4.5.1 Check Memory Size

Check the memory size with the /proc/meminfo command.

```
cat /proc/meminfo | grep MemTotal
MemTotal:        3818520 kB # 4GB RAM
```

4.5.2 Check Huge Pages in the System

You configured huge pages in Chapter 3.

```
cat /proc/meminfo | grep HugePages_
HugePages_Total:    1600
HugePages_Free:     1600 # Huge pages not allocated
```

4.5.3 Check Huge Page Size

```
cat /proc/meminfo | grep Hugepagesize
Hugepagesize:         2048 kB
```

4.5.4 Check Huge Pages After Start of Cluster

```
$ cat /proc/meminfo | grep HugePages_
HugePages_Total:    1600
HugePages_Free:     1592.  # Huge Pages allocated
HugePages_Rsvd:       63
```

4.6 Parameter Settings

PostgreSQL has around 350 configurable parameters that affect the behavior and performance of the database. The optimal values for these parameters can vary depending on the application workload and hardware configuration of the database server. The number of user sessions defaults to 100 during the install. You have to increase the value for the `max_connections` parameter. You identified the maximum number of user connections based on the instance type in a previous chapter. Adjust this parameter with the instance type.

4.6.1 Expand Shared Buffers Memory

During the default installation of the PostgreSQL cluster, 128MB of memory is allocated for shared buffers, where the database buffers are kept for query access. Depending on the availability of memory in the OS, you have to increase the size of the shared buffers. In the following example, you expand the shared memory from 128MB to 1024MB. You must reboot the server to make a memory parameter change..

CHAPTER 4 POSTGRESQL SOFTWARE INSTALLATION ON AMAZON EC2/AZURE VM LINUX

Check the allocated memory before shared_buffers with the psql command.

```
psql -c " show shared_buffers;"
```

The database parameter shared_buffers is changed by two methods: modifying values in postgresql.conf or using the alter system command.

4.6.2 Modify Parameters in the postgresql.conf File

With the sed command, you can replace any values in the postgresql.conf file. The following is the command:

```
sed -i 's/shared_buffers = 128MB/shared_buffers = 1024MB/g' $PGDATA/postgresql.conf
```

You can validate the change with the grep command.

```
$grep shared_buffers $PGDATA/postgresql.conf
shared_buffers = 1024MB                    # min 128kB
```

After rebooting the cluster, check the size of the shared buffers and huge pages.

```
pg_ctl restart -D $PGDATA
psql -c " show  shared_buffers;"
```

Listing 4-19 shows the output of the commands.

Listing 4-19. Allocated Shared Buffers

```
shared_buffers
----------------
 1GB
(1 row)
```

4.6.3 Modify Parameters with the Alter System

You can modify the shared buffers with methods to alter commands:

```
psql -c "alter system set shared_buffers to '1024MB';"
```

or

connect to Postgres with psql and run the alter command.
```
postgres=# alter system set shared_buffers to '1024MB'
```

> **Note** The changes made by the `alter system` command are registered in the `postgresql.auto.conf` file, which is used during the restart of the PostgreSQL cluster.

4.6.4 New Parameters Between Versions 14-16

With each release, based on the enormous research by the developer community, new features and functionality are added to the PostgreSQL cluster software.

Figures 4-7 and 4-8 show the major parameters introduced for each version. The deprecated features are in red.

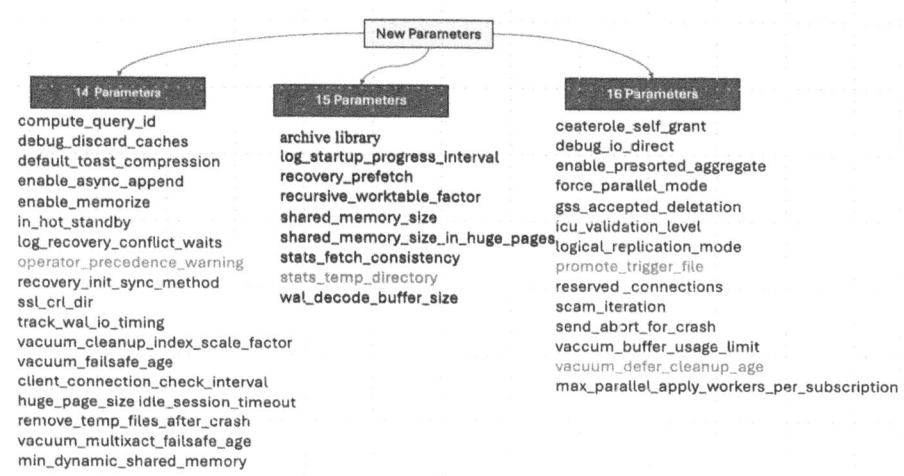

Figure 4-8. PostgreSQL parameters

```
pg_stat_statements.track = all
shared_preload_libraries = 'pg_stat_statements'
pg_stat_statements.max = 10000
```

Figure 4-9. pg_stat_statements in postgresql.conf

4.7 Create Extensions

Extensions are additional software modules added on the base server. The important extension you have to create after the installation of PostgreSQL cluster is pg_stat_statements, which will record the SQL elapsed time details in the database in the view pg_stat_stements. You have to make the entries in Figure 4-10 in the postgresql.conf file to configure the extension.

CHAPTER 4 POSTGRESQL SOFTWARE INSTALLATION ON AMAZON EC2/AZURE VM LINUX

```
postgres=# explain analyze select * From pgbench_accounts where aid=1;
                                      QUERY PLAN
-----------------------------------------------------------------------------------
 Index Scan using pgbench_accounts_pkey on pgbench_accounts  (cost=0.29..8.31 rows=1 width=97) (actual time=4.
298..4.30
1 rows=1 loops=1)
   Index Cond: (aid = 1)
 Planning Time: 13.215 ms
 Execution Time: 4.321 ms
(4 rows)
```

Figure 4-10. *Explain command*

Load sample data with the command pgbench -i postgres to examine the SQL statement profile and select the execution time with SQL statement in Script 4-1. pgbench is a client command used to generate the benchmark metrics for data load.

This example script configures the pg_stat_statements extension, reboots the PostgreSQL server, loads sample data, and selects the query details.

Script 4-1. pg_stat_statements Configuration

```
#!/bin/bash

# Check if pg_stat_statements extension is available
extstat=$(psql -t -A -c "SELECT name from pg_available_
extensions where name='pg_stat_statements';")

if [ "$extstat" != "pg_stat_statements" ]; then
  echo "Install Contrib package"
else
  # Create the pg_stat_statements extension
  psql -c "CREATE EXTENSION IF NOT EXISTS pg_stat_statements;"

  # Add the pg_stat_statements extension settings to
postgresql.conf
```

CHAPTER 4 POSTGRESQL SOFTWARE INSTALLATION ON AMAZON EC2/AZURE VM LINUX

```
  echo "shared_preload_libraries = 'pg_stat_statements'" >> 
$PGDATA/postgresql.conf
  echo "pg_stat_statements.max = 10000" >> $PGDATA/
postgresql.conf
  echo "pg_stat_statements.track = all" >> $PGDATA/
postgresql.conf

  # Restart PostgreSQL to apply changes
  pg_ctl restart -D $PGDATA
 # Load sample data
  pgbench -i postgres
  psql -c "SELECT query, total_exec_time,rows  FROM pg_stat_
statements limit 2;"
  psql -c "explain SELECT  * FROM pgbench_accounts 
WHERE aid=1;"
fi
```

https://drive.google.com/file/d/1H6MVXLwlnDleGZcTo6TxeOGUahp5-m5y/view?usp=sharing

It is worth noting the explain command, which analyzes the query access path and suggests the cost of executing the query. The cost is a measure used by the optimizer's cost model as compared with similar other queries and is not the economic cost. You can view the query plan of the SQL statements executed in the database. The query column of pg_stat_statements records the SQL statements. Figure 4-11 shows the explain command.

CHAPTER 4 POSTGRESQL SOFTWARE INSTALLATION ON AMAZON EC2/AZURE VM LINUX

```
postgres=# \timing
Timing is on.
postgres=# select * From pgbench_accounts where aid=1;
 aid | bid | abalance |                                         filler
-----+-----+----------+-----------------------------------------------
   1 |   1 |        0 |
(1 row)

Time: 0.878 ms
```

Figure 4-11. The timing command

In the plan details, an index plan is performed on the primary key index. The first, cost=0.29, indicates the time to get the first row whereas 8.31 indicates the total cost for all rows. The actual time is measured in milliseconds, which is 4.3ms and total time = planning time + execution time.

By setting the timing on in the psql shell, you obtain the query elapsed time. See Figure 4-12.

```
$ ps -ef | grep -i post
postgres    1388       1  0 01:20 ?        00:00:00 /usr/local/pgsql/bin/postgres -D /postgres/pgdata
postgres    1389    1388  0 01:20 ?        00:00:00 postgres: checkpointer
postgres    1390    1388  0 01:20 ?        00:00:00 postgres: background writer
postgres    1392    1388  0 01:20 ?        00:00:00 postgres: walwriter
postgres    1393    1388  0 01:20 ?        00:00:00 postgres: autovacuum launcher
postgres    1394    1388  0 01:20 ?        00:00:00 postgres: logical replication launcher
```

Figure 4-12. PostgreSQL OS processes

Here is an additional reference about extensions:
https://docs.google.com/document/d/1u18mgBTO0fF3FBcHANKmTYoF5BL2eZOH/edit?usp=sharing&ouid=117618855868897795502&rtpof=true&sd=true.

4.8 Postgres Operating System Process Details

Linux uses shared memory and semaphores to assign memory to the PostgreSQL operating system process. The process is a running job in the operating system. The main process running the job is postgres -D, which is a Postmaster process assigned the 3805 process id in the operating system. You can examine the operating system resource allocation by viewing the status of the process. You may notice Postmaster in certain instances, which is a legacy program. See Figure 4-13.

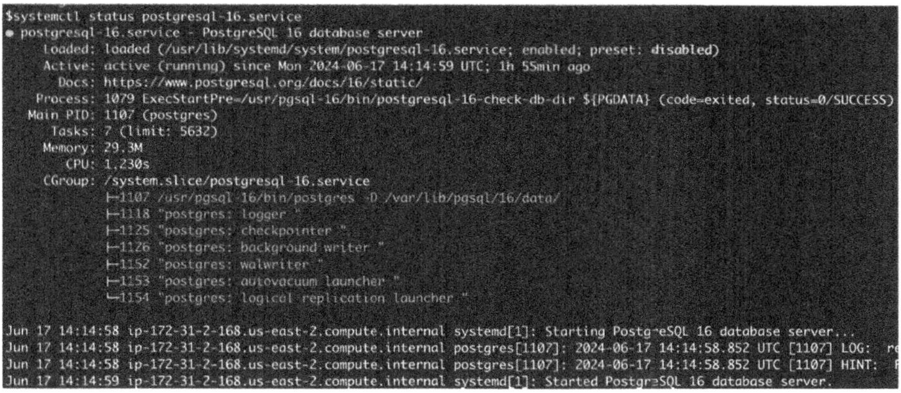

Figure 4-13. systemctl details of PostgreSQL process

With the command `systemctl status postgresql-[version].status`, you can view all details such as Postmaster process (pid 1107), child processes, and start time. See Figure 4-14.

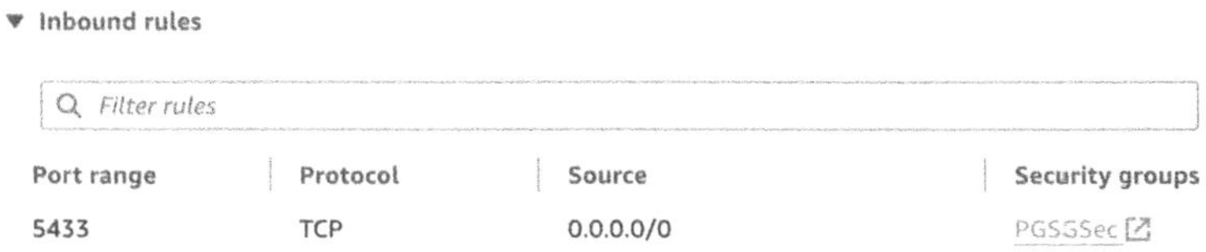

Figure 4-14. systemctl details of the PostgreSQL process

Use `systemctl --help` to understand all of the features, which integrates service management, which starts, stops, restarts, and reloads system and daemons and process monitoring plus initialization tasks.

```
systemctl --help
systemctl [OPTIONS...] COMMAND ...
```

Query or send control commands to the system manager.

4.8.1 Process Memory Details

For multiple instances, you can obtain the virtual memory usage with the following command. The process status details are defined in the /proc/[processed]/status directory. You can calculate the total virtual memory allocated to PostgreSQL clusters from process status file with this command:

```
for proc in $(ps -ef | grep postgres | grep D | grep -v auto |awk '{print $2}' ); do cat /proc/$proc/status | grep VmPeak | awk '{print $2}'; done | awk '{sum += $1} END {print sum}'

Output: 1582852 Kb
```

4.9 Multiple Instances of PostgreSQL

For business requirements of separate instances with different maintenance windows, you can create multiple instances. To create multiple instances on same host, you have to follow two steps:

1. Create a separate directory, preferably a different file system, and initialize the cluster with `initdb -D [new file system]`.

CHAPTER 4   POSTGRESQL SOFTWARE INSTALLATION ON AMAZON EC2/AZURE VM LINUX

2. Change the port number in postgresql.conf in each new data directory. As 5432 is taken by the default installation, you can create ports from 5433 onwards.

Follow these steps:

1. Create an instance with intdb -D /postgres/data01 # New Directory

2. Change the port in the postgres.conf file to 5433 or higher number.

3. Start the instance with pg_ctl start -D /postgres/data01.

4. Connect to the instance with psql -p 5433.

```
$ps -ef | egrep 'postgres -D' | grep -v auto
postgres    5344       1  0 22:24 ?        00:00:00 /usr/
pgsql-15/bin/postgres -D /postgres/pgdata15
postgres    5456       1  0 22:27 ?        00:00:00 /usr/
pgsql-14/bin/postgres -D /postgres/pgdata14
postgres    5487       1  0 22:29 ?        00:00:00 /usr/
pgsql-13/bin/postgres -D /postgres/pgdata13
postgres    5598       1  0 22:30 ?        00:00:00 /usr/
pgsql-12/bin/postgres -D /postgres/pgdata12
postgres    5728       1  0 22:36 ?        00:00:00 /usr/
pgsql-16/bin/postgres -D /postgres/pgdata16
```

4.10 Create a Non-Default Security Group

For security considerations, you have to create a non-default security group for Postgres client access. The default 5432 port is well known universally, so you must use a different port number. There is no option to add rules for non-default port with templates in AWS, as AWS can't assume the non-default port numbers. The only option is to create a new security group, add a port number, and assign it to the instance.

4.10.1 Create a Security Group From AWS

The following are the steps to create the security group in AWS EC2 with a non-default port:

1. ```
   aws ec2 create-security-group --group-name
   PGSGSec --description "Security group for
   PostgreSQL on port 5433"
   ```

2. ```
   aws ec2 authorize-security-group-ingress
   --group-name PGSGSec --protocol tcp --port
   5433 --cidr 0.0.0.0/0. # change your
   IP range
   ```

3. Obtain a security group id with the query command.

   ```
   aws ec2 describe-security-groups --query
   "SecurityGroups[*].[GroupId,GroupName]" --output table
   | grep PGSGSec
   result
   sg-08c06aa7fdd308f50
   ```

4. ```
   aws ec2 modify-instance-attribute
   --instance-id i-123ioooi0abcdef0 --groups
   sg-08c06aa7fdd308f50
   ```
   ```

CHAPTER 4　POSTGRESQL SOFTWARE INSTALLATION ON AMAZON EC2/AZURE VM LINUX

Security group validation from the AWS console is shown in Figure 4-15.

```
c:\Users\pvadl\Downloads>"c:\Program Files\PostgreSQL\16\bin\psql" -h 3.149.235.237 -U devuser -d sales
Password for user devuser:
psql (16.1, server 16.2)
WARNING: Console code page (437) differs from Windows code page (1252)
         8-bit characters might not work correctly. See psql reference
         page "Notes for Windows users" for details.
Type "help" for help.

sales=> \conninfo
You are connected to database "sales" as user "devuser" on host "3.149.235.237" at port "5432".
sales=> \! hostname
ven
```

Figure 4-15. *Non-default security group*

4.10.2　Azure Security Group

An Azure security group is created by the command `az network nsg rule create`. Listing 4-20 shows the code that allows PostgreSQL to access from non-default port 5433 with default values.

Listing 4-20. Azure Network Rules

```
az network nsg rule create \
  --resource-group demo \
  --nsg-name  PGdev-nsg \
  --name Allow-PostgreSQL-5433 \
  --priority 1000 \
  --direction Inbound \
  --access Allow \
  --protocol Tcp \
  --source-address-prefixes '*' \
  --source-port-ranges '*' \
  --destination-address-prefixes '*' \
  --destination-port-ranges 5433
```

Output
```
{
  "access": "Allow",
  "destinationAddressPrefix": "*",
  "destinationAddressPrefixes": [],
  "destinationPortRange": "5433"
:::: Lines truncated
"type": "Microsoft.Network/networkSecurityGroups/securityRules"
}
```

After changing the port number in postgresql.conf, access the PostgreSQL running on port 5433. See Figure 4-16.

```
[postgres@PGdev data]$ psql -p 5433
psql (16.3)
Type "help" for help.

postgres=#
```

Figure 4-16. Connect to a non-default port

4.11 Post Installation Tasks

You have to work or validate several tasks after the installation and configuration of PostgreSQL on the Red Hat OS.

4.11.1 Create a Database

The end result of all the tasks on EC2/Azure VM on Red Hat is to facilitate creation of databases to store user data.

To create a database, you must use the command `createdb`, which is a client application. With the `createdb` command, you can create a database where user data resides. See Listing 4-21. The default location is `$PGDATA/base`. You can assign a tablespace to a database. The tablespace creation details are covered in the subsequent chapters.

Listing 4-21. Create a Database

```
createdb -help
createdb creates a PostgreSQL database.
Usage:
  createdb [OPTION]... [DBNAME] [DESCRIPTION]
postgres=# CREATE DATABASE demo;
CREATE DATABASE


$ psql -c " select datname From pg_database;"
   datname
-----------
 postgres
 demo
 template1
 template0
 finance
```

4.11.2 Validate Access from a Remote Client

The final validation of the install of PostgreSQL is to validate access from the remote client machine. Figure 4-17 shows the screen image of the connection from a client to PostgreSQL Server.

CHAPTER 4　POSTGRESQL SOFTWARE INSTALLATION ON AMAZON EC2/AZURE VM LINUX

```
$cd /usr/pgsql-16/
$ls -l
total 16
drwxr-xr-x. 2 root root 4096 Jun  7 23:33 bin
drwxr-xr-x. 3 root root   23 Dec 10  2023 doc
drwxr-xr-x. 3 root root 4096 Jun  7 23:33 lib
drwxr-xr-x. 8 root root 4096 Jun  7 23:33 share
```

Figure 4-17. psql client connection

4.11.3 Validate WAL Archiving

The last step of configuration is to validate the Write Ahead Log copy to the archive location by identifying log files in pg_wal, archive_status, and archive directories.

In Listing 4-22, the log file 000000010000000000000001 is archived to the $PGDATA/archive directory.

Listing 4-22. Archive Log Backup

```
$ls $PGDATA/pg_wal
000000010000000000000001   000000010000000000000002
archive_status
$ls $PGDATA/pg_wal/archive_status
000000010000000000000001.done
$ls $PGDATA/archive
000000010000000000000001
```

Congratulations! You have configured PostgreSQL Server for user transactions with point-in-time recovery capability.

4.11.4 Validate Non-Default Block Size

You configured PostgreSQL with a non-default block size of 16k earlier in the chapter. You can validate the 16k block size with the show block_size command, as shown in Listing 4-23.

Listing 4-23. Non-Default Block Size

```
echo $PGHOME
/usr/local/pgsql/bin
[postgres@devpoc data]$ psql -p 5432 -d postgres
psql (16.1)
Type "help" for help.
postgres=# show block_size;
 block_size
------------
 16384
```

4.11.5 Client Connection Details

You can identify all connected user sessions to PostgreSQL Server from Linux with the command ps -ef | grep -i post. Listing 4-24 shows the output of the command.

Listing 4-24. User Process on Linux

```
postgres   31477    31458  0 04:04 ?        00:00:00 postgres: user001 postgres 47.224.119.107(58812) idle
postgres   31482    31458  0 04:05 ?        00:00:00 postgres: user001 postgres 47.224.119.107(58829) idle
```

The inter-process communication between PostgreSQL server and a psql client on a Linux machine is established with sockets. To prevent multiple instances from starting the same port, the instance lock is created in the /tmp directory. You can check available running PostgreSQL servers with the ls -a /tmp command. See Listing 4-25.

Listing 4-25. PostgreSQL Socket Lock

```
ls -a /tmp | grep PGSQL
.s.PGSQL.5432
.s.PGSQL.5432.lock
.s.PGSQL.5439
.s.PGSQL.5439.lock
.s.PGSQL.5482
.s.PGSQL.5482.lock
```

Netstat is a command or utility on Unix, Linux, Mac, and Windows. Install the utility with the command sudo yum install net-tools. It displays the details about active connections to the host. With the netstat -an command, you can identify all client-connected client IP addresses to the Postgres server. See Listing 4-26.

Listing 4-26. Netstat Command

```
Proto Recv-Q Send-Q Local Address         Foreign
Address         State
tcp       0      0 172.38.27.76:5432
47.224.119..107:58829    ESTABLISHED
tcp       0      0 172.38.27.76:5432
47.224.119..107:58812    ESTABLISHED
```

You connect to different instances with psql -p on the local host. See Listing 4-27.

Listing 4-27. PostgreSQL Client to a Non-Default Port

```
psql -p 5439
psql (16.1, server 14.11)
Type "help" for help.
```

4.11.6 Control Data

With `pg_controldata`, you can identify the database system, latest checkpoint, and latest WAL file sequence. Listing 4-28 shows the command to list the PostgreSQL system identification and WAL location.

Listing 4-28. Control Data

```
 pg_controldata | egrep 'identifier|REDO'
Database system identifier:           7364598982571686033
Latest checkpoint's REDO location:    0/30000D8
Latest checkpoint's REDO WAL file:    000000010000000000000003
```

4.12 Uninstall Postgres from a Linux Host

If you wish to remove PostgreSQL from the local machine, see Listing 4-29.

Listing 4-29. Uninstall PostgreSQL from a Linux Host

```
$pg_ctl stop -D $PGDATA
$rm -rf $PGDATA/*
$sudo dnf remove postgresql16*
```

4.13 Keywords

Rpm, dnf install, dnf remove, yum install, initdb, pg_ctl, postgresql.conf, pg_hba.conf, netstat, and pg_stat_statements.

4.14 Summary of Learning

You learned how to connect to an EC2/Azure VM host, the configuration of a PostgreSQL environment, the installation of PostgreSQL server software, the creation of a PostgreSQL cluster and how to set up security access, modify database parameters, configure extensions, and validate client access. You worked with pg_ctl to start and stop a PostgreSQL cluster. This concludes all the tasks required to set up a PostgreSQL cluster in an EC2/Azure environment.

4.15 Practice Chapter 4

1. Install a PostgreSQL cluster with the dnf method.
2. Install a PostgreSQL cluster with an RPM.
3. Initialize a PostgreSQL database with the initdb or pg_ctl method.
4. Configure the pg_hba.conf file to allow access from your laptop IP address
5. Configure remote access in the postgres.conf file.
6. Configure access to a PostgreSQL cluster from a non-default port.
7. Configure a pg_stat_statement extension.
8. Modify shared buffers to 40% of RAM.

4.16 Questions Chapter 4

1. How can you check the allocated memory on the Linux host?
2. How can you check the number of CPUs on a Linux host?
3. How do you check the installed PostgreSQL packages?
4. How do you change the block size to 32K?
5. How do you connect to multiple PostgreSQL clusters on a Linux host?
6. What are the steps to create a non-default port for PostgreSQL access?
7. How do you check the available extensions?
8. Where do you check for multiple instances of Postgres servers?

References

1. Bruce Momjian, page 187, Chapter 17 *Programming Interfaces PostgreSQL Introduction and Concepts*, Addison-Wesley, 2001.
2. PostgreSQL documentation on configuration settings: www.postgresql.org/docs/current/config-setting.html

CHAPTER 5

Client Tools

5.1 Abstract

The availability of free PostgreSQL client tools allows database application developers to connect to the PostgreSQL cluster database. In addition, DBAs can use these tools with database resources in the cloud. ODBC or JDBC must be installed on the client machine to use these free software tools. The PostgreSQL installation package includes both server and client software. You can install only the PostgreSQL client on Linux from Red Hat 8 onwards. The advantage of using the psql client tool over PGAdmin or SQLJ is that it is an interactive command line tool useful for managing complex database tasks. As a DBA, you have to work with the application team and data analysts to configure client connectivity to PostgreSQL databases.

5.2 Objectives of Learning

- Installation and configuration of SQLJ
- Installation and configuration of PGAdmin
- Installation and configuration of the PostgreSQL client on Windows

CHAPTER 5   CLIENT TOOLS

- Installation and configuration of ODBC software on Linux and Windows clients
- Installation and configuration of PostgreSQL client software on Linux
- Set up Git Bash and run AWS CLI commands to start/stop EC2

5.3 Introduction

The client tools allow users to connect to a PostgreSQL database and perform various database-related tasks such as querying, managing databases, and monitoring performance. The libpq protocol laid the foundation for client server computing on Unix/Linux for PostgreSQL with its rich set of client libraries for data exchange, followed by Open Database Connectivity (ODBC), which provides a universal interface to databases, and Java Database Connectivity (JDBC), allowing Java applications. The data is secured over the Internet by Hypertext Transfer Protocol Secure (HTTPS), which uses the Secure Socket Layer (SSL) protocol, which encrypts the data transmitted over the Internet. In the realm of cloud computing, you have to work with command line interface tools to manage resources provided by AWS and Azure.

The main functions of client-server communication are to allocate a handle, have the driver connect to a database, execute the query, bind column variables, fetch the data, and release the handle.

Standard Application Program Interface calls (API) allow applications to access the database systems. Each database vendor provides ODBC and JDBC and they work on all operating systems such as Windows, Mac, and Linux as with many programming languages such as C, C++, Java, and Python.

The libpq is native PostgreSQL client server protocol without any install, whereas for ODBC and JDBC, separate software is installed on client computers. The libpq, ODBC, and JDBC have similar functionalities; however, JDBC works only with the Java language.

The most popular open-source client tools are pgAdmin, SQLJ, and psql. See Figure 5-1.

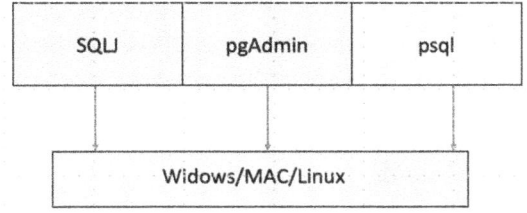

Figure 5-1. Postgres client tools

5.4 pgAdmin

The pgAdmin client tool is an open-source product that has evolved over decades. It's been overseen by the PostgreSQL Global Development team and is widely used by application developers for its rich GUI features. It is a client tool mainly installed on Windows PCs and Mac PCs to support PostgreSQL development as well as administrative tasks using libpq protocol for client-server communication. pgAdmin installs and starts a local web server on the local host. It creates databases, offers extensions, backs up databases, restores databases, and generates ERD diagrams. A query tool and a PGSQL tool are among the features of the pgAdmin tool.

CHAPTER 5   CLIENT TOOLS

Download the software from www.postgresql.org/ftp/pgadmin/pgadmin4/v8.6/windows/ and extract the software to your Windows PC and install it. For a Mac, download from www.pgadmin.org/download/pgadmin-4-macos/.

5.4.1 Create a New Server

After extracting the software, the first task is to create a new server. Click on the servers icon and choose Register server. Choose Server > Register > Server, as shown in Figure 5-2.

Figure 5-2. Register a server

In the general tab, enter the server identifier. You can restrict a specific database or set of databases in the Advanced option. For instance, a Sales Force application has thousands of databases where you have to choose the ones you would like to work. See Figure 5-3.

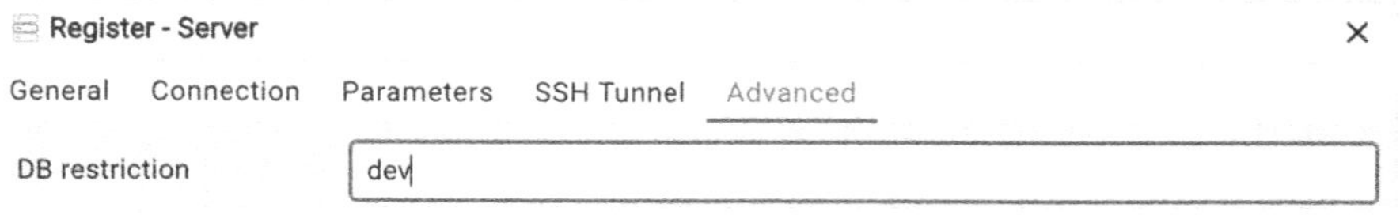

Figure 5-3. Restrict a database for selection

5.4.2 Provide the Host IP Address and User Connection Details

Provide an IP address or service name of the PostgreSQL server or localhost, port, username, and password in the connection. Then click to save the settings. See Figure 5-4.

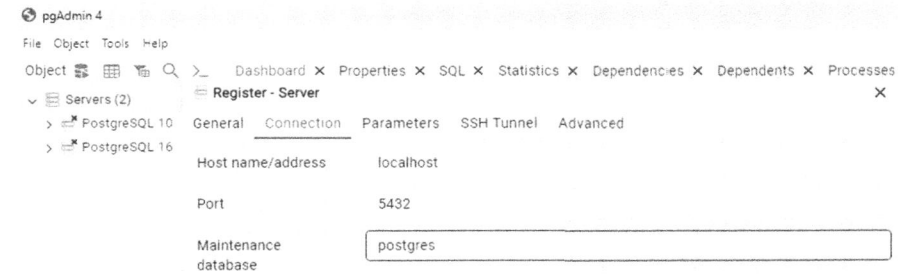

Figure 5-4. *PostgreSQL connection details*

5.4.3 Query Tool

After connecting to PostgreSQL, choose the user database and right-click the database, which displays all the available options to work with PGAdmin. Open the query window from the tool menu. See Figures 5-5 and 5-6.

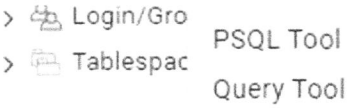

Figure 5-5. *PSQL and the Query Tool*

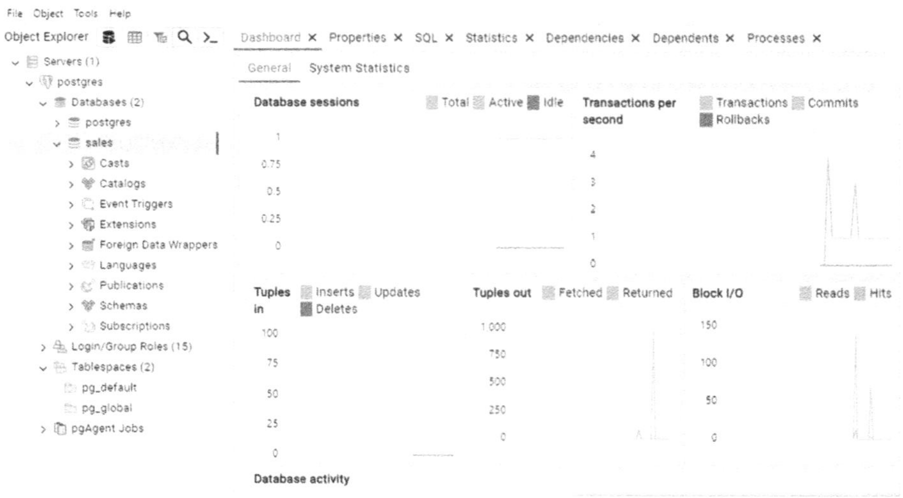

CHAPTER 5   CLIENT TOOLS

Figure 5-6. Dashboard

5.4.4 PSQL

PSQL is an interactive psql command tool. It's a preferred tool for DBAs who like to work on the command line, for ease and comfort of toggling between databases, for using meta commands. You will learn psql meta commands in subsequent chapters.

From the Tools option, choose PGSQL Tool to launch the tool. Figure 5-7 shows the screen image from a Mac.

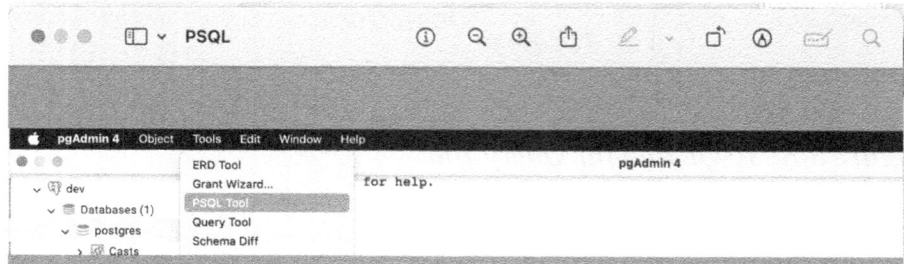

Figure 5-7. Choose the PSQL Tool

CHAPTER 5 CLIENT TOOLS

The PSQL tool launches a PostgreSQL shell, like the Linux terminal from the PGAdmin tool. Figure 5-8 is the screen image of the psql shell.

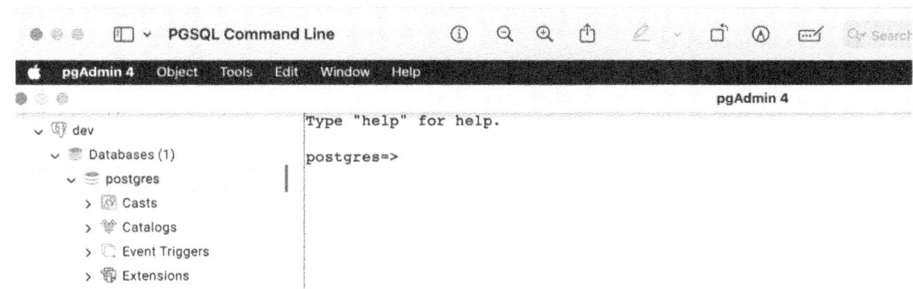

Figure 5-8. PostgreSQL shell

5.5 psql Client on Windows

The psql client tool is shipped by EDB with its PostgreSQL distribution for the Windows OS. Go to www.enterprisedb.com/downloads/postgres-postgresql-downloads.

5.5.1 PostgreSQL Executable

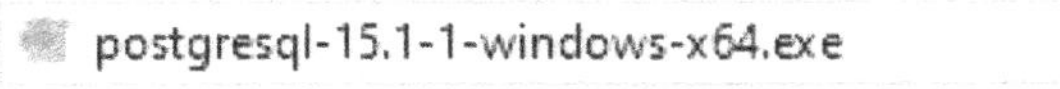

postgresql-15.1-1-windows-x64.exe

Figure 5-9. PostgreSQL Windows executable file

After extracting the PostgreSQL Cluster software (Figure 5-9), choose the command line option to install client tools on the Windows computer.

After installing the PostgreSQL client on Windows, you can perform all admin tasks such as create database, create user, and so on. Figure 5-10 is the screen image of database creation from the Windows PostgreSQL client. It is best to install command line tools when installing the server.

179

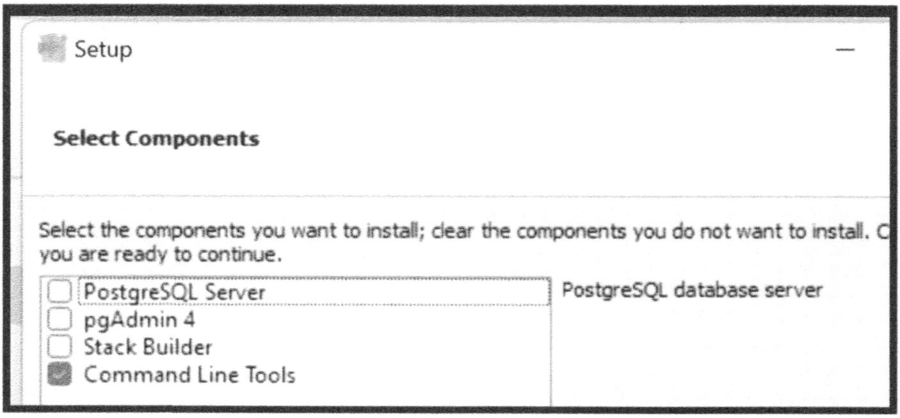

Figure 5-10. Choose command line tools

After successfully installing client software, validate the client software by working with the commands. One such command is createdb. See Figure 5-11.

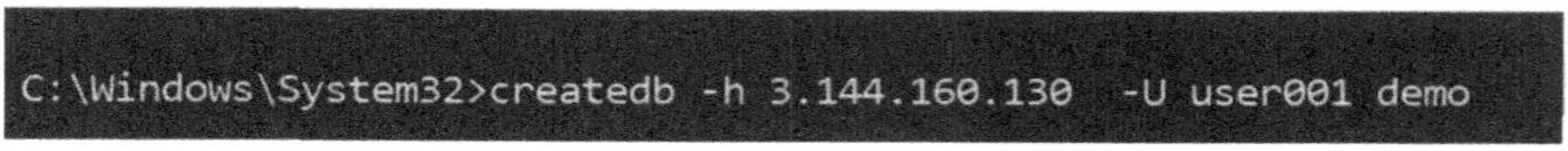

Figure 5-11. Create a database from a client machine

5.6 SQLJ Workbench

Mount Peter (UK) created the first version of JDBC drivers in 2000, which later on went with several changes. The main features of SQLJ are database explorer, data pumper, schema explorer, workspace creation and management, complex SQL execution management with macros, bookmarks, data display, data formatting, DbTree, file tree, SQL formatter and SQL generation.

5.6.1 Download Software

You have to download two software products to install SQLJ Workbench:

1. SQLJ software from the site at www.sql-workbench.eu/download-archive.html

2. JDBC drivers from the PostgreSQL site at https://jdbc.postgresql.org/download/#latest-versions

5.6.2 Manage JDBC Drivers

After extracting the software, click the SQLWorkbench, which will spawn a connection profile window. Choose the PostgreSQL driver in the Manage Drivers option. See Figure 5-12.

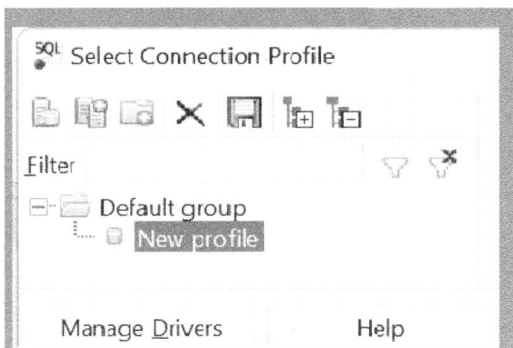

Figure 5-12. *Manage drivers*

Choose PostgreSQL driver, as shown in Figure 5-13.

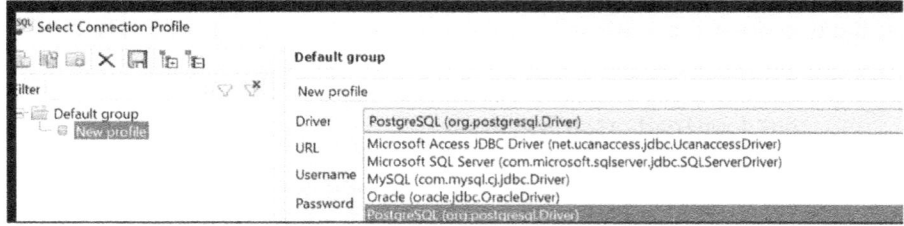

Figure 5-13. *PostgreSQL driver*

Enter the name for the profile; choose the PostgreSQL driver; enter the hostname, port, and database name in the URL; enter the username and password; and click the test button. See Figure 5-14.

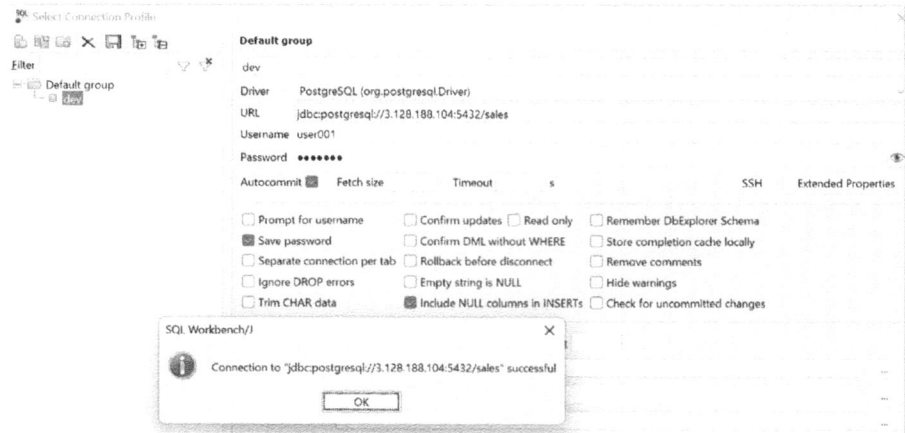

Figure 5-14. *SQLJ connection options*

CHAPTER 5 CLIENT TOOLS

Note The connection parameters could be different based on different user types. Furthermore, there is no option to toggle between databases. For each database connection, you have to create a different profile. You have to open the statement tab to query the database. From the Database Explorer tab, right-click to choose the Add tab menu, which will create a statement window.

5.6.3 Statement Tab

After establishing the connection, you will be launched into the Database Explorer. See Figure 5-15.

Figure 5-15. Statement tab

You can toggle between Database Explorer to view the data objects, the object DDL, and object data. From the Database Explorer, you can view all the attributes of a table with the details shown in Figure 5-16.

CHAPTER 5   CLIENT TOOLS

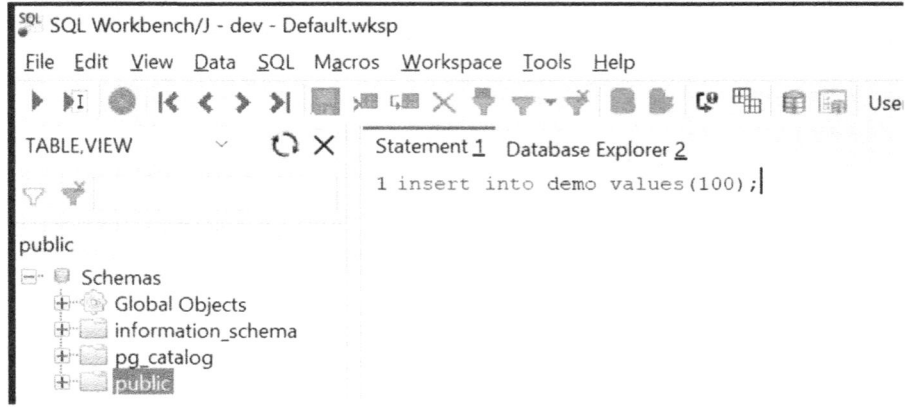

Figure 5-16. *SQLJ Database Explorer*

From the database explored, you can view the attributes of a table, as shown in Figure 5-17.

Columns SQL source Data Indexes References Referenced by Triggers Dependencies Partitions

Figure 5-17. *Database Explorer options*

pgAdmin, SQL Workbench, and psql have their own sets of features, suitable to development, administrative, and analysts roles in an organization. While pgAdmin is more geared towards database developers, data analysts prefer SQLJ and DBAs prefer psql. Table 5-1 show the comparative features of these tools.

Table 5-1. pgAdmin, SQL Workbench, and psql Comparative Features

Feature	pgAdmin	SQL Workbench	psql
Usage	Developer choice with multiple windows to several database clusters	Database schema and data management	DBAs' choice for interactive tool
Target users	Database administrators and developers	Database developers, data scientists, data analysts, and business analysts	Database administrators and developers
Main Features	Visual query builder, monitoring, GUI tools, ability to monitor multiple clusters	Advanced SQL editing, scripting capabilities, and enhanced schema view	Direct command execution and scripting.
GUI	Yes	No	No
Workspace	No	Yes	No
Performance Tuning	Robust GUI metrics for performance tuning	Custom scripts	Custom scripts

5.7 AWS CLI on Windows

You can manage a fleet of computers with the AWS CLI client utility. You can work on all tasks with the AWS CLI such as managing EC2, RDS, and S3 tasks.

CHAPTER 5   CLIENT TOOLS

5.7.1 Create an IAM User Account

To begin the process, you have to connect to the AWS console, set up an AWS account, create a user account with AWS Identity and Access Management (IAM), and download the AWS access key ID and secret access key, which can be obtained from the AWS IAM console. In order to use the AWS CLI, you have to download the AWS CLI software from AWS, which can be installed on Linux, Windows, and Mac operating systems. After creating the user in IAM, you have to grant necessary permission such as EC2 full access and RDS and S3 full access to work on CF templates to the AWS user. Figure 5-18 shows the grants assigned from the IAM console.

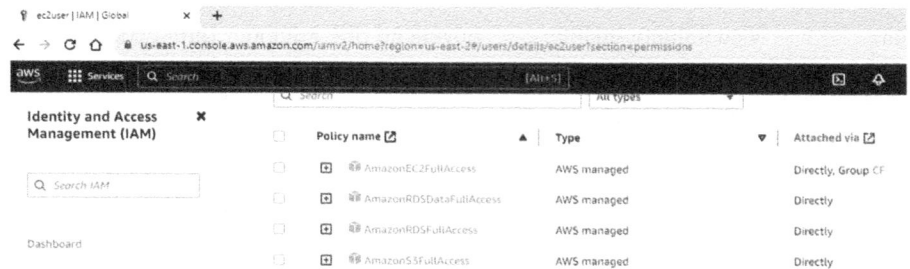

Figure 5-18. IAM roles

5.7.2 Download AWS CLI

You can download the msi package for Windows from the AWS site. Figure 5-19 shows the command to download AWS.

Figure 5-19. Set up AWS CLI on a Windows PC

5.7.3 Configure AWS CLI

After installing AWS CLI software, you have to work with the `aws configure` command, which establishes communication from the local machine to work on tasks in the AWS cloud environment. Figure 5-20 is the screen image of the AWS configure command.

The `aws configure` command is used to set up the AWS CLI on a local machine. It requires the AWS access key ID and secret access key, which can be obtained from the AWS IAM (Identity and Access Management) console. Additionally, the default region can also be specified during the configuration process. Once configured, the AWS CLI can be used to interact with various AWS services such as EC2, S3, and RDS.

```
C:\Users\pvadl>aws configure
AWS Access Key ID [****************C6KS]:
AWS Secret Access Key [****************24Zf]:
Default region name [us-east-2]:
Default output format [None]:
```

Figure 5-20. Configure the AWS CLI

5.7.4 AWS CLI on a Mac

The AWS CLI is my favorite choice for working on cloud-related tasks because I can work with command line utilities as well as connect to Linux with ssh. Download the following package (Figure 5-21) on a Mac, which will install the AWS CLI: https://awscli.amazonaws.com/AWSCLIV2.pkg.

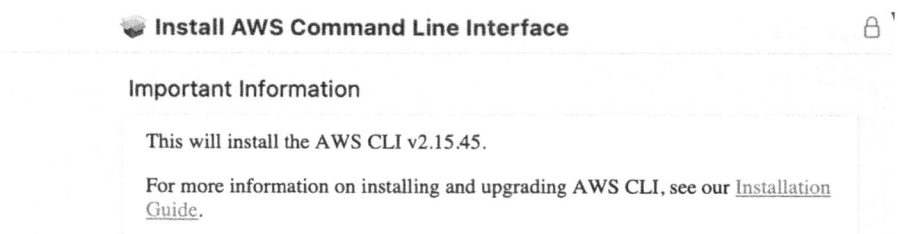

Figure 5-21. *AWS C5.LI software install on Mac*

After installing the package, proceed with aws configure by providing the AWS access key id, AWS secret access key, and default region.

5.7.5 AWS CLI Install on Linux

Like Windows and Macs, you can install the AWS CLI on Linux. Open a CloudShell terminal and run the command in Listing 5-1, which will install the AWS CLI on Linux. After install, proceed with aws configure. Note: If an earlier version exists, the update flag must be used.

Listing 5-1. AWS CLI Install on Linux

```
curl "https://awscli.amazonaws.com/awscli-exe-linux-x86_64.zip" -o "awscliv2.zip"
unzip awscliv2.zip
sudo ./aws/install
```

```
  % Total    % Received % Xferd  Average Speed   Time    Time     Time  Current
                                 Dload  Upload   Total   Spent    Left  Speed
100 57.7M  100 57.7M    0     0   120M      0 --:--:-- --:--:-- --:--:--  120M
::::: Lines omitted
aws --version
aws-cli/2.15.45 Python/3.11.8 Linux/5.14.0-362.18.1.el9_3.x86_64 exe/x86_64.rhel.9 prompt/off
```

5.8 Windows Git Bash

You can run all Linux shell commands from Git Bash on Windows. Git Bash emulates the bash Linux command line interface on Windows. You can work with Red Hat OpenShift Containers and Crunch Data Operators with Git Bash shell. In section 7, you will learn about containers. You will learn about these programs in the subsequent chapters. This allows users to get familiar with Linux commands, work on shell script, variables, loops, use editors such as awk, grep, sed, and more.

5.8.1 Download Software

Download the software from `https://git-scm.com/download/win`. After the download, click the Git icon to complete the installation process.

Like Linux commands, you can submit similar commands on Windows. The Git Bash shell supports all GIT commands. It's a useful interface to open shift containers from a client machine after installing the CLI. After completion of installation, from all programs choose Git > Git Bash icon. See Figure 5-22.

CHAPTER 5 CLIENT TOOLS

Figure 5-22. Git Bash program

The default directory of Git is /c/users/[pcusaname].

5.8.2 Start EC2 from Windows Git Bash Shell

You can perform all cloud admin tasks from the Git Bash shell. Figure 5-23 shows the example of starting the EC2 instance from the Git Bash shell. Create a directory called scripts, cd to scripts, and create a file start_ec2.sh with these details:

aws ec2 start-instances --instance-ids i-02e8b750920e7dda5

You can list all the files with the ls -l command such as ls -l start_ec2.sh.

```
aws ec2 start-instances --instance-ids i-0e51b5e8284fc4189

pvadl@ven MINGW64 ~/scripts
$ ./start_ec2.sh
{
    "StartingInstances": [
        {
            "CurrentState": {
                "Code": 0,
                "Name": "pending"
            },
            "InstanceId": "i-0e51b5e8284fc4189",
            "PreviousState": {
                "Code": 80,
                "Name": "stopped"
            }
        }
    ]
}
```

Figure 5-23. Git Bash command to start EC2

5.8.3 Query S3

With the AWS CLI, you can perform all task. Here is an example to query S3 bucket:

```
$ aws s3 ls s3://
2022-04-19 08:10:52 palos123
```

> **Note** You can work either from the Windows command prompt or from Windows Git Bash to start/stop.

5.9 ODBC

ODBC (Open Database Connectivity) for Windows was created by Microsoft in 1992. It's an interface that allows applications to access and interact with various database management systems. You may have to configure ODBC connectivity for some of the client-server applications such as Informatica to connect to the PostgreSQL database. While libpq works only with PostgreSQL and C/C++, ODBC supports many databases, and many languages including C, C++, Java, and Python require drivers to install and configure. ODBC does not have features like pg_bouncer to connect load balancing. Figure 5-24 shows the main flow of ODBC configuration.

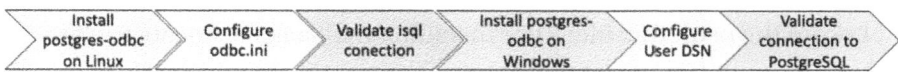

Figure 5-24. ODBC configuration on Linux/Windows

CHAPTER 5 CLIENT TOOLS

5.9.1 Configuration of ODBC on Linux

Connect to a Linux host with root credentials and install the ODBC software with the command sudo yum install postgresql-odbc, which will install libpq, libtools, postgres odbc, and unix odbc packages. Note that through the book I am using Red Hat OS as an example. The command may be similar on other Linux distributions.

The following is the command and install log. See Listing 5-2.

Listing 5-2. ODBC Install on Linux

```
sudo yum install postgresql-odbc
Updating Subscription Management repositories.
::::: Lined Omitted
Installing:
 postgresql-odbc           x86_64           12.02.0000-6.
el9          rhel-9-appstream-rhui-rpms         453 k
Installing dependencies:
 libpq                     x86_64           13.11-1.el9
rhel-9-appstream-rhui-rpms         206 k
:::::Lines Omitted
Installed:
  libpq-13.11-1.el9.x86_64      libtool-ltdl-2.4.6-45.el9.
x86_64    postgresql-odbc-12.02.0000-6.el9.x86_64
  unixODBC-2.3.9-4.el9.x86_64
Complete!
```

Locate the psqlodbc file: After installing the package, locate the file psqlodbc.so, which is the ODBC driver software with the find command:

```
$ sudo find . -name psqlodbc.so
./usr/lib64/psqlodbc.so
```

CHAPTER 5 CLIENT TOOLS

Edit odbc.ini: Upon identification of the *.so file, add entries in the /etc/odbc.ini file for driver location, database name, username, and userpassword.

Listing 5-3 is an example.

Listing 5-3. obdc.ini

```
/etc/odbc.ini
[MyPostgresDSN]
Description = PostgreSQL ODBC driver
Driver =/usr/lib64/psqlodbc.so
ServerName = localhost
Port = 5432
Database =postgres
Username =demo
Password = MyStrong$pwd
```

The isql connection: The last step is to validate the odbc configuration with isql [dsnname]. Figure 5-25 shows an example of the isql command.

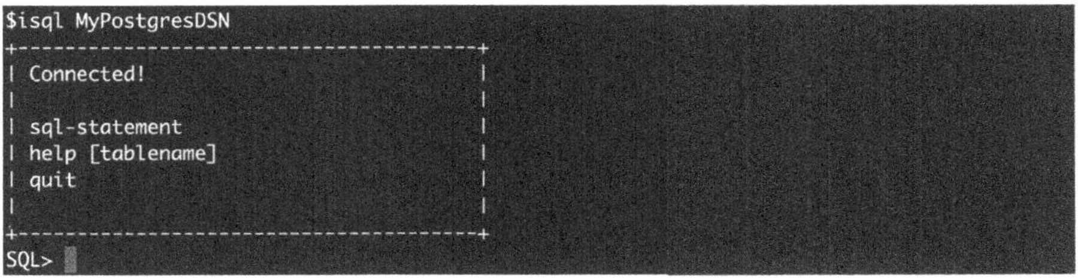

```
$isql MyPostgresDSN
+---------------------------------------+
| Connected!                            |
|                                       |
| sql-statement                         |
| help [tablename]                      |
| quit                                  |
|                                       |
+---------------------------------------+
SQL>
```

Figure 5-25. *isql connection*

5.9.2 Configuration of ODBC on a Windows Client

For configuration of PostgreSQL ODBC on Windows, follow these steps:

CHAPTER 5   CLIENT TOOLS

1. Download the software from the site: www.
   postgresql.org/ftp/odbc/releases/
   REL-16_00_0004/

2. Download the latest file or choose the file of
   your choice.
   psqlodbc_x64.msi or psqlodbc-setup.exe

3. After unzipping the file, execute the program
   psqlodbc-setup.exe.

4. Type for ODBC data sources in the search bar,
   choose User DSN, and choose the Add button,
   which will take you to the Create New Data Source
   window. See Figure 5-26.

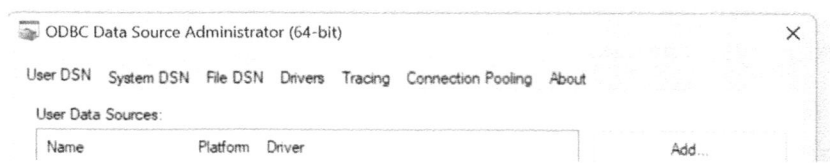

Figure 5-26. *ODBC DSN*

In the Create New Data Source window, choose PostgreSQL Unicode(x64) driver. See Figure 5-27.

CHAPTER 5 CLIENT TOOLS

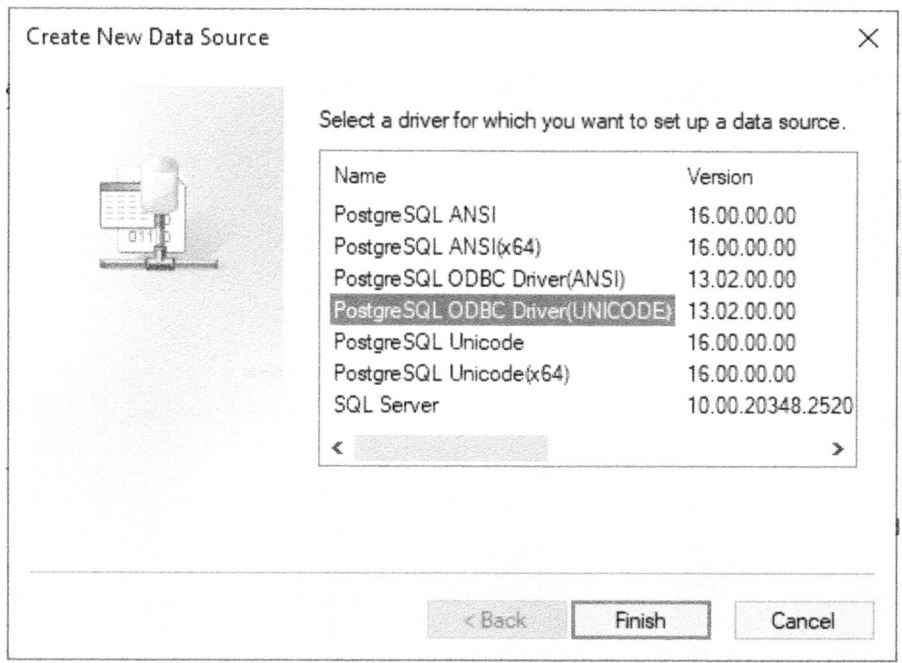

Figure 5-27. PostgreSQL data source

After choosing the PostgreSQL driver, the psqlODBC window is displayed. Provide a name for data source, database name, PostgreSQL server IP address or domain name, username, password and default for port and clock the Test icon to validate the connection. See Figure 5-28.

CHAPTER 5   CLIENT TOOLS

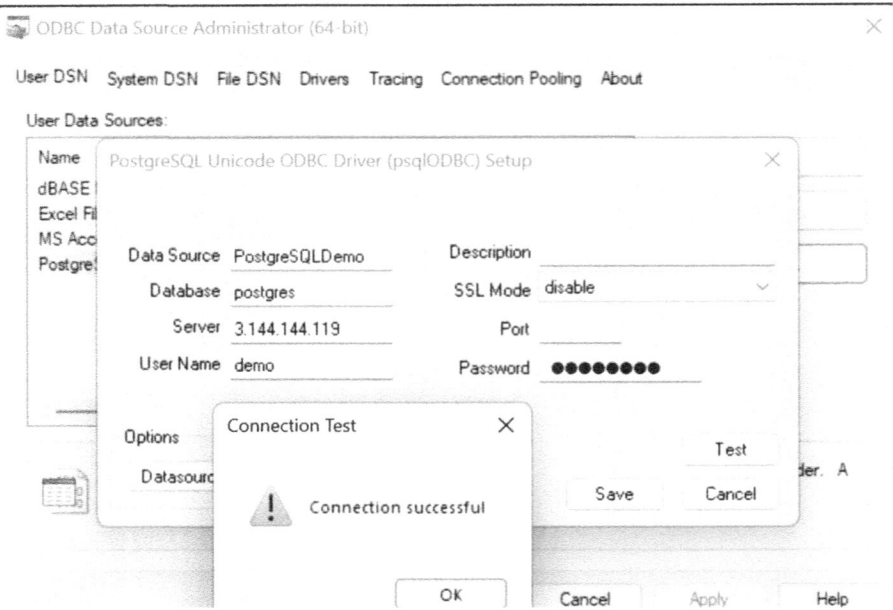

Figure 5-28. ODBC connection test

5.9.3 ODBC with Configuration Option

For the additional options to configure odbc on Linux, follow these steps:

1. Download the software with the wget command:

   sudo wget https://www.postgresql.org/ftp/odbc/
   versions.old/src/psqlodbc-16.00.0000.tar.gz

2. After downloading the psqlodbc, the next step is to configure it on the Linux host.
   Here are the steps to configure ODBC on Linux:

   % tar -zxvf psqlodbc-xx.xx.xxxx.tar.gz
   % cd psqlodbc-xx.xx.xxxx
   % ./configure

```
% make
% make install
edit /etc/odbc.ini and provide values for database
connection and validate with isql [data source name]
```

Source: https://odbc.postgresql.org/docs/unix-compilation.html.

> **Note** psqlODBC can also be installed with StackBuilder.

5.10 Install PostgreSQL Client on Linux

The PostgreSQL client is used by database users to connect to PostgreSQL residing on remote machines. Like client software on Windows, you can work with client software on a Linux host, which takes less resources compared to full-blown server install. As client software is installed on the application server, you can restrict it to create a local PostgreSQL server on the Linux host. You can perform all database tasks such as creation of databases and users plus backup recovery operation from the PostgreSQL client software.

Beginning from the Red Hat 8.0 release, you can install the PostgreSQL client separately on the Linux host. In the earlier versions, you had to install PostgreSQL Server binaries to work with client program such as psql.

Here are the steps:

1. Install the latest repositories from the PostgreSQL site:

   ```
   sudo dnf install -y https://download.postgresql.org/
   pub/repos/yum/reporpms/EL-8-x86_64/pgdg-redhat-repo-
   latest.noarch.rpm
   ```

CHAPTER 5   CLIENT TOOLS

```
:: Lines omitted
Installed:
  pgdg-redhat-repo-42.0-43PGDG.noarch
```

2. Install the PostgreSQL client (see Figure 5-29).

   Install PostgreSQL client with this command:

   ```
   sudo dnf install postgresql16.
   ::: Line omitted
   ```

```
Dependencies resolved.
================================================================================
=================
 Package                       Architecture     Version                 Repository
        Size
================================================================================
=================
Installing:
 postgresql16                  x86_64           16.3-1PGDG.rhel9        pgdg16
        1.7 M
Installing dependencies:
 libicu                        x86_64           67.1-9.el9              rhel-9-baseos-rhui-rpms
        9.6 M
 lz4                           x86_64           1.9.3-5.el9             rhel-9-baseos-rhui-rpms
        62 k
 postgresql16-libs             x86_64           16.3-1PGDG.rhel9        pgdg16
        333 k

Transaction Summary
================================================================================
=================
Install  4 Packages

Total download size: 12 M
Installed size: 44 M
Is this ok [y/N]: y
```

```
           :::: Lines omitted
```

```
Installed:
  libicu-67.1-9.el9.x86_64                     lz4-1.9.3-5.el9.x86_64        postgresql16-16.3-1PGDG.r
hel9.x86_64
  postgresql16-libs-16.3-1PGDG.rhel9.x86_64

Complete!
```

Figure 5-29. *PostgreSQL client install on Linux*

The installed software is in the directory /usr/pgsql-16/bin. Listing 5-4 shows the client binaries.

Listing 5-4. PostgreSQL Client Binaries

psql,clusterdb,dropdb,pgbench,pg_dumpall ,pg_restore,reindexdb, created, dropuser, pg_config pg_isready, pg_waldump , vacuumdb, createuser, pg_basebackup , pg_dump and pg_receivewal

> **Note** The reference to initdb and pg_ctl is missing in client libraries.

5.11 Azure Client

With Azure CLI, you can perform all administrative tasks on the cloud to manage a fleet of VMs and Azure SQL databases.

Download the software from this link and install it: https://learn.microsoft.com/en-us/cli/azure/install-azure-cli-windows?tabs=azure-cli.

5.11.1 Azure CLI

After installing the software, disconnect the Window Ad login to a new dos shell with Administrator access and submit the command az. See Figure 5-30.

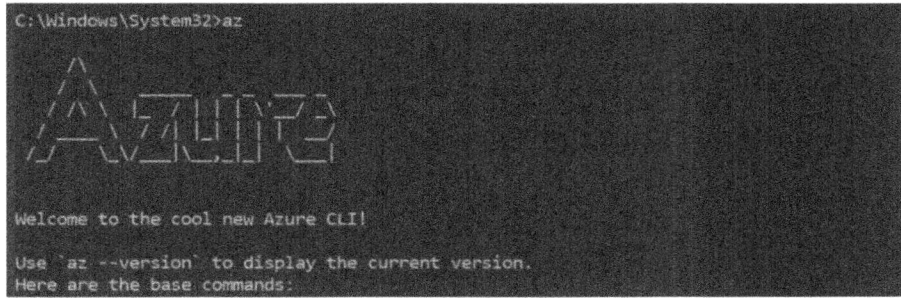

Figure 5-30. Azure CLI

Run the `az login` command, which will prompt for your Microsoft username and password.

Use `az --version` to display the current version.

Here are the base commands:

`account`: Manage Azure subscription information.

`acr`: Manage private registries with Azure Container Registries.

`ad`: Manage Microsoft Entra ID (formerly known as Azure Active Directory, Azure AD, AAD) entities needed for Azure role-based access control (Azure RBAC).

::: Partial list

5.12 Keywords

PGAdmin, psql client, SQLJ, Git Bash, AWS CLI, AWS configure, Azure CLI, ODBC, isql, odbcinst.ini, and EC2 instances

5.13 Summary of Learning

You have learned how to install and configure PostgreSQL client software tools PGAdmin, SQLJ and psql. You set up AWS and Azure command line tools. You installed and worked with git bash on Windows. You installed and configured ODBC on Linux and Windows. You installed the PostgreSQL client on Linux.

5.14 Practice Chapter 5

1. Install and configure PGAdmin on a Windows PC to access a PostgreSQL database.

2. Install and configure SQLJ on a Windows PC to access a PostgreSQL database.

3. Download putty and configure puttygen to access to a PostgreSQL database.
4. Connect to PostgreSQL from a psql client.
5. Deploy scripts from a PC.
6. Install a PostgreSQL client on a Windows laptop.
7. Install and configure psql ODBC drivers on a Linux host.
8. Configure odbc.ini to access the PostgreSQL database.
9. Configure a user DSN from a laptop to access a PostgreSQL database.
10. Configure AWS and Azure command line software.
11. Create a shell script in Git bash to start and stop EC2 instances.

5.15 Questions Chapter 5

1. What are the different methods available to restrict access to a specific database in PGAdmin when the PostgreSQL luster contains over 1000 databases?
2. Can you provide step-by-step instructions on configuring access restrictions for a specific database in PGAdmin when dealing with many databases in the PostgreSQL cluster?
3. Which driver is commonly used to establish a connection to PostgreSQL using SQLJ, and what are its key features or advantages?

CHAPTER 5   CLIENT TOOLS

4. What are the specific steps to connect to a PostgreSQL cluster on EC2 or Azure VM from a Windows host? And what additional requirements or settings are necessary for the connection to be successful?

5. How do you connect to the PostgreSQL Cluster on EC2 or Azure VM host from a Linux host? Are there any differences in the connection process compared to other operating systems?

6. What are the benefits and drawbacks of different access methods for toggling between multiple databases in PostgreSQL?

CHAPTER 6

PostgreSQL on AWS RDS/Azure SQL Database

6.1 Abstract

The relational database service (RDS) offered by cloud provider AWS and the Azure SQL database offered by Microsoft Azure are fully managed services that perform the underlying tasks of provisioning of virtual or physical machines, PostgreSQL cluster software, applying patches, upgrades, migration, security, backup, and recovery tasks, with provisioning for high availability across regions and zones. A fleet of database services are created or automated with cloud scripting templates. After network security rules are provisioned by the network team, the DBA can work on provisioning PostgreSQL services on the cloud.

6.2 Objective of Learning

- Understand the provisioning of managed database services on the cloud
- Provision RDS with the console and templates
- Provision Azure SQL databases with the console and templates
- Create parameter and option groups
- Performance monitoring with cloud tools
- RDS proxy configuration

6.3 Introduction

The traditional roles of administrators managing the infrastructure, storage, networking, and databases are redefined in the cloud, as most functions are now performed as a managed service by cloud providers. The system administrator does not have access to the computer where the PostgreSQL database resides and database-related tasks such deploying RDS, performance tuning, query optimization and scripts deployment are performed by the enterprise DBA.

As you can see in Figure 6-1, computers, network, storage, and security are provisioned by the cloud providers, along with the replication of data in multiple availability zones.

CHAPTER 6 POSTGRESQL ON AWS RDS/AZURE SQL DATABASE

Amazon Relational Database Service(RDS) / Azure RDS

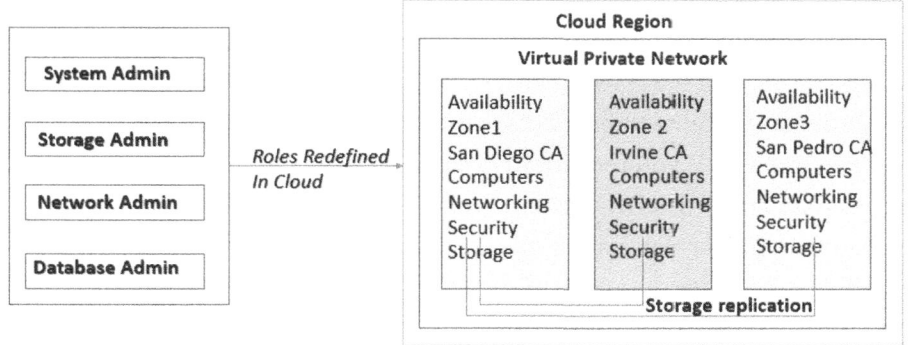

Figure 6-1. *Roles in the cloud*

As database services are managed by cloud providers, the roles of system administration, storage administration, and network administration are redefined and geared toward governance. The enterprise DBA is responsible for provisioning database resources, managing storage space, and implementing security rules provided by Networking team.

6.4 AWS RDS

AWS is a prime mover in the cloud industry because it extensively provisions computer hardware infrastructure and software across numerous regions and availability zones globally.

6.4.1 Database as a Service Architecture

With Database as a Service (DaaS), you can provision PostgreSQL lusters across the globe, although provisioning from nearby region reduces the latency more than using remote regions. You can provision database

CHAPTER 6 POSTGRESQL ON AWS RDS/AZURE SQL DATABASE

replicas in multiple regions. The RDS replication services are configured inter-region as well as intra-region. Any updates or changes made to the primary cluster in the East Coast region will be automatically replicated to the replica within the same region, ensuring data consistency. The high availability of database service is ensured by replicating the data to one or two availability zones. This is the default configuration on RDS with PostgreSQL. If you require RDS clones for read access, AWS provides Aurora RDS ➤ Aurora DB cluster cloning for this requirement. Aurora DB is a paid service for database software due its HA features, whereas there is no license cost for open source PostgreSQL. In the event of failure of the primary database, the standby site will assume the role of the primary. In summary, you can create DB instances and DB snapshots, point-in-time restores and backups. DB instances running PostgreSQL support multi-AZ deployments, read replicas, provisioned IOPS, and can be created inside a virtual private cloud (VPC). You can also use Secure Socket Layer (SSL) to connect to a DB instance running PostgreSQL [1]. See Figure 6-2.

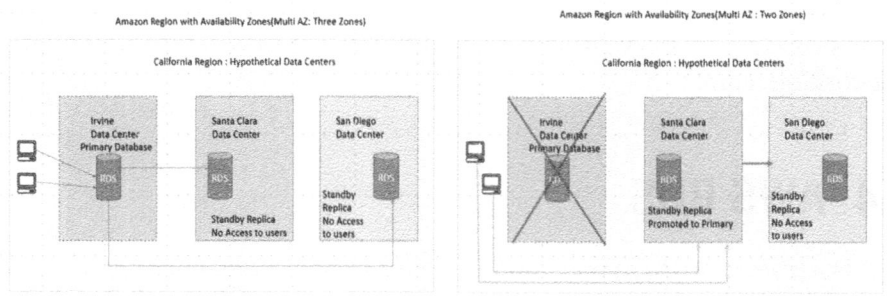

Figure 6-2. *RDS availability zones and failover*

In the above diagram, the primary database is configured with two replicas, where you have no access to the replica databases. In the event of failure of the primary site, one of the available replicas will be promoted to the primary role.

6.4.2 RDS PostgreSQL Creation Methods

RDS environments can be configured using the AWS Management Console or the command-line interface (CLI). The CLI offers programmatic control to automate a fleet of RDS instances as well as for snapshot cloning and read replicas. The standard method in corporations is to use the CloudFormation or Azure templates to create PostgreSQL instances, where the contents of the template are thoroughly validated by all stakeholders adhering to security as well as to software lifecycle compliance procedures. See Figure 6-3.

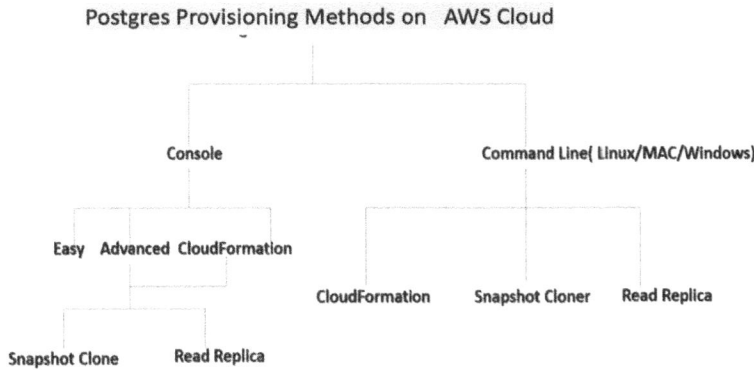

Figure 6-3. *Postgres RDS provisioning methods*

In Figure 6-3, all of the available methods to provision Postgres RDS are illustrated. CloudFormation is the preferred method to deploy Postgres RDS in the cloud for ease and scalability, where the script is thoroughly validated by the DBA, System Admin and Security Admin, although the console is a much easier method for learning and training purposes.

CHAPTER 6   POSTGRESQL ON AWS RDS/AZURE SQL DATABASE

6.4.3 PostgreSQL RDS Creation Procedure from the Console

After connecting to the AWS console, choose Services ➤ Database ➤ RDS and click DB Instances on the Dashboard ➤ Resources page. Click Create Database and select the EasyCreate method. Choose PostgreSQL ➤ Dev/Test. See Figure 6-4.

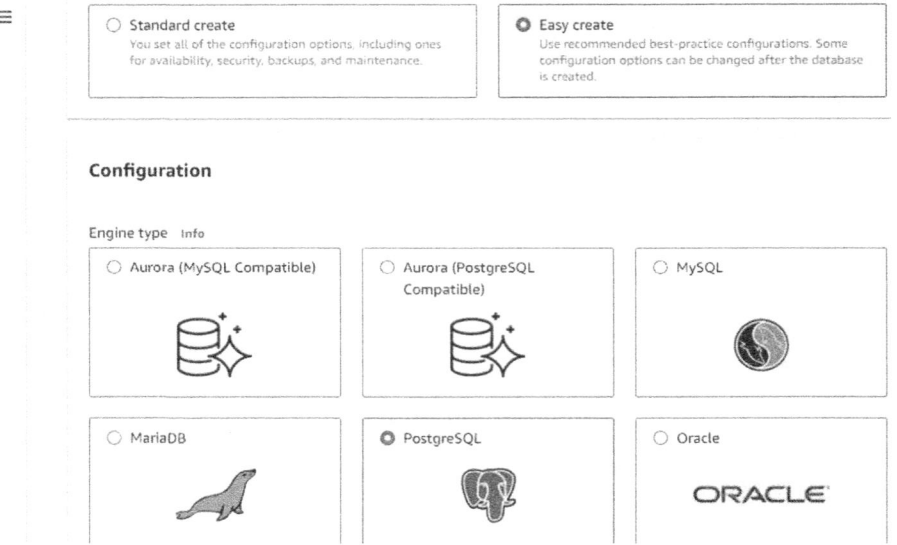

Figure 6-4. AWS RDS PostgreSQL creation option

Please check the full install instructions from this AWS page:
https://aws.amazon.com/getting-started/hands-on/create-connect-postgresql-db/

Connect from the Client tool to RDS

The first step after creating RDS is to validate access from the client. The host endpoint is obtained from the console. Here is the command to connect to RDS from the psql client (and see Figure 6-5):

CHAPTER 6   POSTGRESQL ON AWS RDS/AZURE SQL DATABASE

```
$psql -h hh2-demodbinstance-ozbtancteuxb.c87h7wvm7a78.us-
east-2.rds.amazonaws.com -U USER1 -d postgres
```

```
postgres=> \conninfo
You are connected to database "postgres" as user "USER1" on host "hh2-demodbinstance-ozbtancteuxb.c87h7wvm7a78.us-ea
t-2.rds.amazonaws.com" (address "18.117.36.100") at port "5432".
SSL connection (protocol: TLSv1.3, cipher: TLS_AES_256_GCM_SHA384, compression: off)
postgres=>
```

Figure 6-5. *Connect to RDS from a Windows client*

Immediately after provisioning RDS, the first task is to view the contents of pg_hba.conf rules. As you have no access to the OS, query the contents from the query select file_name,database,user_name,address,auth_method from pg_hba_file_rules. You can change the client authentication method by creating a parameter group. You can view the password authentication method by selecting the password_encryption column of the pg_settings view. See Figure 6-6.

```
postgres=> select file_name,type,database,user_name,address,auth_method from pg_hba_file_rules;
         file_name              |  type   |  database   | user_name  | address  | auth_method
--------------------------------+---------+-------------+------------+----------+--------------
 /rdsdbdata/config/pg_hba.conf  | local   | {all}       | {rdsadmin} |          | peer
 /rdsdbdata/config/pg_hba.conf  | local   | {all}       | {all}      |          | scram-sha-256
 /rdsdbdata/config/pg_hba.conf  | host    | {all}       | {rdsadmin} | all      | reject
 /rdsdbdata/config/pg_hba.conf  | host    | {rdsadmin}  | {all}      | all      | reject
 /rdsdbdata/config/pg_hba.conf  | hostssl | {all}       | {all}      | all      | md5
 /rdsdbdata/config/pg_hba.conf  | host    | {replication} | {all}    | samehost | md5
(6 rows)
```

Figure 6-6. *PostgreSQL host-based authentication query*

In Figure 6-6, the authentication by hostssl, all, all, all and m5 in the line number 5 from enforces md5 authentication by PostgreSQL server. The recommended security authentication method is the scram-sha-256 method. In corporation for the address, you allow by specific IP addresses.

CHAPTER 6   POSTGRESQL ON AWS RDS/AZURE SQL DATABASE

6.4.4 Create RDS from the Command Line

AWS provides several functions to manage RDS environment such as create, describe, start, stop, delete, and restore. Use the `aws rds help` command to list all available commands to manage PostgreSQL RDS. Figure 6-7 shows the categories of RDS commands.

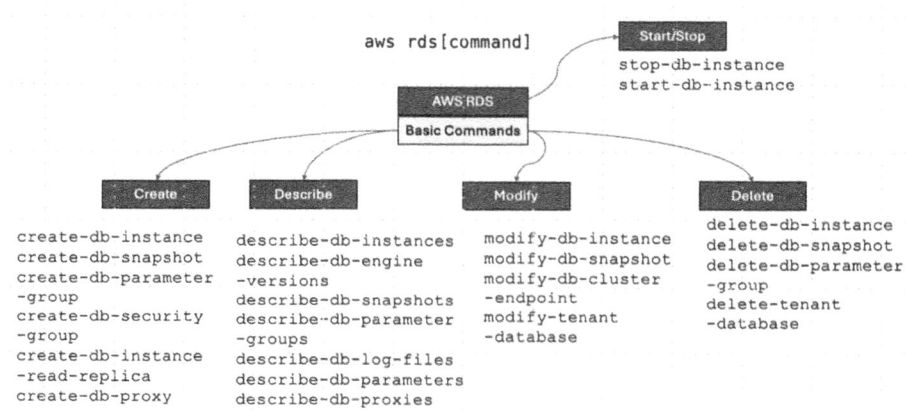

Figure 6-7. *Basic RDS commands*

One of the useful commands is `aws rds describe`, where you can query all the attributes of the RDS environment. You can execute the following command from CloudShell or from any other machines where AWS client software is installed. This command queries the instance class, instance id, and instance status example (and see Figure 6-8):

   aws rds describe-db-instances --query "DBInstances[*].{DBInstanceIdentifier:DBInstanceIdentifier,DBInstanceClass:DBInstanceClass,DBInstanceStatus:DBInstanceStatus}" --output table

```
$aws rds describe-db-instances --query "DBInstances[*].{DBInstanceIdentifier:DBInstanceIdentifier,DBInstanceClass:DBInstanceClass,
DBInstanceStatus:DBInstanceStatus}" --output table
```

	DescribeDBInstances	
DBInstanceClass	DBInstanceIdentifier	DBInstanceStatus
db.t3.micro	devrds01-demodbinstance-ghfkfft25q0u	stopped
db.t3.micro	dev-rds-postgres-instance	stopped
db.t3.micro	mydevres-demodbinstance-vqsii3zaoqrc	stopped

Figure 6-8. RDS query instance

Create RDS from the Command Line

An easy and simple method is to create RDS from the command line with the API method. You have to provide six mandatory required parameters: instance name, instance type, engine, master username and password, and storage size. Unless you have multiple VPCs, the default VPC and subnet is used for the RDS instance creation in the default region. For multiple availability zones, use the flag --multi-az. See Listing 6-1.

Listing 6-1. Create RDS Instance

```
aws rds create-db-instance --db-instance-identifier dev2-
rds-postgres-instance --db-instance-class db.t3.micro --engine
postgres --master-username USER1 --master-user-password
Monitor10177 --allocated-storage 20 --publicly-accessible
```

With the above command, you are creating a default RDS with t3.micro instance type with 20GB of storage. Figure 6-9 shows the output of the above command.

```
$aws rds create-db-instance --db-instance-identifier dev2-rds-postgres-instance --db-instance-class db.t3.micro --eng
ine postgres --master-username USER1 --master-user-password Monitor10177 --allocated-storage 20 --publicly-accessible
{
    "DBInstance": {
        "DBInstanceIdentifier": "dev2-rds-postgres-instance",
        "DBInstanceClass": "db.t3.micro",
```

Figure 6-9. RDS creation from API output

CHAPTER 6 POSTGRESQL ON AWS RDS/AZURE SQL DATABASE

Upon creation of the RDS instance, you can query the instance attributes. See Listing 6-2.

Listing 6-2. Describe RDS Instance

```
aws rds describe-db-instances --query 'DBInstances[*].
[DBInstanceIdentifier, DBInstanceClass, DBInstanceStatus,
AllocatedStorage, Endpoint.Address, Engine, EngineVersion]'

::: partial outout
"dev2-rds-postgres-instance",
"dev2-rds-postgres-instance.c87h7wvm7a78.us-east-2.rds.
amazonaws.com"
```

The AWS console view of RDS provides comprehensive details about the instance.

For the complete create database instance, go to https://docs.aws.amazon.com/cli/latest/reference/rds/create-db-instance.html.

Create RDS from YAML Template

You worked with AWS CloudFormation in Chapter 3 to install EC2 or Azure VM. CloudFormation also allows you to automate the entire lifecycle of your RDS environments from provisioning to updating and deletion.

With YAML you can configure over 50 parameters for building a complex RDS environment. The YAML configuration consists of two components: the Resources section, which is mandatory with optional parameters, which are referenced from Resources section. In the section 4.8 of Chapter 4, you created a non-default port PGSGSec. When creating new RDS instances, you can import the security group definitions with the !ImportValue prefix. In the Resource section, you define rules for the variables, which are referenced with the !Ref prefix. The YAML file can run into hundreds of lines if you add all 50 parameters while building an RDS instance. You can use a CloudFormation template to validate the YAML file.

Listing 6-3 shows a simple RDS to create a basic instance.

Listing 6-3. RDS Creation from YAML

```
Parameters:
  RDSName:
   Type: String
   Default: 'DEVRDS1'
  RDSUser:
   Type: String
   Default: 'USER1'
  RDSPass:
   Type: String
   Default: 'Monitor10177'
   Description: SOX
Resources:
  DemoDbInstance:
    Type: 'AWS::RDS::DBInstance'
    Properties:
      DBName: !Ref RDSName
      MasterUsername: !Ref RDSUser
      MasterUserPassword: !Ref RDSPass
      Engine: Postgres
      DBInstanceClass: db.t3.micro
      StorageType: gp2
      PubliclyAccessible: true
      AllocatedStorage: '20'
      VPCSecurityGroups:
        !ImportValue "PostgresSecurityGroup"
```

The deploy command creates CloudFormation stack with the YAML file at a specified location.

CHAPTER 6　POSTGRESQL ON AWS RDS/AZURE SQL DATABASE

After creating the YAML script, validate it with the CloudFormation Application Composer Template.

Listing 6-4 shows the command and image of YAML CloudFormation deployment to create PostgreSQL RDS instance. See Figure 6-10 also.

Listing 6-4. CloudFormation Deployment

```
aws cloudformation deploy --template-file /Users/Venkat/rds.yaml --stack-name mydevres2
```

```
$aws cloudformation deploy --template-file /Users/venkat/rds.yaml --stack-name  mydevres
Waiting for changeset to be created..
Waiting for stack create/update to complete
Successfully created/updated stack - mydevres
```

Figure 6-10. *RDS creation from the YAML template output*

Listing 6-5 is a basic script to create RDS instance in the AWS Cloud, where parameter definitions are referred as !Ref [Parameter Name]. Listing 6-5 shows the example of enforcing the instance type with parameter allowed values rule.

Listing 6-5. YAML Parameter for Instance Type

```
Parameters:
  InstanceType:
    Type: String
    Description: 'EC2 instance type'
    Default: 't3.micro'
    AllowedValues:
      - 't2.micro'
      - 't2.small'
    ConstraintDescription: 'Valid values are: t3.micro/t2.micro/t2.small'
```

Note IaC (Infrastructure as Code) is used because it is easier to share and review the configuration. In corporations, all RDS deployments are done with a YAML or JSON template file where all template definitions along with parameter values are approved by infrastructure provisioning resources. Listing 6-6 shows the JSON template file to deploy PostgreSQL RDS.

Listing 6-6. RDS Creation with JSON

```json
{
  "Parameters": {
    "RDSName": {
      "Type": "String",
      "Default": "DEVRDS"
    },
    "RDSUser": {
      "Type": "String",
      "Default": "USER1"
    },
    "RDSPass": {
      "Type": "String",
      "Default": "Monitor10177",
      "Description": "SOX"
    }
  },
  "Resources": {
    "DemoDbInstance": {
      "Type": "AWS::RDS::DBInstance",
      "Properties": {
        "DBName": { "Ref": "RDSName" },
```

```
        "MasterUsername": { "Ref": "RDSUser" },
        "MasterUserPassword": { "Ref": "RDSPass" },
        "Engine": "Postgres",
        "DBInstanceClass": "db.t3.micro",
        "StorageType": "gp2",
        "PubliclyAccessible": true,
        "AllocatedStorage": "30"
      }
    }
  }
}
```

With the `aws cloudformation` command you provision RDS as per the details of the JSON file.

Here is the command and screen image (Figure 6-11) of the deployment status:

```
aws cloudformation deploy --template-file rds.json --stack-name mydevres2
```

```
$aws cloudformation deploy --template-file rds.json --stack-name mydevres21

Waiting for changeset to be created..
Waiting for stack create/update to complete
Successfully created/updated stack - mydevres21
```

Figure 6-11. *JSON script deployment*

After deployment, view the Summary section of the AWS console to check the database status, as shown in Figure 6-12.

CHAPTER 6   POSTGRESQL ON AWS RDS/AZURE SQL DATABASE

Summary

DB identifier	Status	Role	Engine
mydevres21-demodbinstance-ep5mkd5yfgzr	⊙ Available	Instance	PostgreSQL
	Class	Current activity	Region & AZ
	db.t3.micro	0 Connections	us-east-2b
CPU			
3.56%			

Figure 6-12. RDS console view

Start and Stop of RDS Instances with a Script

You can manage a fleet of RDS instances with scripting solutions. The script in Listing 6-7 uses the command `aws rds describe-db-instances –query` to obtain instance details. Depending on the outcome of the status, you can either start or stop the instance. The user is prompted to choose db instance and press Return for no action. Listing 6-7 shows the script to start or stop RDS instances

Listing 6-7. RDS Start/Stop Script

```
#Script to start  RDS"
echo " Available Instance Status"
aws rds describe-db-instances --query 'DBInstances[*].[DBInstanceIdentifier,DBInstanceStatus]' --output text
echo " Press return for no action "
echo " Start or Stop Depending on the status for this instance ...."
for db in $(aws rds describe-db-instances --query 'DBInstances[*].[DBInstanceIdentifier]' --output text)
do
```

```
echo $db
 echo " enter choice"
 read ans
    if [ "$ans" == "start" ]
    then
    echo " proceeding .... to $ans ....$db."
      aws rds $ans-db-instance --db-instance-identifier $db
     elif [ "$ans" == "stop" ]
     then
    aws rds $ans-db-instance --db-instance-identifier $db
    fi
done
```

The command to start and stop the instance is `aws rds [start/stop] --db-instance-identifier [instance name]`.

Figure 6-13 shows the output of the above script.

```
$ ./rd.sh
 Available Instance Status
devrds01-demodbinstance-ghfkfft25q0u      stopped
dev-rds-postgres-instance            stopping
mydevres-demodbinstance-vqsii3zaoqrc      stopped
 Press return for no action
 Start or Stop Depending on the status for this instance ....
devrds01-demodbinstance-ghfkfft25q0u
 enter choice
start
 proceeding .... to start ....devrds01-demodbinstance-ghfkfft25q0u.
{
    "DBInstance": {
        "DBInstanceIdentifier": "devrds01-demodbinstance-ghfkfft25q0u",
```

Figure 6-13. *RDS start and stop script output*

RDS Access From a Non-Default Port

While creating the RDS instance, you can choose the PostgresSecurityGroup for access with a non-default port such as 5433, which you created earlier in Chapter 3. Here is the command to use a non-default port after the creation of RDS:

```
aws rds modify-db-instance --db-instance-identifier
your-instance-identifier --db-parameter-group-name
PostgresSecurityGroup --apply-immediately
```

To create a non-default security group, you can use the AWS CLI or AWS SDKs. Specify the desired inbound and outbound rules to control access to your RDS instance.

6.4.5 Modification to RDS

If you want to extend the basic configuration of RDS, you have to modify two configuration parameters: the options group, which provide additional extensions and features such as `enable pg_cron` to run database jobs, and the parameter group, which is used to define new values to the database parameters such as increasing the default limit of processes from 100 to 1000. Each RDS instance is associated with one options group and one parameter group. Figure 6-14 exhibits the relationship between parameter groups, option groups, and RDS instances.

CHAPTER 6 POSTGRESQL ON AWS RDS/AZURE SQL DATABASE

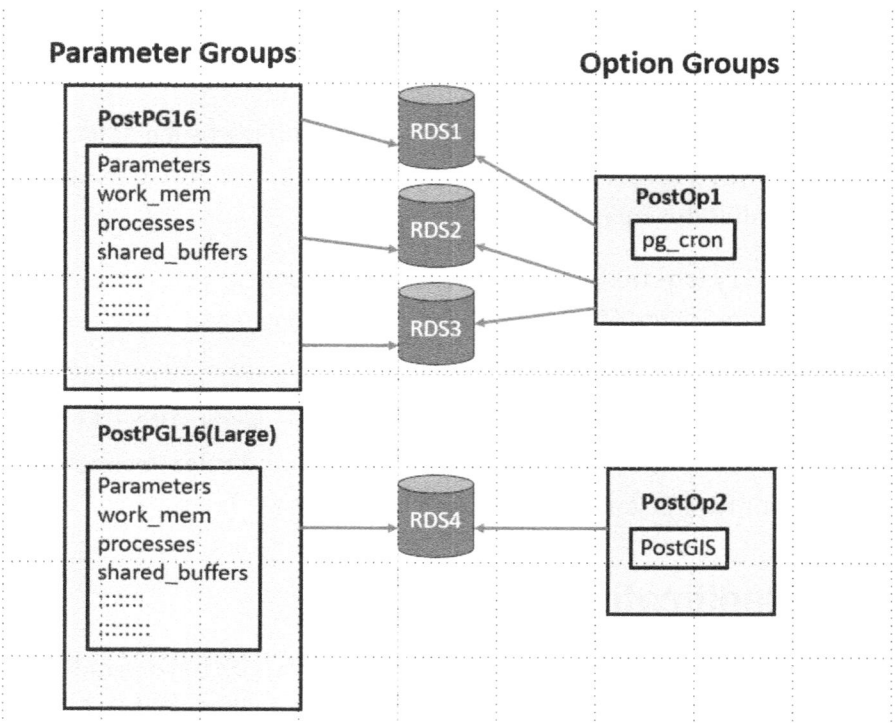

Figure 6-14. Parameter and option groups

Parameter Group

RDS has a default parameter group, which cannot be modified. In RDS, you cannot use an alter command because you must create a new parameter group and modify the command to make changes to database parameters. The default PostgreSQL is configured with basic values for memory parameters. Create a custom parameter group for each version to modify parameter values.

The new parameter group will inherit the properties from the default parameter group. The following is an example of setting values for work_mem in the parameter group for the Postgres 16 release. work_mem is a dynamic parameter that will take immediate effect . The creation of a parameter group is a one-time task for each version of PostgreSQL, whereas you can modify over 350 parameters with the modify option for each parameter group.

Parameter Modification from RDS API

There are three steps to change values in RDS:

1. Create a parameter group.
2. Modify a parameter group.
3. Modify the instance with a new parameter group.

The following is the procedure:

1. `aws rds create-db-parameter-group --db-parameter-group-name Postgresdb16 --db-parameter-group-family postgres16 --description "pgdb16parameter changes."`

2. `aws rds modify-db-parameter-group \ --db-parameter-group-name Postgresdb16 \ --parameters "ParameterName=work_mem,ParameterValue=2097152,ApplyMethod=immediate"`

3. `aws rds describe-db-parameters --db-parameter-group-name Postgresdb16 --query 'Parameters[?ParameterName==’work_mem’].ParameterValue'`

4. `aws rds modify-db-instance --db-instance-identifier [instanceid] --db-parameter-group-name Postgres16 --apply-immediately`

For detail references on parameter groups, refer to these AWS URLs:
https://docs.aws.amazon.com/cli/latest/reference/rds/create-db-parameter-group.html,

https://docs.aws.amazon.com/cli/latest/reference/rds/modify-db-cluster-parameter-group.html,

https://docs.aws.amazon.com/cli/latest/reference/rds/modify-db-instance.html, and

https://docs.aws.amazon.com/cli/latest/reference/rds/describe-db-parameters.html.

Modify an AWS Parameter Value From the Console

The database parameters can be modified with the AWS console. The procedure is Create Parameter Group ➤ Modify Parameter Group ➤ Modify Instance.

Options Group

Similar to the parameter group, you have to create a new option group and assign it to an instance. Listing 6-7 shows the command to add pgaudit to new options groups.

Listing 6-7. Create Options Groups

```
aws rds create-option-group \
    --option-group-name PostOpt1
    --engine-name postgres \
    --major-engine-version 16 \
    --option-group-description "New Options Group"
aws rds add-option-to-option-group \
    --option-group-name  PostOpt1\
    --options "OptionName=pgaudit" \
    --apply-immediately
```

> **Note** You have to install pgaudit extension to add it to an options group.

6.4.6 RDS PostgreSQL Logs View

The RDS error logs are visible from the AWS console. From RDS choose Database ➤ instancename ➤ Log&Events to view the log files.

Log View from the AWS CLI

With the aws describe-db-log-file and aws rds downloads-db-log-file-portion AWS CLI you can view the full or a portion of the error log. You can identify the last file and file portion with the tail command. Listing 6-8 shows the commands to view the partial error log contents. As PostgreSQL created on an hourly basis, substitute with your date.

Listing 6-8. RDS Logs View

```
$aws rds describe-db-log-files --db-instance-identifier dev2-rds-postgres-instance | tail -6
            "LogFileName": "error/postgresql.log.2024-05-26-04"
$aws rds download-db-log-file-portion --db-instance-identifier dev2-rds-postgres-instance --log-file-name error/postgresql.log.2024-05-26-04 --output text | tail -5
2024-05-26 04:24:27 UTC::@:[709]:LOG:  checkpoint starting: time
```

6.4.7 RDS Performance Monitoring

Figure 6-15. *RDS performance monitoring*

The main benefit of working with databases on the cloud is to leverage the capabilities of monitoring tools provided by cloud vendors for the analysis of real-time and historical data about operating system, database metrics, and database wait events. Metrics (Figure 6-15) are the measures that provide throughput and response time details to understand the health of the database as well as the operating system for performance tuning analysis. The major metrics include CPU utilization, free memory, I/O latency, disk usage, I/O throughput, response time, latency, vacuum progress, replication latency, and database cache hit ratio. Database wait events, along with metrics, provide the overall health of the database system.

6.4.8 AWS Performance Insights

Performance Insights is a new feature to provide additional monitoring capabilities in AWS. After signing into the AWS console, choose the Modify option to enable Performance Tuning metrics. See Figure 6-16.

CHAPTER 6   POSTGRESQL ON AWS RDS/AZURE SQL DATABASE

Monitoring

Performance Insights Info

☑ Turn on Performance Insights

Retention period   Info

| 7 days (free tier) ▼ |

Figure 6-16. Choose Performance Insights

Next, choose the Performance insights menu option, which is called the Metrics screen. See Figure 6-17.

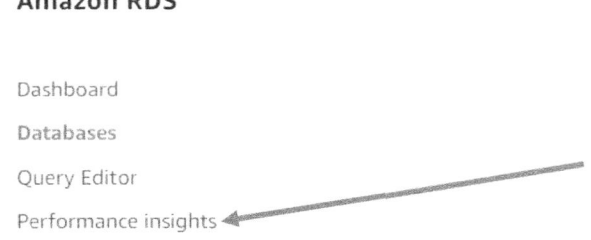

Figure 6-17. Metrics screen

Metrics Dashboard

The Performance Insights Metrics is a paid service which provides a detailed view of performance metrics of the database with real-time data analysis for query tuning, which help in identifying any performance bottleneck at the OS and database layers. You can effectively trace each and every SQL statement execution plan and query throughput

6.4.9 Dimensions Menu

The Dimensions menu has options for observing the SQL statement details. See Figure 6-18.

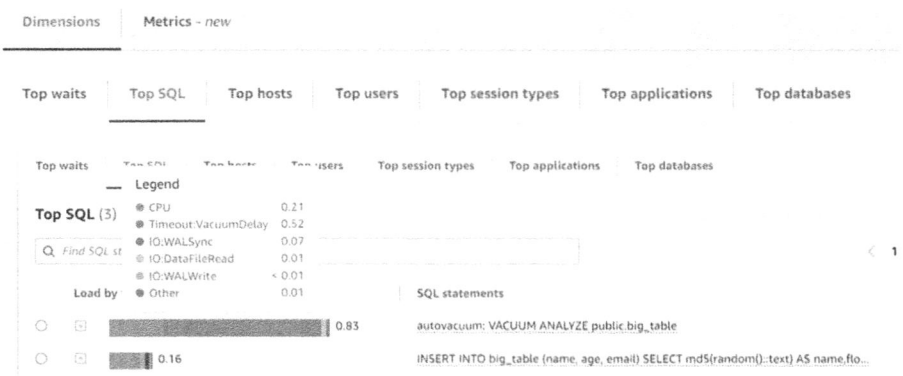

Figure 6-18. *Top SQL*

6.4.10 PostgreSQL Dynamic View for Metrics

The database wait events are recorded in the view `pg_stat_activity`. The column wait event type displays details about activity, I/O, lock, buffer pin, and client wait events. See Figure 6-19.

CHAPTER 6 POSTGRESQL ON AWS RDS/AZURE SQL DATABASE

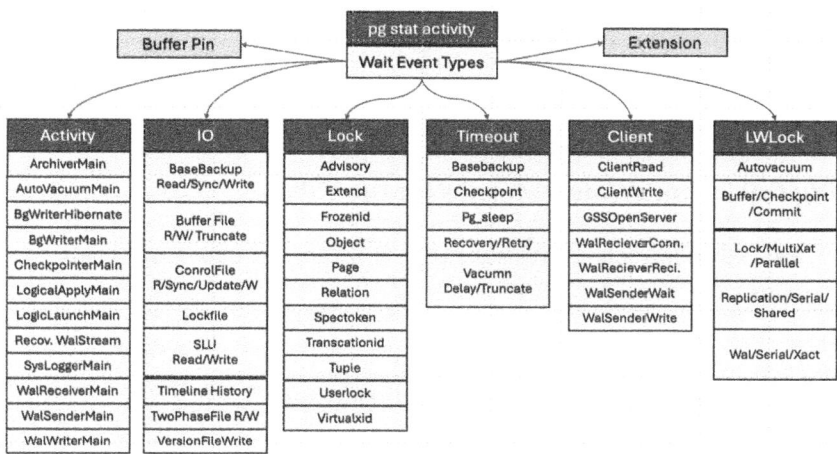

***Figure 6-19.** PostgreSQL wait event types*

The performance tuning process is to identify and resolve the wait events in the database.

Refer to the following documentation for additional details:

www.postgresql.org/docs/current/monitoring-stats.html#MONITORING-PG-STAT-ACTIVITY-VIEW.

6.4.11 Performance Monitoring with the AWS CLI

If you want to monitor a fleet of RDS servers, the easy and simple method is to use the AWS CLI looping for all RDS instances for the examination of the metric thresholds.

AWS Metrics

You can obtain full metrics with the command aws cloudwatch list-metrics. Query to get CPU-related metrics. See Listing 6-9.

Listing 6-9. CloudWatch Metrics for the CPU

```
$   aws cloudwatch list-metrics | grep -i cpu | sort -u
    Output:
                "Value": "vCPU"
        "MetricName": "CPUCreditBalance",
        "MetricName": "CPUCreditUsage",
        "MetricName": "CPUSurplusCreditBalance",
        "MetricName": "CPUSurplusCreditsCharged",
        "MetricName": "CPUUtilization",
```

6.4.12 AWS CLI JSON Metrics Monitoring

Listing 6-10 shows the JSON template to report CPU utilization for an instance based on a time range. You can monitor over 500 monitored metrics with templates. The maximum number of data points returned from a single call is 1,440 [2].

Listing 6-10. CloudWatch Metrics Data

```
# Database Metric Data for CPU and Disk usage across all RDS instances
for db in $(aws rds describe-db-instances --query 'DBInstances[*].{DBInstanceIdentifier:DBInstanceIdentifier}' --output text)
 do
 echo "Processing CPU/Storage Metrics for ....$db"
aws cloudwatch get-metric-data --cli-input-json '{
```

```
"MetricDataQueries": [
  {
    "Id": "cpu_avg",
    "MetricStat": {
      "Metric": {
        "Namespace": "AWS/RDS",
        "MetricName": "CPUUtilization",
        "Dimensions": [
          {
            "Name": "DBInstanceIdentifier",
            "Value": "'"${db}"'"
          }
        ]
      },
      "Period": 3600,
      "Stat": "Average",
      "Unit": "Percent"
    },
    "ReturnData": true
  },
  {
    "Id": "freeStorageSpace",
    "MetricStat": {
      "Metric": {
        "Namespace": "AWS/RDS",
        "MetricName": "FreeStorageSpace",
        "Dimensions": [
          {
            "Name": "DBInstanceIdentifier",
            "Value": "'"${db}"'"
```

CHAPTER 6   POSTGRESQL ON AWS RDS/AZURE SQL DATABASE

```
            }
          ]
        },
        "Period": 3600,
        "Stat": "Average"
      },
      "ReturnData": true
    }
  ],
  "StartTime": "2024-04-25T10:00:00+00:00",
  "EndTime": "2024-04-27T10:00:00+00:00"
}'
done

Output
"Id": "cpu_avg",
            "Label": "CPUUtilization",
            "Timestamps": [
                "2024-04-27T07:00:00+00:00",
                "2024-04-27T06:00:00+00:00"
            ],
            "Values": [
                9.914633079830264,
                15.274274662842958
"Id": "freeStorageSpace",
            "Label": "FreeStorageSpace",
            "Timestamps": [
                "2024-04-27T07:00:00+00:00",
                "2024-04-27T06:00:00+00:00"
            ],
            "Values": [
                19629370880.0,
```

        19721681920.0
    ]

6.4.13 AWS CLI API

Another method to view metrics data is from `aws cloudwatch get-metric-statistics` to view the metrics from a fleet RDS instance, where you have to provide one metric at a time. Listing 6-11 shows the example script to monitor the CPU.

Listing 6-11. CloudWatch Metric Data for a Single RDS Instance

    aws cloudwatch get-metric-statistics --metric-name CPUUtilization --start-time 2023-09-12T10:00:00+00:00 --end-time 2023-09-12T14:05:00+00:00 --period 3600 --namespace AWS/RDS --statistics Maximum --dimensions Name=DBInstanceIdentifier,Value=devrds2-demodbinstance-drtzsxzfoiea

6.4.14 Script for Metric Data

You can create a script that goes through all instances to obtain metrics for a fleet of instances. Listing 6-12 is the script that queries all RDS instances and provides input to CPU utilization metrics function.

Listing 6-12. CloudWatch Metrics Data for All Instances

```
# Query CPU usage data for RDS instances on hourly usage
# Change date for the sample window
for db in $(aws rds describe-db-instances --query
'DBInstances[*].{DBInstanceIdentifier:DBInstanceIdentifier}'
--output text)
```

```
  do
     echo " cpu usage $db"
       aws cloudwatch get-metric-statistics --metric-name 
CPUUtilization --start-time 2024-04-26T10:00:00+00:00 --end-
time 2024-04-27T11:05:00+00:00 --period 3600 --namespace AWS/
RDS --statistics Maximum --dimensions Name=DBInstanceIdentifier
,Value=$db
  done
```

6.4.15 RDS Extensions

RDS provides additional extensions beyond the dbase ones provided by PostgreSQL.

```
postgres=> select count(*) from pg_available_extensions;
 count
-------
    92
```
https://docs.aws.amazon.com/AmazonRDS/latest/PostgreSQLReleaseNotes/postgresql-extensions.html

6.5 Azure SQL Database

PostgreSQL cluster is provided within the Azure environment as a fully managed database service called Azure SQL Database. It covers all PostgreSQL database tasks such as installation, configuration, updates, migration, backup, and recovery, as well as ensuring high availability both within and across regions through geo-redundant data replication. Azure offers two options to manage PostgreSQL in the cloud: Single Server for the open source and Flexible Server for added performance tuning capabilities. You can work with these database services from

Azure Console, Azure CLI from CloudShell, Linux, Mac, and Windows environments. Minimal services are offered from the Single Server option, whereas full performance tuning capabilities are added in the Flexible Service option. To manage a fleet of computers, you can deploy templates with Bicep, ARM, and Terraform formats. You can provision Azure SQL Database from the console or from command line options.

6.5.1 Azure SQL Database for PostgreSQL

With Azure SQL Database you can provision PostgreSQL cluster with simple steps, where the provision of hardware and software is taken care of by Microsoft. Like AWS, there are regions spread across all over the globe, where there are two or three availability zones in each region and each region is a dedicated data center provisioned with a fleet of computers, network interfaces, and storage subsystems.

> **Note** In the workload type, when selecting computer hardware, you have only three options to choose from on the Azure console, such as Standard_B1ms, Standard_D4ds_v4, and Standard_E4ds_v4.

To review a list of all available computer hardware, you have to work with the command line with the command `az vm list-skus --location eastus --output table`. The command line options are detailed in section 2. For training and testing, choose the base model called Standard_B1ms, which is not eligible for upgrade from an Azure SQL database for PostgreSQL.

6.5.2 Azure PostgreSQL Creation Steps

Figure 6-20. Azure PostgreSQL creation process

After connecting to the Azure console (Figure 6-20), choose SQL database service, which will spawn the screen, as shown in Figure 6-21.

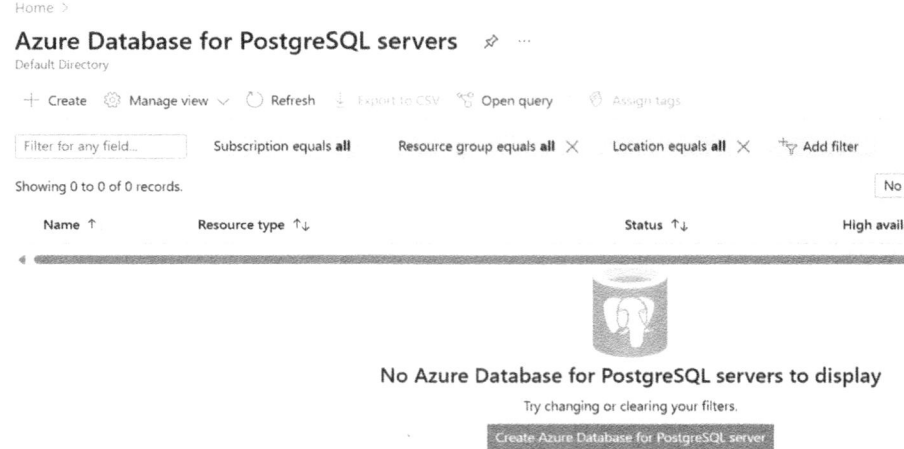

Figure 6-21. Azure database for PostgreSQL Server

Go to this URL to complete the PostgreSQL Server creation on Azure: https://learn.microsoft.com/en-us/azure/postgresql/flexible-server/quickstart-create-server-portal.

Enable public access for initial testing and configuration. In corporations, databases are never exposed to public access directly and database access is configured through a web service, which connects to the database internally by private network. To create a test environment only, you allow public access. The databases always reside in private network in corporations accessed internally by web/application servers. The security to a PostgreSQL database is granted with a combination of IP address and netmask. For instance, the IP 172.238.12/16 with subnet mask 16 translates to the range of IP addresses from 172.238.0.0 to 172.238.255.255 where you can allocate 65,545 host addresses. The subnet mask prefix ranges between 1 to 32. If you wish to allow only one computer to the database, the netmask is 32, which is 172.238.12/32.

It is worth noticing the netmask ranges with this URL:

https://learn.microsoft.com/en-us/azure/postgresql/flexible-server/quickstart-create-server-portal.

After completion of PostgreSQL, you can view the details from All services ➤ Postgresql Flexible Server option. See Figure 6-22.

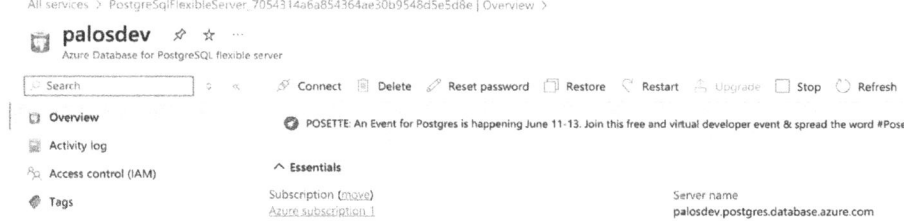

Figure 6-22. PostgreSQL Flexible Server completion view

After completion of PostgreSQL, the first step is to validate access from the client machines.

6.5.3 psql Connection From a Windows Laptop

Figure 6-23 shows the connection example from a Windows client.

```
postgres=> \conninfo
You are connected to database "postgres" as user "pgAdmin" on host "palosstg2.postgres.database.azure.com" (address "20.
172.211.193") at port "5432".
SSL connection (protocol: TLSv1.3, cipher: TLS_AES_256_GCM_SHA384, compression: off)
postgres=>
```

Figure 6-23. Connection to PostgreSQL from a Windows PC

6.5.4 Azure PostgreSQL CLI

All administrative tasks of PostgreSQL on Azure are performed by az postgres flexible-server commands. Figure 6-24 lists Azure commands to manage PostgreSQL databases.

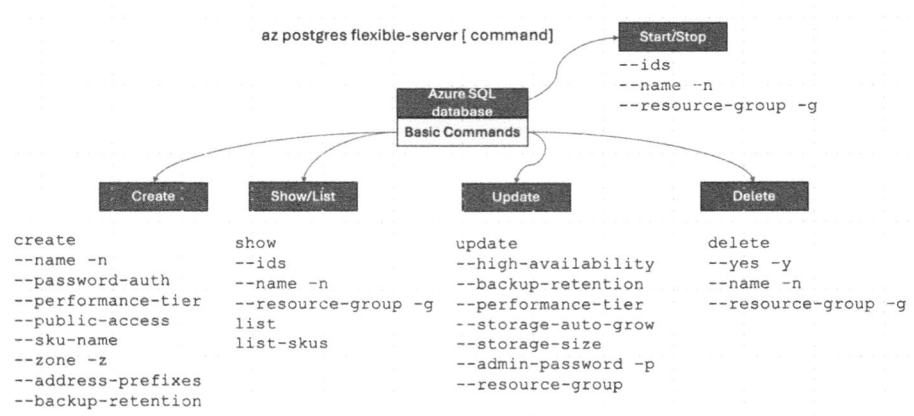

Figure 6-24. Azure PostgreSQL Flexible Server commands

Refer to the following URL for a detailed description of the command az postgres flexible-server: https://learn.microsoft.com/en-us/cli/azure/postgres/flexible-server?view=azure-cli-latest.

6.5.5 Create a PostgreSQL Single Server

PostgreSQL Single Server is an open-source Postgres cluster software. The supported version is 11. The following is the command to create PostgreSQL Single Server:

venkat [~]$ az postgres server create --resource-group myRsourceGroup --name palosdev --admin-user postdev --admin-password Post10177 --sku-name B_Gen5_1 --version 11

Partial output is shown in Figure 6-25.

```
venkat [ ~ ]$ az postgres server create --resource-group myRsourceGroup --name palosd
ev --admin-user postdev --admin-password Post10177 --sku-name B_Gen5_1 --version 11
Checking the existence of the resource group 'myRsourceGroup'...
Resource group 'myRsourceGroup' exists ? : False
Creating Resource Group 'myRsourceGroup'...
```

Figure 6-25. *Azure PostgreSQL Single Server creation*

6.5.6 Create PostgreSQL Flexible Server Azure CLI

Microsoft added additional features and functionalities in Flexible Server. The following is the command to create PostgreSQLFlexible Server (and see Figure 6-26):

venkat [~]$ az postgres flexible-server create --resource-group demo --name palosdemo --admin-user postdev --admin-password Post10177 --version 16 --high-availability Enabled

```
venkat [ ~ ]$ az postgres flexible-server  create --resource-group demo --name palosd
emo --admin-user postdev --admin-password Post10177  --version 13
Checking the existence of the resource group 'demo'...
Resource group 'demo' exists ? : False
Creating Resource Group 'demo'...
```

Figure 6-26. *The Azure PostgreSQL Flexible Server CLI*

6.5.7 Create PostgreSQL Flexible Server with a Template

Creation of PostgreSQL with templates is the industry standard for mass deployment and to deploy per organizational standards.

Bicep Template

Bicep is a domain-specific language (DSL) that uses declarative syntax to deploy Azure resources [3]. In the declarative syntax, the user requests what they want to provision and how it is provisioned is transparent to the user and taken care of by the cloud providers. The Bicep domain-specific language is an open-source initiative by Microsoft to simplify the definition of Azure Resource Manager (ARM) templates, which are used to manage PostgreSQL on the cloud along with other resources. With reusable parameters, variables, and resources, you deploy the code to provision databases. The resource is the basic unit of a Bicep template, with property definitions for each type of resource such as Flexible server, VM, and firewall rules. You can deploy complex environments with loops and programmatic constructs with Bicep.

In Listing 6-13, for US East location, PostgreSQL Flexible Server is provisioned with Standard_B1ms virtual machine and firewall rules are open to all. If not already created, create a resource group with the command az group create --name demo --location eastus and execute the following Bicep script. Change the location to your geography.

Listing 6-13. Azure Bicep Example

```
param location string = 'eastus'
resource server 'Microsoft.DBforPostgreSQL/flexibleServers@2023-03-01-preview' = {
  name: 'palosstg5'
  location: location
  sku: {
    name: 'Standard_B1ms'
    tier: 'Burstable'
  }
```

```
  properties: {
    administratorLogin: 'pgAdmin'
    administratorLoginPassword: 'Admin10177'
    createMode: 'default'
    storage: {
      storageSizeGB: 32
    }
    version: '15'
  }
}
resource firewallRule 'Microsoft.DBforPostgreSQL/
flexibleServers/firewallRules@2023-03-01-preview' = {
  name: 'allowAll'
  parent: server
  properties: {
    startIpAddress: '0.0.0.0'
    endIpAddress: '255.255.255.255'
  }
}
```

After creating the bicep template, with the `az deployment` command you can provision PostgreSQL Server. See Figure 6-27.

```
venkat [ ~ ]$ az deployment group create --resource-group demo --template-file azds.b
icep
  Running ..
```

Figure 6-27. *PostgreSQL Flexible Server creation with a Bicep template*

JSON Template

In Azure, JSON deployment templates use schema definitions for syntax verification. Check for the latest version of schema management template on the Microsoft site when deploying code in JSON.

In Listing 6-14, the password for the Administrative user is prompted with a parameter definition. The unique instance name is generated by variables and PostgreSQL Flex Server is created by basic configuration. The resources are defined in square [] brackets, which refers to forward declaration of parameters and variables. See Listing 6-15 also.

Listing 6-14. JSON Template

```
{
  "$schema": "https://schema.management.azure.com/schemas/2019-08-01/deploymentTemplate.json#",
  "contentVersion": "1.0.0.0",
  "parameters": {
    "administratorLoginPassword": {
      "type": "securestring", //  prompt for password
      "metadata": {
        "description": "The password for the postgres
        administrator login."
      }
    }
  },
  "variables": {
// Generate unique string from resource group name
    "uniqueSuffix": "[substring(uniqueString(resourceGroup().id), 0, 5)]",
//Append unique suffix to instance name
    "postgresInstanceName": "[concat('palos', variables('uniqueSuffix'))]"
  },
  "resources": [
    {
      "type": "Microsoft.DBforPostgreSQL/flexibleServers",
      "apiVersion": "2023-03-01-preview",
```

CHAPTER 6   POSTGRESQL ON AWS RDS/AZURE SQL DATABASE

```
      "name": "[variables('postgresInstanceName')]",
      "location": "eastus",
      "sku": {
        "name": "Standard_B1ms",
        "tier": "Burstable"
      },
      "properties": {
        "administratorLogin": "pgAdmin",
        "administratorLoginPassword": "[parameters('administrat
        orLoginPassword')]",
        "createMode": "default",
        "storage": {
          "storageSizeGB": 32
        },
        "version": "15"
      }
    }
  ]
}
```

Listing 6-15. Azure JSON Deployment

```
az deployment group create --resource-group demo --template-
file azds.json
```

After creating a JSON template, execute the command `az deployment` to provision PostgreSQL Sever. See Figure 6-28.

```
venkat [ ~ ]$ az deployment group create --resource-group demo --template-file azds.json
Please provide securestring value for 'administratorLoginPassword' (? for help):
{
```

Figure 6-28. *PostgreSQL Flexible Server creation with a JSON template*

241

CHAPTER 6   POSTGRESQL ON AWS RDS/AZURE SQL DATABASE

6.5.8 Enable PostgreSQL Parameter for Logging

The next step after creating the PostgreSQL cluster database is to enable logging of cluster events of the database in the database log, which is called error.log. By default, PostgreSQL will create one error per day with a date timestamp. There are over 20 options to customize logging of database event in the error log. See Figure 6-29.

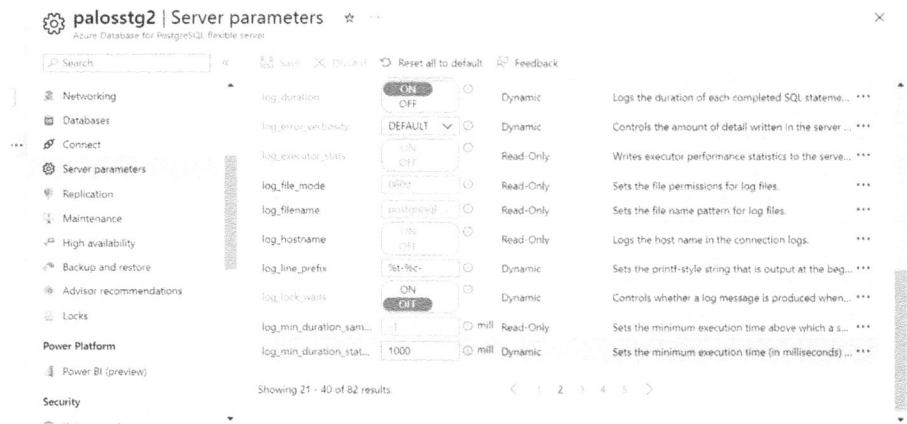

Figure 6-29. PostgreSQL parameter enabling

6.5.9 Enable Azure Database Logging

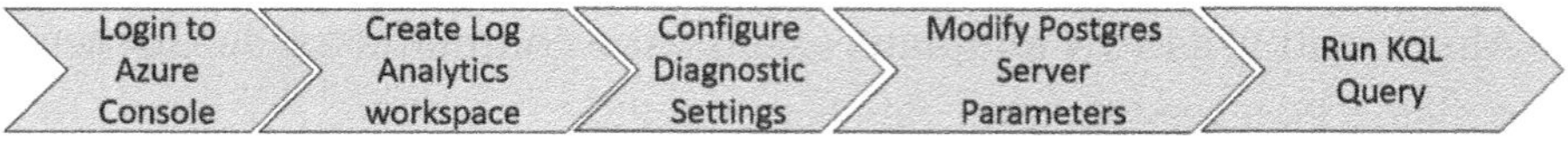

Figure 6-30. Enable Azure Database logging procedure

The PostgreSQL data service logs are not automatically visible in the Azure console. You have to execute a custom Kusto Query Language.

The destination to log files are in the Log Analytics workspace, storage account, event hub and partner solutions. There are two sections in the Diagnostic settings: Logs and Metrics. In the Logs category, there are two category groups, audit and all logs, and several categories for PostgreSQL Server logs, schema statistics, and PostgreSQL remaining transactions. In the Metrics category, you can choose all metrics options. There are over 100 monitoring metrics. You will review the metrics in detail in the Performance Tuning section.

The first step is to create a new space name for the Log Analytics workspace.

The following are the images to create the PostgreSQL logs in the Log Analytics Workspace.

6.5.10 Create Analytics Workspace

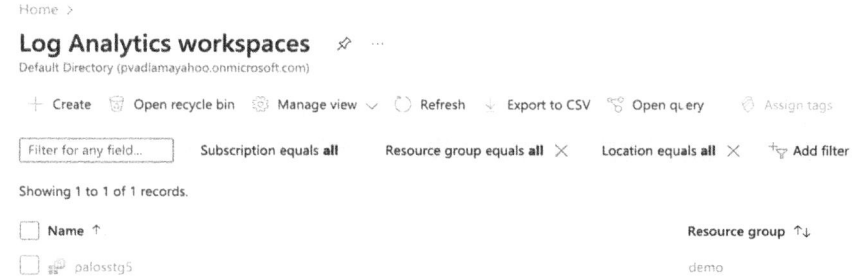

Figure 6-31. *Create the Analytics workspace*

After creating the Log Analytics workspace (Figure 6-31), the next step is to choose Diagnostics settings and to choose the logs, categories, and metrics to capture the details to it.

CHAPTER 6 POSTGRESQL ON AWS RDS/AZURE SQL DATABASE

6.5.11 Enable Diagnostic Setting

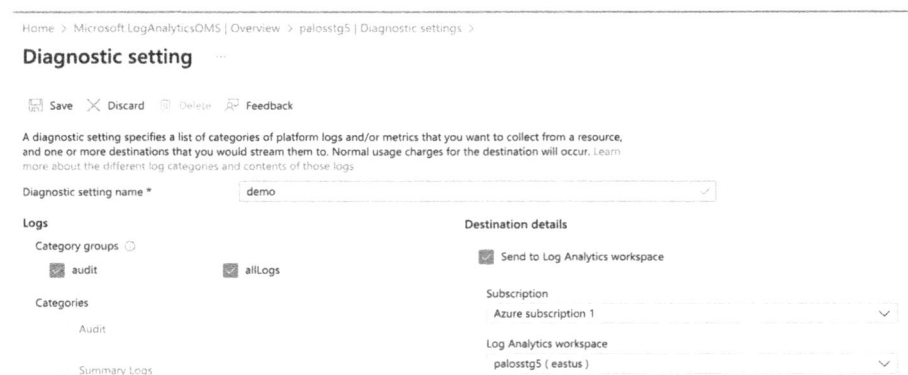

Figure 6-32. *Enable diagnostic settings*

After customizing the diagnostics settings (Figure 6-32), choose the logs option to run the KQL query to examine the PostgreSQL Cluster Diagnostics data.

For Azure Monitor Logs, logs are sent to the workspace you selected. Kusto Query Language (KQL) is a powerful language used to query data set is integrated with Azure landscape. You have to run KQL to view the log files of PostgreSQL. The basic syntax is [tablename] | where [column]='value1'| where columnname='value2'. The output of one pipe is input to another pipe.

Figure 6-33 shows running a KQL script from Instancename ➤ logs ➤ New Query menu.

6.5.12 Run KQL

Figure 6-33. *KQL*

You can add additional Azure Diagnostics to examine the Auto vacuum details.

6.6 Keywords

AWS region, RDS easy creation, metrics dashboard, dimensions menu, Azure create resource group and Azure Flexible Server, Azure database logging

1. https://docs.aws.amazon.com/AmazonRDS/latest/UserGuide/CHAP_PostgreSQL.html

2. https://docs.aws.amazon.com/cli/latest/reference/

3. https://learn.microsoft.com/en-us/azure/azure-resource-manager/

4. https://docs.aws.amazon.com/cli/latest/reference/cloudwatch/get-metric-statistics.html

CHAPTER 6   POSTGRESQL ON AWS RDS/AZURE SQL DATABASE

6.7 Summary of Learning

You learned about the creation of database services from AWS and Azure console and the command line, the setup of RDS Proxy, plus the setup of database security, monitor performance, view logging, and more.

6.8 Practice Chapter 6

1. Create PostgreSQL RDS with high availability in three availability zones in AWS from a YAML template.

2. Enable security access from a laptop IP address.

3. Create PostgreSQL DS with high availability in three availability zones in Azure with a Bicep template

4. Enable security access from a laptop IP address to Azure.

5. Configure an Azure Data Service snapshot backup for 14-day retention.

6. Write a JSON script to monitor five metrics in AWS.

7. Write a Bicep script to monitor five metrics in Azure.

6.9 Questions Chapter 6

1. What are the different methods of provisioning RDS?

2. What are the different methods of provisioning Azure SQL databases?

CHAPTER 6   POSTGRESQL ON AWS RDS/AZURE SQL DATABASE

3. How do you create and assign non -default port 5467 for psql access?

4. How do you disable public access to RDS?

5. Outline the steps to create RDS Proxy.

6. What is the difference between port address suffix 16/24/32 in an IP address assignment?

CHAPTER 7

PostgreSQL on Docker

7.1 Abstract

Containers in Docker, combined with the Kubernetes framework, provide capabilities for high availability (HA) and disaster recovery (DR) in containerized environments. Kubernetes, as a container orchestration platform, offers features such as automatic scaling, load balancing, and self-healing, which contribute to the high availability of applications running in containers. Through Kubernetes, containers can be deployed across multiple nodes or hosts, distributing the workload and ensuring redundancy. If a container or node fails, Kubernetes can automatically reschedule and restart the affected containers on healthy nodes, minimizing downtime and maintaining service availability.

7.2 Objective of Learning

- Introduction to Docker
- Docker software for PostgreSQL
- Docker software installation and configuration

The original version of the chapter has been revised. A correction to this chapter can be found at https://doi.org/10.1007/979-8-8688-0817-3_18

© Venkateswara Vadlamani 2024, corrected publication 2025
V. Vadlamani, *PostgreSQL Skills Development on Cloud*,
https://doi.org/10.1007/979-8-8688-0817-3_7

CHAPTER 7   POSTGRESQL ON DOCKER

- Connect to Docker from the OS host
- Kubernetes and Docker
- Backup and recovery of Docker
- Docker monitoring tool and the desktop

7.3 Introduction

Docker is an open-source software. It runs on Linux, Mac, and Windows, which allows you to create multiple machines in the physical or virtual hardware infrastructure. This means you can separate your database applications from your infrastructure [1] so that you can deploy database software and application software quickly.

Figure 7-1 shows the docker architecture.

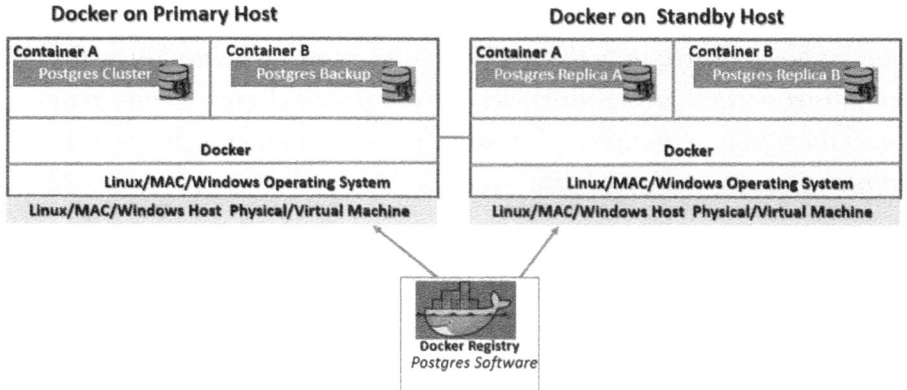

Figure 7-1. *Docker environment*

7.4 Installation

You can install Docker on any platform. If you are working on the Red Hat operating system, you can install the Docker from the Docker site and then install PostgreSQL on a Docker environment. Docker is like a virtual machines (VM) where you partition a computer into multiple isolated environments with isolated networking, storage, and computer resources. The main difference is that Docker containers share the host OS kernel and support only one OS (such as Linux, Windows, or macOS), making them lightweight and efficient, whereas VMs use a hypervisor to run multiple full operating systems independently, which uses more resources.

You can develop your application with PostgreSQL database on a Mac in Docker, which you can move to Linux Docker without any change. Docker allows rapid application development to support the agile application development methodology.

7.5 Docker Platform

Docker is a platform that enables deployment of PostgreSQL clusters in isolated containers, addressing high availability, scalability, backup and recovery, and performance tuning requirements. It offers easy deployment and management, simplified scaling and upgrading, as well as improved security and isolation. The container in Docker has its own IP address, storage, memory allocation, software libraries, and isolation from other containers. From a DBA perspective, Docker helps in isolating the environments to improve fault tolerance and scalability.

A typical application has several containers for application servers, web servers, and database servers in the cloud environment. The basic docker commands are `cp, create, cp, diff, events, ecport, history, import, inspect, kill, load, logs, pause, port, rename, restart, rm, rmi, save, start.stats, stop, tag, top, unpuse, update, and wait`.

Docker services are essential for high availability, disaster recovery, backup and recovery, monitoring, and load balancing of PostgreSQL cluster databases. Docker compose is a tool to manage all container administration in a single host, which reads configuration from a YAML file.

There are two steps to configure Docker in the Linux environment: configure a yum repository and install Docker.

7.5.1 Docker Info

After installing and configuring docker on Linux, the command to check for docker software is `docker info`. As the root user or a user with sudo privilege you can work with Docker. `docker info` displays information about one container, which is not running. See Listing 7-1.

Listing 7-1. The docker info Command

```
[ec2-user@node1172 ~]$
root@ip-172-31-32-62 ~]# docker info
Client:
 Context:    default
 Debug Mode: false
 Plugins:
  buildx: Docker Buildx (Docker Inc., 0.0.0+unknown)
Server:
 Containers: 1
  Running: 0
  Paused: 0
  Stopped: 1
 Images: 1
 Server Version: 20.10.23
 : : : : : : :
```

7.5.2 Docker pull

With the `docker pull` command you can download the PostgreSQL Docker image from the public repository. After installing the Docker environment, you can proceed with pulling the Docker image of PostgreSQL and running the PostgreSQL container to set up PostgreSQL on the Docker environment. Both from AWS EC2 and Azure VM, the steps are to pull the docker image and create a PostgreSQL cluster from this image.

The OS command to pull PostgreSQL is `docker pull postgres:latest` to download the PostgreSQL cluster and Docker's latest version, which is 16 as of writing the book. See Listing 7-2.

Listing 7-2. Docker pull

```
$sudo docker pull postgres:latest
latest: Pulling from library/postgres
f11c1adaa26e: Pull complete
::::Lines omitted
95c2c2ef9f02: Pull complete
Digest: sha256:0aafd2ae7e6c391f39fb6b7621632d79f54068faebc726c
af469e87bd1d301c0
Status: Downloaded newer image for postgres:latest
docker.io/library/postgres:latest
```

7.5.3 Docker Registry

The Docker images are software copies of the PostgreSQL cluster, which are available in the centralized repository for download purposes. After pulling the image from the public repository, you can check the image inventory with the command `docker images`. Listing 7-3 shows the output of the `docker images` command.

Listing 7-3. Docker images

```
$ docker images
REPOSITORY      TAG        IMAGE ID         CREATED        SIZE
dev             latest     661045193646     3 weeks ago    371MB
<none>          <none>     8897ad7628aa     3 weeks ago    379MB
<none>          <none>     bb344044f395     3 weeks ago    371MB
postgres        15         0c88fbae765e     4 weeks ago    379MB
postgres        latest     0c88fbae765e     4 weeks ago    379MB
```

After pulling the image, the next step is to run a container with the necessary configurations to deploy a PostgreSQL cluster in the Docker environment.

7.5.4 Create a PostgreSQL cluster in Docker

The next step after installing the PostgreSQL software is to create the PostgreSQL cluster. docker run is a command to create a PostgreSQL cluster where you can specify the PostgreSQL container name, admin username, admin user password, postgres port, and container storage location for the data directory.

Here is the command to create a PostgreSQL cluster in a Docker environment:

```
$sudo docker run --name postgresql -e POSTGRES_USER=myusername -e POSTGRES_PASSWORD=mypassword -p 5439:5432 -v /data:/var/lib/postgresql/data1 -d postgres
```

The above command creates a container named postgresql on the Docker host, along with the specified environment variables for the user and password, exposes port 5432 for communication, and maps the data directory to a local directory (/data).

CHAPTER 7 POSTGRESQL ON DOCKER

After the successful creation of PostgreSQL Docker, you can identify the running status by the command docker ps -a. See Listing 7-4.

Listing 7-4. Docker Process Command

```
# docker ps -a
CONTAINER ID   IMAGE      COMMAND                  CREATED
  STATUS           PORTS
NAMES
8bbf6454e67f   postgres   "docker-entrypoint.s..."   3 minutes ago
  Up 3 minutes   0.0.0.0:5432->5432/tcp, :::5432->5432/tcp
postgresql
```

After installing the PostgreSQL cluster on the Docker host, connect to the database by the command docker exec -it postgresql psql -U username. See Listing 7-5.

Listing 7-5. Docket Connection from psql

```
$ sudo docker exec -it postgresql psql -U myusername
psql (16.3 (Debian 16.3-1.pgdg120+1))
Type "help" for help.

myusername=# \du
List of roles
Role name | Attributes
------------+-------------------------------------------------
myusername | Superuser, Create role, Create DB, Replication,
Bypass RLS

myusername=#
```

255

CHAPTER 7 POSTGRESQL ON DOCKER

To select data from Docker, run the command (assuming the sales database and t1 table exist in the PostgreSQL cluster) `$docker exec -it postgresql psql -U myusername -d sales -c "select * from t1;"`. See Figure 7-2.

```
 id
-----
 100
(1 row)
```

```
 id
-----
 100
(1 row)
```

Figure 7-2. *Docker connect to PostgreSQL from local host*

Direct connection to the Docker host is not required, as authentication is done by the host staging the docker. You can connect to Docker from a local host where the database is staged as well as from remote machines. Once connected, you can create a new database, create tables, and insert data using SQL commands. Listing 7-6 shows an example of connecting to PostgreSQL on Docker from a Windows PC. The `-h` refers to the Docker host.

Listing 7-6. Docker Connection from a Remote PC Client

```
c:\Program Files\PostgreSQL\15\bin>psql -h 18.116.230.186 -U myusername
Password for user myusername:
psql (15.2)
Type "help" for help.
myusername=# \du
```

CHAPTER 7 POSTGRESQL ON DOCKER

```
                         List of roles
 Role name  |                      Attributes                      | Member of
------------+------------------------------------------------------+----------
 demo       |                                                      | {}
 myusername | Superuser, Create role, Create DB, Replication, Bypass RLS | {}
 postgres   |                                                      | {}
```

7.5.5 Docker Compose

With Docker compose, you can deploy a fleet of containers in a single host. The details are defined in the file `docker-compose.yaml` file. The `docker-compose.yaml` file in Listing 7-7 creates three containers in the Docker host listening on three different ports for PostgreSQL and one container for SQL Server. You have to provide the image name, container name, admin username and password, port name and volume location in the compose file. The SQL Server container serves as a use case to copy data between docker containers.

Listing 7-7. docker-compose.yaml File

```
docker-compose.yaml
version: '3.8'
services:
  sql_server:
    image: mcr.microsoft.com/mssql/server:latest
    container_name: sql_server1
    environment:
```

CHAPTER 7   POSTGRESQL ON DOCKER

```
      ACCEPT_EULA: "Y"
      MSSQL_SA_PASSWORD: "Konitor10177"
    ports:
      - "1433:1433"
    volumes:
      - sql_data:/var/opt/mssql
  postgreslatest:
    image: postgres:latest
    container_name: sales
    environment:
      POSTGRES_USER: postgres
      POSTGRES_PASSWORD: Konitor10177
      POSTGRES_DB: postgres
    ports:
      - "5439:5432"
    volumes:
      - postgres_data1:/var/lib/postgresql/data
  postgres15:
    image: postgres:15
    container_name: mkt
    environment:
      POSTGRES_USER: postgres
      POSTGRES_PASSWORD: Konitor10177
      POSTGRES_DB: postgres
    ports:
      - "5440:5432"
    volumes:
      - postgres_data2:/var/lib/postgresql/data
  postgres14:
    image: postgres:14
    container_name: fin
    environment:
```

```
      POSTGRES_USER: postgres
      POSTGRES_PASSWORD: Konitor10177
      POSTGRES_DB: postgres
    ports:
      - "5444:5432"
    volumes:
      - postgres_data3:/var/lib/postgresql/data
volumes:
  sql_data:
  postgres_data1:
  postgres_data2:
  postgres_data3:
```

All the containers are started with the docker compose up command, shown in Listing 7-8.

Listing 7-8. Docker compose up Output

```
$docker compose up
[+] Running 4/0
 ✓ Container fin          Created                           0.0s
 ✓ Container shipping     Created                           0.0s
 ✓ Container sales        Created                           0.0s
 ✓ Container mkt          Created                           0.0s
Attaching to fin, mkt, sales, shipping
:::Continued
mkt       | 2024-07-04 01:12:14.489 UTC [1] LOG:  database system is ready to accept connections
sales     | 2024-07-04 01:12:14.580 UTC [1] LOG:  database system is ready to accept connections
fin       | 2024-07-04 01:12:14.639 UTC [1] LOG:  database
```

system is ready to accept connections
2024-07-04 01:12:22.11 spid23s   Server is listening on ['any' <ipv6> 1433] accept sockets 1

7.5.6 Docker Process

The point of interest in the Docker command is the reference docker container id as well as the name, which are the first and last fields in the docker ps -a command. You need the container id for backup as well as for removing the docker. You need a docker name for connection to any Postgres cluster residing in the docker host. The container name is highlighted in yellow color in Listing 7-9.

Listing 7-9. Docker Process with Multiple Containers

```
docker ps -a
CONTAINER ID    IMAGE
COMMAND                     CREATED         STATUS          PORTS
NAMES
3264a5f65c17    postgres:14                                 "docker-
entrypoint.s..."   26 seconds ago   Up 24 seconds
   0.0.0.0:5444->5432/tcp, :::5444->5432/tcp    fin
656ad823574c    mcr.microsoft.com/mssql/server:latest   "/opt/
mssql/bin/perm..."   26 seconds ago   Up 24 seconds
   0.0.0.0:1433->1433/tcp, :::1433->1433/tcp    sql_server1
28004de163ec    postgres:latest                             "docker-
entrypoint.s..."   26 seconds ago   Up 24 seconds
   0.0.0.0:5439->5432/tcp, :::5439->5432/tcp    sales
6f6fcf556bfc    postgres:15                                 "docker-
entrypoint.s..."   26 seconds ago   Up 24 seconds
   0.0.0.0:5440->5432/tcp, :::5440->5432/tcp    mkt
```

7.5.7 psql Connection to a Docker Local Host

After installing the Docker containers on the local host, you can connect to psql program on each Docker with the command sudo docker -exec it [docker name] psql -U [username]. The command in Listing 7-10 illustrates the connection to three containers in the Docker host environment. I have installed four containers (post14, post15, postlatest, and sql_server1) on a Linux host, which are isolated environments to segregate business-specific data. The listing is an example of connecting to two different databases residing on two different Docker containers.

Listing 7-10. Connect to psql on a Docker Host

```
$sudo docker exec -it sales  psql -U postgres -c "select version();"
                          version
------------------------------------------------------------------
 PostgreSQL 16.1 (Debian 16.1-1.pgdg120+1) on x86_64-pc-linux-gnu, compiled by gcc (Debian 12.2.0-14) 12.2.0, 64-bit
(1 row)

$sudo docker exec -it fin  psql -U postgres -c "select version();"
                          version
------------------------------------------------------------------
 PostgreSQL 14.10 (Debian 14.10-1.pgdg120+1) on x86_64-pc-linux-gnu, compiled by gcc (Debian 12.2.0-14) 12.2.0, 64-bit
(1 row)
```

7.5.8 psql Connection from a Remote Laptop

You can connect to multiple Postgres servers in containers in the Docker host by referring to different ports, as each Postgres server will listen to a dedicated port. In section 4, you saw multiple PostgreSQL servers running on different ports. In a Linux host without Docker, the PostgreSQL cluster is resolved to respective ports, whereas in Docker, all the non-default ports are bound through 5432. Although Docker is considered as a dedicated host for PostgreSQL with its local ports, for external connections to Docker, all connections are bound through port 5432. This binding is observed in Docker Compose YAML definitions such as "5433:5432". In the following example, notice the connection to the PostgreSQL cluster from the default port 5432 as well as from port 5433.

Figure 7-3 shows the example of a connection established to a Postgres container on non-default port 5433 on a Docker host.

```
SQL Shell (psql)
Server [localhost]: 3.16.164.76
Database [postgres]:
Port [5432]: 5433
Username [postgres]:
Password for user postgres:
psql (15.4, server 15.3 (Debian 15.3-1.pgdg110+1))
WARNING: Console code page (437) differs from Windows code page (1252)
         8-bit characters might not work correctly. See psql reference
         page "Notes for Windows users" for details.
Type "help" for help.

postgres=#
```

Figure 7-3. Connect to Docker from a non-default port

7.5.9 Docker Utility

The essential database tasks that can be performed by the Docker utility are pulling of docker from a repository and creating databases, users, scripts deployment, and backup. The Docker utility is available in the AMI. Refer to the AMI documentation for further details.

7.6 Backup and Recovery of Docker

Figure 7-4 shows the steps to back up and recover Docker for a Postgres image.

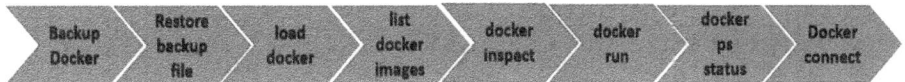

Figure 7-4. *Backup and recovery of Docker*

7.6.1 Back Up Docker

The backup of the container is performed by the command `docker export`. The container id is identified by `docker ps -a`. Listing 7-11 shows the command to back up Docker in the tar format.

Listing 7-11. Docker export

```
$docker export f656f2ba6d09  > fin.tar
$ls -l  fin.tar
-rw-r--r--. 1 ec2-user ec2-user 416779776 Jul  4 01:23 fin.tar
```

Additional reference can be found at https://docs.docker.com/reference/cli/docker/container/export/.

7.6.2 Recover Docker

You can recover Docker in local as well as in remote locations where you have already installed and configured the Docker environment. The recovery is done with two methods: with the `docker load` command or with the `docker import` command. The `import` command restores the contents of the backup tar file as a Docker container in the local filesystem from the backup of the remote system. The `load` command is used for restoring Docker containers on the same host. For instance, the image of PostgreSQL running on a Linux host can be loaded into Docker running on a Windows host or MAC host.

Full details of all import options are mentioned in the docker documentation at https://docs.docker.com/engine/reference/commandline/import/.

7.6.3 Docker Restore on a Local Host

The responsibility of a DBA is to know setup, backup, and recovery procedures and to test them periodically to recover database(s) from planned or unplanned outages. With the `docker load` command with the -i argument, you can restore the backup container in the same host..

After performing a backup, the steps to recover are: 1) `docker load`, 2) check the image, 3) inspect the image, 4) run the container, and 5) check the status of the container.

The `docker load` is a simple and straightforward command where the recovery of Docker will be completed unless you have other unknown issues. After successfully loading the Docker image, you can inspect the metadata of the Docker container for username, password, Postgres version, path, container id, and path of Postgres data directory.

The following are the Docker restore details in the following order:

Backup

```
docker commit 1869a4addec5 stage_image
$docker stop 1869a4addec5
$docker save -o stage.tar stage_image
$docker rm 1869a4addec5
```

See Listing 7-12.

Listing 7-12. Backup and Recovery Docker Procedures

```
$docker load -i stage.tar
Loaded image: stage_image:latest
$docker run -d --name restoredev -e POSTGRES_PASSWORD=mysecretpassword stage_image:latest /usr/lib/postgresql/14/bin/postgres -D /var/lib/postgresql/data
docker exec -it restoredev bash
postgres@4eb6ff6b06a9:/$ exit
exit
$docker exec -it restoredev psql -U postgres
psql (14.10 (Debian 14.10-1.pgdg120+1))
Type "help" for help.
postgres=# \l
                        List of databases
  Name     |  Owner   | Encoding  | Collate | Ctype |   Access privileges
-----------+----------+-----------+---------+-------+---------------------
 devdocker | postgres | SQL_ASCII | C       | C     |
```

Figure 7-5 shows the screen image of the backup and recovery of Docker on the same host.

```
$docker commit 1869a4addec5 stage_image
sha256:8d82ab44152215c2607ca8fc254fccc28b57071b9bee19cb148f9bd75396caa8
$docker stop 1869a4addec5
1869a4addec5
$docker save -o stage.tar stage_image
$docker rm 1869a4addec5
1869a4addec5
$docker load -i stage.tar
Loaded image: stage_image:latest
$docker run -d --name restoredev -e POSTGRES_PASSWORD=mysecretpassword stage_image:latest /usr/lib/postgresql/14/bin/postgres -D /var/lib/postgresql/data
4eb6ff6b06a9d1aaa6e2021961e69d148e3ac75c405c944a20d43727e8f60f32
$docker logs restoredev
2024-07-06 23:48:50.520 UTC [1] LOG:  starting PostgreSQL 14.10 (Debian 14.10-1.pgdg120+1) on x86_64-pc-linux-gnu, compiled by gcc (Debian 12.2.0-14) 12.2.0, 64-bit
```

Figure 7-5. *Docker save and load*

7.7 Orchestration Framework

There are orchestration frameworks to the Docker technology, which extend the functionality of Docker for high availability and scalability. There are three main frameworks: Kubernetes, OpenShift, and Amazon EKS. In addition to the above, Docker Registry is a repository for all open-source software.

7.7.1 Remove Docker

To remove Docker, run this command to identify the Docker id. The docker should be stopped.

```
docker rm [container id]
```

The commands to stop and remove Docker is `docker stop` and `docker rm`.

You have to identify the docker container id and then stop and remove it. See Listing 7-13.

Listing 7-13. Remove a Docker Container

```
# docker rm 8bbf6454e67f
8bbf6454e67f
```

The Docker commands reference is at `https://docs.docker.com/reference/cli/docker/image/import/`.

7.7.2 Kubernetes

Kubernetes is an open-source container orchestration platform that helps manage and automate the deployment, scaling, and management of containerized applications across a cluster of machines. K3 is lightweight Kubernetes. Install Kubernetes full or preferably the lightweight version

CHAPTER 7 POSTGRESQL ON DOCKER

k3sa framework for deploying and running containers, load balancing, scaling applications, and managing storage and networking. Kubernetes is highly flexible, scalable, and portable, allowing applications to be run consistently across different environments, which can be a collection of physical and virtual machines. Kubernetes software can detect the failed nodes and restart nodes on predefined time intervals.

The first step for Kubernetes is to create a namespace; *namespaces* provides a mechanism for isolating groups of resources within a single cluster (https://kubernetes.io/docs/concepts/overview/working-with-objects/namespaces/).

After creating the namespace, the next task is to configure the resources in the YAML file with the `apply` command to create the resources in the Kubernetes cluster environment.

The main command in the Kubernetes environment, `kubectl`, controls the Kubernetes cluster manager, which takes several arguments to get details about the pods. The major commands to manage Kubernetes with kubectl are the following:

```
kubectl get services                # List all services in
                                      the namespace
kubectl get pods --all-namespaces   # List all pods in all
                                      namespaces
kubectl get pods -o wide            # List all pods in the
                                      current namespace, with
                                      more details
kubectl get deployment my-dep       # List a particular
                                      deployment
kubectl get pods                    # List all pods in the
                                      current namespace
kubectl get pod my-pod -o yaml
[https://kubernetes.io/docs/reference/kubectl/cheatsheet/]
```

Kubernetes Cluster ➤ Pods ➤ Containers. In a Kubernetes cluster, you can have multiple pods, and each pod can have one or more containers. This structure allows for efficient management, scalability, and coordination of containerized applications within a cluster.

A **pod** is the smallest and most basic unit in Kubernetes. It represents a logical group of one or more closely related containers that are deployed together on the same node.

Pods provide a way to organize containers in an encapsulated manner that need to work together and share resources.

Containers are the runtime instances of applications within pods such as a database server, web server, and application server. Each container represents a lightweight and isolated environment required towards the application and its dependencies. Containers run within pods and share the same network namespace, IPC namespace, and other resources within the pod.

In Figure 7-5, notice the Kubernetes cluster master node and three client nodes. The master node monitors the health of the client mode with the client Kubelet process, works on load balancing, starts any client nodes that are in the stopped state, destroys nodes that are no longer responding, and quickly spawns another node based on the configuration.

7.7.3 Kubernetes Cluster Infrastructure

Kubernetes has a master node and worker nodes, and worker nodes where the master node monitors the worker node workload and availability and will spawn new worker nodes in the event of errors or non-availability of pods in the node. The master nodes are designed in odd numbers such as 3, 5, 7, or more. Kubernetes seamlessly moves the underlying pods in case of issues with any of the pods defined in the infrastructure. In a typical production environment, you have a cluster of nodes managing the environment. Figure 7-6 shows a simple infrastructure diagram with one master node with three worker nodes.

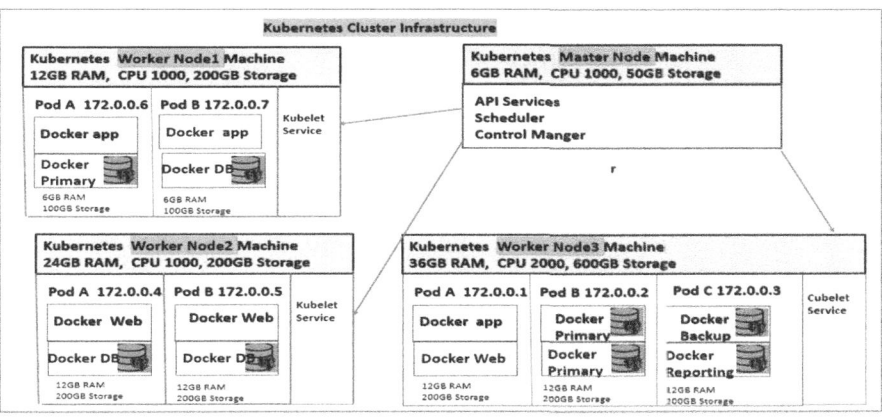

Figure 7-6. Kubernetes infrastructure architecture

7.7.4 Kubernetes Application Access

The microservice application connects to multiple containers residing on one or many pods. In case of any issues to pods or containers, the Kubernetes process will destroy the failed container or pod and will spawn new pods or containers based on the registry information. Microservices are the way to go in the cloud, where business services such as subscription-specific features are aligned with a database, which resides in a pod, and can be turned on or off depending on the user subscription model.

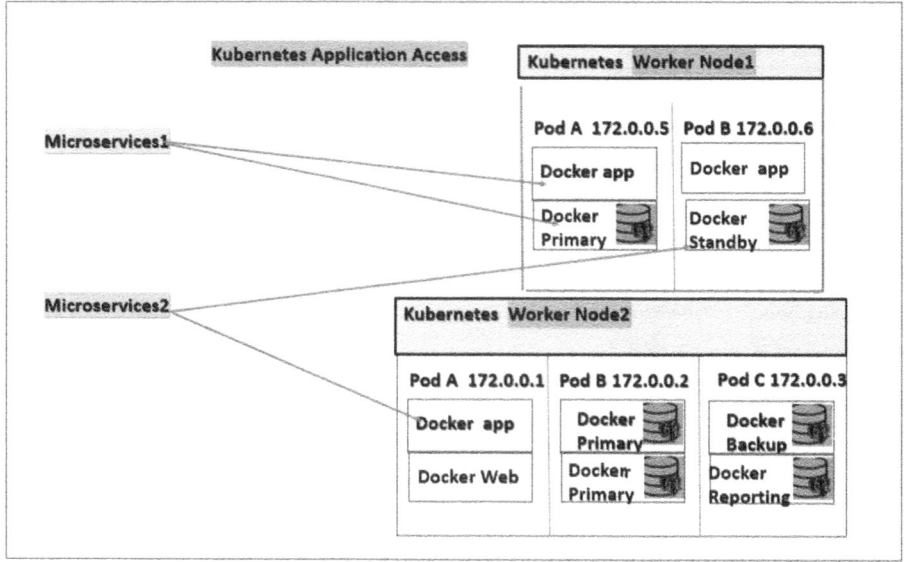

Figure 7-7. *Microservices connection to Kubernetes*

In Figure 7-7, notice that microservices can access any pod in the Kubernetes cluster.

7.7.5 Kubernetes Postgres Creation YAML

Listing 7-14 shows a sample YAML file in Kubernetes to create a Postgres cluster.

Listing 7-14. Kubernetes YAML File to Create PostgreSQL

```
apiVersion: v1
kind: Pod
metadata:
  name: postgres-pod
spec:
```

```
containers:
  - name: postgresql
    image: postgres
    env:
      - name: POSTGRES_PASSWORD
        value: TopSecret(%
# Apply changes
kubectl apply -f
```

7.8 OpenShift

OpenShift is a container platform developed by Red Hat that builds upon the open-source Kubernetes framework. It offers additional features and functionalities such as integrated development tools, source code management, continuous integration and continuous deployment (CI/CD) pipelines, and a web-based user interface. OpenShift provides an end-to-end platform for building, deploying, and managing containerized applications. It offers enterprise-level security, multi-tenancy, and enhanced developer experience.

Like Kubernetes, the first command is to create a namespace, create a pod, and apply a configuration.

The major OpenShift commands are as follow:

```
oc login    # logon to Open Shift
oc create   # create  pod defined in *.yaml or *.json
oc apply # apply configuration in *.yaml or *.json
oc get pods # get all the pods
oc get pods -o wide # get details of pod
oc get -f *.yaml # apply configuration to pod
```

(https://docs.openshift.com/container-platform/4.12/cli_reference/openshift_cli/developer-cli-commands.html)

7.9 Amazon EKS

Amazon EKS (Elastic Kubernetes Service) is a managed Kubernetes service provided by Amazon Web Services (AWS). Kubernetes is the de facto framework for container orchestration [3]. It simplifies the deployment and operation of Kubernetes clusters on AWS. EKS handles the management of the control plane, including security patches, scaling, and updates, while users are responsible for managing the worker nodes. EKS integrates with other AWS services, allowing you to leverage their capabilities alongside Kubernetes. Kubernetes with AWS EKS includes provisioning a cluster, using Fargate, setting up cluster auto scaling, using elastic load balancing (classic, network, application), configuring logging, using persistent storage on EBS, and using ALB Ingress Controller [2].

Amazon EKS commands are as follows:

```
aws eks create-cluster # with input json file
aws eks delete-cluster  #delete cluster
aws eks describe-cluster # describe cluster attributes
aws eks list-clusters  # list available clusters
aws eks update-cluster-config # update cluster configuration defined in json file
```

 (https://docs.aws.amazon.com/cli/latest/reference/eks/)

CHAPTER 7 POSTGRESQL ON DOCKER

7.10 Docker Desktop

Docker Desktop is a popular software tool that enables developers to build, test, and deploy applications using containers. It provides an easy-to-use graphical user interface (GUI) and command-line interface (CLI) for managing Docker containers and images on Windows and macOS operating systems. If you prefer to use a GUI for ease of commands, Docker Desktop is the way to go, where you perform all your administrative tasks with ease and comfort. In Figure 7-7, there are two docker images, MySQL and Postgres, and SQL Server, in which Postgres and SQL server are in use, which you can access from your local desktop. Docker Desktop includes Docker Compose along with Docker Engine and Docker CLI.

In the above example, I configured SQL Server and PostgreSQL Docker containers with Docker Desktop. With Docker Desktop, you can view all the details about available container images, data volumes, the status for the Docker application in user or unused, to efficiently work with all the available components for management. Figure 7-8 shows Docker Desktop on a Mac, after loading a backup of Docker from Linux.

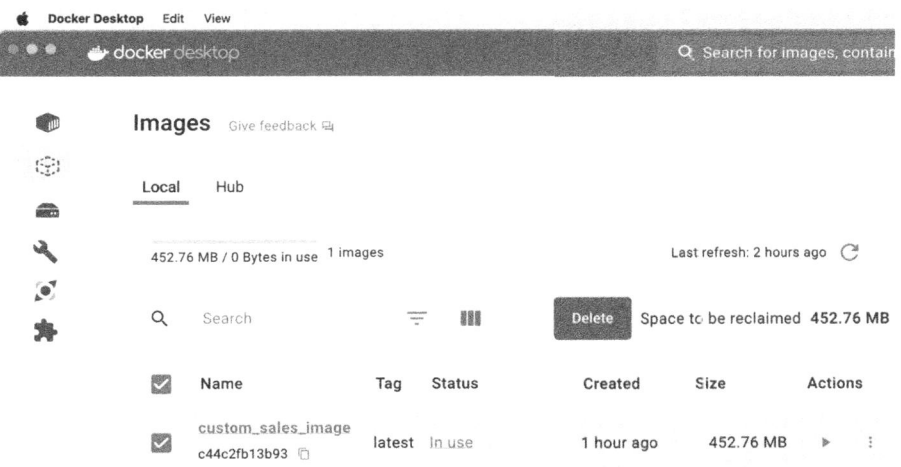

Figure 7-8. Docker Desktop image of Postgres for a Mac

273

CHAPTER 7   POSTGRESQL ON DOCKER

After importing the docker from Linux, the next step is to start the container.

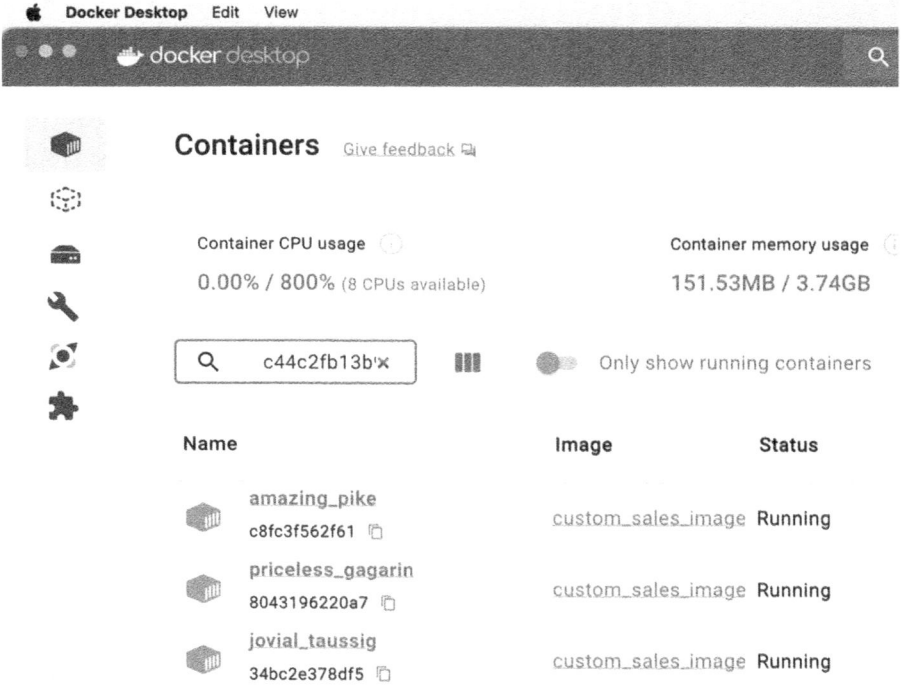

Figure 7-9. *Docker containers on a Mac*

Figure 7-9 shows the screen image of starting Docker on MAC, which is a random name generated by Docker. From a single image, I built three containers for testing and training purposes.

For scalability and load balancing you can create multiple containers with the same image. See Listing 7-15.

Listing 7-15. Running Docker Images

```
$docker ps -a
CONTAINER ID    IMAGE
COMMAND                         CREATED                 STATUS
PORTS       NAMES
34bc2e378df5    custom_sales_image:latest   "/usr/
lib/postgresql..."    6 minutes ago    Up 6 minutes
jovial_taussig
8043196220a7    custom_sales_image:latest   "/usr/
lib/postgresql..."    12 minutes ago   Up 12 minutes
priceless_gagarin
c8fc3f562f61    custom_sales_image:latest   "/usr/
lib/postgresql..."    26 minutes ago   Up 26 minutes
amazing_pike
```

After starting all Docker images, you can connect to respective PostgreSQL databases. See Listing 7-16.

Listing 7-16. psql Connection to Docker

```
$docker exec -it jovial_taussig  psql -U postgres
psql (14.10 (Debian 14.10-1.pgdg120+1))
Type "help" for help.
postgres=# exit
$docker exec -it amazing_pike psql -U postgres
psql (14.10 (Debian 14.10-1.pgdg120+1))
Type "help" for help.
postgres=# exit
$docker exec -it priceless_gagarin psql -U postgres
psql (14.10 (Debian 14.10-1.pgdg120+1))
Type "help" for help.
```

CHAPTER 7   POSTGRESQL ON DOCKER

You can perform all administrative tasks from Docker Desktop. Figure 7-10 shows connecting to the container host from Docker Desktop.

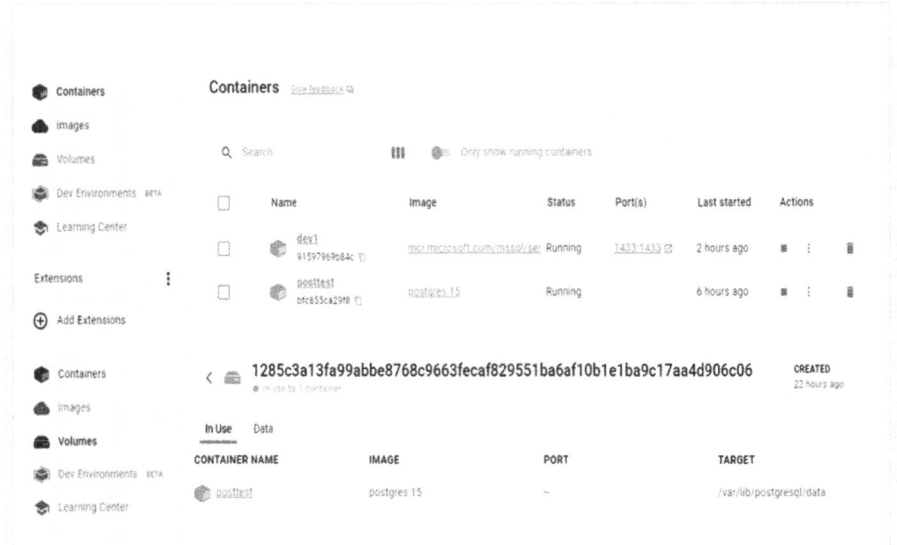

Figure 7-10. Docker Desktop storage on Windows Docker

7.10.1 Docker Export from a Mac and Import to Linux

See Listings 7-17 and 7-18.

Listing 7-17. Table Count in Docker Before Export

```
(1) $sw_vers
ProductName:            macOS
ProductVersion:         14.1.1
(2) sudo docker exec -it  amazing_pike  psql -U postgres  -d
devdocker -c "select count(*) From userdasa;"
```

CHAPTER 7 POSTGRESQL ON DOCKER

```
  count
-------
     66

$sw_vers |head -2
ProductName:            macOS
ProductVersion:         14.1.1
$sudo docker exec -it amazing_pike psql -U postgres -d devdocker -c "select count(*) From userdasa;"
 count
-------
    66
(1 row)
```

Listing 7-18. Docker Export

```
(1) $docker ps -a
CONTAINER ID    IMAGE                         COMMAND
CREATED         STATUS         PORTS NAMES
c8fc3f562f61    custom_sales_image:latest     "/usr/lib/
postgresql..."  4 hours ago    Up 4 hours    amazing_pike

(2) docker export c8fc3f562f61 > mac.tar
(3) scp -i "redaws.pem" mac.tar ec2-user@3.144.126.148:/home/
ec2-user/scripts
```

Linux: Docker import, start PostgreSQL, and connect to psql. See Listing 7-19.

Listing 7-19. Docker Import

```
(1) $docker import mac.tar mac_post1
(2) $docker images
REPOSITORY                    TAG         IMAGE
ID         CREATED        SIZE
mac_post1                     latest      5f683672538d    8 minutes
ago    462MB
```

(3)docker run -d --name mycontainer1 -e POSTGRES_PASSWORD=mysecretpassword --user postgres mac_post1 /usr/lib/postgresql/14/bin/postgres -D /var/lib/postgresql/data=
(4)sudo docker exec -it mycontainer1 psql -U postgres -d devdocker -c "select count(*) From userdasa;"
 count
66

Here is a link to a video recording of a Docker container copy from macOS to Linux:
https://us02web.zoom.us/rec/share/x869M5iYROIztmiYkgopG6OE5idsn5rMX3dVMI7G_BgndnF3BEcIybTtNas9fPA8.Vaf1px-PgWKd1Tt0

7.11 Summary of Learning

Docker is a powerful tool that allows for easy deployment and management of Postgres clusters in a containerized environment. With Docker, you can easily set up and configure Postgres databases, set up HA, and configure backup solutions. Keep learning about amazing Docker technology in the cloud. Refer to Docker tools to learn about data copying from SQL Server to Postgres procedures.

7.11.1 Keywords

Docker host, docker container, docker run, docker registry, docker info, docker images, docker ps command, docker pull, docker export, docker load, docker import, docker-decompose, docker-exec it, Kubernetes, pods, and containers

7.12 Practice chapter 7

1. Install and configure Docker on a Linux host.
2. Download Postgres and SQL Server images.
3. Validate the Docker registry inventory software.
4. Configure `compose.xml` to start multiple Postgres clusters.
5. Back up and restore Docker containers between Linux hosts.
6. Back up Docker from Linux and import into a Windows host.
7. Install and configure Docker Desktop.
8. Uninstall Docker on Linux.

7.13 Questions Chapter 7

1. Identify the following exhibit of connecting to psql from Linux. Explain why a password is required for psql to connect to the localhost and not to the docker host. Review the `pg_hba.conf` from Docker and the local host. The Postgres docker cust is running on port 5434 binding to 5432 on the local host.

   ```
   $docker ps -a | grep fin
   ee23b560af8a    postgres:14
   "docker-entrypoint.s..."   7 months ago    Up 37
   minutes                0.0.0.0:5434->5432/tcp, :::5434-
   ```

CHAPTER 7 POSTGRESQL ON DOCKER

```
>5432/tcp      fin
$sudo docker exec -it  fin psql  -U postgres
psql (14.10 (Debian 14.10-1.pgdg120+1))
Type "help" for help.

postgres=# select distinct type,database,auth_method
from pg_hba_file_rules;
 type  |   database      |  auth_method
-------+-----------------+---------------
 local | {all}           | trust
 host  | {all}           | trust
 host  | {all}           | scram-sha-256
 host  | {replication}   | trust
 local | {replication}   | trust
$psql -p 5432 -U postgres
Password for user postgres:
psql (11.18, server 12.18)
postgres=# select distinct type,database,auth_method
from pg_hba_file_rules;
 type  |   database      |  auth_method
-------+-----------------+---------------
 local | {all}           | scram-sha-256
 host  | {all}           | trust
 host  | {all}           | scram-sha-256
 host  | {replication}   | trust
 local | {replication}   | trust
```

2. How do you download Docker software?

3. What steps are required to install Postgres Docker?

4. What is the Docker registry?

5. How do you backup and restore Docker images?

6. Can you migrate Docker between multiple operating systems?
7. What is the difference between a pod and a container in the Kubernetes environment?
8. If a Docker is destroyed, how is it recognized in the Kubernetes environment?
9. How do you connect to the postgres database in Docker?
10. How do you deploy scripts in a Docker container?
11. What configuration changes do you have to make to grant access to ports 5433, 5434 and 5435 on the Postgres container residing on the Docker host?
12. How do you uninstall all components from Docker?

References

1. https://docs.docker.com/get-started/overview
2. www.amazon.com/Practical-Amazon-Elastic-Kubernetes-Service-ebook/dp/B086GZYYD7/ref=sr_1_5?crid=2VQW4HJ8IK6RO&dib=eyJ2IjoiMSJ9.R_jbCW1h9Y65vyXn2scC1pjc_KMZIbCOq2kAxfc9HExOPpQo8qndOUdQ9oS6k_pCMR4vbWN51fdlOSg-k9KqEL8PwHBPhVwm1FE7Tx59zfZ1R4gSqXNYOKVWnwJZexqb_-xwiItyPb5CfLtjObt1IS-ht54O26fOE_EXWTCLDtuoAttNSEUBDyceVcGnUNKS9O_IaUZgblDkKSCugtyNhXyqO1nXlSsuB_JBI_54WVg.bHiiawFGIvsQwYUPXkZlpZSEGxrvMSQxpS2E1YLISHI&dib_tag=se&keywords=EKS&qid=1715785769&sprefix=eks+%2Caps%2C162&sr=8-5

3. www.amazon.com/Practical-Amazon-Elastic-Kubernetes-Service-ebook/dp/B086GZYYD7/ref=sr_1_5?crid=2VQW4HJ8IK6RO&dib=eyJ2IjoiMSJ9.R_jbCW1h9Y65vyXn2scC1pjc_KMZIbC0q2kAxfc9HEx0PpQo8qnd0UdQ9oS6k_pCMR4vbWN51fdl0Sg-k9KqEL8PwHBPhVwm1FE7Tx59zfZ1R4gSqXNYOKVWnwJZexqb_-xwiItyPb5CfLtj0bt1IS-ht54O26f0E_EXWTCLDtuoAttNSEUBDyceVcGnUNKS9O_IaUZgblDkKSCugtyNhXyq01nXlSsuB_JBI_54WVg.bHiiawFGIvsQwYUPXkZlpZSEGxrvMSQxpS2E1YLISHI&dib_tag=se&keywords=EKS&qid=1715785769&sprefix=eks+%2Caps%2C162&sr=8-5

CHAPTER 8

Postgres Cluster and Database Backup

8.1 Abstract

The identification of backup requirements for critical data recovery in the event of an outage or disaster is a collaborative effort involving project managers, business application owners, and database administrators (DBAs). The key aspects in designing backup solutions are determining the amount of data that can be lost in case of a failure or disaster, as well as the time it takes to recover the system to make it operational again. Project managers, business application owners, and DBAs work together to understand the criticality of the data and the impact of downtime. Backups are essential for restoring user data, before database upgrades, for cloning databases on other systems, to set up replicas, and to implement high availability.

8.2 Objectives of Learning

- Backup methods
- Backup setup and configuration

- Integration with AWS S3
- Sample script
- RDS backup (see Figure 8-1)

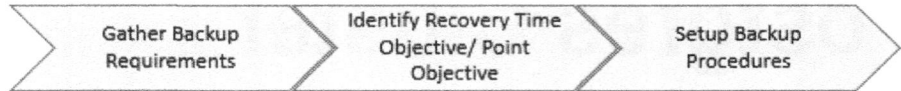

Figure 8-1. *Backup configuration*

8.3 Introduction

Setting up a reliable backup and recovery strategy is crucial for critical production environments to ensure business continuity in case of unexpected events such as hardware failure, natural disasters, or human errors.

The Recovery Time Objective (RTO) and Recovery Point Objective (RPO) are two important benchmarks that help define the backup and recovery strategy. The RTO defines the acceptable duration of time for the recovery of data from a backup that the organization can tolerate in case of a disaster, and the RPO defines the maximum acceptable amount of data loss that the organization can tolerate in case of a disaster.

To meet the RTO and RPO requirements, you have to set up a backup and recovery solution to satisfy the Service Level Agreements (SLA) of the organization. For example, if the RTO or RPO SLA requirement is 15-30 minutes, then a backup and recovery solution with high availability features such as real-time replication and point-in-time recovery should be considered. The backup solutions are different between AWS-EC2/Azure VM and RDS environments. In an AWS/EC2/Azure VM, you can

CHAPTER 8 POSTGRES CLUSTER AND DATABASE BACKUP

set up backups to go to S3/Data Blob for reliable storage or set up data replication with high availability of a PostgreSQL cluster. The RDS/Azure Data Service comes with read replicas and multi-AZ configurations.

There is no provision to backup or restore database tables in the AWS Relational Database Service/Azure SQL Database Service backup architecture, as the backups are performed with the snapshot methodology. If you need to restore a table from a backup, the process is to clone the instance with a different name, back up the database with pg_dump and restore it with either the psql or pg_restore command. Plan your backup strategy with your application requirements. See Figure 8-2.

Postgres Cluster Database RPO and RTO

Available Database Backup files
Full Backup Completion Date 03/20/2023 23:00:00
Log Backup Completion Date 03/20/2023 23:15:00
Log Backup Completion Date 03/20/2023 23:30:00
Log Backup Completion Date 03/20/2023 23:45:00
Log Backup Completion Date 03/21/2023 00:15:00

RPO: Availability of backup files for restore
Recovery Point Objective
Latest Available Backup File
03/21/2023 00:15:00

Database Crash at 03/21/2023 00:20:00

RTO
Recovery Time Objective : Total time to restore the database

Restore Time to Restore Hardware +
Restore Time for Backup Files from Tape/Disks Media + Database Recovery time. Hypothetical for Hardware restore 4 is hours is Tape/disk restore of backup files 2 hours + Database recover time of 1 hour= 7 hours of RTO

***Figure 8-2.** Database RPO and RTP*

Postgres provides three utilities to back up databases to disk: pg_dump, which back ups individual databases; pg_dumpall for backup of all databases; and pg_basebackup to back up cluster datafiles and software, which serves as a point-in-time recovery of a Postgres cluster where you can apply transaction logs for the required time of recovery. The concepts and description of pg_dumpall and pg_basebackup will be covered in subsequent chapters. For this section, the objective is to understand how the pg_dump utility works.

Figure 8-3 shows a backup flow chart in AWS/EC2/Azure VM.

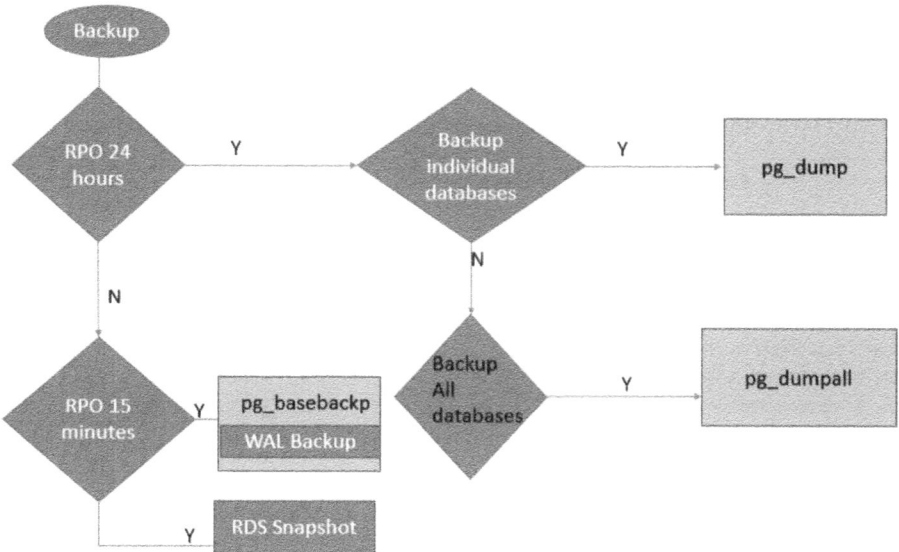

Figure 8-3. Backup flow chart

8.4 pg_dump

The pg_dump program backs up individual databases as well as individual tables to disk from a Postgres cluster database on Linux, Unix, macOS, or Windows. You can copy DDL scripts as well as a full database copy of all databases with pg_dump. There are several arguments to the pg_dump utility, which you have to use depending on the requirements. Depending on the size of the database, you can use the parallel option as well as run backup jobs in the Linux background shell to leverage parallel CPUs to speed up the backup job. The pg_dump program will not copy user accounts, passwords, and privileges. You have to work with another program called pg_dumpall for this requirement.

Listing 8-1 shows the important commands of the pg_dump utility. For a complete listing, use pg_dump -help.

Listing 8-1. pg_dump Options

```
$
pg_dump dumps a database as a text file or to other formats.
Usage:
  pg_dump [OPTION]... [DBNAME]
General options:
  -f, --file=FILENAME          output file or directory name
F, --format=c|d|t|p output file format (custom, directory, tar,
  -j, --jobs=NUM               use this many parallel
                               jobs to dump
Connection options:
  -d, --dbname=DBNAME       database to dump
  -h, --host=HOSTNAME       database server host or socket
                            directory
  -p, --port=PORT           database server port number
  -U, --username=NAME       connect as specified database user
  -w, --no-password         never prompt for password
  -W, --password            force password prompt (should happen
                            automatically)
  --role=ROLENAME           do SET ROLE before dump
```

8.4.1 Back Up a Database

The backup of the database with `pg_dump` at a minimum takes two arguments: the backup file location with the `-f` flag and the name of the database.

The following are the commands to make a backup of the database to disk with the `pg_dump` command:

> On Linux connected as postgres user, use the command `pg_dump -f postgres.sql postgres`.
>
> On macOS, use the command `pg_dump -f postgres.sql postgres`.
>
> On Windows, use the command `pg_dump -U postgres -f demo.sql postgres`.

8.4.2 Back Up a Database to S3

The best practice for databases configured on AWS is to back up database files to S3. The s3 bucket needs to be created in advance. You have to use several commands to back up the database to AWS s3: the `pg_dump` program to back up the database, gzip to compress the backup file, and `aws s3 cp` to copy the backup to s3. With pipe commands, the output of the backup is passed to gzip, which is copied to s3. The command after cp "-" specifies to copy the input file to the s3 location. A unique file is created in the format of Year/Month/date/Hour/Minute/Second. If you are connected as a postgres OS user and depending on the `pg_hba.conf` rules, you can run `pg_dump` without providing any password.

The following is the script to back up a database to S3:

```
pg_dump demo | gzip | aws s3 cp - s3://palos123/demo_$(date +%Y%m%d%H%M%S).sql.gz
```

You can customize several database backups to go to S3 with the shell script.

8.4.3 Back Up One or Many Tables

Backing up of one or many tables takes three arguments to the pg_dump command: the output file name, the table or tables, and the database name. Make sure that the backup directory exists on the Linux or Windows host.

The following is the command that specifies the backup filename on the local host with the -f argument, for each table name with the -t argument, and finally the database name:

pg_dump -f /[backup directory]/demo.pgbench_acct_brnch.sql -t pgbench_accounts, -t pgbench_branches demo

The following is the command to back up individual tables similar to the description in section 8.1.2 where the backup file is compressed and copied to s3, without creating a copy on the local host:

pg_dump -t pgbench_accounts -t pgbench_branches demo | gzip | aws s3 cp - s3://palos123/demo_pgbench_acct_branch_$(date +%Y%m%d%H%M%S).sql.gz

8.4.4 Back Up a Database for Table Restore

There are two programs to restore database(s) or table(s) from backup media: psql and pg_restore. The backup is performed as a text file with pg_dump without any options and is restored from a psql program, where the entire contents of the backup file are restored; you have no ability to restore individual databases or tables. To restore a subset of tables from the full database backup, you have to use Fc (Format custom) with the pg_dump command which is suitable for pg_restore.

The following is the command:

```
pg_dump -Fc -f demo_full.bk demo
```

With this command, you have the ability to restore any table from the demo database.

8.4.5 Back Up DDL

To back up only the schema of the database and tables to generate DDLs for import, you have to pass the -s flag to the pg_dump program. With the -s argument, no data is copied as object definitions are copied. To back up the DDL command, use the -s option in the pg_dump command.

```
pg_dump -s -f [backup directory]/demo.pgbench_accounts_DDL.sql
-t pgbench_accounts demo
```

> **Note** RDS does not support a full table-level database backup. You have to work with a snapshot backup approach to back up all databases. The pg_dump and pg_restore utilities may not be suitable for the following use cases if your database size is greater than 100GB or you want to avoid downtime.

8.4.6 Parallel Backup Configuration

The pg_dump can back up large databases with parallel options, based on the CPU count. Depending on the number of CPUs you can adjust the database maximum parallel workers parameter. The script in Listing 8-2 gathers the maximum number of CPUs from the /proc/cpuinfo command and assigns it to the cpu_count variable. If the cpu_count variable is greater than 1, the script alters the system with the maximum CPU count for the max_paralle_workers parameters. This is a preparatory step for parallel backup. If max_parallel_workers is set to the available CPU count, please ignore this script.

Listing 8-2. Parallel Backup Configuration

```
# Check the OS CPU's and adjust parallelism at the database
 cpu_count=$(grep -c "^processor" /proc/cpuinfo)
if [ $cpu_count -gt 1 ]; then
   echo "number of CPU's: $cpu_count"
   psql -c "ALTER SYSTEM SET max_parallel_workers = $cpu_count;"
   psql -c "SELECT pg_reload_conf();"
   psql -c "show  max_parallel_workers;"
else
   echo " No parallelism with $parallel_jobs"
fi
```

8.4.7 Parallel Backup Script

To perform a parallel backup, you have to use the -Fd command with pg_dump, which copies backup data to a directory. The arguments for parallel backup job are

pg_dump -Fd [databasename]   -j [cpu count]   -f [backup directory]

> **Note** The directory names have to be unique.

Listing 8-3 is the simple shell script that sets the max_parallel_workers based on CPU count, prompts for the directory name for the parallel backup, creates a backup directory, compresses the backup file, and records the elapsed time of the backup duration for a single database assuming postgres user does not require password for access.

Listing 8-3. Simple Backup Script

```bash
#!/bin/bash
# Prompt the user to enter the database name for backup
echo "Enter database for backup:"
read db
# Define a function for PostgreSQL backup
pg_backup_parallel() {
    # Get the current date and time in minutes and seconds
    dd=`date +%M%s`
    # Get the number of parallel workers for the
    PostgreSQL server
    parallel_count=$(psql -t -c "show max_parallel_workers;")
    echo "Running pg_backup with $parallel_count CPUs"
    # Create a backup directory name using the database name
    and current time
    backup_dir=$db$dd
    # Record the start time of the backup process
    start_time=$(date +%s)
    # Run pg_dump with directory format, using parallel
    workers, and save to the backup directory
    pg_dump -Fd $db -j $parallel_count -f $backup_dir
    # Compress the backup directory into a tar.gz file
    tar -czvf $backup_dir.tar.gz $backup_dir
    # Record the end time of the backup process
    end_time=$(date +%s)
    # Calculate the elapsed time for the backup process
    elapsed_time=$(expr $end_time - $start_time)
    # Print completion messages and timings
    echo "Backup of $db completed."
    echo "Start Time: $(date -d @$start_time)"
    echo "End Time: $(date -d @$end_time)"
```

```
    echo "Elapsed Time: $elapsed_time seconds"
}
# execute the function
pg_backup_parallel
```

In a typical production environment, you would have around 100 databases or more. You have to work on a script to backup all databases to disk. As you reviewed in chapter 3, you have to work with variables to perform the backup of databases from a Postgres cluster.

Listing 8-4 is the simple backup script. It assumes a backup directory, a loop through all user databases, and a backup of all databases and it compresses the backup file and displays the backup file upon successful completion.

Listing 8-4. Backup Script

```
# Create unique file name with database and date format
export sdate=$(date "+%m%d%Y%H%M%S")
# Backup directory
bkdir=/appl/postgres/backup  # enter your backup directory
# Obtain database name from database catalog
dbname=$(psql -t -c "select datname from pg_database where datname not like 'template%';")
# backup of each database to local disk in for loop
for db in $dbname
do
echo "Backup of database:$db in progress"
# backup database with pg_dump command
pg_dump  -d $db | gzip > $bkdir/$db.$sdate.sql.gz
# Check the backup status
```

```
if [ $? -eq 0 ]
 then
 echo " Backup of database $db completed"
 echo " Backup file ::::"
 ls -l $bkdir/$db.$sdate.sql.gz
fi
done

[postgres@node2 ~]$ ./exp.sh
Backup of database::::postgres in progress
 Backup of database postgres completed
 Backup file ::::
-rw-r--r--. 1 postgres 72766390 Aug  6 02:39
```

8.5 pg_dumpall

The pg_dumpall program is used to copy the contents of all databases into a text file for later recovery in an AWS/EC2/Azure VM environment. You cannot restore individual databases or tables with a backup performed by pg_dumpall. Furthermore, it should be noted that in an RDS or Azure SQL databases environment, you cannot restore an individual user login using the pg_dumpall program since database logins are not copied by the utility. You can perform a full backup of PostgreSQL cluster databases into Amazon S3 or Azure for cloning of other environments or for restoring the source database for AWS/EC2 or Azure VM. It is important to note that this is not a point-in-time recovery method, as you can only go back to the time of completion of the backup.

Use pg_dumpall --help to obtain all options. An essential one is -f for file name and optional ones are -s for schema only without data or -a for data only, along with several options as per your requirements. See Figure 8-4.

CHAPTER 8 POSTGRES CLUSTER AND DATABASE BACKUP

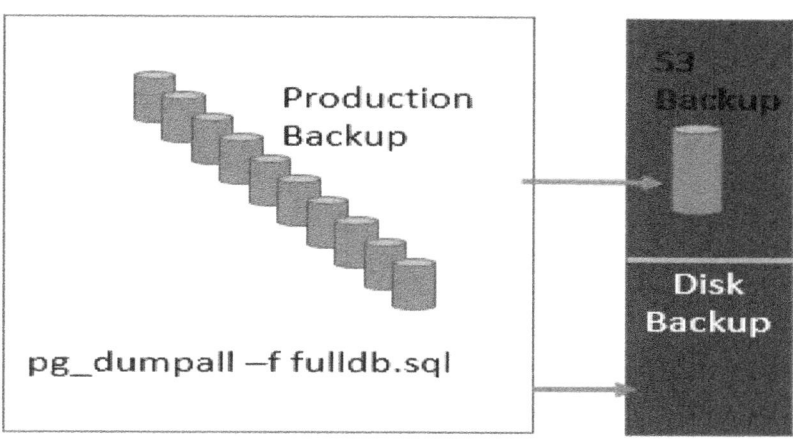

Figure 8-4. pg_dumpall

8.5.1 pg_dumpall Shell Script for S3

You have to create a bucket in S3 for the backup file from the `pg_dumpall` program.

The following simple shell script performs a full database backup to the local disk using the `pg_dumpall` utility, creates a unique backup file, compresses it, copies the backup file to S3, and removes the backup from disk upon successful backup to S3. Run the program in the backup directory where there is available space for the backup. The script hints for an S3 bucket name.

```
function bk_all() {
    echo "command pg_dumpall backupfile"
# enter s3 bucket
    echo "S3 bucket list"
# list the contents of s3 for hit for s3 folder
```

```
    aws s3 ls s3://
    echo "Enter bucket for backup"
    read bucket
    dd='date +%Y%m%d_%H_%M'
    echo "Dump in progress ..."
# pg_dumpall to local disk
    $PGHOME/pg_dumpall | gzip > full_database.dump.$dd | pv -pt
    if [ $? -eq 0 ]
    then
        echo "Backup completed"
    fi
    echo "Backup to S3 in progress"
# Backup file copy to s3
    aws s3 cp full_database.dump.$dd s3://$bucket | pv -pt
    if [ $? -eq 0 ]
    then
        echo "Backup to S3 completed"
    fi
    echo "S3 bucket list"
# displays the backup bucket contents
    aws s3 ls s3://$bucket
# remove backup file from disk
    echo "Removing backup data from disk"
    rm full_database.dump.$dd
    echo "Press enter to continue menu"
    read x
}
#execute the function
bk_all;
```

8.5.2 pg_dumpall Shell Script for Azure

If PostgreSQL is installed on an Azure VM, the cloud storage is an Azure Blob container for backup files.

You reviewed the Azure Data Blob storage in Chapter 2. Use the procedure to create Azure Data Blob for storing backup files. The script in Listing 8-5 displays the available Azure Data Blob containers, reads the container name, performs the pg_dumpall to local disk, uploads the backup files to the Azure Data Blob container, and removes the local copy upon completion of backup.

Listing 8-5. Azure Backup Script

```
function bk_all() {
    echo "command pg_dumpall backupfile"
    echo "Azure Blob container list"
    az storage container list --output table
    echo "Enter container for backup"
    read container
    dd=$(date +%Y%m%d_%H_%M)
    echo "Dump in progress ..."
    $PGHOME/pg_dumpall | gzip > full_database.dump.$dd | pv -pt
    if [ $? -eq 0 ]; then
        echo "Backup completed"
    fi
    echo "Backup to Azure Blob Storage in progress"
    az storage blob upload --account-name <your_account_name> --container-name $container --type block --source full_database.dump.$dd --name full_database.dump.$dd | pv -pt
    if [ $? -eq 0 ]; then
        echo "Backup to Azure Blob Storage completed"
    fi
```

```
        echo "Azure Blob container list"
        az storage blob list --container-name $container
        --output table
        echo "Removing backup data from disk"
        rm full_database.dump.$dd
        echo "Press enter to continue menu"
        read x
}
```

8.5.3 pg_dumpall Shell Script for Disk Copy

You need the super user privilege to back up a PostgreSQL databases. Make sure you are assigned the super user privilege before running the pg_dumpall program.

The script in Listing 8-6 reads the disk location provided by the user to perform a pg_dumpall backup to local disk storage while compressing the backup file.

Listing 8-6. Back Up to Disk

```
function bk_all() {_
    echo "disk location for backup"
    read ldisk
    dd=`date +%Y%m%d_%H_%M`
    echo "Dump in progress ..."
    $PGHOME/pg_dumpall | gzip>  $ldisk/full_database.dump.$dd
    | pv -pt
    if [ $? -eq 0 ]
    then
        echo "Backup completed"
    fi
}
```

8.6 pg_basebackup

The pg_basebackup program performs an online copy of a running PostgreSQL cluster's $PGDATA directory, along with write-ahead log (WAL) files. Use the help command to check for all options. At a minimum, -D , -F, and -t are required.

```
$pg_basebackup --help
pg_basebackup takes a base backup of a running
PostgreSQL server.
Usage:
  pg_basebackup [OPTION]...
Options controlling the output:
  -D, --pgdata=DIRECTORY receive base backup into directory
  -F, --format=p|t       output format (plain (default), tar)
::::: Lines omitted
```

WAL records all the committed changes to the database, which are replayed to reconstruct the data since the last checkpoint. This backup can be used to restore the cluster to the point in time when the backup was taken, as well as to apply available WAL backups to restore the database to a later point in time. When running pg_basebackup, it is important to specify a backup directory that is separate from the $PGDATA directory to avoid overwriting any existing data in the cluster. You have to create a directory before proceeding with backup.

Along with pg_basebackup, you must also backup archive logs generated in the archive directory by WAL files. The frequency of WAL backups determines the recovery point objective (RPO). The pg_basebackup copies only one WAL file along with the backup. For the point in time requirement, back up the subsequent WAL file generated after the backup. See Figure 8-5.

CHAPTER 8   POSTGRES CLUSTER AND DATABASE BACKUP

However, there is no provision for incremental backup with this utility. For incremental backup, third-party tools need to be used. Additionally, the pg_basebackup utility also does not provide individual database backup; only full cluster backup is supported.

Name	Date modified	Type
base	7/4/2024 7:09 PM	File folder
global	7/4/2024 7:09 PM	File folder
log	7/4/2024 7:09 PM	File folder
pg_commit_ts	7/4/2024 7:09 PM	File folder
pg_dynshmem	7/4/2024 7:09 PM	File folder
pg_logical	7/4/2024 7:09 PM	File folder
pg_multixact	7/4/2024 7:09 PM	File folder
pg_notify	7/4/2024 7:09 PM	File folder
pg_replslot	7/4/2024 7:09 PM	File folder
pg_serial	7/4/2024 7:09 PM	File folder
pg_snapshots	7/4/2024 7:09 PM	File folder
pg_stat	7/4/2024 7:09 PM	File folder
pg_stat_tmp	7/4/2024 7:09 PM	File folder
pg_subtrans	7/4/2024 7:09 PM	File folder
pg_tblspc	7/4/2024 7:09 PM	File folder
pg_twophase	7/4/2024 7:09 PM	File folder
pg_wal	7/4/2024 7:09 PM	File folder
pg_xact	7/4/2024 7:09 PM	File folder
backup_label	7/4/2024 7:09 PM	File
backup_manifest	7/4/2024 7:09 PM	File
current_logfiles	7/4/2024 7:09 PM	File

Figure 8-5. PGATA directory contens

8.6.1 pg_basebackup Script

The first step is to create a backup directory which should be empty along with a variable to store date in YearMonthDayHourMinute format, dd=`date +%Y%m%d_%H_%M`, and run the following command:

pg_basebackup -D /appl/postgres/backup/'hostname'$dd -F t &

While pg_basebackup is running, notice the two OS processes running related to the backup - pg_basebackup and postgres: walsender postgres [local] sending backup "pg_basebackup base backup". The pg_basebackup process is responsible for performing the backup, while the postgres: walsender process is used to send the backup to another location or server.

pg_basebackup with argument -F t creates two files, one for the backup of the PGDATA directory and another for the WAL directory.

```
$ ls -l /appl/postgres/backup/node1172.22.71.25
total 340052
-rw--------. 1 postgres     183359 Feb 25 21:47 backup_manifest
-rw--------. 1 postgres  331246080 Feb 25 21:47 base.tar
-rw--------. 1 postgres   16778752 Feb 25 21:47 pg_wal.tar
```

8.6.2 Backup Manifest File Details

The backup program creates a backup manifest file, which records metadata about the backup. From the backup manifest file, you can obtain details about the WAL file log sequence numbers, which serve as a reference during the restoration of the database. During restoration, the log sequence numbers from the manifest file help in identifying the necessary WAL segments to restore to a specific point in time. Furthermore, it checksums details for determining the validity of the backup file during recovery. See Listing 8-7.

Listing 8-7. Backup Manifest

```
cat backup_manifest
{ "Path": "pg_xact/0000", "Size": 8192, "Last-Modified":
"2023-02-25 21:45:26 GMT", "Checksum-Algorithm": "CRC32C",
"Checksum": "259f510e" },
{ "Path": "pg_logical/replorigin_checkpoint", "Size": 8, "Last-
Modified": "2023-02-25 21:45:26 GMT", "Checksum-Algorithm":
"CRC32C", "Checksum": "c74b6748" },
],"WAL-Ranges": [
{ "Timeline": 1, "Start-LSN": "0/B000028", "End-LSN":
"0/B000138" }
],
```

8.6.3 Incremental Backup

Available from version 17 which copies only changed blocks since last full backup with pg_basebackup command. Preparation: Enable archive log of the server, followed by enabling summarize_wal, and reload the configuration.

Listing 8-8. Summarize WAL setting

```
psql -c "ALTER system SET summarize_wal = ON;"
psql -c "SELECT pg_reload_conf();"
```

Perform full backup followed by incremental backup by including manifest file with -i argument.

Listing 8-9. Incremental Backup

```
export sdate=$(date "+%m%d%Y%H%M%S")
echo "Start Backp:::$sdate" > /tmp/bk
pg_basebackup -D /appl/postgres/backup/full_$sdate -Ft # full backup
```

```
pg_basebackup --i /appl/postgres/backup/full_$sdate/backup_
manifest -D /appl/postgres/backup/inc_01_$sdate -Ft
# incremental backup
export edate=$(date "+%m%d%Y%H%M%S")
echo "End Backup :::$edate" >> /tmp/bk
```

8.7 RDS Backup

The RDS backup is based on snapshot backup technology, which offers quick recovery. After the completion of the RDS creation, the initial full database backup is taken by AWS through a snapshot, which serves as a base backup. Subsequent backups are based on the incremental changes to the original snapshot. Automated backups are enabled by RDS, in accordance with the definitions of the snapshot configuration. See Figure 8-6.

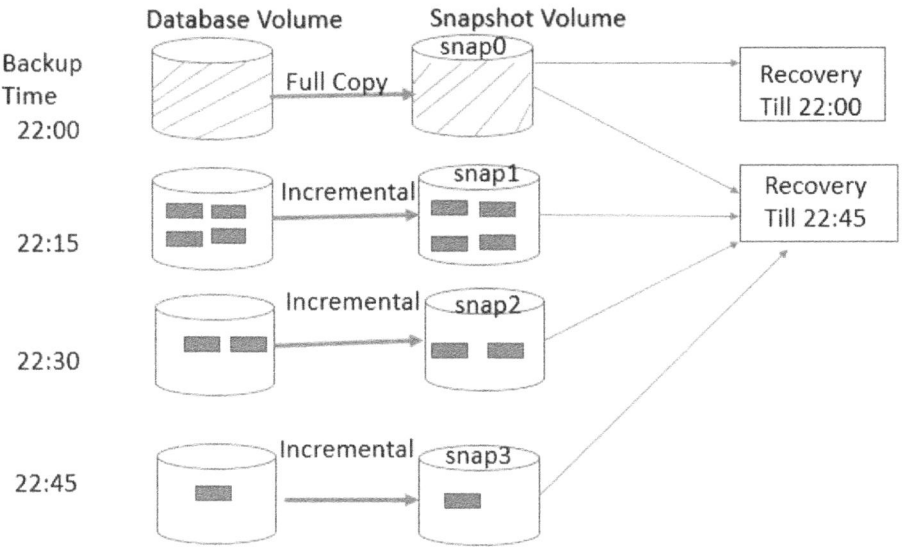

Figure 8-6. Snapshot backup

CHAPTER 8 POSTGRES CLUSTER AND DATABASE BACKUP

The initial full backup is complemented by capturing the incremental changes to the database blocks. In Figure 8-6, only changes that took place to the database at 22:15, 22:30, and 22:45 were copied as snap1, snap2, and snap3, ignoring the original snap0 backup, thereby significantly reducing the backup time.

8.7.1 RDS Backup from the AWS Console

To configure automated RDS backups, choose the modify option, enter the values for the Backup retention period option, and choose the daily start time. See Figure 8-7.

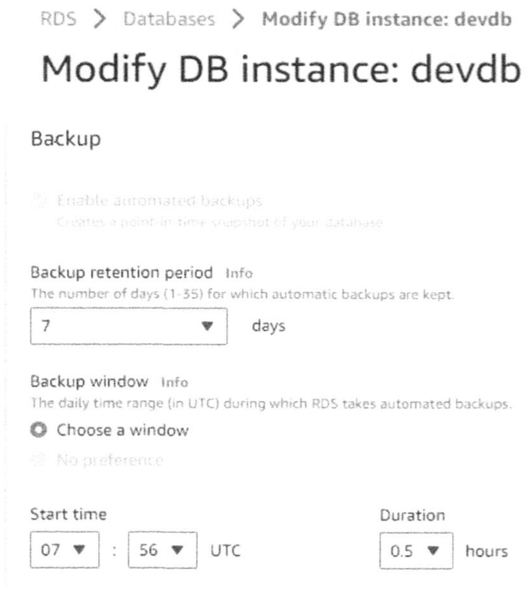

Figure 8-7. Modify database instance backup retention

Confirm the changes to the backup configuration.

8.7.2 RDS Backup from AWS CLI

There will be requirements to take a manual snapshot such as during upgrades or for data copy to different RDS instances. The following is the AWS CLI command:

    aws rds create-db-snapshot --db-instance-identifier devdb --db-snapshot-identifier devdb-snapshot-2024-03-05

After successful completion of the RDS snapshots, you can query the available snapshots by the command `aws rds describe-db-snapshots --db-instance-identifier devdb`. Once the initial snapshot is taken, subsequent snapshots as well as log backup are taken by AWS automatically, without any involvement of the DBA.

8.7.3 Backup from Azure Linux Host

Like AWS, you can back up only user databases with `pg_dump`. Note that `pg_dumpall` does not back up user logins as Azure does not grant access to pg_auth tables in Azure SQL databases. As a result, user logins, passwords and other credentials will be missing during a restore. Listing 8-10 is a simple backup script from Azure SQL Database. Change the `bkdir` to your backup directory. You should be a super user to perform the backup of the database. As users do not have access to an Azure database, ignore this database along with template databases.

Listing 8-10. Postgres Backup of Azure Red Hat

```
# Create unique file name with database and date format
export sdate=$(date "+%m%d%Y%H%M%S")
# Backup directory
bkdir=/appl/postgres/backup   # Enter your backup directory
# Obtain database name from database catalog
```

```
dbname=$(psql -t 'host=palosdev.postgres.database.azure.
com dbname=postgres user=pgAdmin password=Admin10177
sslmode=require'  -c "select datname From pg_database where
datname not like 'az%' and datname not like 'temp%';")
# backup of each database to local disk in for loop
for db in $dbname
do
echo "Backup of database:$db in progress"
# backup database with pg_dump command
pg_dump 'host=palosdev.postgres.database.azure.com user=pgAdmin
password=Admin10177 sslmode=require' -f $bkdir/$db.$sdate.
sql -d $db
# check the backup status
if [ $? -eq 0 ]
 then
 echo " Backup of database $db completed"
 echo " Backup file ::::"
 ls -l $bkdir/$db.$sdate.sql
fi
done
```

8.7.4 Back Up a Database from Azure DS to Azure Blob

Azure Blob is a durable storage to keep all the backup data. Listing 8-11 shows a script that backs up databases from Azure DS to Azure Blob storage. Create a container "backup" in your Azure account. Provide the account name to this script, as the container name is hard-coded in the script. Change the script to accommodate another Blob directory. You should be the owner of Blob storage to copy backup data.

Listing 8-11. Back Up to Azure Blob

```
# Create unique file name with database and date format
export sdate=$(date "+%m%d%Y%H%M%S")
# Backup directory
bkdir='pwd'
# Obtain database name from database catalog
dbname=$(psql -t 'host=palosdev.postgres.database.azure.com dbname=postgres user=pgAdmin password=Admin10177 sslmode=require'  -c "select datname From pg_database where datname not like 'az%' and datname not like 'temp%' and datname not like 'postgres%';"
# backup of each database to local disk in for loop
for db in $dbname
do
echo "Backup of database:$db in progress"
# backup database with pg_dump command
pg_dump -d $db -f $db.$sdate.sql -h palosdev.postgres.database.azure.com -U pgAdmin
# Check the backup status
if [ $? -eq 0 ]
 then
 echo " Backup of database $db completed"
 echo " Backup file ::::"
 ls -l $bkdir/$db.$sdate.sql
fi
az storage blob upload \
    --overwrite \
    --account-name cs4109889998hyuul \
    --container-name backup \
    --name $db \
    --file $bkdir/$db.$sdate.sql
done
```

CHAPTER 8   POSTGRES CLUSTER AND DATABASE BACKUP

8.7.5 Azure Snapshot Backup

Azure does not offer a snapshot backup feature for customers. All snapshots are managed by Azure internally. By default, Azure Database for PostgreSQL flexible server enables automated backups of your entire server (encompassing all databases created) with a default retention period of seven days [1].

8.7.6 Backup Tool

You can simulate all backup and recovery scenarios with the Backup Tool available in the AMI. Figure 8-8 shows the tool options.

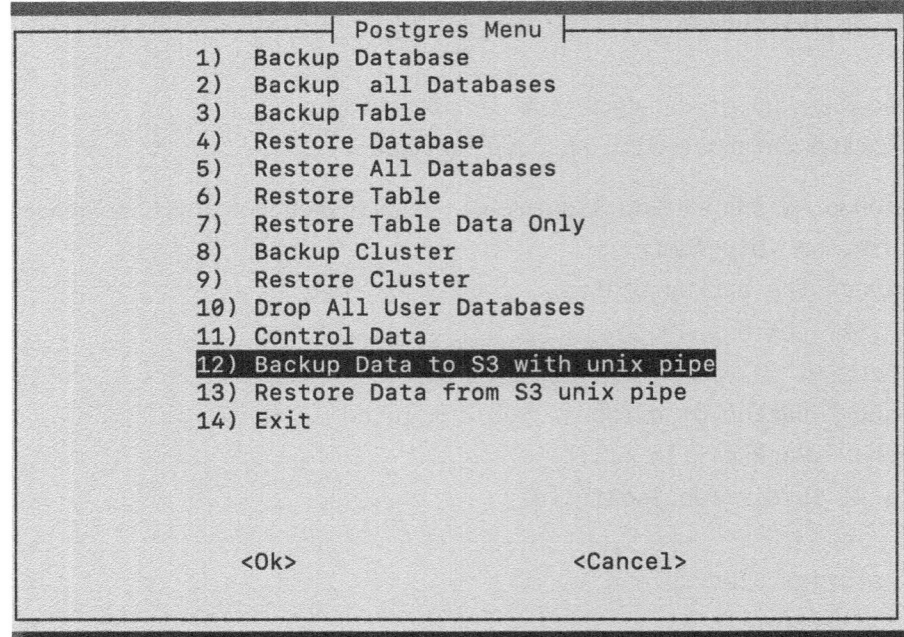

Figure 8-8. PostgreSQL AMI tool: backup section

Listing 8-12 shows the backup log.

Listing 8-12. Backup Log

```
2024-05-15 03:56:26
 Backup of database sales .....
 mkfifo
 gzip of fifo /appl/postgres/scripts/sales05241518
 Run the backup in the background
gzip /appl/postgres/scripts//sales05241518.gz
 Checksum for validate during restore::
30c5f3a1c666b2b27f378a3048c67224
upload: ./sales05241518.gz to s3://palos123/sales05241518.gz
 End of sales backup
2024-05-15 03:56:27
INSERT 0 1
```

Key points: fifo, gzip,checksum, etc.

8.7.7 Keywords

RTO, pg_dumpall, RPO, pg_dump, pg_basebackup, backup to Azure Blob, and RDS snapshot backup.

8.8 Summary of Learning

You now know the difference between RPO and RTO, plus you've identified different backup methods provided by Postgres and several scripting examples of `pg_dump`, `pg_dumpall`, and `pg_basebackup`. Furthermore, you explored backup copy to S3 procedures, the RDS clone procedure, and how to make an Azure copy to Blob storage.

8.9 Practice Chapter 8

1. Back up all databases to S3 from AWS/EC2.
2. Back up all databases to an Azure Blob container from Azure VM.
3. Perform pg_basebackup to S3.
4. Perform pg_basebackup to an Azure Blob container.
5. Perform a parallel backup to disk.
6. Create a Postgres cluster backup either on RES or on an Azure Data Service.

8.10 Questions Chapter 8

1. Can you explain the distinction between the pg_dumpall and pg_dump backup utilities in PostgreSQL?
2. What is the purpose of the pg_dumpall utility, and how does it differ from pg_dump?
3. Can you provide step-by-step instructions on how to back up all databases from PostgreSQL to Amazon S3?
4. Are there any specific considerations or prerequisites when performing a backup of all databases to Amazon S3 in PostgreSQL?

5. How do you back up only the schema or DDL (Data Definition Language) statements in PostgreSQL?

6. Can you explain the process of selectively backing up specific database schemas or DDL statements in PostgreSQL?

7. What are the recommended backup compression parameters available in PostgreSQL?

8. How do you configure and enable backup compression in PostgreSQL?

9. Are there any performance considerations or trade-offs when using backup compression in PostgreSQL?

10. Can you provide examples of the different backup compression methods and their respective compression ratios in PostgreSQL?

11. How do you enable parallel backup and parallel restore procedures?

12. Is there any procedure to estimate the backup size of a Postgres cluster?

13. Is there a database-level file backup for a point-in-time restore?

14. Provide step-by-step procedures to copy data from Postgres to Azure Blob Storage

References

1. https://learn.microsoft.com/en-us/azure/postgresql/flexible-server/concepts-backup-restore

   Additional references

   www.postgresql.org/docs/15/app-pgdump.html
   www.postgresql.org/docs/15/app-pg-dumpall.html
   www.postgresql.org/docs/15/app-pgbasebackup.html
   https://docs.aws.amazon.com/AmazonRDS/latest/UserGuide/USER_CreateMultiAZDBClusterSnapshot.html
   https://learn.microsoft.com/en-us/azure/backup/backup-azure-database-postgresql
   https://us02web.zoom.us/rec/share/WObtToeyHnhRBhDvQ5LCV0-GGoERyEKcYVgu8kHS7ApsTQMhQsTk_NDtQ64bd7tn.u7Is21LsdOjup9Q6

CHAPTER 9

PostgreSQL on Windows Server in Cloud

9.1 Abstract

Windows is a robust operating system with a graphical user interface, multitasking, virtual desktops, Active Directory, Task Manager, virtual machines with App-V, UE-V and Hyper-V, NTFS (New Technology File Systems), FAT (File Allocation Table), and NFS (Network File Systems). It is a suitable choice to stage a PostgreSQL cluster database for multi-user and concurrent access requirements in the AWS and Azure cloud environments. Windows is scalable in AWS and Azure environments, where you can upgrade to high instance types and increase or decrease RAM to adjust to a dynamic application workload. Windows works in a container environment for rapid application deployment along with Postgres database components.

CHAPTER 9   POSTGRESQL ON WINDOWS SERVER IN CLOUD

9.2 Objective of the Chapter

- Overview of Windows
- Verification of Windows for the installation of a Postgres cluster
- Installation of Postgres on Windows
- Configuration of Postgres on Windows
- AWS AMI of a Postgres cluster
- Azure virtual machine image
- Backup of a Postgres database to the cloud

9.3 Postgres on the Windows Operating System

Windows is a proprietary operating system designed by Microsoft. PostgreSQL gained official support for Windows with the release of version 8.0 in January 2005. In addition to Unix/Linux, the PostgreSQL community has expanded its support to the Windows operating system. This expansion includes the provision of bug fixes, performance enhancements, and new features with each release. The support includes parallelism, partitioning, ACID-compliant concurrency control mechanisms, and object-relational database models. This comprehensive support extends to database configuration in the Windows registry and services.

Although Windows presents several user interface and administration tools which may benefit various applications, PostgreSQL does not heavily rely on graphical user interfaces, as many PostgreSQL users from Unix/Linux background prefer to use command-line tools and scripts for tasks such as database maintenance, database administration, and database automation.

CHAPTER 9   POSTGRESQL ON WINDOWS SERVER IN CLOUD

Windows is a powerful and robust operating system to support all the PostgreSQL database activities. Windows was created to cater the needs of two distinct users: personal users and enterprise users. The installation of Postgres on a PC is for personal knowledge about a Postgres database, the features, functionality, programs, and utilities. The enterprise version is for corporations, small or large organizations that required multi-user concurrent access to the Postgres cluster databases. For PC versions, Postgres cluster is available from Vista (released in 2007) up to the latest, Windows 11, whereas for the enterprise versions, the PostgreSQL support is available from Server 2008 up to the latest, Server 2022. Figure 9-1 list the Windows OS versions.

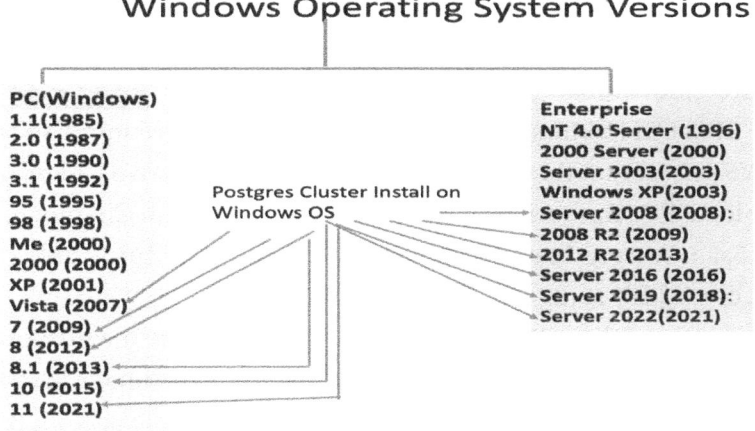

Figure 9-1. *Windows OS versions*

CHAPTER 9　POSTGRESQL ON WINDOWS SERVER IN CLOUD

9.3.1 Install Windows on AWS

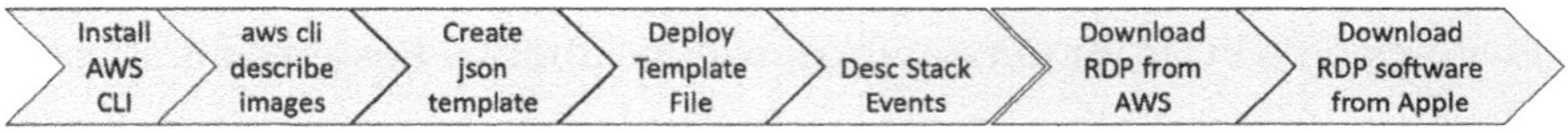

Install AWS CLI	aws cli describe images	Create json template	Deploy Template File	Desc Stack Events	Download RDP from AWS	Download RDP software from Apple

Figure 9-2. *Install Windows*

This chapter covers installing Windows on the AWS cloud, installing PostgreSQL software, downloading and configuring client tools, and configuring a backup of a PostgreSQL database to the AWS cloud. See Figure 9-2.

The first step is to install Windows Operating system which you can install from a Mac, Windows client or server, Amazon Cloud Shell Linux, and Azure Cloud Shell.

The AWS CLI (command line interface) program is required to work with AWS services on the cloud. You have to set up the AWS CLI program on your local PC. You reviewed AWS CLI configuration in Chapter 5, section 5.4.3. You can install AWS CLI from this URL: `https://aws.amazon.com/cli/9.1.2`.

After successfully validating the AWS client program, the next task is to query the Windows image from AWS. You require the image id to build Windows. You can query the image from the AWS console or from the `aws ec2 describe` command.

The following describe-image example returns the image id for Windows Server 2022. You must configure a region when configuring AWS CLI.

```
aws ec2 describe-images --owners amazon --filters
"Name=name,Values=Windows_Server-2022-English-Full-Base-*"
--query "Images[0].ImageId" --output text
```

The output of the above command is the following Amazon Machine Image:

ami-063f64fd624326307.

Note that the Amazon Machine Image (AMI) varies from this output. AWS may provide the latest AMI.

9.3.2 JSON Template File

You have to create a simple JSON or YAML template file to create Windows 2022 ec2 image in AWS. The following JSON example file in Listing 9-1 creates a Windows OS EC2 instance on AWS from a Mac terminal. Install and configure aws CLI to execute the below script, which creates EC2 with t2.micro instance type. The Windows instance will be created in your default VPC. Some changes need to be made to the script such as KeyName. Use your own key with the script.

Listing 9-1. Deploy Windows OS from CloudFormation

```
win22.json
 {
  "AWSTemplateFormatVersion": "2010-09-09",
  "Description": "Create a Windows Server 2022 instance with defaults",
  "Resources": {
    "MyInstance": {
      "Type": "AWS::EC2::Instance",
      "Properties": {
        "InstanceType": "t2.micro",
        "ImageId": " ami-063f64fd624326307",
        "KeyName": "redaws"
      }
    }
  }
}
```

```
$aws cloudformation deploy --template-file  /Users/venkat/
work1/work/win22.json --stack-name win22
Waiting for changeset to be created..
Waiting for stack create/update to complete
Successfully created/updated stack - win22
```

After successful completion of the Windows 2022 OS, you can check the stack with the command describe-stack-events. See Listing 9-2.

Listing 9-2. Describe Stack Events

```
$     aws cloudformation describe-stack-events --stack-
name win22
{
    "StackEvents": [
        {
            "LogicalResourceId": "win22",
::::::::::::::::::::: Lines omitted
0b24eb32c43d56c23\",\"InstanceType\":\"t2.micro\"}"
        }
```

Azure Windows VM creation consists of two steps: create a resource group and create a VM. See Listing 9-3.

Listing 9-3. Create a Resource Group and an Azure VM

```
venkat [ ~ ]$ az group create --name WRG --location eastus
{
  "id": "/subscriptions/682277887-oiiooi-788d223c603/
resourceGroups/WRG",
  "location": "eastus",
:::::
"type": "Microsoft.Resources/resourceGroups"
}
```

```
az vm create \
  --resource-group WRG \
  --name PostVM \
  --image MicrosoftWindowsServer:WindowsServer:2022-Datacenter:latest \
  --admin-username azureuser \
  --admin-password Konitor10177$
{
  "fqdns": "",
  "id": "/subscriptions/68
::::
"zones": ""
}
```

9.3.3 RDP Download from AWS Console

Your Windows or Mac should support Windows Remote Desktop (RDP). After the installation of a new EC2 instance type of Windows 2022 is created, the next step is to download RDS based on your preference of OS. Your Windows OS must support Remote Desktop to be able to use RDP (see https://learn.microsoft.com/en-us/windows-server/remote/remote-desktop-services/clients/remote-desktop-supported-config).

9.3.4 AWS Details for Windows OS

You can examine the details for Windows by clicking the Details tab of the AWS Console. See Figure 9-3.

CHAPTER 9 POSTGRESQL ON WINDOWS SERVER IN CLOUD

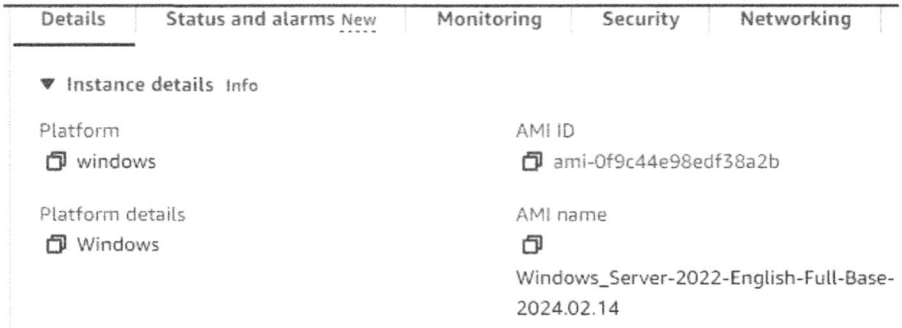

Figure 9-3. Windows OS details

9.3.5 Download the RDP Client

Choose the connect option in the EC2 instances, which will take you to RDP client menu. Download the RDP client to your local machine. See Figure 9-4.

Figure 9-4. Connect to the client

9.3.6 Windows Admin Password

You can obtain the windows Admin password by clicking the connect icon and choosing the RDP client. Click the Get password tab, which will prompt for the *.pem key. After providing the key, you have to click Decrypt password, which will display the password. See Figure 9-5.

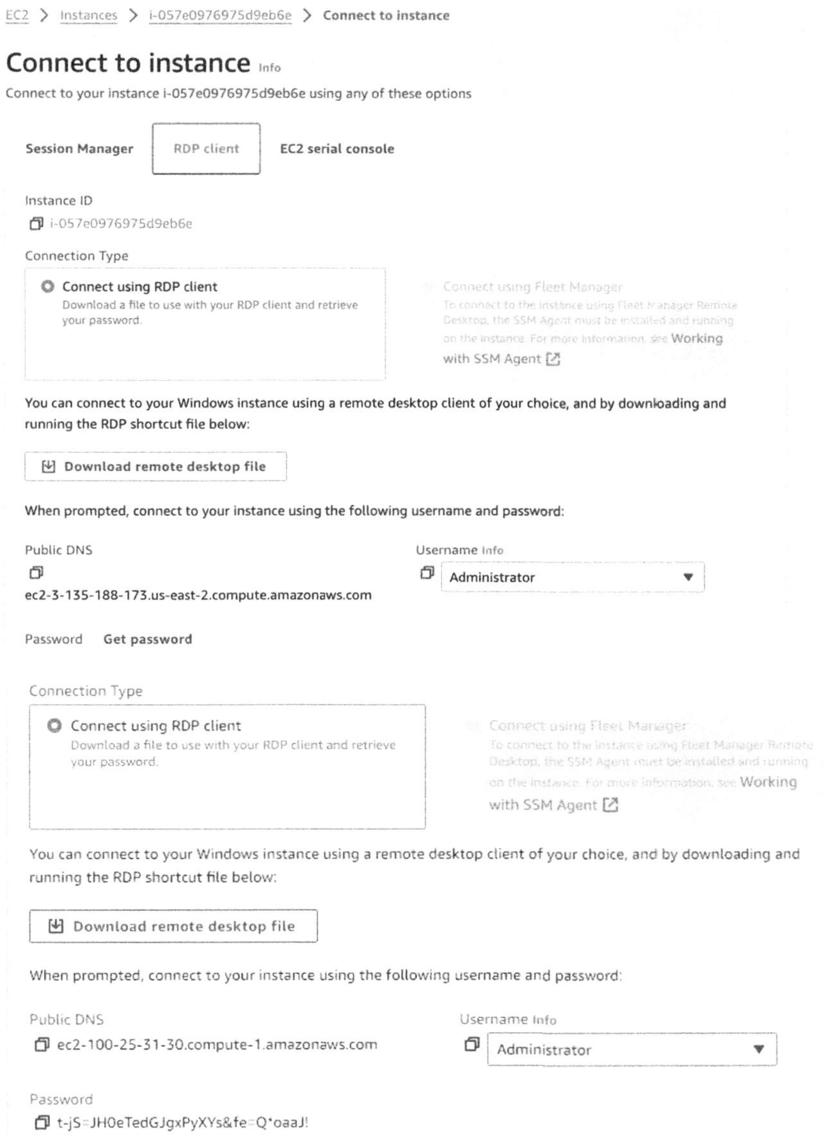

CHAPTER 9   POSTGRESQL ON WINDOWS SERVER IN CLOUD

Figure 9-5. Windows RDP configuration

9.3.7 Download RDP from the Apple Site

You have to download the Microsoft remote desktop software from the Apple store in order to open the RDP downloaded on the Mac. Here is the link to download the Mac software for Microsoft Remote Desktop:

https://apps.apple.com/us/app/microsoft-remote-desktop/id1295203466?mt=12.

9.3.8 Connect to Windows Server

The Window OS must support Remote Desktop access. The connection to Windows Server involves clicking the downloaded rdp file, which will request the Administrators password, which you have already obtained in the previous task. See Figures 9-6 through 9-9.

Windows RDP:

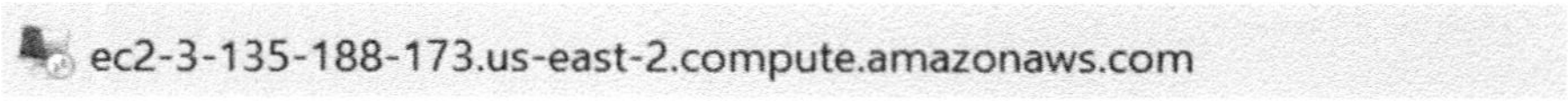

ec2-3-135-188-173.us-east-2.compute.amazonaws.com

Figure 9-6. *Windows RDP client*

MAC RDP:

 ec2-18-219-31-102.us-east-2.compute.amazonaws.com.rdp

Figure 9-7. *Mac RDP*

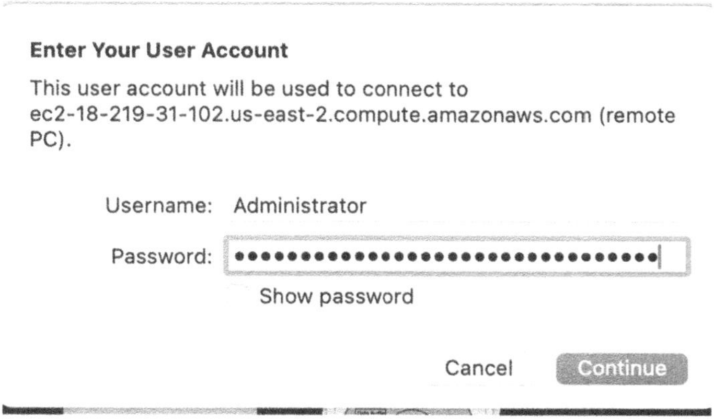

CHAPTER 9   POSTGRESQL ON WINDOWS SERVER IN CLOUD

Enter Your User Account

This user account will be used to connect to ec2-18-219-31-102.us-east-2.compute.amazonaws.com (remote PC).

Username: Administrator
Password: ●●●●●●●●●●●●●●●●●●●●●●●●●●●●●●●●●●
Show password

Cancel   Continue

Figure 9-8. Windows connection

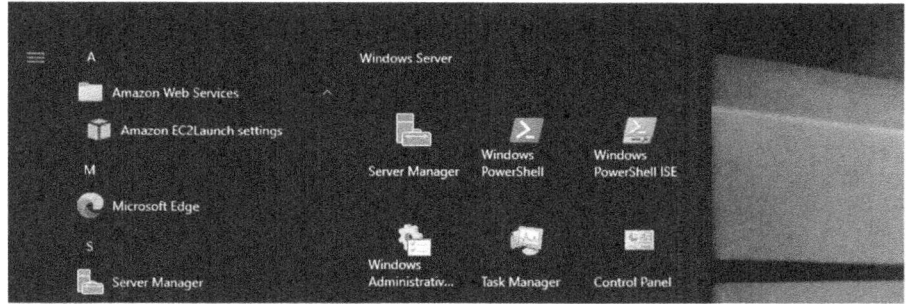

Figure 9-9. Windows on EC2

9.4 Postgres Configuration on Windows

After the installation of Windows, the next step is to install Postgres cluster software. Refer to the Postgres install details for Windows from Chapter 1, section 1.7.

9.4.1 psql Shell

psql is a client program to connect to Postgres databases. After installation, you can connect to the default spql shell program created during installation.

9.4.2 PostgreSQL Configuration Files

Refer to Chapter 4, sections 4.2.2, 4.2.6, 4.2.6.1, and 4.2.6.2 to work on the configuration of the postgresql.conf and pg_hba.conf files.

9.4.3 Stop/Start Windows Server

You can manage all EC2 instance tasks from client machines with aws ec2 commands.

The following is the command to stop the Windows EC2 VM (and see Figure 9-10):

    aws ec2 stop-instances --instance-id i-057e0976975d9eb6e

```
$aws ec2 stop-instances  --instance-id  i-057e0976975d9eb6e
{
    "StoppingInstances": [
```

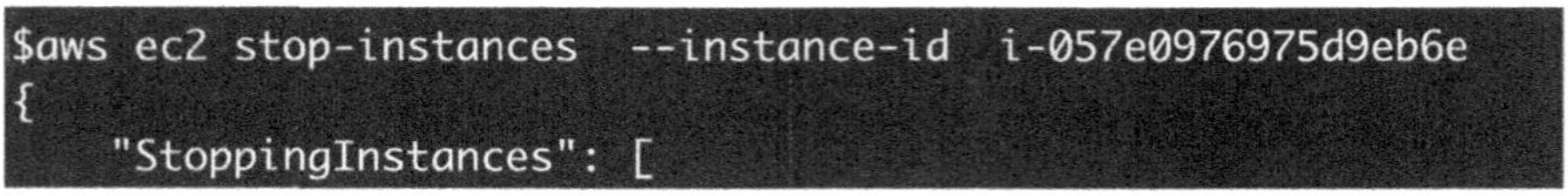

Figure 9-10. *Stopping Windows on EC2*

Like the stop command, you can start the Windows EC2 VM. See Figure 9-11.

aws ec2 start-instances --instance-id i-00101e2ddcdb99eec

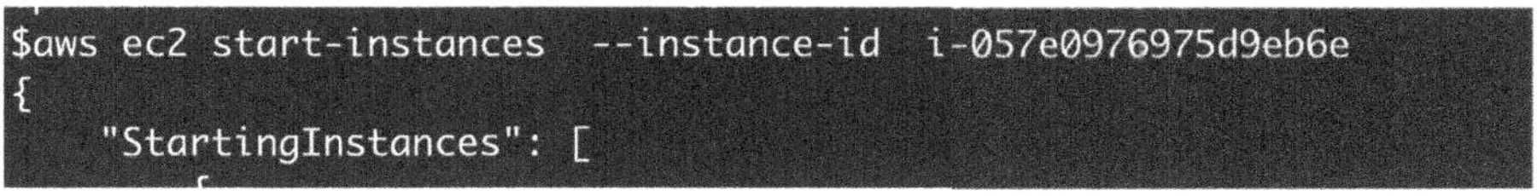

```
$aws ec2 start-instances   --instance-id  i-057e0976975d9eb6e
{
    "StartingInstances": [
```

Figure 9-11. Starting Windows on EC2

9.4.4 Initialize the Postgres Cluster

The initialization of the PostgreSQL cluster is discussed in Chapter 4. The procedure is same on the Windows OS. The Postgres cluster is initialized with the initdb command with -D for the instance directory and -U for the Postgres user's name for installation. Refer to detailed instructions from Chapter 4.

Listing 9-4 shows the command to initialize the Postgres cluster.

Listing 9-4. Initialize PostgreSQL Cluster

```
c:\data>initdb -D qa  -U postgres
syncing data to disk ... ok
Success. You can now start the database server using:
    pg_ctl -D qa -l logfile start
```

9.4.5 Start and Stop of Postgres Cluster

The pg_ctl command or utility is used to start, stop, restart, initialize a Postgres cluster, reload, logrotate, and kill the Postgres process. On Windows, you can start and stop Postgres with services.

The following are the commands to stop Postgres Server running on default and non-default ports, which you reviewed in Chapter1.

Set the PATH with the setx command. Refer to section 1.7.4.

```
"C:\Program Files\PostgreSQL\16\bin\pg_ctl" stop -D "C:\Program Files\PostgreSQL\16\data".
waiting for server to shut down... done
```

It is best to use the environmental variable with the traditional method for PGDATA and PATH variables. See Figures 9-12 and 9-13.

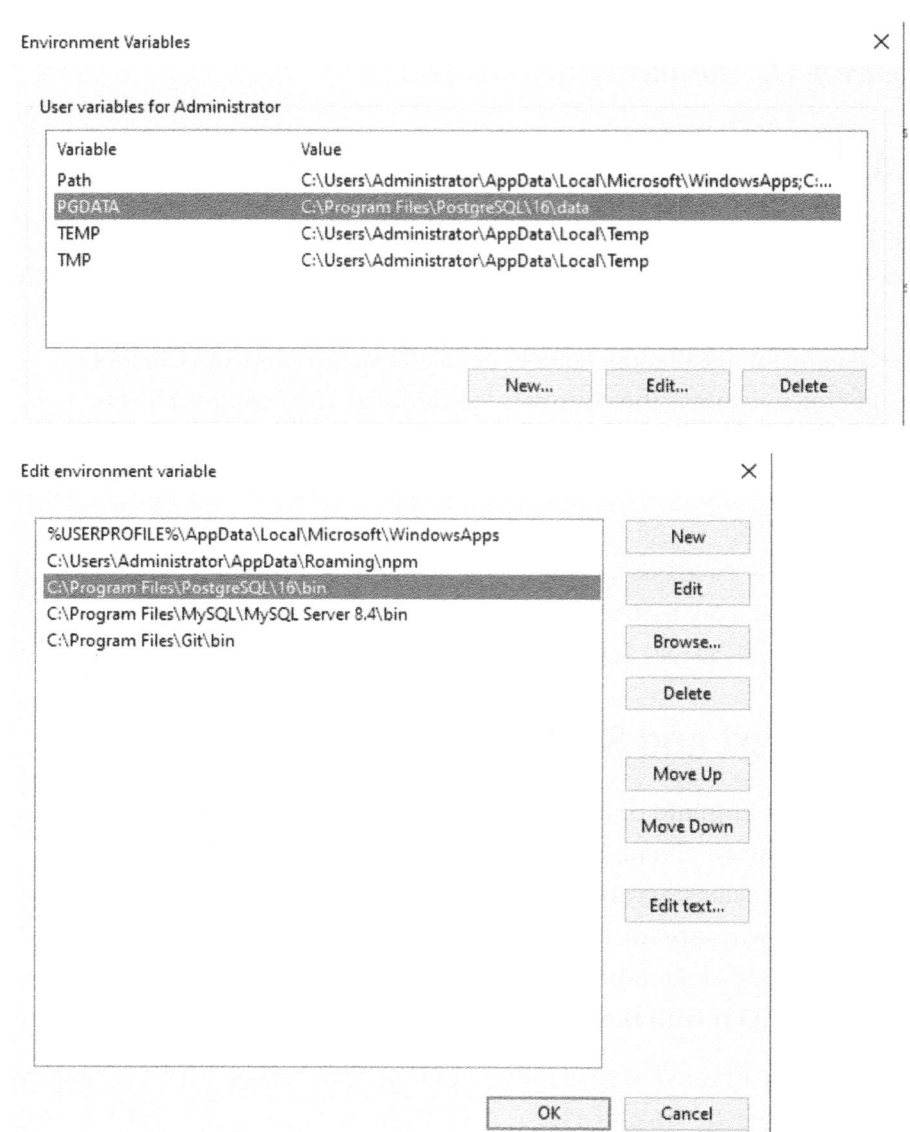

Figure 9-12. Set environmental variables

CHAPTER 9 POSTGRESQL ON WINDOWS SERVER IN CLOUD

```
c:\data>psql -p 5433 -U postgres
psql (16.1)
WARNING: Console code page (437) differs from Windows code page (1252)
         8-bit characters might not work correctly. See psql reference
         page "Notes for Windows users" for details.
Type "help" for help.

postgres=# exit
```

Figure 9-13. psql connect to a non-default port

9.4.6 PowerShell Commands to Manage a Postgres Cluster

For PostgreSQL management on Windows, PowerShell is similar to the shell in Linux. PowerShell provides a command-line interface and scripting language to support functions, loops, variables, conditional logic, and error handling to manage PostgreSQL on Windows. You have to work with PowerShell to perform a backup to S3.

In the search box, type "powershell" to invoke the PowerShell terminal. See Figure 9-14.

Figure 9-14. PowerShell terminal

The last step after installing and configuring a Postgres cluster on Windows is to configure database backup to S3. The backup of Postgres databases is done with a Windows PowerShell script.

Listing 9-5 is the power shell script for a backup. The steps are as follows:

1. Define values for the S3 bucket.
2. Get a list of databases,
3. Assign a date value for the variable.
4. Back up the database to disk.
5. Copy the backup data to S3.

Listing 9-5. PowerShell Backup Script

```
Set the path to "C:\Program Files\PostgreSQL\16\bin"
$s3BucketName = 'palos123'
$databaseNames = .\psql -U postgres -d postgres -t -c " SELECT
datname FROM pg_database WHERE datistemplate = false;"
Write-Host $databaseNames
# Split the query result into an array of database names
$databaseNamesArray = $databaseNames -split "`n"
foreach ($databaseName in $databaseNamesArray) {
    $databaseName = $databaseName.Trim()  # Remove any leading/
    trailing whitespace
    $timestamp = Get-Date -Format 'yyyyMMddHHmmss'
    $backupFileName = "backup_${databaseName}_$timestamp.sql"
    # Execute pg_dump without Invoke-Expression
    .\pg_dump  -f $backupFileName -U postgres  $databaseName
    if ($?) {
    Write-Host "Backup  succedded to disk"
       aws s3 cp $backupFileName s3://$s3BucketName
} else {
   Write-Host " Backup  failed"
}
```

```
if ($?) {
    Write-Host "Backup to S3 completed"
    rm $backupFileName
} else {
    Write-Host "Backup to S3 failed"
}
}
cd c:\scripts
```

9.4.7 Power Shell Execution

Figure 9-15 shows the execution.

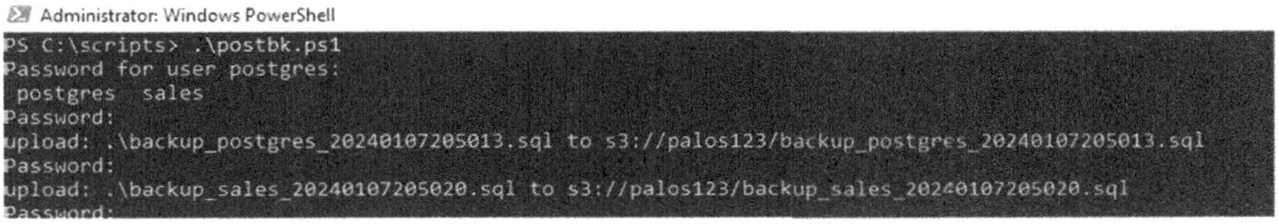

Figure 9-15. PowerShell backup output

9.4.8 Postgres Data Directory Files

The database data is stored in the base directory and the database log files are stored in the pg_wal directory. See Figure 9-16.

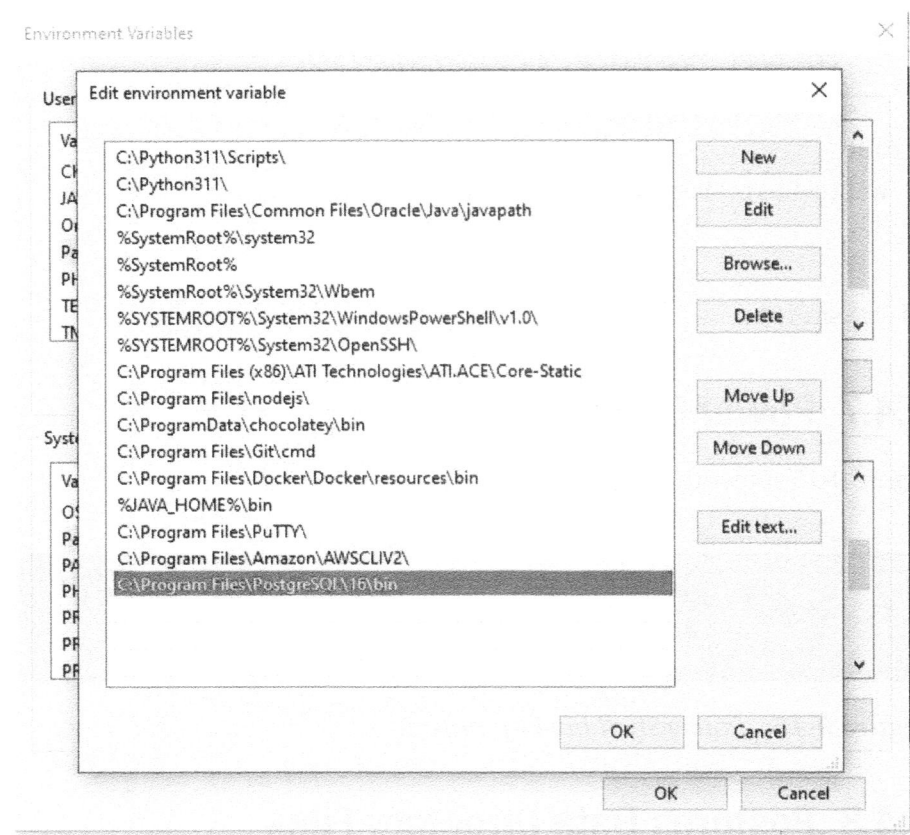

Figure 9-16. *PostgreSQL path*

9.4.9 Registry Entry

The parameters related to the Postgres installation on Windows are stored in the registry. If you look at Figure 9-17, you'll see the base directory, data directory, server version, service ID, and the database port. Search for regedit and choose Computer\HKEY_LOCAL_MACHINE\SOFTWARE\ PostgreSQL\Installatoins\postgresql-x64-14 to identify the data directory, version, root user, version, and service ID details

CHAPTER 9   POSTGRESQL ON WINDOWS SERVER IN CLOUD

If multiple PostgreSQL clusters are installed, search under the installation folder for the details of the data directory, version, root user, version, and service ID details. See Figures 9-18 and 9-19.

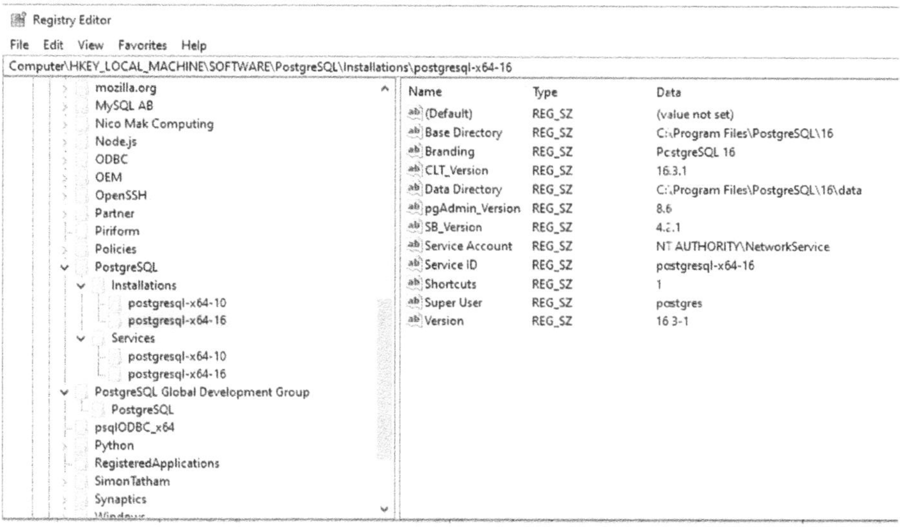

Figure 9-17. Registry entry for PostgreSQL 16

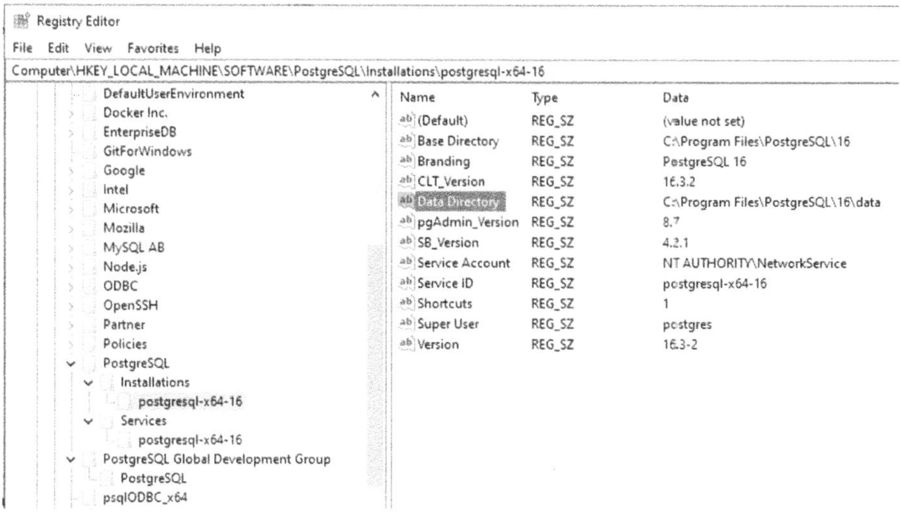

Figure 9-18. PostgreSQL registry values

CHAPTER 9   POSTGRESQL ON WINDOWS SERVER IN CLOUD

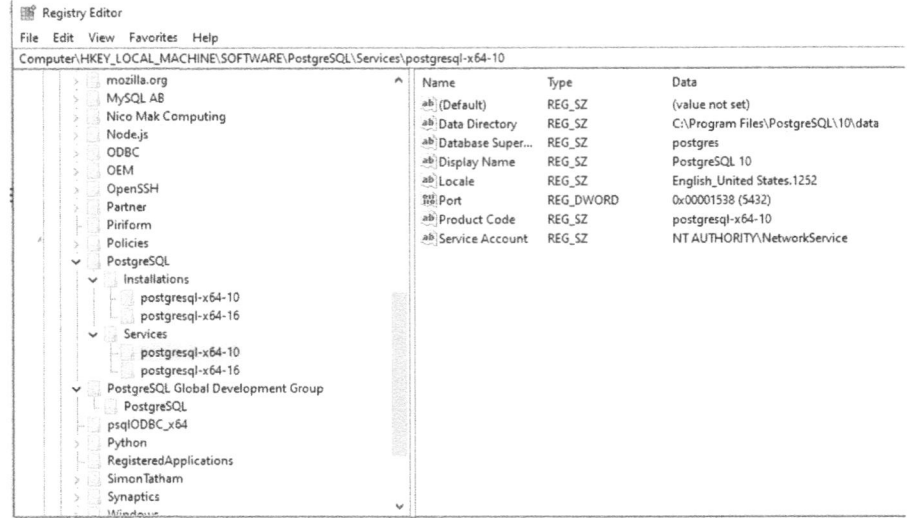

Figure 9-19. Registry entry for PostgreSQL 10

9.4.10 The forfiles Command

As a DBA, you are responsible for identifying and removing large files that are not required for Postgres databases. With the `forfiles` command you can find the size of files on the computer disk.

To find files greater than 10000000 bytes, use this code and see Figure 9-20:

```
forfiles /s /m * /c "cmd /c if @fsize gtr 10000000 echo @path"
```

CHAPTER 9 POSTGRESQL ON WINDOWS SERVER IN CLOUD

```
Administrator: Windows PowerShell
Windows PowerShell
Copyright (C) Microsoft Corporation. All rights reserved.

Install the latest PowerShell for new features and improvements! https://aka.ms/PSWindows

PS C:\Users\Administrator> forfiles /s /m * /c "cmd /c if @fsize gtr 10000000 echo @path"
"C:\Users\Administrator\edb_languagepack_4.exe"
"C:\Users\Administrator\edb_pgagent_pg16.exe"
"C:\Users\Administrator\edb_pgbouncer.exe"
"C:\Users\Administrator\edb_pgjdbc.exe"
"C:\Users\Administrator\edb_psqlodbc.exe"
"C:\Users\Administrator\postgresql_16.exe"
"C:\Users\Administrator\AppData\Local\Google\Chrome\User Data\Default\Cache\Cache_Data\data_3"
```

Figure 9-20. The forfiles command

9.4.11 Delete Large Files

With the `forfiles` command, you can delete files from a specified folder. In the following code, you are deleting the files in the `downloads` directory that are greater than 10000000 bytes. Please check for any important files in the `downloads` directory before executing this code.

```
PS C:\Users\Administrator> forfiles /p "C:\Users\Administrator\Downloads" /m * /c "cmd /c if @fsize gtr 10000000 del @path"
```

9.4.12 Identify Postgres Process

You have to identify the process ID of Postgres Server to terminate the process for maintenance requirements. With the `Get-Process` command, you can identify the process details. Here is an example to identify the Windows OS process for a Postgres cluster (see Figure 9-21 also):

```
PS C:\Users\Administrator>     Get-Process | Where-Object { $_.ProcessName -like "*postgres*" }
```

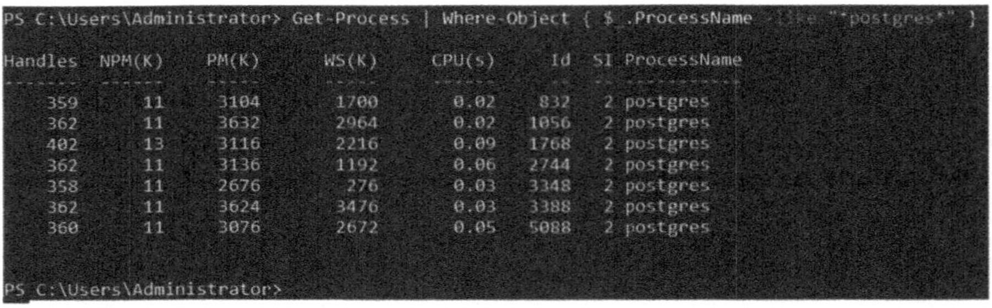

Figure 9-21. PostgreSQL processes

9.4.13 Terminate Postgres Process

With the Stop-Process command you can terminate the Postgres Server Process. With proper permissions you can terminate the Windows OS process. Note that I am running as Administrator to execute this command:

```
PS C:\Users\Administrator> Stop-Process -Id 5088
Confirm
Are you sure you want to perform the Stop-Process operation on the following item: postgres (2688)?
[Y] Yes  [A] Yes to All  [N] No  [L] No to All
```

9.4.14 Tail the Log File

With Get-Content-Path and the wait flag, you can view the contents of the Postgres log file while the data is being written. See Figure 9-22.

CHAPTER 9　POSTGRESQL ON WINDOWS SERVER IN CLOUD

```
PS C:\Users\Administrator> cd "C:\Program Files\PostgreSQL\16\data\log"
PS C:\Program Files\PostgreSQL\16\data\log> Get-ChildItem

    Directory: C:\Program Files\PostgreSQL\16\data\log

Mode                 LastWriteTime         Length Name
----                 -------------         ------ ----
-a----         6/26/2024   5:59 PM           1065 postgresql-2024-06-26_174447.log
-a----         6/26/2024   6:20 PM            875 postgresql-2024-06-26_181914.log
-a----         6/26/2024   9:33 PM           8747 postgresql-2024-06-26_182149.log
-a----         6/27/2024   7:58 PM           2372 postgresql-2024-06-27_195750.log
-a----         6/27/2024   8:16 PM            826 postgresql-2024-06-27_201143.log
-a----         6/28/2024   6:25 PM           3827 postgresql-2024-06-28_175516.log
-a----         6/28/2024   9:28 PM           1289 postgresql-2024-06-28_212858.log
-a----         6/29/2024   6:17 PM           7599 postgresql-2024-06-29_171753.log
-a----         7/2/2024    5:49 PM           1540 postgresql-2024-07-02_170439.log
-a----         7/4/2024    7:00 PM           3168 postgresql-2024-07-04_181402.log
-a----         7/4/2024    7:03 PM           1564 postgresql-2024-07-04_190129.log
-a----         7/4/2024    7:09 PM           1185 postgresql-2024-07-04_190748.log

PS C:\Program Files\PostgreSQL\16\data\log>
```

Figure 9-22. PostgreSQL logs

```
PS C:\Users\Administrator> Get-Content -Path "C:\Program Files\
PostgreSQL\16\data\log\postgresql-2024-01-08_051308.log" -Wait
>>
2024-01-08 05:13:08.531 UTC [2280] LOG:  starting PostgreSQL
16.1, compiled by Visual C++ build 1937, 64-bit
2024-01-08 05:13:08.742 UTC [4184] LOG:  database system was
interrupted; last known up at
```

9.4.15 Windows PostgreSQL Service

The auto start of PostgreSQL is done by Windows services, which synchronizes with Windows Server reboot. You can create multiple PostgreSQL instances on Windows OS, each running on a port other than 5432. The steps to add another windows service are as follows:

1. `pg_ctl.exe register -N "PostgreSQL" -U "NT AUTHORITY\NetworkService" -D "C:/data" -w`

2. `icacls "C:/data" /grant "NT AUTHORITY\NetworkService:(OI)(CI)F"`. The `c:/data` is another data directory running on port 5444. See Figure 9-23.

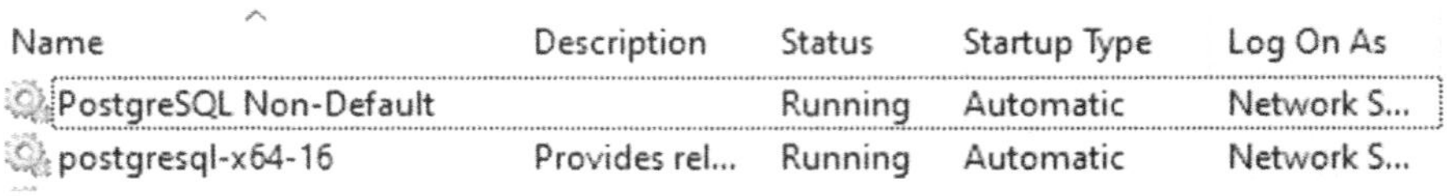

Name	Description	Status	Startup Type	Log On As
PostgreSQL Non-Default		Running	Automatic	Network S…
postgresql-x64-16	Provides rel…	Running	Automatic	Network S…

Figure 9-23. *Windows Services*

9.5 Keywords

Apple Remote Desktop software, psql shell, forfiles, Azure Blob storage, Get-Process, aws s3 storage, Stop-Process, aws ami, Windows RDP client, aws configure, Windows Registry, aws ec2 describe images, aws cloudformation deploy, aws cloudformation describe-stack-events, aws ec2 stop-instances, and aws ec2 start-instances .

9.6 Summary of Learning

You identified the Windows AWS AMI, installed Windows 2022 on EC2, installed Windows 2022 on AWS/EC2, installed a PostgreSQL cluster, configured RDP, make a PowerShell backup to S3, started and stopped Windows 2022, and started and stopped a Postgres cluster in this chapter.

9.7 Chapter 9 Practice

1. Connect to the AWS console, create a user with IAM, grant admin privileges, and download the credentials.

2. Create a Windows 2022 VM from the AWS command line.

3. Download a parallel desktop for a Mac.

4. Connect to the Azure console, connect to Cloud Shell, and create an Azure VM Windows 2022 Server.

5. Download and install Postgres on an AWS Windows VM and Azure VM.

9.8 Chapter 9 Questions

1. How do you to enable `pg_hba.conf` to allow access from your laptop IP?

2. How do you enable `postgres.conf` to allow access from all hosts?

3. What are the steps to set up a Postgres database backup to a local disk and Amazon S3?

4. What are the steps to set up a Postgres database backup to Azure Blob storage?

5. What are the commands to start and stop Azure Windows 2022 from the command line?

6. What are the commands to start and stop AWS Windows 2022 from the command line?

7. Outline the procedure to back up a Windows 2022 server from AWS and Azure.

CHAPTER 10

PostgreSQL Post-Installation Tasks

10.1 Abstract

On a day-to-day basis, several tasks are performed by the DBA to support the PostgreSQL database environment. With the command-line interactive psql program you can work on all administrative tasks of PostgreSQL. You can deploy all scripts interactively or with a crontab scheduler. The DBA is responsible for deploying all scripts in the production environment. Day-to-day tasks include the creation of user databases, users, schemas, grants, and roles on database objects along with table copy procedures and providing database object size estimates.

10.2 Objectives of Learning

- Overview of the psql program
- Database onboarding procedures

- Database schemas
- Data copy procedures
- Dynamic SQL

10.3 Introduction

After successfully installing and configuring PostgreSQL, the next tasks are to understand the features of psql; create PostgreSQL schemas; create user databases and database objects; grant roles; grant access to the database based on roles; and create scripts to automate database object grants.

10.4 psql

The psql program is an interactive command-line terminal for working on both local and remote PostgreSQL database tasks such as creating DDL statements, working with DML statements, data loading from the database, data import from the database, and script deployment.

Figure 10-1 shows the flags to use psql programs.

psql usage

```
psql --help
General options
-c —command
-d, --dbname=DBNAME
-f, --file=FILENAME
-l, --list available databases
-v, --set=, --variable=NAME
-V, --version
-?, --help[=options]
Input and output options
-a, --echo-all
-b, --echo-errors
-e, --echo-queries
-E, --echo-hidden
-L, --log-file=FILENAME
-n, --no-readline
-o, --output=FILENAME
-q, --quiet
-s, --single-step
-S, --single-line
```

```
Output format options
-A, --no-align
--csv
-F, --field-separator=STRING
-H, --html
-P, --pset=VAR[=ARG]
-R, --record-separator=STRING
-t, --tuples-only
-T, --table-attr=TEXT
-x, --expanded
-z, --field-separator-zero
-0, --record-separator-zero
Connection options
-h, --host=HOSTNAME
-p, --port=PORT
-U, --username=USERNAME
-w, --no-password
-W, --password
```

Figure 10-1. plsql usage

You can check all available commands of psql with the `help` command.

With scripting, you can use psql with OS variables to retrieve data from the database for tasks such as backup and recovery, perform dynamic SQL execution, implement conditional logic, use loops and programming structures, generate logs, and send output from the database to the local disk. As reviewed already, psql is a client program. With the `-h` flag, you can access remote hosts. If you are not connected as a postgres operating system user, provide `-U` for username. Assuming the server is running at 127.0.0.1 and accepting connections on TCP/IP port 5432, with the `-c` flag you can specify a SQL command, such as `psql -c "select datname from pg_database;"`. If you connect as a user other than postgres on Linux, use `sudo su - postgres -c "select datname from pg_database;"`.

```
    datname
-----------
 postgres
 sales
 template1
 template0".
```

You reviewed script deployment with psql in Chapter 1. You can deploy DDL or DML statements with begin and end markers with the example in Figure 10-2.

```
$psql -d sales  <<eof
create table t1(id integer);
insert into t1 values(100);
eof
CREATE TABLE
INSERT 0 1
```

Figure 10-2. *psql DDL and DML*

You can work with two types of variables: Linux variables and database variables.

Linux variables:

Consider the example of a psql version stored and displayed from a database version OS variable. See Listings 10-1 and 10-2.

Listing 10-1. Linux Variable

```
$ dbversion=$(psql -t -c "select version();")
$ echo $dbversion
PostgreSQL 16.2 on x86_64-pc-linux-gnu, compiled by gcc (GCC) 11.4.1 20230605 (Red Hat 11.4.1-2), 64-bit
$
```

Listing 10-2. psql Variable

```
postgres=# \set date_var `date`
postgres=# \echo :date_var
Thu May 30 04:44:47 AM UTC 2024
```

Reference: Bruce Momjian, page 181, *PostgreSQL: Introduction and Concepts*, 2001.

Note Bruce, who made significant contributions for PostgreSQL over three decades, illustrated the command to set a date to a variable. The example dates to 1994 in Bruce's illustration of assigning values to a variable. In essence, assigning a value to PostgreSQL variable dates back 30 years. There are four broad categories of usage of psql commands: general, input and output, output format, and connection.

10.4.1 psql Connection from a Host

As you saw in earlier chapters, the command to connect to a Postgres server is psql -h[hostname] -U [username] -p[port].

With the psql --help command, you can view all the options for using this powerful utility.

10.4.2 psql –help

After connecting to the database with the psql program, you can view all the Postgres features with the inbuilt help syntax help for all DDL commands. You check for syntax help with the psql --help command. A DBA's work is all about understanding the SQL commands and using them to manage all database tasks.

CHAPTER 10 POSTGRESQL POST-INSTALLATION TASKS

```
postgres=# \help commit;
```

    Command: COMMIT
    Description: commit the current transaction
    Syntax:

```
COMMIT [ WORK | TRANSACTION ] [ AND [ NO ] CHAIN ]
URL: https://www.postgresql.org/docs/16/sql-commit.html
```

A DBA will work with basic commands to support Postgres administration tasks. The most used commands are Create Table, Alter Table, Create Index, Alter Index, Create View, Create Schema Alter System, Create User, Create Procedure, Create Function, Create Trigger, Drop Table, Drop Procedure, Drop Trigger, and Drop Schema. See Figure 10-3.

CHAPTER 10 POSTGRESQL POST-INSTALLATION TASKS

```
postgres=# \h
Available help:
  ABORT                              CREATE FOREIGN DATA WRAPPER    DROP ROUTINE
  ALTER AGGREGATE                    CREATE FOREIGN TABLE           DROP RULE
  ALTER COLLATION                    CREATE FUNCTION                DROP SCHEMA
  ALTER CONVERSION                   CREATE GROUP                   DROP SEQUENCE
  ALTER DATABASE                     CREATE INDEX                   DROP SERVER
  ALTER DEFAULT PRIVILEGES           CREATE LANGUAGE                DROP STATISTICS
  ALTER DOMAIN                       CREATE MATERIALIZED VIEW       DROP SUBSCRIPTION
  ALTER EVENT TRIGGER                CREATE OPERATOR                DROP TABLE
  ALTER EXTENSION                    CREATE OPERATOR CLASS          DROP TABLESPACE
  ALTER FOREIGN DATA WRAPPER         CREATE OPERATOR FAMILY         DROP TEXT SEARCH CONFIGURATION
  ALTER FOREIGN TABLE                CREATE POLICY                  DROP TEXT SEARCH DICTIONARY
  ALTER FUNCTION                     CREATE PROCEDURE               DROP TEXT SEARCH PARSER
  ALTER GROUP                        CREATE PUBLICATION             DROP TEXT SEARCH TEMPLATE
  ALTER INDEX                        CREATE ROLE                    DROP TRANSFORM
  ALTER LANGUAGE                     CREATE RULE                    DROP TRIGGER
  ALTER LARGE OBJECT                 CREATE SCHEMA                  DROP TYPE
  ALTER MATERIALIZED VIEW            CREATE SEQUENCE                DROP USER
  ALTER OPERATOR                     CREATE SERVER                  DROP USER MAPPING
  ALTER OPERATOR CLASS               CREATE STATISTICS              DROP VIEW
  ALTER OPERATOR FAMILY              CREATE SUBSCRIPTION            END
  ALTER POLICY                       CREATE TABLE                   EXECUTE
  ALTER PROCEDURE                    CREATE TABLE AS                EXPLAIN
  ALTER PUBLICATION                  CREATE TABLESPACE              FETCH
  ALTER ROLE                         CREATE TEXT SEARCH CONFIGURATION  GRANT
  ALTER ROUTINE                      CREATE TEXT SEARCH DICTIONARY  IMPORT FOREIGN SCHEMA
  ALTER RULE                         CREATE TEXT SEARCH PARSER      INSERT
  ALTER SCHEMA                       CREATE TEXT SEARCH TEMPLATE    LISTEN
  ALTER SEQUENCE                     CREATE TRANSFORM               LOAD
  ALTER SERVER                       CREATE TRIGGER                 LOCK
  ALTER STATISTICS                   CREATE TYPE                    MOVE
  ALTER SUBSCRIPTION                 CREATE USER                    NOTIFY
  ALTER SYSTEM                       CREATE USER MAPPING            PREPARE
  ALTER TABLE                        CREATE VIEW                    PREPARE TRANSACTION
  ALTER TABLESPACE                   DEALLOCATE                     REASSIGN OWNED
  ALTER TEXT SEARCH CONFIGURATION    DECLARE                        REFRESH MATERIALIZED VIEW
  ALTER TEXT SEARCH DICTIONARY       DELETE                         REINDEX
  ALTER TEXT SEARCH PARSER           DISCARD                        RELEASE SAVEPOINT
  ALTER TEXT SEARCH TEMPLATE         DO                             RESET
  ALTER TRIGGER                      DROP ACCESS METHOD             REVOKE
  ALTER TYPE                         DROP AGGREGATE                 ROLLBACK
  ALTER USER                         DROP CAST                      ROLLBACK PREPARED
  ALTER USER MAPPING                 DROP COLLATION                 ROLLBACK TO SAVEPOINT
  ALTER VIEW                         DROP CONVERSION                SAVEPOINT
  ANALYZE                            DROP DATABASE                  SECURITY LABEL
  BEGIN                              DROP DOMAIN                    SELECT
  CALL                               DROP EVENT TRIGGER             SELECT INTO
  CHECKPOINT                         DROP EXTENSION                 SET
  CLOSE                              DROP FOREIGN DATA WRAPPER      SET CONSTRAINTS
  CLUSTER                            DROP FOREIGN TABLE             SET ROLE
  COMMENT                            DROP FUNCTION                  SET SESSION AUTHORIZATION
  COMMIT                             DROP GROUP                     SET TRANSACTION
  COMMIT PREPARED                    DROP INDEX                     SHOW
  COPY                               DROP LANGUAGE                  START TRANSACTION
  CREATE ACCESS METHOD               DROP MATERIALIZED VIEW         TABLE
  CREATE AGGREGATE                   DROP OPERATOR                  TRUNCATE
  CREATE CAST                        DROP OPERATOR CLASS            UNLISTEN
  CREATE COLLATION                   DROP OPERATOR FAMILY           UPDATE
  CREATE CONVERSION                  DROP OWNED                     VACUUM
  CREATE DATABASE                    DROP POLICY                    VALUES
  CREATE DOMAIN                      DROP PROCEDURE                 WITH
  CREATE EVENT TRIGGER               DROP PUBLICATION
  CREATE EXTENSION                   DROP ROLE
```

Figure 10-3. psql commands

CHAPTER 10   POSTGRESQL POST-INSTALLATION TASKS

10.4.3 psql Meta-Commands

The psql meta-commands have been shipped with the product for the past 25 years, allowing users to type simple commands to view database metadata. You can use \? in psql to list available meta-commands. For example, \l lists available databases, \c connects to a database, \dt lists table names, and \d displays table details. These meta-commands eliminate the need to remember complex catalog queries to view metadata about database objects. Additionally, you can export and import operating system data using the psql \copy command. By using the -E option, you can identify the internal commands generated by psql. See Figure 10-4.

```
postgres=# \l
                                                  List of databases
   Name    |  Owner   | Encoding | Locale Provider |  Collate   |   Ctype    | ICU Locale | ICU Rules | Access priv
ileges
-----------+----------+----------+-----------------+------------+------------+------------+-----------+-------------
 postgres  | postgres | UTF8     | libc            | en_US.UTF-8| en_US.UTF-8|            |           |
 sales     | postgres | UTF8     | libc            | en_US.UTF-8| en_US.UTF-8|            |           |
 template0 | postgres | UTF8     | libc            | en_US.UTF-8| en_US.UTF-8|            |           | =c/postgres
           |          |          |                 |            |            |            |           | postgres=CTc/
postgres
 template1 | postgres | UTF8     | libc            | en_US.UTF-8| en_US.UTF-8|            |           | =c/postgres
           |          |          |                 |            |            |            |           | postgres=CTc/
postgres
(4 rows)
```

Figure 10-4. *Database listing*

In summary, meta-commands simplify catalog queries and provide an easy way to access database catalog details. Figure 10-5 shows an example of a psql meta-command.

```
$psql -E
psql (16.3)
Type "help" for help.

postgres=# \dt
********* QUERY **********
SELECT n.nspname as "Schema",
  c.relname as "Name",
  CASE c.relkind WHEN 'r' THEN 'table' WHEN 'v' THEN 'view' WHEN 'm' THEN 'materialized view' WHEN 'i' THEN 'index' WHE
N 'S' THEN 'sequence' WHEN 't' THEN 'TOAST table' WHEN 'f' THEN 'foreign table' WHEN 'p' THEN 'partitioned table' WHEN
'I' THEN 'partitioned index' END as "Type",
  pg_catalog.pg_get_userbyid(c.relowner) as "Owner"
FROM pg_catalog.pg_class c
     LEFT JOIN pg_catalog.pg_namespace n ON n.oid = c.relnamespace
     LEFT JOIN pg_catalog.pg_am am ON am.oid = c.relam
WHERE c.relkind IN ('r','p','')
      AND n.nspname <> 'pg_catalog'
      AND n.nspname !~ '^pg_toast'
      AND n.nspname <> 'information_schema'
  AND pg_catalog.pg_table_is_visible(c.oid)
ORDER BY 1,2;
**************************

         List of relations
 Schema | Name | Type  | Owner
--------+------+-------+----------
 public | t1   | table | postgres
```

Figure 10-5. psql meta command

10.4.4 psql Command Prompts

If you are connected as a root user of PostgreSQL, the psql prompt is #. If you use a begin and end block, the prompt for root user is #*. The chosen database is echoed in the prompt "[databasenae=]. If you connect as a regular user, the prompt is $. Listing 10-3 shows the example of a root user prompt.

Listing 10-3. psql Prompt

```
Postgres root user prompt is # connected to fin database
psql
psql (16.3)
Type "help" for help.
fin=#
Inside Block in fin database
fin=*#
Regular  user prompt is =>
fin=>
```

10.4.5 psql Background Job

For long-running SQL statements, you can disconnect from the session after submitting the background job with the nohup command. Redirection 1 refers to sending the standard output and 2 refers to sending the error. In Listing 10-4, the standard error and output is sent to /tmp/count.log. The listing shows the help command to use nohup.

Listing 10-4. nohup help Command

```
$ nohup --help
Usage: nohup COMMAND [ARG]...
  or:  nohup OPTION
Run COMMAND, ignoring hangup signals.

--help     display this help and exit
--version  output version information and exit

If standard input is a terminal, redirect it from an
unreadable file.
If standard output is a terminal, append output to 'nohup.out'
if possible,
'$HOME/nohup.out' otherwise.
If standard error is a terminal, redirect it to
standard output.
To save output to FILE, use 'nohup COMMAND > FILE'.
```

NOTE: your shell may have its own version of nohup, which usually supersedes the version described here. Please refer to your shell's documentation for details about options its supports.

Listing 10-5 shows the nohup command.

Listing 10-5. psql nohup Command

```
sudo -u postgres createuser -s $USER
createdb
 nohup psql -c "select count(*) from pg_tables;" 2>&1 > /tmp/count.log &
[1] 17019
 nohup: ignoring input and redirecting stderr to stdout

nohup psql -c "select count(*) from pg_tables;" 2>&1 > /tmp/count.log
$ cat /tmp/count.log
count
-------
68

(1 row)
```

10.5 Postgres Schemas

As a DBA, you will be working most of the time with application developers on schema-related tasks. In PostgreSQL, schemas can be compared to subject areas or domains within a business, such as shipment, order, marketing, claim, and warranty. Each schema represents a specific area of focus and may contain tables, views, functions, and other database objects related to that subject area. The default schema is public, where all user objects are created. When you create a table, by default it is created in the public schema.

Schemas enable different business units to have their own view of the same data. For example, the marketing team might have a different view of customer data compared to the finance team. Although tables are unique within a database, schemas allow for the creation of tables with the same name in different schemas. This separation allows the same object name to be used for different business units or business domains. By default, there is a public schema where user objects are created in each and every database. You do not have to prefix the public when referencing the objects in the public schema. Note that starting with version 15 of Postgres, due to security concerns, except DBA privileged accounts, all other accounts have revoked access on the public schema. DBAs have to explicitly grant permissions on the public schema.

The best practice is to create named schemas such as marketing, sales, finance, and human resources. For example, if you have a table named `customer` in the `marketing` schema, you will refer to it as `marketing.customer`, whereas in the sales schema, it is referenced as `sales.customer`. With the `set` or `set search path` commands, you can conveniently access the objects in respective schemas. The search path is an ordered list of schemas that PostgreSQL searches when resolving object names. By setting the search path appropriately, you can simplify the way you reference objects within schemas, reducing the need for explicit schema qualification in your queries. By granting all schema objects, you do not have to grant access to each and every object in the schema to application users.

10.5.1 Schema Definition

In Listing 10-6, two schemas, `sales` and `finance`, are created. A `logs` table is created in each schema. By setting a search path, you access the same table in different schemas.

Listing 10-6. Deploy DDL and DML Statements

```
-- connect to pre existing  shipment database
\c shipment;
\echo create schema finance and sales - echo command to print
on the screen.
create schema finance;
create schema sales;
\echo create table logs in finance schema
CREATE TABLE finance.logs
(
log_id integer NOT NULL GENERATED ALWAYS AS IDENTITY,
logname   varchar(40),
logdate   date,
CONSTRAINT pk_logs_id PRIMARY KEY(log_id)
);
\echo insert 1 record into finance schema log tables
insert into finance.logs(logname,logdate) values('financelog','
jan-01-2024');
 -create table logs in sales schema
CREATE TABLE sales.logs
(
log_id integer NOT NULL GENERATED ALWAYS AS IDENTITY,
logname   varchar(40),
logdate   date,
CONSTRAINT pk_logs_id PRIMARY KEY(log_id)
);
\echo Insert  1 record into sales schema log table.
insert into sales.logs(logname,logdate)
values('saleslog','jan-01-2024');
```

10.5.2 Create a Read-Only User

In production or critical systems, there is no requirement for a user to create any database objects. You can restrict users from creating database objects with the set default_transaction_read_only command. See Listing 10-7.

Listing 10-7. Create Read-Only User

```
CREATE USER user01 with password 'Mystrong$pwd';
GRANT SELECT on sales.logs to user01;
ALTER USER user01 SET default_transaction_read_only = on;
```

Read-only access users can't create any DDL or DML commands. Figure 10-6 shows the screen image of the command psql -h 18.117.137.57 -U user01 -d shipment -c "create table t1(id integer);.

```
[postgres@nodel172 dev]$ psql -h 18.117.137.57 -U user01 -d shipment -c "select * From finance.logs;"
Password for user user01:
 log_id | logname |  logdate
--------+---------+------------
      1 | applog  | 2022-01-01
(1 row)

[postgres@nodel172 dev]$ psql -h 18.117.137.57 -U user01 -d shipment -c "create table t1(id integer);"
Password for user user01:
ERROR:  cannot execute CREATE TABLE in a read-only transaction
```

Figure 10-6. *Read-only session grants*

10.5.3 Schema Search Path

With the search path setting, you set the order of tables for a query. In our example, the logs table is in both the finance and sales schemas. PostgreSQL begins searching with public, followed by the schema name in the order specified in the query. The psql meta-command \dn displays the available schemas in the database. With the command set search_path, you can set the query search path to the schemas for table selection. In the following example, you are connected to the database shipment. After identifying the schemas with the \dn meta-command, you set the path to the schema finance with the command set search_path. With the command show search_path, you identify the default schema, which is $user, followed by public.

10.5.4 Set Search Path to Schema

You can set the search path to your desired schema with the set search_path command. See Listing 10-8.

Listing 10-8. Schema Search Path

```
shipment=# set search_path to '$user','public','sales','finance';
SET
shipment=# show search_path;
       search_path
----------------------------------
 "$user", public, sales, finance
(1 row)
shipment=# select * from logs;
 log_id | logname  | logdate
--------+----------+------------
      1 | saleslog | 2022-01-01
set search_path to '$user','public','finance','sales';
select * from logs
 log_id | logname    | logdate
--------+------------+------------
      1 | financelog | 2022-01-01
```

In summary, by switching between schemas, you access the same table in different schemas.

CHAPTER 10 POSTGRESQL POST-INSTALLATION TASKS

10.5.5 PostgreSQL Database Onboarding Process Summary

Figure 10-7 shows the database onboarding process.

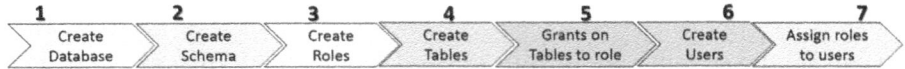

Figure 10-7. Database onboarding process

Create Database

Postgres names are case sensitive. You have to enclose in quotes to preserve uppercase and lowercase characters. Consider the following example of creating databases (see also Figure 10-8):

create database "Sales";
create database sales;

```
postgres=# create database "Sales";
CREATE DATABASE
postgres=# create database Sales;
CREATE DATABASE
postgres=# \l
                                               List of databases
   Name    |  Owner   | Encoding | Locale Provider |  Collate    |   Ctype     |
-----------+----------+----------+-----------------+-------------+-------------+
 Sales     | postgres | UTF8     | libc            | en_US.UTF-8 | en_US.UTF-8 |
 postgres  | postgres | UTF8     | libc            | en_US.UTF-8 | en_US.UTF-8 |
 sales     | postgres | UTF8     | libc            | en_US.UTF-8 | en_US.UTF-8 |
 template0 | postgres | UTF8     | libc            | en_US.UTF-8 | en_US.UTF-8 |
           |          |          |                 |             |             |
 template1 | postgres | UTF8     | libc            | en_US.UTF-8 | en_US.UTF-8 |
           |          |          |                 |             |             |
```

Figure 10-8. Create databases

The created database uses the template database template0 for user database structure. The default character set is UTF8, which accommodates multibyte character sets. The storage is limited to available space in the file system for the base directory.

Create a Schema

The schemas are isolated namespaces that store user data in the database (see Listing 10-9).

DDL: Create schema east;

Listing 10-9. Create a Schema

```
postgres=# \c "Sales"
psql (16.1, server 12.18)
You are now connected to database "Sales" as user "postgres".
Sales=# Create schema east;
CREATE SCHEMA
```

Create Roles

Create two roles: read only and read write. See Listing 10-10.

DDL : Create role readonly;
DDL : Create role readwrite;

Listing 10-10. Create Roles

```
Sales=# CREATE ROLE readonly;
CREATE ROLE
Sales=# CREATE ROLE readwrite;
CREATE ROLE
```

Create a Table

Create tables in a schema. See Listing 10-11.

Listing 10-11. Create a Table in a Schema

```
Sales=# CREATE TABLE east.test2(id integer);
CREATE TABLE
Sales=# set search_path to east;
SET
Sales=# CREATE TABLE test1(id integer);
CREATE TABLE
```

Grants

Create grants on a schema object. See Listing 10-12.

Listing 10-12. Grants

```
Sales=# GRANT SELECT  ON east.test2 to readonly;
GRANT
Sales=# GRANT SELECT,INSERT,UPDATE,DELETE ON east.test1 to readwrite;
GRANT
```

Create Users

```
Sales=# CREATE USER user001 with password 'String#pwd';
CREATE ROLE
Sales=# GRANT readonly to user001;
GRANT ROLE
Sales=# CREATE USER  user002 with password 'String#pwD';
CREATE ROLE
```

Object Grants

Listing 10-13 shows object grants.

Listing 10-13. Grants

```
grant usage on schema east to user001;
Sales=# CREATE USER user002 with password 'String#pwD';
CREATE ROLE
Sales=# GRANT readwrite to user002;
GRANT ROLE
Sales=# grant all on schema east to user002;
```

If you want users to create objects in a schema, provide grant all on the schema. For DML tasks, grant select, insert, update, and delete to the database role.

Object Size

The maximum size of the database object is 64 bytes. The long object name is truncated to 64 bytes.

```
postgres=# create table mylong123456789101112131415161718192021
22232425262728293031323334353637383940314243 44(mylongcol1234
5678910111213141516171819202122232425262728293031323334353637 38
394031424344 integer);
NOTICE:  identifier "mylong12345678910111213141516171819202122 2
32425262728293031323334353637383940314243 44" will be truncated
to "mylong1234567891011121314151617181920212223242526272829 30
313233"
NOTICE:  identifier "mylongcol1234567891011121314151617181920
2122232425262728293031323334353637383940314243 44" will be
truncated to "mylongcol123456789101112131415161718192021222324 2
52627282930313
```

10.6 Schema Data Move Procedure

There will be requirements to copy data from one schema to another schema. Figure 10-9 shows a schema copy.

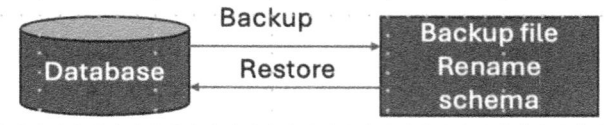

Figure 10-9. *Schema copy*

10.6.1 Postgres Schema Clone Procedure

If there is a requirement to clone a schema to another schema, the procedure is to back up the database, change the reference of the old schema in the backup file, and restore the database. There is no option to rename the schema while doing the import. Listing 10-14 shows the steps.

Listing 10-14. Schema Rename

```
# Create new schema
psql -d demo1 -c "create schema qa;"
# Backup database
pg_dump -f demo1_full.sql demo1
# Replace reference of schema public with qa with sed command 
in the backup file
sed 's/public/qa/g' demo1_full.sql > demo1_DDL.sql
# Backup public schema to old
psql -d demo1 -c " alter  schema public rename  to public_old;"
# Restore database
psql -d demo1 < demo1_DDL.sql
```

```
#Validate the table row count from qa schema
psql -d demo1 -c "select count(*) from qa.pgbench_accounts;"
# Rename old public schema
psql -d demo1 -c " alter  schema public_old rename  to public;"
# Validate the count from
psql -d demo1 -c "select count(*) from public.pgbench_accounts;"
dropdb demo1
rm demo1_full.sql
rm demo1_DDL.sql
Note: If the size of the database is large and you can't use
sed command, the procedure is to rename original schema,
restore database to original schema, rename it to desired
schema and rename the original schema to its old name. Rename
constraints if present.
```

Another simple procedure is to rename public schema to old, import the data to default public, rename public to the new schema, and rename old to the public schema.

10.6.2 Table Copy to a Different Schema

The public schema has security issues and this is widely known for hackers. As a good practice, you have to move the tables to different schemas, such as qa1 in this example. Listing 10-15 shows the procedure to move objects from the public schema to a user-defined schema.

Listing 10-15. Table Schema Rename

```
# create database
createdb demo1
# Create schema qa1
CREATE schema qa1
```

```
# Load test data with pgbench utility. The -i option of pgbench
initializes the database.and #loads  benchmark data.
pgbench -i demo1
# Create desired sehema
psql -d demo1 -c "create schema qa1;"
# Backup 2 tables
pg_dump -f demo1_tab.sql
 -t pgbench_history -t pgbench_tellers demo1
# Change reference to public with qa1
sed 's/public/qa1/g' demo1_tab.sql > demo1_tabDDL.sql
psql -d demo1 < demo1_tabDDL.sql
psql -d demo1 -c "select count(*) from qa.pgbench_accounts;"
psql -d demo1 -c "select count(*) from public.pgbench_accounts;"
```

10.7 Dynamic psql

You can generate SQL statements from psql. Assuming you have more than 100 tables to be granted to a specific role, with Dynamic SQL you can generate the SQL statements for all grants.

The following is the example of PostgreSQL dynamically creating SQL statement grants on tables to a schema user account. The dynamic SQL scripts are created in two methods: create SQL with a script and create with variables.

10.7.1 Dynamic SQL script1

In the script, you must use single quotes inside your statement. which is like a comment in which the statement is literally reproduced. In the following example, after the select statement, specify a single quote

CHAPTER 10 POSTGRESQL POST-INSTALLATION TASKS

before grant and after end of the phrase. The SQL statement returns a set of queries along with the quoted text appended to it. In the following example, you are granting select to the appro role with tables with the sales prefix. See Listing 10-16.

Listing 10-16. Dynamic Script for Grants

```
--- Create output file on Operating System
     shipment=# \o salesgrant.sql
--- Create a grant command from select statement
shipment=# select 'grant select on finance.'||tablename||' to appro;'
shipment-# from pg_tables
shipment-# where tablename like 'sales%';
shipment=# exit
# read the contents of grant script
$ cat salesgrant.sql
 grant select on finance.sales to appro;
 grant select on finance.sales202301 to appro;
 # You can run the grant script from psql with \i inputfile
After the script is generated, execute the sql with \i from the
psql statement.
psql -t -d shipment
psql (13.10)
Type "help" for help.
shipment=# \i salesgrant.sql
GRANT
GRANT
:::::::
You can check the grants with \z meta command on the database
table for the read only role granted to appro role.
shipment=# \z finance.sales
 finance | sales | table | postgres=arwdDxt/postgres+|           |
         |       |       | appro=r/postgres          |           |
```

10.7.2 Dynamic SQL script2

In the Listing 10-16 example, the output of the select statement is written to the OS file for later usage. With psql variables, you can store the results of the select command to a variable and execute the SQL statement dynamically with `execute command`. You can execute the Dynamic SQL from a file or from a variable.

You can generate Dynamic SQL from the database block. The procedural language for PostgreSQL is PL/pgSQL, which is a structured programming language with control structure along with variable declaration. PL/pgSQL is a block-structured language. The complete text of a function body must be a *block[1]*. The following PL/pgSQL block grants select on all tables in a particular database for schema named `sales`. You can substitute `sales` with any other schema name.

In the following example, there are three sections: declaration of variables, the begin and end block, and the loop and execution. The results of the table names are stored in the `dtab` variable and grants are assigned on the selected tables and a stored in a dsql variable, which is executed to grant select on selected tables. See Listing 10-17.

Listing 10-17. psql execute Command

```
DO $$
DECLARE
    dsql text;
    dtab text;
BEGIN
---- Generate a list of tables and loop till the end of search
    FOR dtab IN (SELECT tablename FROM pg_tables WHERE schemaname='sales')
    LOOP
--- Generate the grants on the selected tables in the variable dtab
```

```
        dsql := 'GRANT SELECT ON  sales.' || dtab || ' TO
        readonly';
           -- Execute the dynamic SQL statement
        EXECUTE dsql;
    END LOOP;
END $$;
```

Upon executing above code, you can validate the read-only user access with the \dp command. See Listing 10-18.

Listing 10-18. View Grants

```
postgres=# \dp sales.logs;
                                    Access privileges
 Schema | Name | Type |      Access privileges      | Column
privileges | Policies
--------+------+------+-----------------------------
+------------------+
 sales  | logs | table | postgres=arwdDxt/postgres+
|                  |
        |      |      | user01=r/postgres         +
|                  |
        |      |      | readonly=r/postgres
|
```

10.7.3 Dynamic SQL script3

The requirement of the script is: for each database, identify the sequence names and grant usage and then select all sequences to a specific role. Some of the recently created roles may not have access to sequences; as a result, they can't read primary key data in the table. The shell in Listing 10-19 loops through all databases, identifies sequence names, and assigns grants to a database role.

CHAPTER 10 POSTGRESQL POST-INSTALLATION TASKS

Listing 10-19. Dynamic Sequence Grant Script

```
--- store the database names in the db variable
db=$(psql  -t -c "SELECT DATNAME FROM PG_DATABASE WHERE
datistemplate = false and datname not in ('postgres');")
# Loop and change ownership for tables in user databases
# Loop for each database
for DATABASE in $db; do
  echo " Grant select on sequences to : $DATABASE"
--- store the sequence names in the variable
    SEQ=$(psql -d $DATABASE -t -c "SELECT  sequencename from
pg_sequences;" |tr -d '|')
# Loop for each sequence
for seq in $SEQ
    do
      echo "grant usage,select on  $seq to approle;"
 ---- Grants  on sequence to role
      psql -d $DATABASE -c "grant usage,select on  $seq to
temprole01;"
    done
done
```

The script in Listing 10-20 displays the sequence grant scripts on the console. You can save it to a file and execute it later on.

Listing 10-20. Grants on Sequences

```
--- Get user database names in to a variable
db=$(psql 'host=dev.rds.amazonaws.com user=adminuser
dbname=postgres password=MyStrongPwd#'  -t -c "SELECT DATNAME
FROM PG_DATABASE WHERE datistemplate = false and datname not in
('postgres','rdsadmin');")
# Loop for each database, identify sequence name and assign it
```

to a role
for DATABASE in $db; do
  echo " Grant select on sequences to : $DATABASE"

psql -t 'host=dev.rds.amazonaws.com user=adminuser dbname=postgres password=MystorntgP3&&6''<<eof
\c $DATABASE
select 'grant select,usage on '||sequencename||' to devrole;' from pg_sequences;
eof
done

10.7.4 Table Row Count Dynamic Script

The shell script in Listing 10-21 computes the size of database tables by the SQL script created by the Dynamic SQL script.

Listing 10-21. Schema Table Count Script

Database row count for Postgres Cluster Database
Generate *.sql script and execute it
rowcount.sh
echo " Enter host"
read host
echo " Enter database"
read db
echo " Enter user"
read user
echo " Enter schema"
read schema
psql -t -h $host $db -U $user <<eof
\o tabcount.sql
select 'select count(*)from '||tablename||';' from pg_tables

```
where schemaname='$schema';
select 'select pg_relation_size('''||tablename||''');' from pg_
tables where schemaname='$schema';
select 'select pg_table_size('''||tablename||''');' from pg_
tables where schemaname='$schema';
select 'select pg_total_relation_size('''||tablename||''');' from
pg_tables where schemaname='$schema';
eof
psql -a -t -h $host $db -U $user -c "\i tabcount.sql" >>
$db.$user.table.lst
cat $db.$user.table.lst
rm tabcount.sql
```

10.7.5 Dynamic SQL Variable

It is a common requirement to obtain the usage of allocated space of each table in the database. The table size estimation is performed by three functions: pg_relation_size, which takes the table as an argument, pg_table_size, and pg_total_relation_size. The script gets all the tablenames and computes the size. Furthermore, the script provides table statistics such as insert, delete, update count from the view pg_stat_all tables.

The script in Listing 10-22 generates the table counts using operating system variables. See Figure 10-10.

Listing 10-22. Table Count of All Databases

```
#!/bin/bash
# Get the list of database names
echo "Enter database name"
read db
  # Get the list of table names in the public schema
```

```
    tables=$(psql -t -d "$db" -c "SELECT tablename FROM pg_
    tables where schemaname not in ('information_schema','pg_
    catalog');")
    # Iterate through each table
    for table in $tables
    do
       # Execute the queries and store the results in variables
       # Query to get the row count of the table
       count=$(psql -t -d "$db" <<EOF
SELECT COUNT(*) FROM "$table";
EOF
)
       # Query to get the size of the table's main data file
       (excluding indexes and associated objects)
       relation_size=$(psql -t -d "$db"  -c "SELECT pg_relation_
       size('$table');")
       # Query to get the size of the table, including all indexes
       and associated objects
       table_size=$(psql -t -d "$db" -c "SELECT pg_table_
       size('$table');")
       # Query to get the total size of the table, including the
       main data file, indexes, and associated objects
       total_size=$(psql -t -d "$db" -c "SELECT pg_total_relation_
       size('$table');")
       stats=$(psql -d "$db" -c "select n_live_tup,n_tup_ins,n_tup_
       upd,n_tup_del,last_vacuum,last_analyze from  pg_stat_all_
       tables where relname='$table';")

       # Display the results
       echo "Database: $db"
       echo "Table: $table"
       echo "Count: $count"
```

```
    echo "Table size : $relation_size"
    echo "Table Size  including large objects : $table_size"
    echo "Total Size including indexes: $total_size"
    echo "Table : $table stats: $stats"
    echo
done
```

```
Enter database name
sales
Database: sales
Table: pgbench_accounts
Count:  100000
Table size :         13434880
Table Size  including large objects :      13467648
Total Size including indexes:              15728640
Table : pgbench_accounts stats:  n_live_tup | n_tup_ins | n_tup_upd | n_tup_del |           last_vacuum
    |        last_analyze
------------+-----------+-----------+-----------+-------------------------------+-----------------------------
--
     100000 |    100000 |        0 |         0 | 2024-05-30 06:00:44.117939+00 | 2024-05-30 06:00:44.150173+0
0
(1 row)

Database: sales
Table: pgbench_branches
Count:   1
Table size :              8192
Table Size  including large objects :         40960
Total Size including indexes:                 57344
Table : pgbench_branches stats:  n_live_tup | n_tup_ins | n_tup_upd | n_tup_del |           last_vacuum
    |        last_analyze
------------+-----------+-----------+-----------+-------------------------------+-----------------------------
          1 |         1 |        0 |         0 | 2024-05-30 06:00:44.11348+00  | 2024-05-30 06:00:44.11392+00
(1 row)
```

Figure 10-10. *Table size estimate*

10.7.6 Table Rename Script

The script in Listing 10-23 renames the table ownership in all databases for a specified user.

Listing 10-23. Table Owner Change Script

```
# Rename table  owner
NEW_OWNER="$1"
```

```
psql  -c "CREATE ROLE $NEW_OWNER;"
# Get a list of databases
db=$(psql  -t -c "SELECT DATNAME FROM PG_DATABASE WHERE
datistemplate = false and datname not in ('postgres');")
# Loop and change ownership for tables in user databases
for DATABASE in $db; do
  echo " Renaming tables in db: $DATABASE"
    TABLES=$(psql -d $DATABASE -t -c "SELECT  tablename
    FROM pg_tables where schemaname not in ('pg_
    catalog','information_schema')" |tr -d '|')
    for TABLE in $TABLES; do
     echo  "renaming table .... $TABLE"
        psql  -d $DATABASE -c "ALTER TABLE  $TABLE  owner TO
        $NEW_OWNER"
    done
done
```

10.7.7 Session Termination Script

During database maintenance tasks, you may have to terminate user sessions accessing a database. You can run the output of the SQL statement to terminate all user sessions accessing a database.

```
postgres=# select  'select pg_terminate_backend('||''''||p
id||''''||');' from pg_stat_activity
where datname='sales';
```

Output.
```
select pg_terminate_backend('23157');
 select pg_terminate_backend('23163')
```

10.8 Data Copy and Load

Data load and copy are simple steps to copy to the OS and copy back from the OS to a database table.

10.8.1 Table Copy to OS

As a DBA, you get requirements from the application team to copy table data to the OS and vice versa. With a copy command from psql, you can back up a table data to csv or other format files as full table data or selective data based on the where condition. Listing 10-24 shows the partial help command to copy data from a database to the OS file.

Listing 10-24. Help for the copy Command

```
postgres-# \help copy
Command:         COPY
Description: copy data between a file and a table
Syntax:
COPY table_name [ ( column_name [, ...] ) ]
    FROM { 'filename' | PROGRAM 'command' | STDIN }
    [ [ WITH ] ( option [, ...] ) ]
    [ WHERE condition ]
::: Truncated

where option can be one of:

    FORMAT format_name
    FREEZE [ boolean ]
    DELIMITER 'delimiter_character'
    NULL 'null_string'
::::::::: continued
```

Here is an example script to copy table data to the OS file, where you have to provide tablename and copy path along with the file format:

```
$ psql -d sales -c "\COPY pgbench_accounts to '/appl/backup/pgbench_accounts.csv' WITH CSV HEADER;"
COPY 100000
```

10.8.2 Truncate Table

The truncate is a DDL statement that removes the table data efficiently by releasing space to the database immediately, whereas Delete is a DML statement that deletes data row by row and creates a vacuum activity to claim space. Delete the contents of the table with the truncate command.

```
$ psql -d sales -c "truncate table pgbench_accounts;".
```

10.8.3 Table Copy from the OS

The procedure to copy data from file to table is similar, except for the FROM clause in the copy command.

```
$ psql -d sales -c "COPY pgbench_accounts FROM  '/appl/backup/pgbench_accounts.csv' DELIMITER ',' CSV HEADER;"
COPY 10000
```

10.9 Large Objects

The procedure is to use the lo_import function to load to the database. With lo_ulink you can delete the large object reference in the database. The catalog view pg_largeobject displays the large object data. Copy a test file to the /tmp directory from the scp program from a mac or winscp from Windows before running the script in Listing 10-25.

Listing 10-25. Large Object Details

```
CREATE TABLE Auto (name CHAR(30), image OID);
INSERT INTO Auto values('Benz',lo_import('/tmp/Marcedes.jpg'));
postgres=# select * From auto;
-[ RECORD 1 ]------------------------
name  | Benz
image | 19838
select * from pg_largeobject  where loid=19838 limit 1;
loid   | 19838
pageno | 0
data   | \xffd8ffe000104a464946000101010048004800000ffe20c5849434
35f50524f46494c4500010100000c484c696e6f021000006d6e747252474220
58595a2007ce0002000900060031000061637370d53465400000000494543
20735247420000000000000000000000000000f6d6000100000000d32d48502
02000000000000000000000000000000000000000000000000000000000000
postgres=# SELECT lo_unlink(19838);
-[ RECORD 1 ]
lo_unlink | 1
postgres=# select * From auto;
-[ RECORD 1 ]------------------------
name  | Benz
image | 19838
postgres=# select * from pg_largeobject  where loid=19838;
(0 rows)
https://www.postgresql.org/docs/current/lo-funcs.html
```

10.10 SQL Overload Function

With PostgreSQL overloading, the same function takes multiple arguments. You can reuse the function to provide multiple arguments based on your requirements or for dynamic search criteria where the column or field names are not known in advance. In Listing 10-26, the overload creates a table with a different number of columns by executing the DDL statement dynamically or at runtime.

Listing 10-26. Overload Function

```
create or replace function cr_tab1(tabname text,colname1
text,datatype1 text)
RETURNS BOOLEAN AS $$
DECLARE stat text;
stmt text;
begin
stmt = 'create table '||tabname||'('||colname1||' '||datatype1||')';
RAISE NOTICE '%' , stmt;
EXECUTE stmt;
return stat;
end;
$$ LANGUAGE plpgsql;
create or replace function cr_tab1(tabname text,colname1
text,datatype1 text,colname2 text,datatype2 text)
RETURNS BOOLEAN AS $$
DECLARE stat text;
stmt text;
begin
stmt = 'create table '||tabname||'('||colname1||'
'||datatype1||','||colname2||' '||datatype2||')';
RAISE NOTICE '%' , stmt;
EXECUTE stmt;
return stat;
end;
$$ LANGUAGE plpgsql;
```

```
--- Execute the function
postgres=# select cr_tab1('customersales','salevalue','text');
NOTICE:  create table customersales(salevalue text)
 cr_tab1
---------

(1 row)
postgres=# select cr_tab1('customerfinance','invoice','text','amount','text');
NOTICE:  create table customerfinance(invoice text,amount text)
 cr_tab1
---------

(1 row)
postgres=# \d+ customersales;
                                        Table "public.customersales"
  Column   | Type | Collation | Nullable | Default | Storage | Compression | Stats target | Description
-----------+------+-----------+----------+---------+---------+-------------+--------------+-------------
 salevalue | text |           |          |         | extended |            |              |
Access method: heap
postgres=# \d+ customerfinance;
                                        Table "public.customerfinance"
```

```
 Column   | Type | Collation | Nullable | Default | Storage  |
Compression | Stats target | Description
---------+------+-----------+----------+---------+----------+
-------------+--------------+-------------
 invoice | text |           |          |         | extended |
            |              |
 amount  | text |           |          |         | extended |
            |              |
Access method: heap
postgres=#
```

10.11 Postgres System Functions

A rich set of system functions are available to obtain PostgreSQL details for session information functions, access privilege inquiry functions, schema visibility inquiry functions, system catalog information functions, object information and addressing functions, comment information functions, data validity checking functions, transaction ID and snapshot information functions, committed transaction information functions, and control data.

Reference: www.postgresql.org/docs/16/functions-info.html

You can call the function switch select [function_name] like so:

```
select current_database();
 current_database
------------------
 demo
```

Furthermore, a rich set of date functions are available. For instance current time is obtained by the current_timestamp function.

```
select current_timestamp;
     current_timestamp
---------------------------------
 2024-07-12 12:58:18.515514-07
```

Reference: www.postgresql.org/docs/16/functions-datetime.html

10.12 Keywords

psql program, Dynamic psql, data copy, schemas, and seach_path.

10.13 Summary of Learning

In this chapter, you got a psql program overview. psql is a command-line interface to interact with PostgreSQL databases locally as well as remotely. You covered the basics of PostgreSQL schemas, which are essential for organizing database objects like tables and views for subject area logical grouping. You reviewed all procedures for copying schema data. You also reviewed the procedures for Dynamic SQL, which constructs values at runtime for various requirements.

10.14 Practice Chapter 10

1. Create multiple schemas with DDL statements, with grants to user accounts.

2. Create two users, one with read write permissions and another with read-only permissions on the schemas.

3. Set the search path and identify the table contents in different schemas.

4. Identify the Postgres catalog with psql -E flag.
5. Backup database tables to CVS files and import data from CSV files.

10.15 Questions Chapter 10

1. How do you check meta-commands from psql?
2. How do you pass database and OS values to variables?
3. What steps are taken to create a read-only user account?
4. Identify uppercase and lowercase objects in the database.
5. How do you to set the search path to navigate to different schemas?
6. What steps are performed to rename objects from publics to different schemas?
7. What is the maximum size of a database object?
8. What procedure is called to import large objects in the database?
9. What are the steps to copy table data to an OS file?
10. What are the steps to copy an OS fie to a database table?

CHAPTER 11

Sequences

11.1 Abstract

In transaction processing systems, the management of sequences is of utmost importance for the database management system. Sequences play a critical role as they are responsible for generating unique primary key values within the database. Databases efficiently manage and allocate sequence numbers to ensure the uniqueness and integrity of the generated values.

The database engine actively manages the allocation and management of sequence numbers for the application. It ensures that each transaction receives a unique sequence value to maintain data integrity and prevent conflicts with concurrent transactions.

By managing sequences, the database engine ensures the proper functioning of the primary key constraint or other data inserts, maintaining data consistency and referential integrity across tables.

11.2 Objectives of Learning

- Creation of sequences
- Sequence manipulation
- Sequences on new and old tables
- Performance tuning of sequences

CHAPTER 11 SEQUENCES

11.3 Introduction

A sequence is a database object that is used to generate unique numbers for primary keys and unique columns and are managed by the database system.

11.4 Sequence Management Procedures

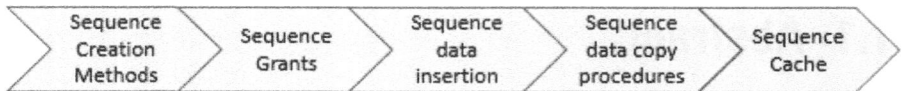

Figure 11-1. *Sequence management*

Sequences play a crucial role in transaction processing by providing transaction identifiers that are obtained from the sequence number. See Figure 11-1.

The Postgres Database Management system ensures that each transaction identifier is unique and can be used to identify specific transactions to provide concurrency control in multi-user environments. The sequences are created with the number data type. The maximum size of the sequence is based the data type such as smallint (-32768 to +32767), integer (-32768 to +32767), bigint (-9223372036854775808 to +9223372036854775807), smallserial (1 to 32767), serial (1 to 2147483647), and bigserial (1 to 9223372036854775807) [1].

Listing 11-1 shows the help on sequences from www.postgresql.org/docs/12/sql-createsequence.html.

Listing 11-1. Sequence Commands

```
postgres=# \h create sequence;
Command:     CREATE SEQUENCE
Description: define a new sequence generator
```

CHAPTER 11 SEQUENCES

```
Syntax:
CREATE [ TEMPORARY | TEMP ] SEQUENCE [ IF NOT EXISTS ] name
    [ AS data_type ]
    [ INCREMENT [ BY ] increment ]
    [ MINVALUE | NO MINVALUE ] [ MAXVALUE | NO MAXVALUE ]
    [ START [ WITH ] start ] [ CACHE ] [ [ NO ] CYCLE ]
    [ OWNED BY { table_name.column_name | NONE } ]
```

By default, only one sequence is cached when creating the sequence. The default start value is 1 unless a different value is specified. Figure 11-2 shows the overview of sequences in the Postgres database with three creation types, four data manipulation functions, and an overriding system function, which will be covered later in this chapter.

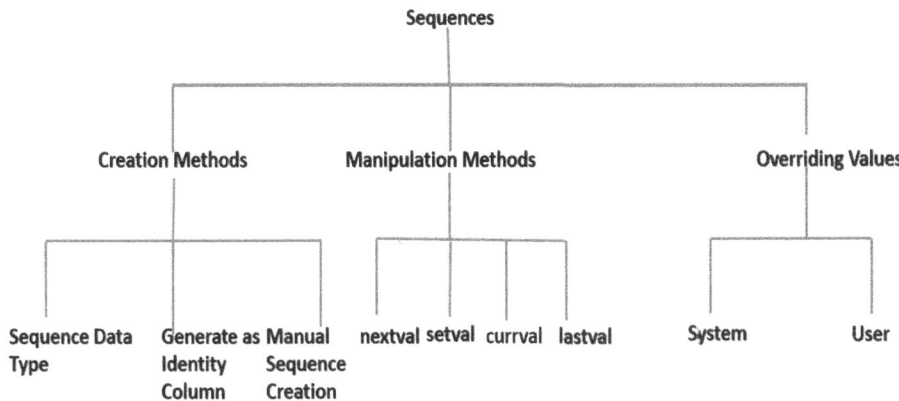

Figure 11-2. Sequences overview

You can create sequences by three methods: with the serial data type, with the GENERATED ALWAYS AS IDENTITY column definition, and with a manual sequence command. I will go through all these three scenarios with detailed examples.

CHAPTER 11 SEQUENCES

The creation of sequences using the serial data type is an old method. GENERATED ALWAYS AS IDENTITY is a recent method used for portability across databases. Manual sequences are suitable for specific instances, particularly to support old code that references the next value.

11.4.1 Serial Data Type Sequence Creation and Grants

You can create a table with a serial data type column, which will be auto incremented by the database. Connect to PostgreSQL with the `psql` command as user1 to the user database and create the table with the serial data type.

Listing 11-2. Sequence Creation with Serial Data type

```
psql -U user1 -d demo
psql (12.5)
Type "help" for help.
demo=>
CREATE TABLE claim01
(
   claim_id     serial not null,
   id integer,
   name varchar(6),
  CONSTRAINT  claim01_pk PRIMARY KEY(claim_id));
```

When you create a sequence using the serial data type or any other sequence data type in PostgreSQL, the sequence is automatically named using the [table_name]_[column_name]_seq naming convention.

For example, if you create a table called `claim01` with a serial column called `claim_id`, the sequence that is automatically created to generate values for that column will be named `claim01_claim_id_seq`.

CHAPTER 11　SEQUENCES

PostgreSQL has a maximum identifier length of 63 characters, which includes the sequence name. So, if the combined length of the table and column names exceeds 63 characters, the sequence name will be truncated to fit within the maximum identifier length.

Type the command \ds to display the sequences in the databases. See Listing 11-3.

Listing 11-3. Sequence Metadata Command

```
postgres=> \ds
                      List of relations
 Schema |            Name             |   Type   | Owner
--------+-----------------------------+----------+-------
 public | claim01_claim_id_seq        | sequence | user1
```

You can select the last assigned values by selecting the last_value from [sequence_name].

The sequence definition is obtained from DDL of the table. See Listing 11-4.

Listing 11-4. Sequence Last Value Command

```
postgres=#SELECT last_value FROM claim01_claim_id_seq;
 last_value
------------
          1
```

Listing 11-5 shows the column created with the serial data type. Notice the nextval auto increment details. You will review the nextval function later in the section. The table definition is obtained from the meta command \d+ [tablename].

Listing 11-5. Serial data type column definition

```
ostgres=# \d+ claim01;

Table "public.claim01"
  Column  |         Type          | Collation | Nullable
|                    Default                            | Storage  |
Compression | Stats target | Description
----------+-----------------------+-----------+----------
+-------------------------------------------+-----------
+------------+--------------+-------------
 claim_id | integer               |           | not null
| nextval('claim01_claim_id_seq'::regclass) | plain
|            |              |
 id       | integer               |           |
|                                           | plain
|            |              |
 name     | character varying(6)  |           |
|                                           | extended
|            |              |
Indexes:
    "claim01_pk" PRIMARY KEY, btree (claim_id)
Access method: heap
```

The sequence association with a given table is derived from the function pg_get_serial_sequence, which takes the table name and column name as arguments. Listing 11-6 shows the command to obtain the associated sequence.

Listing 11-6. pg_get_serial_function Example

```
demo=> select pg_get_serial_sequence('.claim01', 'claim_id');
   pg_get_serial_sequence
------------------------------
 public.claim01_claim_id_seq
```

Grants on the Sequences

When you create a sequence in PostgreSQL, it is a separate database object that is owned by the user who created it. By default, only the owner of the sequence has permission to access it.

In order to allow other roles or users to use the sequence, you need to grant them permission explicitly. You grant the USAGE permission on the sequence, which allows the role or user to use the sequence to generate values, and the SELECT permission, which allows the role or user to retrieve the current value of the sequence. If the user does not have permission to query the last value from the sequence, the DBA has to grant usage permission on the sequence. In Listing 11-7, user dem0 received the sequence permission error while selecting from sequence pseudo column.

Listing 11-7. Sequence Permissions

```
psql -U devuser -d demo
psql (12.5)
Type "help" for help.
demo=> select * From claim01
demo-> ;
 claim_id_sk | id  | name
-------------+-----+------
           1 | 100 | seq1
(1 row)
demo=> SELECT last_value FROM claim01_claim_id_seq;
ERROR:  permission denied for sequence claim01_claim_id_seq
```

You can check the permission on the sequence object in the database with the \z meta command. The owner of the sequence is user1 with no grants on the sequence. See Listing 11-8.

CHAPTER 11   SEQUENCES

Listing 11-8. Sequence Grants View

```
demo=> \z claim01_claim_id_seq
                                          Access privileges
  Schema |         Name          |  Type   | Access privileges
 | Column privileges | Policies
--------+-----------------------+---------+--------------------
+-------------------+----------
 public | claim01 _claim_id_seq | sequence | user1=rwU/user1
   |                    |
```

Grants Permissions on the Sequence

Grants on the sequence to a role or user should be assigned from the owner of the table, which is the demo1 user in Listing 11-9.

Listing 11-9. Sequence Grants View

```
psql -U user1 -d demo
demo=> grant usage, select on sequence claim01_claim_id_seq to readonly;
GRANT
demo=> \z claim01_claim_id_seq
                                          Access privileges
  Schema |         Name          |  Type   | Access privileges
 | Column privileges | Policies
--------+-----------------------+---------+------------------
+-------------------+----------
 public | claim01_claim_id_seq | sequence | user1=rwU/
user1    +|                     |
         |                      |           | readonly=rU/user1
 |                    |
```

As you can see in the above grant, the grant of the sequence is in read-only mode for the role readonly, which is assigned to devuser. The Accel Control Language (ACLs) for r is for read and U is for usage, whereas w stands for write.

Grants on all sequences: The command to grant all the sequences is `GRANT USAGE, SELECT ON ALL SEQUENCES IN SCHEMA public to [user/role]`. Listing 11-10 shows an example of grants on sequences along with validation of the grants.

Listing 11-10. Sequence Grants View

```
postgres=# GRANT USAGE, SELECT ON ALL SEQUENCES IN SCHEMA
public to readonly.
GRANT
postgres=# \z big_table_id_seq
                                          Access privileges
  Schema |        Name       |   Type   |   Access privileges
| Column privileges | Policies
--------+-------------------+----------+----------------------
+-------------------+----------
 public | big_table_id_seq  | sequence | postgres=rwU/postgres+
|                   |
        |                   |          | testrole=U/postgres  +
|                   |
        |                   |          | testuser=rU/postgres
|                   |
(1 row)
postgres=# \z claim08_claim_id_seq
                                          Access privileges
  Schema |        Name       |   Type   |   Access privileges
| Column privileges | Policies
```

CHAPTER 11 SEQUENCES

```
--------+---------------------+----------+---------------------
+------------------+----------
 public | claim08_claim_id_seq | sequence | postgres=rwU/postgres+
|                  |
        |                     |          | testrole=U/postgres  +
|                  |
        |                     |          | testuser=rU/postgres
|                  |
(1 row)
```

You can execute the script in Listing 11-11 to grant select on all sequences in all databases in the rds environment. In Azure, you have to exclude azureadmin from grants. Save the SQL command in a variable and loop through each database grant sequences in the public schema. You can modify the script to include or exclude database names. The first step is to create a Linux SQL variable with a grant command on sequences. The next step is to obtain the database name from the pg_databases view, loop through all databases, and execute the grant command. Listing 11-11 is a shell script to grant sequences to a specified role. In the Azure environment, ignore azureadmin and rdsadmin in AWS as these roles are reserved by the cloud database service. Replace public with your schema.

Listing 11-11. Sequence Grants with a Dynamic Script

```
SQL="GRANT USAGE, SELECT ON ALL SEQUENCES IN SCHEMA public to testrole;"
db=$(psql  -t -c "SELECT DATNAME FROM PG_DATABASE WHERE datistemplate = false and datname not in ('rdsadmin');"
)
for database in  $db
do
psql -t    <<eof
\connect $database
```

```
$SQL
eof
done
```

Check the User Permissions

With the du command you can identify the roles granted to the user account. See Listing 11-12.

Listing 11-12. User Permissions

```
demo=> \du devuser
            List of roles
 Role name | Attributes | Member of
-----------+------------+------------
 devuser   |            | {readonly}
```

Validate Sequence Access

You can validate the access of sequences by selecting the sequence object name. See Listing 11-13.

Listing 11-13. Sequence last_value Function

```
psql -U devuser -d demo
psql (12.5)
Type "help" for help.
demo=> \conninfo
You are connected to database "demo" as user "devuser" via socket in "/var/run/postgresql" at port "5432".
demo=> create table claim04(claim_id   integer   GENERATED ALWAYS AS IDENTITY,
name varchar(6),
CONSTRAINT  claim04_pk PRIMARY KEY(claim_id));
demo=>     SELECT last_value FROM claim04_claim_id_seq;
```

```
 last_value
------------
          1
(1 row)
```

11.4.2 Sequence with Identity column definition

With the generated always identity column, the database will auto increment the sequence number. Listing 11-14 shows a script to generate an identity column example.

Listing 11-14. Sequence with Identity Column

```
CREATE TABLE claim02
(claim_id    integer    GENERATED ALWAYS AS IDENTITY,
id integer,
name varchar(6),
CONSTRAINT  claim02_pk PRIMARY KEY(claim_id));
```

After the creation of the table, you can check the sequence name with the format of [tablename]_[columnname]_[seq] as well as the definition. See Listing 11-15.

Listing 11-15. Sequence Definition

```
postgres=> \ds
                      List of relations
  Schema  |             Name              |   Type   | Owner
----------+-------------------------------+----------+-------
  public  | claim02_claim_id_seq          | sequence | user1
```

```
demo0=# \d+ claim02_claim_id_seq
                Sequence "public.claim02_claim_id_seq"
  Type   | Start | Minimum |  Maximum    | Increment | Cycles?
 | Cache
---------+-------+---------+-------------+-----------+---------
+-------
 integer |   1   |    1    |  2147483647 |     1     | no
 |    1
Sequence for identity column: public.claim02.claim_id
```

11.4.3 Manual Sequence Creation

The manual sequence creation process is for downward compatibility. With this method, the DBA must create sequences manually. Listing 11-16 shows the table creation script.

Listing 11-16. Manual Sequence Increment

```
CREATE TABLE claim05
(
   claim_id    integer not null,
   id integer,
   name varchar(6),
   CONSTRAINT  claim05_pk PRIMARY KEY(claim_id));
postgres=> create sequence claim05_claim_id_seq;
postgres=> SELECT last_value FROM claim05_claim_id_seq;
 last_value
------------
         1
postgres=# insert into claim05 values(nextval('claim05_claim_id_seq'),1018,'seqins');
INSERT 0 1
```

CHAPTER 11 SEQUENCES

11.4.4 Manual Sequence Increment

Although it's not a normal practice to create a gap in the sequence, there are cases and instances where you have to increment the sequence counter with a manual command. There are three commands to manipulate the sequences. They are setval, altering the sequence with the next value, and starting with the identity column. Listing 11-17 shows an example script to illustrate the creation of table with primary key, adding an identity column, and changing the sequence start value.

Listing 11-17. Sequence Increment Example

```
CREATE TABLE claim06
(
   claim_id    integer not null,
   id integer,
   name varchar(6),
  CONSTRAINT   claim06_pk PRIMARY KEY(claim_id));
ALTER TABLE claim06
       ALTER claim_id ADD GENERATED ALWAYS AS IDENTITY
         (START WITH 101);
postgres=> SELECT last_value FROM claim06_claim_id_seq;
 last_value
------------
        101

postgres=> \ds claim06_claim_id_seq
                     List of relations
  Schema  |            Name             |   Type   | Owner
----------+-----------------------------+----------+-------
  public  | claim06_claim_id_seq        | sequence | user1
```

CHAPTER 11 SEQUENCES

Incrementing the sequences with the function setval, which takes 3 arguments such as sequence name, increment number, TRUE/FALSE .

```
postgres=> SELECT setval('claim06_claim_id_seq',10, TRUE);
 setval
--------
     10
(1 row)
```

The current assigned sequence number is obtained by currval function, which takes sequence name as argument.

```
postgres=> SELECT currval('claim06_claim_id_seq');
 currval
---------
      10
(1 row)
```

The next value of the sequence is obtained by nextval function which takes the sequence name as argument.

```
postgres=> SELECT nextval('claim06_claim_id_seq');
 nextval
---------
      11
```

Sequence increment rules:

1. If the column is the identity column, then

    alter [table] alter [column] restart with [number]
    or
    SELECT setval('sequence_name)',[number], TRUE);

2. If the column values are derived from sequence datatype or manual sequence entry, then

    SELECT setval('sequence_name)',[number], TRUE);

393

11.4.5 Data Insertion with Sequences

For each type of sequence, there is a different process to insert the data. The database will auto-populate the data and there's no reference to the column defined as sequence. You have to use the override function to disable the database to auto-generate the incremental sequence numbers.

Data Insertion with the Serial Data Type

When you insert data into a table with a sequence, you can ignore the column that is defined with a serial data type. In our example, the claim04 table has three columns: claim_id, id, and name. The claim_id column is defined with the serial data type, which means that its value is automatically generated by the database.

So, when you insert data into the claim04 table, you can ignore the claim_id column and let the database generate the value for you.

Listing 11-18 shows the example of a sequence increment defined as the serial data type.

Listing 11-18. Serial Data Type Insert

```
demo0=# CREATE TABLE claim04(claim_id serial primary key,
id integer,
name char(30));
CREATE TABLE
demo0=# \d+ claim04;
```

CHAPTER 11 SEQUENCES

```
                                   Table "public.claim04"
  Column    |      Type      | Collation | Nullable |       Default
| Storage  | Compression |
 Stats target | Description
-----------+---------------+-----------+----------+-----------------
+----------+-------------+
--------------+-------------
 claim_id | integer       |           | not null | nextval('claim04_claim_id_seq'::regclass) | plain    |             |
              |
 id       | integer       |           |          |           | plain    |             |
              |
 name     | character(30) |           |          |           | extended |             |
              |
Indexes:
    "claim04_pkey" PRIMARY KEY, btree (claim_id)
Access method: heap
demo0=# INSERT INTO claim04(id,name) values(100,'Auto');
INSERT 0 1
demo0=# SELECT * FROM claim04;
 claim_id | id  |             name
----------+-----+--------------------------------
        1 | 100 | Auto
(1 row)
```

Data Insert with Identity Column

Like the sequence data type, there's no reference to the identity column when inserting data into the table. See Listing 11-19.

Listing 11-19. Sequence Insert with Identity Column

```
postgres=> INSERT INTO claim02(id,name) values(1016,'seqype');
INSERT 0 1
postgres=> SELECT * FROM claim02;
 claim_id_sk |  id  | name
-------------+------+--------
           1 | 1016 | seqype
```

Data Insert with a Manual Sequence

For downward compatibility, the nextval function is used to increment sequence from SQL. Listing 11-20 shows an example of manual sequence increment SQL.

Listing 11-20. Manual Sequence Insertion

```
postgres=> INSERT INTO claim05 values(nextval('claim05_claim_id_seq'),1018,'seqins');
INSERT 0 1
postgres=> SELECT * FROM claim05;
 claim_id_sk |  id  | name
-------------+------+--------
           1 | 1018 | seqins
(1 row)
```

As per the application requirements, you can increase the sequence count. Listing 11-21 shows the command to increment the sequence count.

CHAPTER 11 SEQUENCES

Listing 11-21. Alter sequence with New Value

```
postgres=> ALTER SEQUENCE claim05_claim_id_seq
INCREMENT BY 100;
postgres=> INSERT INTO claim05 values(nextval('claim05_claim_
id_seq'),1019,'se8ins');
After incrementing the sequence to 100, you can notice 101 as
the next value for the sequence.
postgres=> SELECT  * FROM claim05;
 claim_id_sk |  id  |  name
-------------+------+--------
           1 | 1018 | seqins
         101 | 1019 | se8ins
```

Associate Sequence with Database Column

You can associate a sequence with `table.column` to avoid the `nextval` expression for an auto-sequence increment. See Listing 11-22.

Listing 11-22. Sequence Association with Table Column

```
CREATE TABLE t1(id integer, sal integer);
CREATE  SEQUENCE seq1 OWNED BY t1.id;
ALTER TABLE t1 ALTER COLUMN id set default nextval('seq1');

INSERT INTO t1(sal) VALUES(100);
INSERT INTO t1(sal) VALUES(200);
SELECT * FROM t1;
id | sal
------------
 | 100
 | 200
```

CHAPTER 11 SEQUENCES

11.4.6 Data Copy Procedures and Sequence Maintenance

There are several scenarios for data copying between systems during recovery, large table management, and disaster recovery in which the sequence counter number is in confirmation with the business transaction. There are procedures for each scenario such as copy of data from a table with a primary key, a table without a primary key, partitioned and non-partitioned tables, sequence counter reset, and sequence counter increment or decrement depending on data quality and business requirements. When copying data between systems, it is important to ensure that the sequence counter numbers are in alignment with the business transactions.

I am going to cover all the scenarios depicted in Figure 11-3 with scripts and explanations. There are several scenarios when copying the data defined on a column with sequence columns. The possible scenarios are as follows:

1) Table with data and primary key defined

2) Table without data and primary key defined

3) Table without data

4) Partitioned table

5) Non-partitioned table

6) With and without primary key

11-3 illustrates all of the different sequence data copy methods. Depending on the requirements, you can use any of the methods. Examples are provided for all scenarios. Practice all scenarios in the lab to gain a comprehensive understanding of data copy procedures with sequences, as this task is often performed as a part of DBA database table maintenance.

CHAPTER 11   SEQUENCES

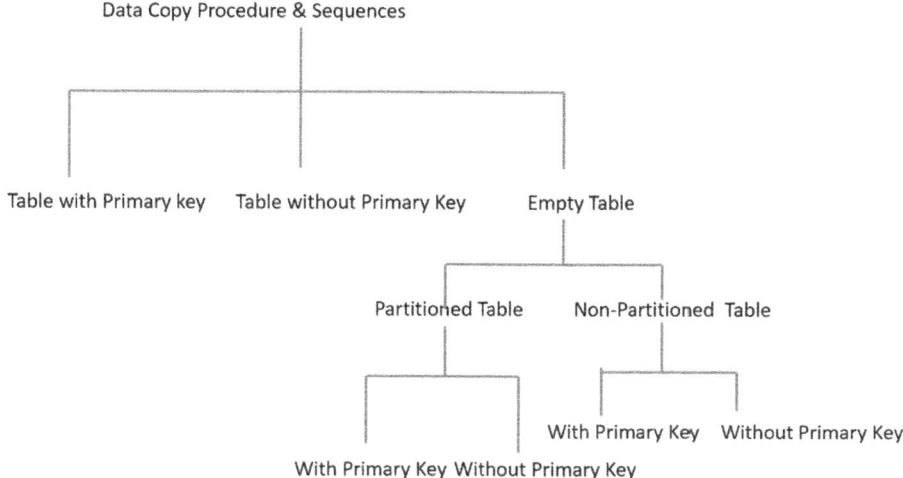

Figure 11-3. *Sequence copy methods*

For the data copy procedure with sequences with a primary key, there will be requests to create a new table from the existing table where sequences are defined as the primary key. The following is the procedure:

1. Rename the original table. Rename all constraints such as the primary key, referential integrity, and unique key. Make sure there are no locks or users accessing the original table.

2. Create a child table with the structure of the primary or source table.

3. Identify the last sequence number from the primary table.

4. Disable the identity or primary key constraint on the child table.

5. Copy the data.

CHAPTER 11 SEQUENCES

6. Rename the original sequence name for access from the child table or drop the identity column on child table.

7. Increment the sequence for the sequence data type and manual created sequences.

8. Add an identity column with a start of sequence with the original table count.

Listing 11-23 shows the script example to create the original table and data insertion and to rename the constraints.

Listing 11-23. Create and Rename Script

```
CREATE TABLE sales
(sales_id    integer    GENERATED ALWAYS AS IDENTITY,
productname varchar(20),
amount integer,
CONSTRAINT   sales_pk PRIMARY KEY(sales_id)
);
INSERT INTO sales(productname,amount) values('product1',101);
INSERT INTO sales(productname,amount) values('product10',1010);
postgres=# \ds
                List of relations
 Schema |          Name          |   Type   |  Owner
--------+------------------------+----------+----------
 public | sales_sales_id_seq | sequence | postgres
SELECT last_value FROM sales_sales_id_seq;
ALTER TABLE sales RENAME TO sales_org;
ALTER  TABLE sales_org REAME CONSTRAINT sales_pk to sales_pk_org;
 ALTER SEQUENCE sales_sales_id_seq REAME TO sales_sales_id_seq_org;
```

Listing 11-24 shows the copy table script.

Listing 11-24. Table Rename with Procedure

```
CREATE TABLE sales
(sales_id    integer not null,
productname varchar(20),
amount integer);
insert into sales select * From sales_org;
ALTER TABLE sales
       ALTER sales_id ADD GENERATED ALWAYS AS IDENTITY;
  ALTER TABLE sales
ADD  CONSTRAINT sales_pk PRIMARY KEY(sales_id);
SELECT setval('sales_sales_id_seq',max(sales_id)) from sales;
 INSERT INTO sales(productname,amount)
values('product11',1011);
SELECT  * FROM sales;
```

Override System Values

If there are gaps in the sequences, you can break the sequence increment or auto sequence creation for the column defined as identity values, with system override value command in the insert statement. Listing 11-25 shows an example of overriding the system value command.

Listing 11-25. Overriding Sequence Values

```
INSERT INTO  sales(sales_id,productname,amount)
OVERRIDING SYSTEM VALUE
values(1000,'product12',1009);
```

CHAPTER 11 SEQUENCES

Increment Sequence Count

After overriding and fixing the sequence gap issue, you can set the value of the sequence to the next counter based on the maximum identification of the columns. Listing 11-26 shows the user setval function.

Listing 11-26. Increment Sequence Values

```
SELECT setval('sales_sales_id_seq',max(sales_id)) from sales;
INSERT INTO  sales(productname,amount)
values('product12',1012);
```

After inserting the data, you can see the increment in the counter values. See Listing 11-27.

Listing 11-27. Increment Sequence Value

```
SELECT * FROM  sales;
 sales_id | productname | amount
----------+-------------+--------
       10 | product10   |   1010
     1000 | product12   |   1009
     1001 | product12   |   1012
```

11.4.7 Data Copy without a Primary Key

Listing 11-28 shows the script to copy data when the primary key is not defined.

> **Note** You can run the script as it is for understanding. The comment is --.

Listing 11-28. *Data Copy without a Primary Key*

```
DROP  table if exists claim08;
DROP table if exists claim08_org;
CREATE TABLE claim08
(claim_id   integer    GENERATED ALWAYS AS IDENTITY,
id integer,
name varchar(6)
);
INSERT INTO   claim08(id,name) values(100,'p1');
INSERT INTO   claim08(id,name) values(200,'p2');
 ALTER TABLE claim08 RENAME TO claim08_org;
CREATE TABLE claim08
(claim_id   integer    GENERATED ALWAYS AS IDENTITY,
id integer,
name varchar(6)
);
\echo review sequence definitions
 \ds claim08_claim_id_seq;
\ds claim08_claim_id_seq1;
 -- identify the sequences
 ---(1) override the system value defined on identity
column or (2)
 INSERT INTO claim08
OVERRIDING SYSTEM VALUE
SELECT * FROM claim08_org;

SELECT * FROM claim_org
claim_id | id | name
----------+-----+------
1 | 100 | p1
2 | 200 | p2
(2 rows)
```

CHAPTER 11 SEQUENCES

```
SELECT last_value FROM claim08_claim_id_seq;
last_value
------------
2
(1 row)
SELECT  last_value FROM claim08_claim_id_seq1;
last_value
------------
1
--Following is the example script.
    SELECT setval('claim08_claim_id_seq1', (SELECT max(claim_id) FROM claim08_org));
--After incrementing the sequence with original values, you can query the last value for the sequence claim08_claim_id_seq1.
 INSERT INTO  claim08(id, name) values(500,'p5');
SELECT  * FROM claim08;
-- Find the difference of values between old and new table with except operator
SELECT * FROM claim08
EXCEPT
SELECT * FROM claim08_org;
```

11.4.8 Sequences with an Empty Table for Data Copy

If you have a million rows in a table, due to performance issues if you are asked to create an empty table with original table structure only and no data, the process is to rename original table and create an empty table with the original table name and definition (which would create a sequence of the original table with a suffix of 1). For instance, if the original table sequence is called temp_id_seq, the empty table will create a sequence called emp_id_seq1. There are three methods to assign the last used sequence number to an empty table: rename the sequence of the original and empty tables, start the empty table sequence with the value of the original table, and use the setval function and pass the maximum value of the original table sequence. See Listing 11-29.

Listing 11-29. Data Copy Procedure with an Empty Table

```
Drop table if exists claim09;
Drop table if exists claim09_org;
CREATE TABLE claim09
(
   claim_id     serial,
   id serial ,
   name varchar(6));
 SELECT pg_get_serial_sequence('public.claim09', 'claim_id');
INSERT INTO claim09(name) values('p1');
INSERT INTO  claim09(name) values('p2');
SELECT last_value FROM public.claim09_claim_id_seq;
ALTER TABLE claim09 rename to claim09_org;
CREATE TABLE claim09
(
   claim_id     serial,
   id serial ,
   name varchar(6));
select pg_get_serial_sequence('public.claim09', 'claim_id');
SELECT last_value FROM public.claim09_claim_id_seq1;
demo=> SELECT setval('claim09_claim_id_seq1',max(claim_id))
from claim09_org;
 setval
--------
      1
```

Method 1: Rename sequences
```
alter sequence  claim09_claim_id_seq1 rename to  claim09_claim_id_seq1_old;
alter sequence claim09_claim_id_seq rename to claim09_claim_id_seq1;
=> SELECT last_value FROM claim09_claim_id_seq1;
 last_value
------------
          8
```
Method 2: Increase the value of claim09_claim_id_seq1
```
SELECT setval('claim09_claim_id_seq1',max(claim_id)) from claim09_org;
demo=> SELECT setval('claim09_claim_id_seq1',max(claim_id)) from claim09_org;
 setval
--------
      8
demo=> SELECT last_value FROM claim09_claim_id_seq1;
 last_value
------------
          8
```

11.4.9 Sequence Truncate Approach

If there is no requirement to preserve the original data, you can truncate the table and increment with old values. See Listing 11-30.

Listing 11-30. Data Copy with the Truncate Table Procedure

```
DROP TABLE IF EXISTS claim08;
CREATE TABLE claim08
(claim_id   integer   GENERATED ALWAYS AS IDENTITY,
id integer,
```

```
name varchar(6)
);
INSERT INTO claim08(id,name) values(100,'p1');
INSERT INTO claim08(id,name) values(200,'p2');
INSERT INTO claim08(id,name) values(300,'p3');
INSERT INTO claim08(id,name) values(400,'p4');
DROP TABLE IF EXISTS claim08_org;
ALTER TABLE claim08 RENAME TO claim08_org;
ALTER  SEQUENCE claim08_claim_id_seq1 RENAME TO claim08_claim_
id_seq_org;
CREATE TABLE claim08
(claim_id    integer    GENERATED ALWAYS AS IDENTITY,
id integer,
name varchar(6)
);
Check Sequence to Table Mapping
postgres=# SELECT  pg_get_serial_sequence('public.claim08',
'claim_id');
   pg_get_serial_sequence
-------------------------------
 public.claim08_claim_id_seq
SELECT start_value FROM pg_sequences
WHERE sequencename='claim08_claim_id_seq';
 start_value
-------------
           1
```
Option 1: Insert id with new start value.
```
INSERT INTO  claim08(id,name) values(500,'p5');
INSERT INTO  claim08(id,name) values(500,'p5');
```

CHAPTER 11   SEQUENCES

```
SELECT * FROM claim08;
 claim_id | id   | name
----------+------+------
        1 | 500  | p5
```
Option 2 : Retain   sequence original values
a) Query last value from catalog, increment the sequence
```
 SELECT last_value FROM pg_sequences
WHERE sequencename='claim08_claim_id_seq_org';
 last_value
------------
          4
```
Set the values to last values
```
SELECT setval('claim08_claim_id_seq',4,true);
 setval
--------
      4
INSERT INTO claim08(id,name) values(500,'p5');
SELECT * FROM claim08;
 claim_id | id   | name
----------+------+------
        5 | 500  | p5
(1 row)
```
Option 3 : Truncate table without rename, keep original sequence
```
DROP table claim08;
CREATE TABLE claim08
 (claim_id    integer    GENERATED ALWAYS AS IDENTITY,
id integer,
name varchar(6)
);
 INSERT INTO claim08(id,name) VALUES(100,'p1');
```

```
INSERT INTO   claim08(id,name) VALUES(200,'p2');
INSERT INTO   claim08(id,name) VALUES(300,'p3');
INSERT INTO   claim08(id,name) VALUES(400,'p4');
TRUNCATE TABLE
TRUNCATE TABLE claim08;
postgres=# INSERT INTO claim08(id,name) values(500,'p5');
postgres=# SELECT * FROM claim08;
 claim_id | id  | name
----------+-----+------
        5 | 500 | p5
(1 row)
```

11.4.10 Sequence Cache

To obtain the last value of the sequence for the next increment, the database must do a read on the sequence column for the maximum value; this can result in performance problems if the data blocks are not cached in the memory. To avoid disk access to obtain the last used sequence number, there is a provision by the database to cache the sequences in the memory, which is used by multiple user sessions in an incremental way. Each session will allocate and cache successive sequence values during one access to the sequence object and increase the sequence object's last_value accordingly. See Listing 11-31.

Listing 11-31. Sequence Cache

```
demo=> ALTER SEQUENCE claim09_id_seq1 CACHE 20;
ALTER SEQUENCE
```

CHAPTER 11   SEQUENCES

11.5 Keywords

\ds, last_value, setval, OVERRIDING SYSTEM VALUES, nextval, create sequence, currval, alter sequence increment, alter sequence cache, serial data type, and GENERATED ALWAYS AS IDENTITY.

11.6 Summary of Learning

Sequences are commonly used for generating auto-incrementing keys, such as primary keys in database tables. There are three methods for generating sequences in PostgreSQL: using the serial data type, creating an IDENTITY column, or manually creating a sequence using the CREATE SEQUENCE command.

To retrieve the current or next value in a sequence, you can use the currval and nextval functions, respectively. The setval function can be used to set the starting value of a sequence. You can override the default sequence number generated by the system by specifying a different value. When you clone a table with a sequence, the sequence name is automatically renamed to follow the [table_name]_[column_name]_seq convention. To use a sequence, you need to have the USAGE privilege on the sequence. Typically, this privilege is granted to the owner of the table or to specific roles that need to access the sequence

11.7 Practice Chapter 11

1. Create a table with a table serial data type column as the primary key. Grant access on the sequence to the user account.

2. Create a partition table, copy data from a non-partitioned table, and add a sequence to the partitioned table.

3. Create a table with the Identity column as the primary key and auto increment the identity column by 10000 numbers.

4. Create a sequence and associate sequence with a database column.

11.8 Questions Chapter 11

1. What is the query for checking the sequence associated with a specific table or partition in a database?

2. Can you explain the command to retrieve information about the grants on a sequence granted to the user?

3. How many methods are available to increment a sequence in a database, and are there any specific commands or functions for this purpose?

4. What is the procedure used to override the default system values associated with a sequence in a database?

5. Can you provide a detailed explanation of how to create a sequence on an empty table in a database, including the necessary syntax and considerations?

6. What steps should be followed to create a sequence on a table with existing values in a database, and how can you ensure proper sequencing of the data?

7. Are there any specific restrictions or limitations when creating a sequence on a table with existing values in terms of conflicts or duplicate values?

8. How do you verify the association of a sequence with a specific table or partition in a database, and are there any system views or catalog tables that provide this information?

References

1. www.postgresql.org/docs/current/datatype-numeric.html

    Additional references:
    www.postgresql.org/docs/current/functions-sequence.html
    www.postgresql.org/docs/current/sql-createsequence.html

CHAPTER 12

Postgres Cluster Upgrade

12.1 Abstract

The choice of upgrade or update methods depends on factors such as the available downtime window and disk space. An update is a minor version change, whereas an upgrade is from one major version to another. In cloud-managed databases services, an update is done at periodic intervals. Some upgrade methods, like in-place upgrades, may require a significant downtime period when the database is inaccessible. After installing a new version of the software, the preferred method is to upgrade on the same host, reusing the already provisioned storage. Other methods, such as logical replication or streaming replication, can minimize downtime by allowing for a phased switchover to the latest version. Version compatibility is essential to ensure a successful upgrade. Examples of upgrades from version 14 and 15 to 16 are provided. In the AWS AMI, you can practice on all version upgrades from 12 to 16. It is necessary to review the release notes and documentation provided by the PostgreSQL cloud vendor to understand any specific requirements or considerations when upgrading between versions. Compatibility issues can arise due to changes in database schemas, data types, or query behavior.

CHAPTER 12   POSTGRES CLUSTER UPGRADE

12.2 Objectives of Learning

- Database upgrade overview
- Upgrade methods
- In-place upgrade
- Logical replication
- Backup and restore method
- Script overview

12.3 Introduction

PostgreSQL supports direct upgrades from version 9.2 onward to the latest version, which is currently version 16, with the pg_upgrade utility. The upgrade is done as a part of DBaaS by the cloud providers. Alternative upgrade methods are pg_dumpall in AWS/EC2 and logical replication. It is a good practice to thoroughly evaluate the upgrade process in a non-production environment before performing it on a production database. An upgrade is an offline activity, which will require downtime during maintenance process. See Figure 12-1.

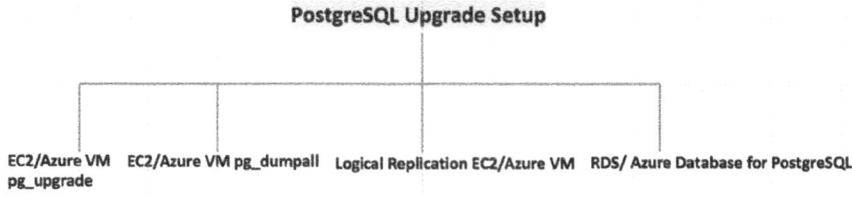

Figure 12-1. Postgres upgrade setup

There are five methods for upgrading:

1. Minor upgrade by cloud providers
2. `pg_dumpall` on AWS/EC2 and Azure VM with more downtime
3. `pg_upgrade` with less downtime
4. Logical replication with no downtime
5. AWS RDS or Azure Database for PostgreSQL

The `pg_upgrade` utility is specifically designed to facilitate upgrades from PostgreSQL 9.2.X and later versions to the latest major release used to upgrade the PostgreSQL cluster in AWS EC2/Azure VM environment. It ensures a smooth transition by preserving your existing data and configurations while upgrading the underlying PostgreSQL binaries. The `pg_upgrade` (formerly called `pg_migrator`) allows data stored in PostgreSQL data files to be upgraded to a later PostgreSQL major version [1]. The `pg_upgrade` name changed from `pg_migrator` started with version 9.0.

12.4 pg_upgrade Method

A common scenario is to upgrade on the same machine as the production database. It will be upgraded to the desired version utilizing the already provisioned storage.

You can upgrade from version 9.x to version 16 using the `pg_upgrade` program. Two clusters will run side by side to perform the upgrade to the new version.

Preparation:

1. Install a new version of the software.

2. Create a new instance of the PostgreSQL cluster and do not create any user databases.

3. Copy `pg_hba.conf` and `postgres.conf` from the old cluster to the new cluster and stop both PostgreSQL clusters. Before proceeding with the upgrade, stop comment crontab on Linux hosts.

This utility requires four arguments: the old binary home, the new binary home, the new data directory, and the old data directory. Amazon RDS and the Azure Postgres data service uses this utility to upgrade the PostgreSQL cluster. With AWS EC2 and Azure VM, you have to call the `pg_upgrade` utility from the command line, whereas in a managed database service Amazon or Azure will pass these arguments in the background.

There are three options available when using `pg_upgrade`:

1. **Upgrade by the copy method**: This method copies the data between the old and new data directories. This method requires additional storage equal to the size of the old instance.

2. **Upgrade by the clone method**: The clone method is like the copy method, which creates hard links to the existing data files in the old data directory.

3. **Upgrade with the link method**: In this method, data is not copied; instead, symbolic links are created between the old and new data directories. This method is particularly useful for large databases exceeding 1TB in size, as it eliminates the need to move or duplicate data.

CHAPTER 12   POSTGRES CLUSTER UPGRADE

> **Note** AWS RDS and Azure SQL Database Service use the link method.

The first mandatory step is performing a full backup of the old database before proceeding with the upgrade. RDS will take a backup before proceeding with upgrade, so no action is required by the DBA in a managed cloud environment. This backup serves as insurance to roll back to old versions.

> **Note** In AWS RDS, you can't roll back to deprecated version 10.x and below.

You can successfully upgrade your PostgreSQL database from version 9.x to version 15 or version 16 or future versions using pg_upgrade. After a successful upgrade, you have to analyze all databases for optimizers to take advantage of the new release.

You can check the available options with the pg_upgrade program help option. The first step in upgrade process is to check the upgrade feasibility with the -c or –check argument of pg_upgrade. See Listing 12-1.

Listing 12-1. pg_upgrade Options

```
Usage:
  pg_upgrade [OPTION]...

Options:
  -b, --old-bindir=BINDIR      old cluster executable directory
  -B, --new-bindir=BINDIR      new cluster executable directory
```

```
-c, --check                   clusters only, don't change any data
-d, --old-datadir=DATADIR     old cluster data directory
-D, --new-datadir=DATADIR     new cluster data directory
-j, --jobs=NUM                number of simultaneous processes or
                              threads to use
-k, --link                    instead of copying files to
                              new cluster
-o, --old-options=OPTIONS     old cluster options to pass to
                              the server
```

There are three methods of upgrading with the pg_upgrade program: clone, copy and link. The copy and clone methods require additional disk space to the size of the original database, as the data is being copied or cloned to a new disk location. The link method requires storage only for PostgreSQL cluster files, which is around 50GB, and there will be a link to old data. Figure 12-2 exhibits the details.

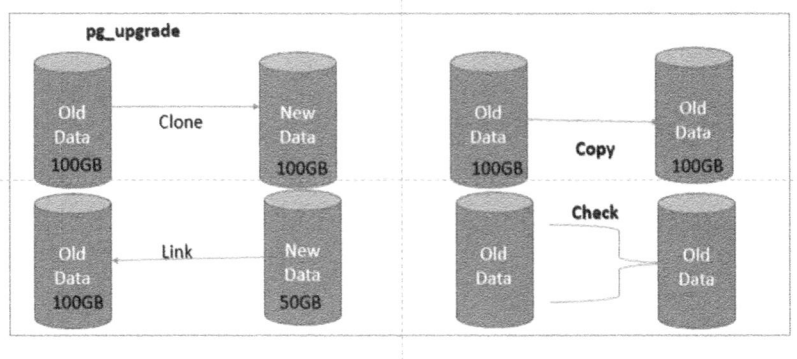

Figure 12-2. pg_upgrade Method

CHAPTER 12 POSTGRES CLUSTER UPGRADE

Note You set up the environment with the version you are working to upgrade the Postgres cluster.

pg_upgrade -d oldCluster/data -D newCluster/data -b oldCluster/bin -B newCluster/bin [link method]

```
$ export PGDATAOLD=oldCluster/data
$ export PGDATANEW=newCluster/data
$ export PGBINOLD=oldCluster/bin
$ export PGBINNEW=newCluster/bin
After setting the above variables proceed with pg_upgarde
with upgrade method
```

Note The pg_upgrade method works on all operating systems where you have to provide old and new cluster details.

$ pg_upgrade

Listing 12-2 is a sample shell script that performs the upgrade between PostgreSQL versions. You have to provide old instance and new instance values to the shell script.

For testing and training with different methods of upgrading, use the script in Listing 12-2. It works in the Linux environment. You can practice upgrading with the PostgreSQL option in the AMI software. You can customize this script to your operating system on Linux.

Listing 12-2. pg_upgrade

```
clear
echo "Enter old Postgres Binary directory : Tip /usr/pgsql-13/bin"
read PGBINOLD
export PGBINOLD
echo "Enter new Postgres Binary directory : Tip /usr/pgsql-16/bin"
read PGBINNEW
export PGBINNEW
echo " Enter New Data Directory : Tip /appl/postgres/data16"
read PGDATANEW
export PGDATANEW
echo "Enter Old Data Directory : Tip  /appl/postgres/data13"
read PGDATAOLD
export PGDATAOLD
  pg_ctl stop -D   $PGDATANEW
  pg_ctl stop -D   $PGDATAOLD
echo  " Upgrade method : Tip clone, link, copy and check"
read method
if [ "$method" == "link" ]
 then
     $PGBINNEW/pg_upgrade --link
 elif [ "$method" == "clone" ]
  then
     $PGBINNEW/pg_upgrade --clone ]
 elif [ "$method" == "copy" ]
  then
      $PGBINNEW/pg_upgrade
 elif  [ "$method" == "check" ]
  then
     $PGBINNEW/pg_upgrade --check
fi
```

CHAPTER 12   POSTGRES CLUSTER UPGRADE

You can simulate the upgrade with the AMI tool. See Figure 12-3.

```
─┤ Postgres Advanced Administration Menu ├─

 Running PostgreSQL instances:
postgres    1423     1  0 00:20 ?         00:00:00 /usr/pgsql-13/bin/postgres -D /var/lib/pgsql/
ta
postgres    1930     1  0 00:36 ?         00:00:00 /usr/pgsql-16/bin/postgres -D /postgres/pgdat
postgres    1968  1960  0 00:36 pts/1     00:00:00 grep pgsql
 Enter old bin directory
/usr/pgsql-13/bin
 Enter new Postgres Binary directory :
/usr/pgsql-16/bin
 Enter New Data Directory :
/postgres/pgdata16
 Enter Old Data Directory :
/var/lib/pgsql/13/data
/run/postgresql:5432 - accepting connections
 New cluster is running: Stopping
waiting for server to shut down.... done
server stopped
/run/postgresql:5432 - no response
 Upgrade method : Tip clone, link, copy and check
check
Performing Consistency Checks on Old Live Server
------------------------------------------------
Checking cluster versions                                    ok
```

Figure 12-3. pg_upgrade check

In the above example, you are checking the compatibility of an upgrade between version 13 and 16.

You can find an upgrade video at https://us02web.zoom.us/rec/share/R3jH9HqRkaEP_-dDSp5uWfsgOAeO8vTU6jlZppHOmQz36YBFoLyUk8CmwTrDeB7P.DsxsPs9XOMkyC-Cr.

Another method of upgrade is by the postgresql-setup --upgrade command, which is available on the Red Hat distribution. It automates the upgrade process. It's essentially a wrapper for pg_upgrade.

12.5 pg_dumpall Upgrade Method

If the size of the database is small, you can proceed with the pg_dumpall utility. The full backup of the database is performed by the pg_dumpall utility and the restore is performed by the psql utility. Note that pg_ dumpall is not supported by Amazon RDS or Azure Data Service because the backup of user logins or passwords are not supported. You may receive an error "failed: ERROR: permission denied for table pg_authid." The main benefit of pg_dumpall in EC2/Azure VM is that you can keep both old and new versions for additional performance testing to establish a baseline performance metrics for cluster upgrades. Upon successful validation of the new cluster, you can delete the old cluster data as well as binaries. Figure 12-4 is a diagram of the pg_dumpall process.

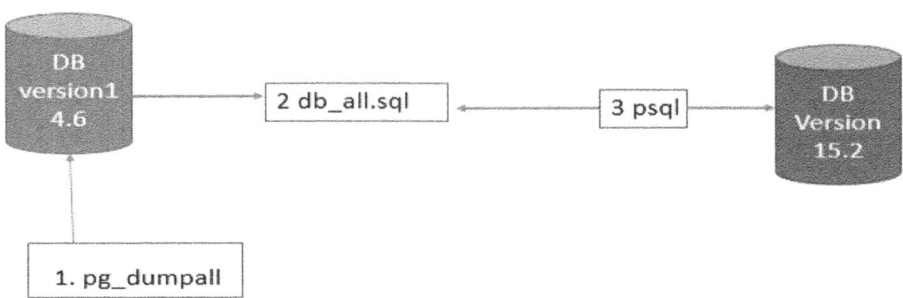

Figure 12-4. pg_dump upgrade method

Note As you saw in the earlier section on the cloud environment, pg_dumpall does copy database logins--not a recommended approach for upgrading a Postgres cluster if you do not have the list of login passwords before the upgrade. The latest release of the database will use `scram-sha-256`, overriding the md5 authentication method. The md5 passwords are used for downward compatibility, meaning the PostgreSQL new cluster honors old passwords and all new passwords are created with scram-sha-256 security encryption.

Some of the jdbc versions do not work with scram-sha-256 encryption after a database upgrade. Check with the jdbc vendor-specific instructions to fix this issue.

The following is the script and output of the backup and recovery option for an upgrade.

12.5.1 pg_dumpall Procedure

The program pg_dumpall creates a file to restore all databases. Use --quote-all-identifiers when a PostgreSQL major version is different from pg_dumpall's, or when the output is intended to be loaded into a server of a different major version (www.postgresql.org/docs/16/app-pg-dumpall.html). Listing 12-3 shows a list of pg_dumpall help commands. You reviewed pg_dumpall in Chapter 8.

Listing 12-3. pg_dumpall

```
pg_dumpall --help

General options:
  -f, --file=FILENAME          output file name
  -v, --verbose                mode
  -V, --version                output version information,
                               then exit
  --lock-wait-timeout=TIMEOUT  fail after waiting TIMEOUT for a
                               table lock
  -?, --help                   show this help, then exit
Options controlling the output content:
Connection options:
  -d, --dbname=CONNSTR         connect using connection string
```

```
-h, --host=HOSTNAME        database server host or socket
                           directory
-l, --database=DBNAME      alternative default database
-p, --port=PORT            database server port number
-U, --username=NAME        connect as specified database user
-w, --no-password          never prompt for password
-W, --password             force password prompt (should happen
                           automatically)
--role=ROLENAME            do SET ROLE before dump
```

12.5.2 Backup a Database with the pg_dumpall Backup Utility

It is recommended to use the same version of pg_dumpall across environments. However, for data migration, you can back up from a higher version where the new binaries are installed, but you cannot back up from lower versions to higher versions

```
pg_dumpall -f all_db.sql
```

12.5.3 Restore a database with pg_dumpall

Set the environment to the latest version, 16, or a version of your choice. Make sure that no user databases are present in the Postgres cluster. Run the command in Listing 12-4 to verify for user databases.

Listing 12-4. PostgreSQL Databases

```
psql -c " select datname from pg_databases where datname not in ('postgres','template0','template1');"
```

12.5.4 Restore a Database with psql

You have to use the psql utility to restore the backup taken from the pg_dumpall utility. Listing 12-5 shows the restore of all databases from the backup.

Listing 12-5. pgdump_all Restore

```
psql < all_db.sql
After restoring, validate the user databases, by ignoring
system databases.
psql -c "select datname from pg_databases where datname not in
('postgres','template0','template1');"
```

12.6 Postgres Upgrade on RDS

The managed database RDS offers an easy and simple approach to upgrading the PostgreSQL cluster, which uses the pg_upgrade utility in the background provided by Postgres cluster software with the link method. To safely upgrade your DB instances, Amazon RDS uses the pg_upgrade utility (https://docs.aws.amazon.com/AmazonRDS/latest/UserGuide/USER_UpgradeDBInstance.PostgreSQL.html).

Note You must drop the view pg_stat_activity_allusers from all databases and recreate after upgrade. Use the following script to identify the view across all databases in RDS. Create a shell script and run the following details in the shell script. The SQL variable stores the SQL statement. The script loops through the user database to check for the view. See Listing 12-6.

Listing 12-6. RDS Check for pg_stat_activity_allusers

```
SQL="select table_name from information_schema.views where table_name='pg_stat_activity_allusers';"
db=$(psql  -t  'host=myrdsdev.amazonaws.com  user=postadmin dbname=postgres password=MyStrong#pwd' <<eof
SELECT DATNAME FROM PG_DATABASE WHERE datistemplate = false;
eof)
for database in  $db
do
psql 'host=myrdsdev.amazonaws.com  user=postadmin dbname=postgres password=MyStrong#pwd' <<eof
\connect $database
$SQL
eof
done
```

Preparation: AWS creates a new parameter file which is called an option file; it is compatible with the version you choose to upgrade to. Before upgrading to a new release, capture the values of parameters with the command `Select name, setting from pg_settings` to preserve the original parameter values before upgrade. After upgrading, run the above command to validate the preservation of original values.

Check the available valid target versions via two options: `aws rds describe` versions or check from the RDS console.

12.6.1 aws describe db Engine

With the `aws rds describe-db-engine-versions` command, you can obtain the available versions for upgrade. See Listing 12-7.

Listing 12-7. Upgrade Version Check

```
$aws rds describe-db-engine-versions \
 --engine postgres \
 --engine-version 15.5 \
 --query "DBEngineVersions[*].ValidUpgradeTarget[*].
{EngineVersion:EngineVersion}" --output text
15.6
15.7
16.1
16.2
16.3
```

Note The current database engine is 15.5, which can be upgraded to either 15.6, 15.7, 16.1, 16.2, or 16.3 versions.

12.6.2 RDS Upgrade Check

You can check the available versions to upgrade from the AWS console. Check the available versions with Figure 12-5. Choose RDS > Databases > choose the instance > modify instance to identify available versions for the upgrade.

CHAPTER 12 POSTGRES CLUSTER UPGRADE

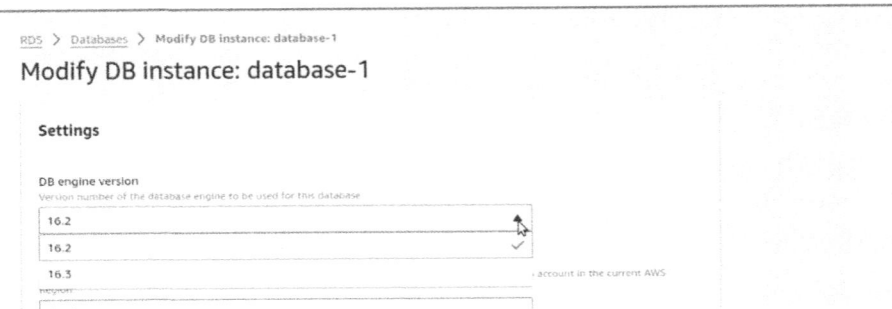

Figure 12-5. Upgrade version check

12.6.3 Upgrade Compatibility Matrix

Verify database compatibility matrix with this URL: https://docs.aws.amazon.com/AmazonRDS/latest/UserGuide/USER_UpgradeDBInstance.PostgreSQL.html#USER_UpgradeDBInstance.PostgreSQL.MajorVersion.

12.6.4 RDS Upgrade

Disconnect the user sessions before proceeding with the upgrade. AWS will take a snapshot backup before proceeding with upgrade operations.

After assessing the required database version to upgrade, follow the steps for upgrading the PostgreSQL cluster:

RDS ➤ Databases ➤ Choose Instance ➤ Modify Instance ➤ Choose Engine Version ➤ Modify DB Instance. See Figure 12-6.

CHAPTER 12   POSTGRES CLUSTER UPGRADE

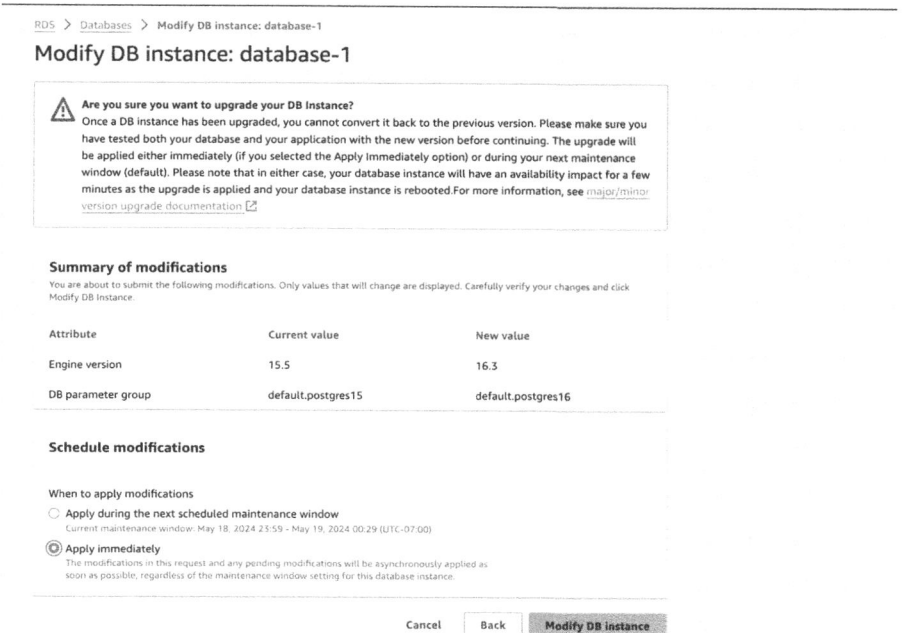

Figure 12-6. Postgres upgrade from the RDS console

After choosing to apply immediately, notice the status of modifying the instance. See Figure 12-7.

DB identifier	Status	Role	Engine
database-1	Modifying	Instance	PostgreSQL

Figure 12-7. Validation of upgraded version

12.7 Upgrade an AWS Instance by AWS CLI

The first step before upgrading is to create the parameter group for the version you are upgrading. See Listing 12-8.

Listing 12-8. Create an RDS Parameter Group

```
$ aws rds create-db-parameter-group --db-parameter-group-name
dbpara16 --db-parameter-group-family postgres15 --description
"RDS parameter changes"
{
    "DBParameterGroup": {
        "DBParameterGroupName": "dbpara16",
        "DBParameterGroupFamily": "postgres16",
        "Description": "RDS  parameter changes",
        "DBParameterGroupArn": "arn:aws:rds:us-east-2:123456678
        901:pg:dbpara16"
    }
}
```

Note After creating the new parameter group, change the values similar to the old parameters and assign them to the new RDS instance.

12.7.1 Upgrade RDS with the Command Line

After the user sessions are disconnected, take a snapshot and proceed with the upgrade with the command in Listing 12-9.

Listing 12-9. Modify the Database Instance for an Upgrade

```
 aws rds modify-db-instance --db-instance-identifier database-1
--engine-version 16.3 --allow-major-version-upgrade --apply-
immediately --db-parameter-group-name dbpara16
{
```

```
"DBInstance": {
"DBInstanceIdentifier": "database-1",
:::: Lines ignored
```

From AWS console, you can view the progress of the upgrade. See Figure 12-8.

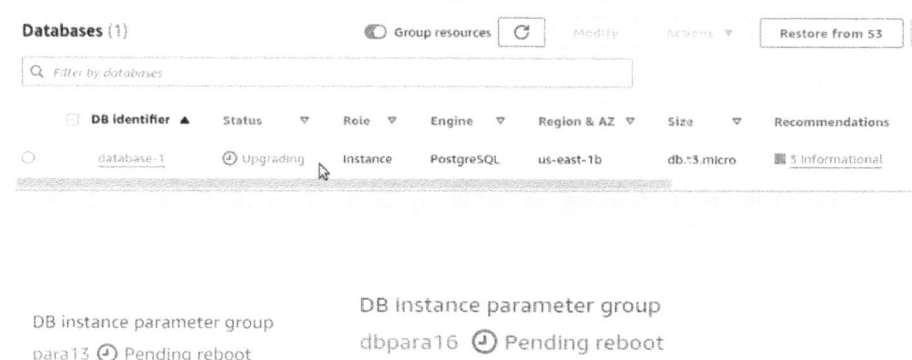

Figure 12-8. *Upgraded instance details*

As a final step, a reboot is performed after the upgrade.

12.7.2 RDS Upgrade Log

The upgrade logs are visible during the course of upgrade from RDS. All cloud vendors follow the `pg_upgrade` program for upgrade of PostgreSQL.

The upgrade details are visible in the two files: internal and server logs. See Figure 12-9 and Listing 12-10.

Name

○ error/pg_upgrade_internal.log.1694894680569

○ error/pg_upgrade_server.log.1694894680569

Figure 12-9. *RDS upgrade log*

CHAPTER 12 POSTGRES CLUSTER UPGRADE

Listing 12-10. RDS Upgrade Log

```
Performing Consistency Checks
-----------------------------
linking "/rdsdbdata/db_old/base/16406/2613" to "/rdsdbdata/db/
base/16406/2613"
  /rdsdbdata/db_old/base/16406/2683
linking "/rdsdbdata/db_old/base/16406/2683" to "/rdsdbdata/db/
base/16406/2683"
"/rdsdbbin/postgres/bin/pg_ctl" -w -D "/rdsdbdata/db" -o
"--config_file=/rdsdbdata/config_new/postgresql.conf" -m smart
stop >> "/rdsdbdata/db/pg_upgrade_output.d/20230916T200416.887/
log/pg_upgrade_server.log" 2>&1
Upgrade Complete
----------------
```

12.7.3 RDS Logs View

RDS logs are generated on an hourly basis. The command in Listing 12-11 is to view the log file from the command line. Change the year, month, day, and hour in the log file name as per your requirements.

Listing 12-11. Postgres Error Log Command

```
aws rds download-db-log-file-portion \
    --db-instance-identifier demoqa \
    --log-file-name error/postgresql.log.2023-06-15-02 \
    --output text > tail.txt
cat tail.txt
```

12.7.4 Analyze Databases

After database upgrade, use the script in Listing 12-12 to analyze all databases in the cluster. If you have hundreds of databases, to save time, split the database and run analyze in parallel. The analyze command is stored in an SQL variable, which is executed against all user databases.

Listing 12-12. Analyze Databases After an Upgrade

```
SQL="ANALYZE VERBOSE;"
db=$(psql  'host= host1 user=user1 dbname=postgres
password=Strong#pwd' -t -c "SELECT datname FROM pg_database
WHERE datistemplate = false;")
for database in $db; do
echo $database
 psql 'host=host1 user=user1 dbname=postgres
password=Strong#pwd'<<eof
\c    $database
$SQL
eof
done
```

12.8 Logical Upgrade Method

A logical upgrade with replication is most suitable when upgrading to a larger database, which is an online activity. Logical replication is a method of data replication in PostgreSQL that operates at the logical level, by replaying all DML commands on a standby host, which will allow you to replicate data between different PostgreSQL clusters. The method used is the publisher and subscribe model. The primary cluster is responsible for the publication of changes, whereas the standby cluster(s) are responsible for subscription of the messages from the primary server. To preserve the

CHAPTER 12 POSTGRES CLUSTER UPGRADE

logs on the primary cluster, a database parameter slot is provisioned for this requirement. The replication slot configuration preserves all required data on the primary site until the subscriber receives these changes.

Replication slot: A replication slot is a mechanism provided by PostgreSQL to keep track of the replication progress. It ensures that the publisher retains the necessary data until all subscribed subscribers have received the changes.

Data Manipulation Language (DML) replication: Logical replication primarily focuses on replicating DML operations such as INSERT, UPDATE, and DELETE statements. These DML changes made on the publisher are captured, transmitted, and applied on the subscriber databases to keep them synchronized.

Figure 12-10 is the high-level diagram of the upgrade process between different versions of the Postgres cluster: Create replication user on source/target ➤ Create publication on source database ➤ Create subscriber on target. The logical replication is performed with the table-by-table data copy process.

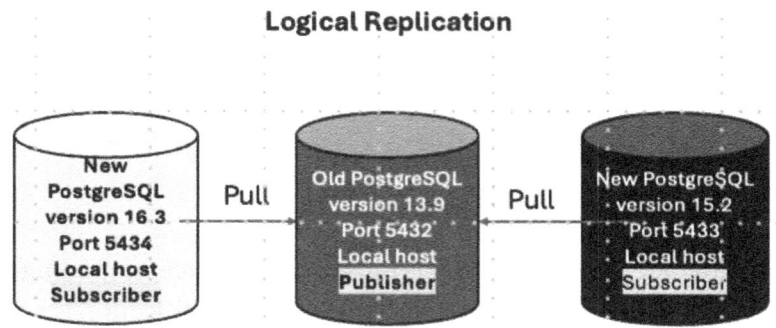

Figure 12-10. Logical replication

12.8.1 Logical Replication Procedure

Listing 12-13 show the logical replication procedure on the same host. The old cluster is version 14.6 running on the default 5432 port, whereas the new cluster version is 15.2 running on port 5433. Create publication on the source old database cluster. Create subscriptions on the target new database cluster. The source port 5432 # change as per your port number. Try post 5433. Only a super user can execute these commands.

Listing 12-13. Replication Configuration Setup

```
Replication configuration:
From psql run below commands on Target and Source server
ALTER SYSTEM SET wal_level = logical;
ALTER SYSTEM SET max_replication_slots = 2;
ALTER SYSTEM SET max_wal_senders = 2;
ALTER SYSTEM SET max_worker_processes = 8;
Add below entry in the pg_hba.conf
host     replication    replicator    172.168.1.10/32   scram-sha-256   # publisher host pg_hba.conf about subscriber host name or IP
host     replication    replicator    172.178.1.10/32   scram-sha-256   # subscriber host pg_hna.conf with publishers host name or IP
create user  replicator with replication  encrypted password 'StrongP4RT';  # on publisher host
```

12.8.2 Replication Configuration

After connecting to the primary host, create publication for all tables, which prepares the database to allow sending data to remote hosts. In Listing 12-14, you are creating a table on the primary remote database and inserting one row at the primary site. With \conninfo validate the primary database port. If you connect to the local host, notice the connection details via socket.

Listing 12-14. Replication Configuration and Validation

Primary Database: Publication
```
--Create Publication
postgres=# \conninfo
You are connected to database "postgres" as user "postgres" via socket in "/var/run/postgresql" at port "5432".
postgres=# CREATE PUBLICATION pub15 FOR ALL TABLES;
CREATE PUBLICATION
CREATE TABLE t (col1 int, col2 int, col3 text NOT NULL DEFAULT 'foo');
postgres=# select * From t;
 col1 | col2 | col3
------+------+------
(0 rows)
postgres=# insert into t values(100,100,'test');
INSERT 0 1
Primary Database: Subscription on same host
-- connect to the new instance onport 5433 on same host
--Create Subscription
You are connected to database "postgres" as user "postgres" via socket in "/var/run/postgresql" at port "5433".
postgres=# CREATE TABLE t (col1 int, col2 int, col3 text NOT NULL DEFAULT 'foo');
CREATE TABLE
postgres=# CREATE SUBSCRIPTION sub15 CONNECTION 'user=postgres host=localhost port=5432 dbname=postgres' PUBLICATION pub15;
NOTICE:  created replication slot "sub15" on publisher
```

```
CREATE SUBSCRIPTION
postgres=# select * from t;
 col1 | col2 | col3
------+------+------
  100 |  100 | test
(1 row)
postgres=# show port;
 port
------
 5433
(1 row)
postgres=# \conninfo
You are connected to database "postgres" as user "postgres" via
socket in "/var/run/postgresql" at port "5433".
```

> **Note** For performance issues, increase the replication slots on the source database.

12.8.3 Replication Slot

The replication slot is created by the function pg_create_logical_replicatio_slot. See Listing 12-15.

Listing 12-15. Replication Slot Configuration

```
SELECT pg_create_logical_replication_slot(
    'my_replication_slot3',
    'pgoutput'
);
```

```
postgres=# postgres(# postgres(# postgres(# pg_create_logical_
replication_slot
-------------------------------------
 (my_replication_slot3,0/80001E8)

(1 row)
SELECT * FROM pg_stat_replication;
SELECT * FROM pg_replication_slots
```

12.8.4 Postgres Log

If the replication is working, you will notice the below message in the error log with reference to WAL from the subscribers log. Use the command SELECT current_setting('log_directory') || '/' || current_setting('log_filename') AS log_path; to identify the log location. The data directory is identified by the command SHOW data_directory;. See Listing 12-16.

Listing 12-16. Replication Details in the Error Log

```
DETAIL:  Streaming transactions committing after 1/22C51F20,
reading WAL from 1/22C51CC8.
 [1313] LOG:  logical replication table synchronization worker
for subscription "sub_pub_pgbench_accounts", table "pgbench_
accounts" has started
 LOG:  logical replication table synchronization worker for
subscription "sub_pub_pgbench_accounts", table "pgbench_
accounts" has finished
```

12.8.5 Remote Database Subscription Details

Connect to psql as a super user and make sure you set all the preparatory steps before setting the logical replication, as illustrated in section 12.5.1 You can subscribe to all tables or individual tables based on your requirements.

Listing 12-17 is an example to view the logs from the primary publisher after the setting up of replication.

Listing 12-17. Replication Configuration

```
Primary
demo=# CREATE TABLE employees (
  id SERIAL PRIMARY KEY,
  name VARCHAR(100),
  age INTEGER,
  department VARCHAR(100)
);demo(# demo(# demo(# demo(# demo(#
CREATE TABLE
demo=# CREATE PUBLICATION employee_publication FOR TABLE
employees;
CREATE PUBLICATION
     demo=# INSERT INTO employees (name, age, department)
VALUES ('John Doe', 30, 'Sales');demo-#
INSERT 0 1
     SELECT pg_create_logical_replication_slot(
    'my_replication_slot4',
    'pgoutput'
);
--Standby Target
--- on the standby provide the primary hostname, primary port,
replication user name and ------password
```

```
    CREATE SUBSCRIPTION employee_subscription
  CONNECTION 'dbname=demo host=remotedb01 port=5439 user=rep password=Monitor'
  PUBLICATION employee_publication;
--Target
CREATE SUBSCRIPTION demo1_subscription
  CONNECTION 'dbname=demo host=remotedb01 port=5439 user=rep password=Monitor'
  PUBLICATION  demo1;
--Target Log
2023-06-08 15:37:32.428 PDT [7094] LOG:  logical replication apply worker for subscription "demo1_subscription" has started
  CONNECTION 'dbname=demo host=remotedb01 port=5439 user=rep password=Monitor'
  PUBLICATION  pub_pgbench_accounts;
pgbench_accounts
```

12.9 Azure Postgres Database Upgrade

You can upgrade Postgres database from the Azure console or from the Azure command line. The upgrade is not an online activity, which requires downtime.

12.9.1 Database Upgrade from Azure Command Line

The command line option is easy and it takes three arguments: the resource group name, the database server name, and the Postgres version. You can check the available options to upgrade with the command `$ az postgres flexible-server upgrade -h`. See Listing 12-18.

Listing 12-18. Azure Flexible Help

```
$ az postgres flexible-server upgrade  -h
Command
    az postgres flexible-server upgrade  -h
Command
    az postgres flexible-server upgrade : Upgrade the major
version of a flexible server.
Arguments
    --version -v [Required] : Server major version.  Allowed
values: 12, 13, 14, 15, 16.
```

12.9.2 Upgrade Command

The upgrade command takes only three arguments: the resource group name, the server name, and the version. Listing 12-19 shows the command to upgrade from v13 to v14.

Listing 12-19. Azure Upgrade Flex Server

```
$ az postgres flexible-server upgrade -g demo -n
palosdemo -v 14
Updating major version in server palosdemo is irreversible. The
action you're about to take can't be undone. Going further will
initiate major version upgrade to the selected version on this
server. (y/n): y
{
  "administratorLogin": "postdev",
  "administratorLoginPassword": null,
  "authConfig": {
    "activeDirectoryAuth": "Disabled",
    "passwordAuth": "Enabled",
    "tenantId": null
```

```
    },
    ::::::::::::::::
    "type": "Microsoft.DBforPostgreSQL/flexibleServers",
    "version": "14"
}
```

12.9.3 psql Connection

After upgrading from Azure, access the database with the psql program and validate the upgraded version:

```
$ psql -h palosdemo.postgres.database.azure.com -U postdev -d postgres
Password for user postdev:
psql (14.8)
SSL connection (protocol: TLSv1.3, cipher: TLS_AES_256_GCM_SHA384, bits: 256, compression: off)
Type "help" for help.

postgres=> SELECT version();
                                                            version
---------------------------------------------------------------------------------------------------------
 PostgreSQL 14.8 on x86_64-pc-linux-gnu, compiled by gcc (Ubuntu 7.5.0-3ubuntu1~18.04) 7.5.0, 64-bit
(1 row)

postgres=>
```

CHAPTER 12 POSTGRES CLUSTER UPGRADE

12.10 Upgrade Extensions

Postgres upgrade software does not upgrade extensions in RDS and EC2/Azure VM environments. You must manually upgrade the configure extensions in the Postgres cluster databases. The extension procedure is provided by RDS at `https://docs.aws.amazon.com/AmazonRDS/latest/PostgreSQLReleaseNotes/postgresql-extensions.html`. For EC2/Azure VM, you can use the alter extension command provided the by Postgres documentation at `https://docs.aws.amazon.com/AmazonRDS/latest/PostgreSQLReleaseNotes/postgresql-extensions.html`.

Some extensions such as `pg_stat_statement` can be dropped and reinstalled, whereas other extensions such as `uuid` can't be dropped because several tables will be using this extension, which requires the `alter extension` command. Depending on the nature of extensions, you have to make a decision whether to drop, create, or alter extensions.

12.11 Keywords

pg_upgrade, RDS upgrade, AWS CLI upgrade, Azure CLI upgrade, pg_dumpall, logical replication upgrade, Azure database upgrade, and upgrade extension.

12.12 Summary of Learning

You reviewed all the upgrade methods, procedures, and commands. You now know how to upgrade of PostgreSQL from different procedures: AWS Console, AWS CLI, Postgres logical replication, Azure CLI, and `pg_dumpall`.

12.13 Practice Chapter 12

1. Upgrade a Postgres cluster by the `pg_upgrade` method with the link and clone procedure on EC2/Azure VM.

2. Upgrade a Postgres cluster by RDS and the Azure DS console as well as from command line options.

3. Configure logical replication between different versions of a Postgres cluster.

4. Upgrade the `pg_stat_statements` extension on RDS.

12.14 Questions Chapter 12

1. What are the recommended best practices for performing a PostgreSQL database upgrade? Can you explain the specific steps and precautions that should be followed to ensure a smooth and successful upgrade?

2. Can you explain the process of rolling back a PostgreSQL database upgrade? What are the steps and considerations involved in reverting to the previous version of the database?

3. How can you migrate data from an older version of PostgreSQL to a newer version during the upgrade process? Are there any specific tools or techniques that can facilitate the data migration?

4. Are there any known compatibility issues or considerations when upgrading from PostgreSQL version 14 to 15?

5. Can you outline the steps involved in configuring and enabling SSL encryption for secure communication in PostgreSQL? Are there any specific settings or certificates that need to be configured?

6. What are the recommended strategies for testing and validating a PostgreSQL database upgrade before performing it in a production environment.

7. How do you validate the data integrity after an upgrade in PostgreSQL? What are the techniques or tools that can be used to ensure data integrity?

8. What user acceptance methods are available after a PostgreSQL database upgrade? How can users or stakeholders validate the upgraded system to ensure it meets their requirements and functions correctly?

References

1. www.postgresql.org/docs/current/pgupgrade.html
2. www.postgresql.org/docs/current/logical-replication.html

CHAPTER 13

PostgreSQL Recovery

13.1 Abstract

PostgreSQL software provides several methods and procedures for database recovery. The choice of recovery method should adhere to the RPO (Recovery Point Objective) and RTO (Recovery Time Objective) of the organization. When planning for recovery, it's important to consider the potential impact on downtime for critical business applications. Some recovery methods, such as point-in-time recovery, can restore the database to the state of the last committed transaction up to a required time or to a specified System Change Number (SCN). It is necessary to review the recovery policies regularly and implement Disaster Recovery (DR) drills periodically to validate the backup media's validity for recovery. Furthermore, a DBA's core competency is judged by their ability to recover databases based on business Service Level Agreements (SLAs).

13.2 Learning Objectives

- Recovery methods
- Point-in-time recovery
- Recovery from `pg_dump` and `dump_all`

CHAPTER 13 POSTGRESQL RECOVERY

- Recovery scripts
- Recovery from AWS Relational Database Service for PostgreSQL and Azure Database for PostgreSQL RDS and Azure Snapshot

13.3 Postgres Cluster Recovery

Recovery is the process of recovering database data from the backup files. Due to a hardware crash or data corruption or application deletes by mistakes, the database will be unusable for user transactions. There are three recovery methods to bring the database to a consistent state: restore (this process involves generating the current database files from backup files), crash recovery or instance recovery (this is used when there is no impact to database files, to restore the database to a consistent state after a crash) and recovery of the database upon restore (this involves restoring the database from a full database backup and applying all write-ahead logs (WAL) for point-in-time recovery, which are generated after full backup).

The WAL files record all the committed transactions to the database, which are applied to roll forward changes to the database after restoring the full backup of the database. For instance, if the full database restore is completed at 22:00 hours, subsequent changes to the database are applied by WAL files. If WAL files are not available, you can restore the database with backup files.

The metadata about the backup is stored in files created at the time of backup. There are no database catalog tables to examine the backup details for each backup. As you saw in the backup chapter, you have to examine the contents of the `00000.*` archive files with the `pg_waldump` command and the `backup_manifest` files created in the `backup` directory. There is no specific command required to restore the Postgres Server from backup, except for the start of the cluster. You have to modify recovery restore parameters in the postgres.conf file based on the requirements, whether to restore to the time of backup or to apply redo logs for the specific point in time or until the application of available logs. The Postgres cluster recovery process involves restoring all databases from the backup files created by the pg_basebackup utility. After pg_basebackup completes the full backup, the WAL files that are subsequently created will be applied to achieve a point-in-time recovery. This recovery process is divided into three stages:

1. This extends until the end of the pg_basebackup for full recovery. During this stage, the database will be in read-only mode to allow for the application of WAL backup files.

2. Complete recovery up to the application of log files.

3. Promote to read-write mode.

13.3.1 Restore Procedure for Postgres Versions 11 and Below

There is no specific command to restore the Postgres cluster from the file created by the pg_basebackup program. The database start command, such as pg_ctl start -D $PGDATA, will proceed with the recovery based on the recovery time depicted in the recovery.conf file.

Listing 13-1 shows the restore procedure in step-by-step order.

Listing 13-1. Recover Database Procedure for PostgreSQL version 11 and below

```
1 ) Abort the database
rm -rf $PGDATA
2) Restore backup file from disk backup
cp base.tar $PGDATA. #copy backup data from tape media
```

```
cd $PGDATA
tar -xvf base.tar
 rm -rf pg_wal     # Remove the old WAL directory. The restore will create the pg_wal.
pg_wal.tar $PGDATA
```
3) Add restore commands in recovery.conf in $PGDATA
```
restore_command = 'cp /appl/postgres/dev/archive/%f %p'
recovery_target_time = '2023-02-25 21:50:00'    # Adjust the recovery time
```

4) Start the database
```
$ pg_ctl start -D $PGDATA
waiting for server to start....2023-02-25 22:11:26.208 UTC [3377] LOG:  redirecting log
2023-02-25 22:11:26.334 UTC [3379] LOG:  checkpoint starting: end-of-recovery immediate wait   database system is ready to accept connections
```

13.3.2 Point-in-Time Recovery

Figure 13-1. Point-in-time recovery procedures

Beginning with PostgreSQL version 12, the recovery configuration file is merged with postresql.conf and you have to create a recovery signal file in the PostgreSQL data directory for the point-in-time recovery requirement. If the signal file is present in the data directory, PostgreSQL treats the database as in recovery mode. Upon completion of the recovery, the signal file is removed by the PostgreSQL database. As you saw in section 4.4.5, recovery methods such as recovery until transaction and log sequence are available from version 12 onwards.

Preparation: Before proceeding with the PostgreSQL cluster restore task, you have to request the systems or storage admin to restore backup files from tape or disk media. You reviewed the pg_basebackup in Chapter 8, which creates three files: base.tar, which consist of a backup of the PGDATA directory, pg_wal.tar, which consist of WAL files, and the backpup_manifest file. Extract the base.tar file in the desired PGDATA directory. Listing 13-2 shows the steps to recover the PostgreSQL cluster.

Listing 13-2. Recover Database Procedure for PostgreSQL Version 12 and Above

1) Abort the database
```
rm -rf $PGDATA
```
2) Restore backup file from disk backup
```
cp base.tar $PGDATA. #copy backup data from tape media
cd $PGDATA
tar -xvf base.tar
 rm -rf pg_wal    # Remove the old WAL directory. The restore will create the pg_wal.
cp pg_wal.tar $PGDATA. #You require a WAL file in pg_wal directory for recovery
cd pg_wal; tar -xvf pg_wal.tar. # Change to  pg_wal directory and extract file
```
3) Add restore commands in postgres.conf   in $PGDATA
```
restore_command = 'cp /appl/postgres/dev/archive/%f %p'
# Adjust the recovery path
recovery_target_time = '2024-06-25 21:50:00'    # Adjust the recovery time
```
4) Create recovery.singal file

5) Remove backup_label file

6) Start the database

[postgres@node1172 pg_wal]$ pg_ctl start -D $PGDATA
checkpoint starting: end-of-recovery immediate wait   database system is ready to accept connections

13.3.3 Backup Metadata File

The backup metadata file records the logfile sequence numbers as well as the start and end time of the backup along with base data directory details with checksums. For a quick summary, you can view the backup_manifest file and for detailed summary, which includes logfile sequence numbers, start and end times, base data directory details with checksums, and additional summary information.

Listing 13-3 is the metadata file, where you can identify start of the WAL file location, the end of the WAL file location, and the checkpoint location (with a checkpoint, all changes are committed to disk).

The backup manifest file has the full details of backup, which includes all WAL files and checksums. All the backup file names, checksum, and WAL ranges with sequences are recorded in the backup manifest file. The tail of the backup_manifest file is Listing 13-3.

Listing 13-3. Backup Manifest File

```
{ "PostgreSQL-Backup-Manifest-Version": 1,
"Files": [
{ "Path": "backup_label", "Size": 225, "Last-Modified":
"2024-06-20 20:42:37 GMT", "Checksum-Algorithm": "CRC32C",
"Checksum": "69e09e76" },
:::::::Lines Omitted
```

```
"WAL-Ranges": [
{ "Timeline": 1, "Start-LSN": "0/4000028", "End-LSN":
"0/4000100" }
],
"Manifest-Checksum": "d59b6209bf80baaea6f361972131c8bfd047860dc
80764e0f92ed06ac1cb3a0d"
```

The restore files consist of all files created during the backup process including base.tar and pg_wal.tar, along with WAL archived files and the backup_manifest file. After completion of the pg_basebackup, a *.backup file is created, which records the backup start time and end time along with begin and end log sequence numbers. In the following exhibit, you can restore a database between log file numbers 000*.5 and 000*.23. See Figure 13-2.

```
000000010000000000000001             00000001000000000000000D        000000010000000000000001B
000000010000000000000002             00000001000000000000000E        000000010000000000000001C
000000010000000000000003             00000001000000000000000F        000000010000000000000001D
000000010000000000000004             000000010000000000000010        000000010000000000000001E
000000010000000000000004.00000028.backup  000000010000000000000011  000000010000000000000001F
000000010000000000000005             000000010000000000000012        000000010000000000000020
000000010000000000000006             000000010000000000000013        000000010000000000000021
000000010000000000000006.00000028.backup  000000010000000000000014  000000010000000000000022
000000010000000000000007             000000010000000000000015        000000010000000000000023
000000010000000000000008             000000010000000000000016        backup_manifest
000000010000000000000009             000000010000000000000017        base.tar
00000001000000000000000A             000000010000000000000018        pg_wal.tar
00000001000000000000000B             000000010000000000000019        qabk.tar.gz
00000001000000000000000C             00000001000000000000001A
```

Figure 13-2. Restore files

With the pg_waldump command, you can examine the details about the transaction ID and log sequence number along with location of the data for the table. A transaction ID is noticed in one or several WAL files. The log sequence numbers are increased or incremented in the WAL files. See Listing 13-4.

Listing 13-4. WAL Dump

```
$pg_waldump 000000010000000000000001 | tail -2
rmgr: Heap2      len (rec/tot):   1215/   1215, tx:        746,
lsn: 0/01FFF770, prev 0/01FFF730, desc: MULTI_INSERT+INIT ntuples:
11, flags: 0x22, blkref #0: rel 1663/16388/16401 blk
1049
rmgr: Heap2      len (rec/tot):     59/     59,
tx:        746, lsn: 0/01FFFC30, prev 0/01FFF770, desc:
VISIBLE snapshotConflictHorizon: 0, flags: 0x03, blkref #0: rel
1663/16388/16401 fork vm blk 0, blkref #1: rel 1663/16388/16401 blk
1049
$

$pg_waldump 000000010000000000000023 | tail -2
rmgr: Heap       len (rec/tot):    152/    152, tx:        761,
lsn: 0/23FFFEA8, prev 0/23FFFE10, desc: INSERT off: 15, flags:
0x00, blkref #0: rel 1663/16388/16411 blk 52127
rmgr: Heap       len (rec/tot):    152/    152, tx:        761,
lsn: 0/23FFFF40, prev 0/23FFFEA8, desc: INSERT off: 16, flags:
0x00, blkref #0: rel 1663/16388/16411 blk 52127
$
```

13.3.4 Recovery Target Methods

To support recovery to the available committed transaction, several recovery methods are provisioned by PostgreSQL. See Figure 13-3.

CHAPTER 13 POSTGRESQL RECOVERY

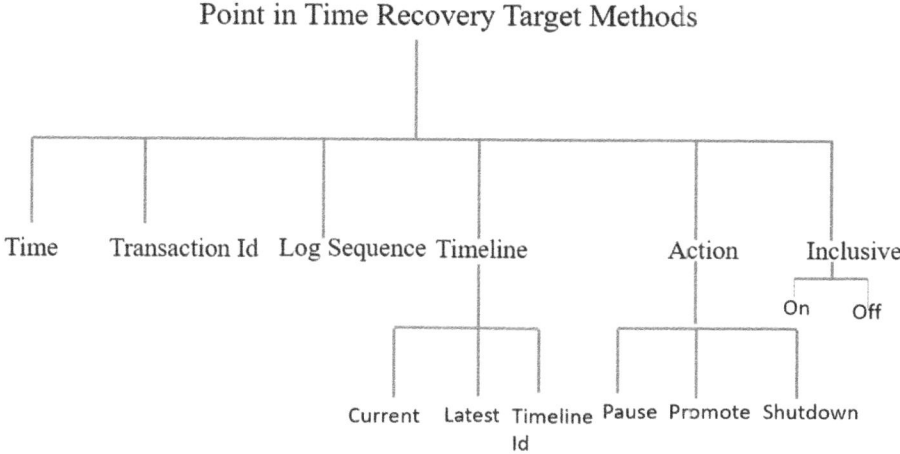

Figure 13-3. *Point-in-time recovery methods*

The recovery methods are time-based recovery, transaction ID-based recovery, log sequence-based recovery, recovery timeline-based recovery, and recovery target timeline. In all recovery methods, there are two stages in the recovery: to reach a consistent recovery state in a read-only mode after the recovery of database until the end of a full backup and to apply available WAL files and promote into read-write mode with command "`select pg_wal_replay_resume();`".

You have to define the required recovery method in the `postgresql.conf` file. Figure 13-4 is a screen image from `postgresql.conf` showing where you can identify the different values for recovery methods. With the `pg_waldump` command, notice the details about log sequence numbers and transaction ID details. The screen image exhibits the log file and transaction ID details from the start and end of the backup.

CHAPTER 13 POSTGRESQL RECOVERY

PostgreSQL Backup Metadata

Full Backup Begin	Full Backup End	WAL Backup Start	WAL Backup Start
2023-10-07 07:05:00	2023-10-07 07:05:03	2023-10-07 07:05:04	2023-10-07 07:06:15
Logfile: 0E	Logfile: 0F	Logfile: 10	Logfile: 2B
Log Sequence:	**Log Sequence**	**Log Sequence**	**Log Sequence**
0/E000028	0/F000060	0/10000028	0/2BFFFCB8
Transaction ID	**Transaction ID**	**Transaction ID**	**Transaction ID**
113064	113065	113065	113068

Transaction ID 113064	**Transaction ID 113065**	**Transaction ID 113068**
Files:	File: 11	Files: 20/21/22/23/24/25/26/27/28
000000010000000000000000E	**Transaction ID 113066**	29/2A/2B
000000010000000000000000F	Files: 12/13/14/15	
0000000100000000000000010	**Transaction ID 113067**	
	Files: 16/17/18/19	

Figure 13-4. *Log dump summary*

As can see, you can restore database until log sequences 0/E000028, 0/F00060,0/10000028, and 0/2BFFFCB8 transaction IDs 113064, 113065, 113066, 113067, and 113068 and until recovery time. Although the standard practice is to recover until the last committed transaction from the latest backup of WAL file, there are instances when you have to restore the cluster to a specific point in time in, situations like a user dropping a table or a user inserting incorrect or inaccurate data in the table. In Figure 13-5, notice the full backup completion time at 23:00 hours with log file backup until 00:15 hours. The database can be recovered until 00:15 hours. You can recover until transaction ID 100700 or the log sequence number.

CHAPTER 13   POSTGRESQL RECOVERY

Postgres Cluster Restore TimeLine

23:00	23:15	23:30	23:45	00:00	00:15
Full Backup End LSN 0100 Transaction id 100000(max)	Log Backup LSN101 Transaction id 1000100	Log Backup LSN102-103 Transaction 1000200	Log Backup LSN104-1200 Transaction id 1000600	Log Backup LSN1201-1230 Transaction id 1000700	Log Backup LSN1231-1340 Transaction id 1000700
Read Only Restore to 23:00	Restore to LSN101 or Transaction id 1000100				Restore to LSN1340 or Transaction id 1000700
Full Recovery Recovery + Log					

Figure 13-5. PostgreSQL cluster recovery timeline

If you want to recover until the end of the full backup, you can recover until the 23 hour when the database will be placed in read-only mode upon completion of the recovery, which you can open in read-write mode if no further logs need to be applied to the base backup. It is a standard practice to apply all available logs for the recovery.

13.3.5 Recovery Parameters

You can identify all recovery parameters in the postgresql.conf file. You have to uncomment and edit the values for the recovery parameter based on your requirements. The mandatory parameter is restore_command where you specify archived the WAL file location. See Figure 13-6 .

```
restore_command = 'cp /postdata16/%f "%p"'        # command to use to restore an archived WAL file
                                                   # placeholders: %p = path of file to restore
#recovery_end_command = ''                         # command to execute at completion of recovery
# Set these only when performing a targeted recovery.
#recovery_target = ''                              # 'immediate' to end recovery as soon as a
#recovery_target_name = ''                         # the named restore point to which recovery will proceed
#recovery_target_time = ''                         # the time stamp up to which recovery will proceed
#recovery_target_xid = '759'                       # the transaction ID up to which recovery will proceed
recovery_target_lsn = '0/15FFE8D8'                 # the WAL LSN up to which recovery will proceed
#recovery_target_inclusive = on                    # Specifies whether to stop:
                                                   # just after the specified recovery target (on)
                                                   # just before the recovery target (off)
#recovery_target_timeline = 'latest'               # 'current', 'latest', or timeline ID
#recovery_target_action = 'pause'                  # 'pause', 'promote', 'shutdown'
#hot_standby = on                                  # "off" disallows queries during recovery
#recovery_min_apply_delay = 0                      # minimum delay for applying changes during recovery
```

Figure 13-6. Recovery parameters

13.3.6 Recovery Until Backup Time

If you do not specify any recovery target parameters except the restore command, the database is recovered until the end of the backup time, as specified in the `backup_manifest` file. In Listing 13-5, notice the Log Sequence Number recovered to bring the database to consistent state.

Add `restore_command = 'cp /[archive log location]/%f "%p"'` in `postgresql.conf` and start the cluster to recover the database till full backup time.

Listing 13-5. Restore Command Parameters

Restore Command	Description
%f	Name of the desired WAL file
%p	Path name relative to current working directory
%%	Embed or add a description

In Listing 13-6, the database is recovered until the end of the log sequence number as noticed in the `backup_manifest` file. This scenario assumes no WAL logs to apply to the database.

Listing 13-6. Database Recovery

```
Backup_manifest WAL Ranges
WAL-Ranges": [
{ "Timeline": 1, "Start-LSN": "0/4000028", "End-LSN":
"0/4000100" }
],
Recovery Log Sequence
2024-06-21 17:32:26.501 UTC [2650] LOG:  redo starts at
0/4000028
2024-06-21 17:32:26.503 UTC [2650] LOG:  completed backup
recovery with redo LSN 0/4000028 and end LSN 0/4000100
2024-06-21 17:32:26.504 UTC [2650] LOG:  consistent recovery
state reached at 0/4000100
2024-06-21 17:32:26.504 UTC [2650] LOG:  redo done at 0/4000100
system usage: CPU: user: 0.00 s, system: 0.00 s, elapse
```

13.3.7 Log Sequence Recovery

The log sequence recovery procedure consists of identifying the log sequence numbers by issuing a pg_waldump command, which takes the WAL file as the input argument. With the head or tail command, you can identify the transaction id, object storage location block id, and recover LSN. With the setting of recovery_target_lsn = '0/14FFFE60' in the postgresql.conf, the database is recovered until this log LSN. See Figure 13-7.

CHAPTER 13 POSTGRESQL RECOVERY

```
2024-06-21 00:45:56.381 UTC [22040] LOG:  starting point-in-time recovery to WAL location (LSN) "0/14FFFE60"
2024-06-21 00:45:56.388 UTC [22040] LOG:  ignoring file "tablespace_map" because no file "backup_label" exist
2024-06-21 00:45:56.388 UTC [22040] DETAIL:  File "tablespace_map" was renamed to "tablespace_map.old".
2024-06-21 00:45:56.388 UTC [22040] LOG:  database system was not properly shut down; automatic recovery in p
rogress
2024-06-21 00:45:56.391 UTC [22040] LOG:  redo starts at 0/4000028
2024-06-21 00:45:56.394 UTC [22040] LOG:  consistent recovery state reached at 0/5000000
2024-06-21 00:45:56.394 UTC [22036] LOG:  database system is ready to accept read-only connections
2024-06-21 00:45:56.416 UTC [22040] LOG:  restored log file "000000010000000000000005" from archive
2024-06-21 00:45:56.482 UTC [22040] LOG:  restored log file "000000010000000000000006" from archive
2024-06-21 00:45:56.545 UTC [22040] LOG:  restored log file "000000010000000000000007" from archive
2024-06-21 00:45:56.721 UTC [22040] LOG:  restored log file "000000010000000000000008" from archive
2024-06-21 00:45:56.893 UTC [22040] LOG:  restored log file "000000010000000000000009" from archive
2024-06-21 00:45:57.064 UTC [22040] LOG:  restored log file "00000001000000000000000A" from archive
2024-06-21 00:45:57.573 UTC [22040] LOG:  restored log file "00000001000000000000000B" from archive
2024-06-21 00:45:58.053 UTC [22040] LOG:  restored log file "00000001000000000000000C" from archive
2024-06-21 00:45:58.647 UTC [22040] LOG:  restored log file "00000001000000000000000D" from archive
2024-06-21 00:45:58.907 UTC [22040] LOG:  restored log file "00000001000000000000000E" from archive
2024-06-21 00:45:59.497 UTC [22040] LOG:  restored log file "00000001000000000000000F" from archive
2024-06-21 00:46:00.104 UTC [22040] LOG:  restored log file "000000010000000000000010" from archive
2024-06-21 00:46:00.691 UTC [22040] LOG:  restored log file "000000010000000000000011" from archive
2024-06-21 00:46:01.552 UTC [22040] LOG:  restored log file "000000010000000000000012" from archive
2024-06-21 00:46:02.158 UTC [22040] LOG:  restored log file "000000010000000000000013" from archive
2024-06-21 00:46:02.787 UTC [22040] LOG:  restored log file "000000010000000000000014" from archive
2024-06-21 00:46:03.402 UTC [22040] LOG:  restored log file "000000010000000000000015" from archive
2024-06-21 00:46:04.230 UTC [22040] LOG:  recovery stopping after WAL location (LSN) "0/14FFFE60"
```

Figure 13-7. Log sequence recovery parameter definition

Log Sequence Recovery Log Details

The above image of the database log displays the details of the point-in-time recovery of the log sequence until 0/14FFE60 as defined in the `postgresql.conf` file. The first phase of recovery is to restore the database until the backup time, which puts the database in read-only mode. The next phase is to apply the available WAL files based on the recovery requirement. After applying the last WAL file required for restore, you have to open the database with the `pg_wal_replay_resume()` function. You must be a superuser or have execute privilege on `pg_wal_replay_resume()` to open the database. In the above database error log file, the database was restored until the 0/14FFFE60 log sequence.

13.3.8 Transaction ID Recovery

A PostgreSQL cluster does not record the transaction IDs in the database tables. You identified transaction ID details in Figure 13-5. In the following example, the `recovery_target_xid` parameter in the `postgresql.conf`

CHAPTER 13 POSTGRESQL RECOVERY

specifies the transaction ID up to which recovery will proceed. In the following example, the database is recovered until transaction id 759 using this parameter's value.

Transaction ID Recovery Log

Figure 13-8 is the screen image of the transaction ID recovery output from the PostgreSQL cluster log until transaction 759.

```
2024-06-21 01:45:36.022 UTC [2663] LOG:  starting point-in-time recovery to XID 759
2024-06-21 01:45:36.025 UTC [2663] LOG:  ignoring file "tablespace_map" because no file "backup_label" exists
2024-06-21 01:45:36.025 UTC [2663] DETAIL:  File "tablespace_map" was renamed to "tablespace_map.old".
2024-06-21 01:45:36.025 UTC [2663] LOG:  database system was not properly shut down; automatic recovery in progress
2024-06-21 01:45:36.030 UTC [2663] LOG:  redo starts at 0/4000028
2024-06-21 01:45:36.032 UTC [2663] LOG:  consistent recovery state reached at 0/5000000
2024-06-21 01:45:36.032 UTC [2659] LOG:  database system is ready to accept read-only connections
2024-06-21 01:45:36.056 UTC [2663] LOG:  restored log file "000000010000000000000005" from archive
2024-06-21 01:45:36.119 UTC [2663] LOG:  restored log file "000000010000000000000006" from archive
2024-06-21 01:45:36.188 UTC [2663] LOG:  restored log file "000000010000000000000007" from archive
2024-06-21 01:45:36.357 UTC [2663] LOG:  restored log file "000000010000000000000008" from archive
2024-06-21 01:45:36.548 UTC [2663] LOG:  restored log file "000000010000000000000009" from archive
2024-06-21 01:45:36.715 UTC [2663] LOG:  restored log file "00000001000000000000000A" from archive
2024-06-21 01:45:37.167 UTC [2663] LOG:  restored log file "00000001000000000000000B" from archive
2024-06-21 01:45:37.436 UTC [2663] LOG:  restored log file "00000001000000000000000C" from archive
2024-06-21 01:45:38.089 UTC [2663] LOG:  restored log file "00000001000000000000000D" from archive
2024-06-21 01:45:38.743 UTC [2663] LOG:  restored log file "00000001000000000000000E" from archive
2024-06-21 01:45:39.018 UTC [2663] LOG:  restored log file "00000001000000000000000F" from archive
2024-06-21 01:45:39.664 UTC [2663] LOG:  restored log file "000000010000000000000010" from archive
2024-06-21 01:45:40.330 UTC [2663] LOG:  restored log file "000000010000000000000011" from archive
2024-06-21 01:45:41.002 UTC [2663] LOG:  restored log file "000000010000000000000012" from archive
2024-06-21 01:45:41.908 UTC [2663] LOG:  restored log file "000000010000000000000013" from archive
2024-06-21 01:45:42.592 UTC [2663] LOG:  restored log file "000000010000000000000014" from archive
2024-06-21 01:45:43.277 UTC [2663] LOG:  restored log file "000000010000000000000015" from archive
2024-06-21 01:45:43.892 UTC [2663] LOG:  recovery stopping after commit of transaction 759, time 2024-06-20 20:53:36.826455+00
2024-06-21 01:45:43.892 UTC [2663] LOG:  pausing at the end of recovery
2024-06-21 01:45:43.892 UTC [2663] HINT:  Execute pg_wal_replay_resume() to promote.
```

Figure 13-8. *Log exhibit of transaction recovery*

13.3.9 Time-Based Recovery

Point-in-time recovery is an easy and simple method where you can recover based on the timestamp. In the cloud environment, time is based on an offset from UTC. For example, UTC-5 is Eastern Standard Time/Central Daylight (https://docs.aws.amazon.com/AmazonRDS/latest/UserGuide/USER_PIT.html).

The parameter `recovery_target_time` is set to the desired time of the recovery subjected to the availability of WAL files.

CHAPTER 13   POSTGRESQL RECOVERY

13.3.10 Recovery to Latest

The "latest" recovery method is to restore the production database from backup and apply logs to bring it to point-in-time recovery. Unless otherwise requested, the standard method is to apply all available logs to the database backup. The log sequence *. 004 is immediately created after completion of a full backup followed by the last archive log sequence *.0028. In Figure 13-9, all logs are applied, which are created after the completion of the full backup.

```
2024-06-20 23:06:10.526 UTC [14315] LOG:  restored log file "000000010000000000000023" from archive
2024-06-20 23:06:11.010 UTC [14315] LOG:  redo in progress, elapsed time: 20.10 s, current LSN: 0/22FFE8A8
cp: cannot stat '/postdata16/000000010000000000000024': No such file or directory
2024-06-20 23:06:11.140 UTC [14315] LOG:  restored log file "000000010000000000000023" from archive
cp: cannot stat '/postdata16/000000010000000000000024': No such file or directory
2024-06-20 23:06:11.648 UTC [14315] LOG:  redo done at 0/23FFFF40 system usage: CPU: user: 2.10 s, system: 0.9
4 s, elapsed: 20.74 s
2024-06-20 23:06:11.651 UTC [14315] LOG:  last completed transaction was at log time 2024-06-20 20:53:44.54509
2+00
2024-06-20 23:06:11.669 UTC [14315] LOG:  restored log file "000000010000000000000023" from archive
cp: cannot stat '/postdata16/00000002.history': No such file or directory
2024-06-20 23:06:11.925 UTC [14315] LOG:  selected new timeline ID: 2
cp: cannot stat '/postdata16/00000001.history': No such file or directory
2024-06-20 23:06:12.203 UTC [14315] LOG:  archive recovery complete
```

Figure 13-9. All logs

::::Lines omitted

```
2024-06-20 23:05:50.803 UTC [14315] LOG:  starting archive recovery
2024-06-20 23:05:50.803 UTC [14315] LOG:  starting backup recovery with redo LSN 0/4000028, checkpoint LSN 0/4
000060, on timeline ID 1
2024-06-20 23:05:50.839 UTC [14315] LOG:  restored log file "000000010000000000000004" from archive
2024-06-20 23:05:50.900 UTC [14315] LOG:  redo starts at 0/4000028
2024-06-20 23:05:50.933 UTC [14315] LOG:  restored log file "000000010000000000000005" from archive
2024-06-20 23:05:51.013 UTC [14315] LOG:  restored log file "000000010000000000000006" from archive
2024-06-20 23:05:51.091 UTC [14315] LOG:  restored log file "000000010000000000000007" from archive
2024-06-20 23:05:51.146 UTC [14315] LOG:  completed backup recovery with redo LSN 0/4000028 and end LSN 0/4000
100
2024-06-20 23:05:51.146 UTC [14315] LOG:  consistent recovery state reached at 0/4000100
2024-06-20 23:05:51.146 UTC [14311] LOG:  database system is ready to accept read-only connections
```

Database Backup Restore with Incremental Backup Files

The procedure is to extract files from the full and incremental backups and combine them into one file. A new program, `pg_combinebackup`, is created to combine the full backup with incremental backups. After restoring backup files from backup to operating system, perform the below steps.

CHAPTER 13   POSTGRESQL RECOVERY

1. Create the original PGDATA directory.

   ```
   mkdir -p /pgdata/devdb
   # create your own PGDATA directory
   chmod 0750 /pgdata/devdb
   # Set the permissions of PGDATA
   chown postgres:postgres /pgdata/dbdev
   ```

2. Extract base backup file from full backup.

   ```
   tar -xvf /appl/postgres/backup/full/base.tar
   # Choose your restore directory
   ```

   1. Extract pg_wal file.

      ```
      mv /appl/postgres/backup/full/pg_wal.tar /appl/postgres/backup/full/pg_wal
      tar -xvf /appl/postgres/backup/full/pg_wal/pg_wal.tar -C /appl/postgres/backup/full/pg_wal
      ```

   2. Remove backup files # remove base.tar and pg_wal.tar as these file are not registered with backup manifest file.

      ```
      rm /appl/postgres/backup/full/pg_wal/pg_wal.tar
      rm /appl/postgres/backup/full/base.tar
      ```

3. Extract files from incremental backup.

   ```
   tar -xvf /appl/postgres/backup/inc_01/base.tar
   ```

   1. Extract pg_wal file.

      ```
      mv /appl/postgres/backup/inc_01/pg_wal.tar /appl/postgres/backup/inc_01/pg_wal
      tar -xvf /appl/postgres/backup/inc_01/pg_wal/pg_wal.tar -C /appl/postgres/backup/inc_01/pg_wal
      ```

CHAPTER 13   POSTGRESQL RECOVERY

2. Remove backup files # remove `base.tar` and `pg_wal.tar` as these file are not registered with backup manifest file.

    ```
    rm /appl/postgres/backup/inc_01/pg_wal/pg_wal.tar
    rm /appl/postgres/backup/inc_01/base.tar
    ```

4. Combine full and incremental backups into a directory.

    ```
    pg_combinebackup -o /pgdata/devdb /appl/postgres/backup/full /appl/postgres/backup/inc_01
    ```

5. Start the PostgreSQL Cluster.

    ```
    $pg_ctl start -D /pgdata/devdb

    waiting for server to start....2024-10-01 14:42:46.123 UTC [53003] LOG: redirecting log output to logging collector process
    ```

13.3.11 Reset Logs

In the event of non-availability of archive logs in PG_WAL, a crash recovery can be performed with the reset logs option using the `pg_resetwal` command. This option allows you to discard any existing WAL files and start a new timeline for WAL files. However, it is important to note that the database will not be available for user transactions after the reset. To perform a recovery with the reset logs option, you can follow these general steps:

1. Stop the PostgreSQL cluster.

2. Use the `pg_resetwal` command to reset the WAL logs, which was formerly the `reset log` command. This command should be run as the same user that owns the PostgreSQL cluster.

3. Export the database using `pg_dumpall`.

4. Initialize a new PostgreSQL cluster.

5. Perform a full backup with `pg_dumpall -f resetlog.sql`.

6. Restore the database using the command `psql < resetlog.sql`.

In the event of non-availability of any WAL backups until the required time, the only available option is to restore the database without the WAL files, where you can bring the database to consistent state, without rollback or roll forward the changes from the WAL files. During this process, some data or all data may be lost. Listing 13-7 shows the procedure.

Listing 13-7. Reset WAL

```
$ pg_ctl stop -D $PGDATA
$ pg_resetwal -f -D $PGDATA
$ pg_ctl start -D $PGDATA
waiting for server to start....2024-02-25 22:58:55.665
UTC [3975] LOG:  redirecting log output to logging
collector process
2024-02-25 22:58:55.665 UTC [3975] HINT:  Future log output
will appear in directory "db_log".
```

13.3.12 The pg_dumpall and recovery

It is a standard practice to schedule a backup of `pg_dumpall` at the end of the day for recovery to the source as well as to remote locations. The backup of production is restored in development environments created by the `pg_dumpall` backup with the psql command `psql < backupfile.sql`. Create a shell PostgreSQL cluster with the default system database and restore with the psql command.

CHAPTER 13   POSTGRESQL RECOVERY

The database is restored to the state it was in at the completion time of the pg_dumpall backup. PostgreSQL uses snapshot isolation to ensure a consistent state of the database during the backup process.. You can make a backup to S3 of Azure data Blob storage. With the psql command, the database is restored from the backup file created by pg_dumpall. See Figure 13-10.

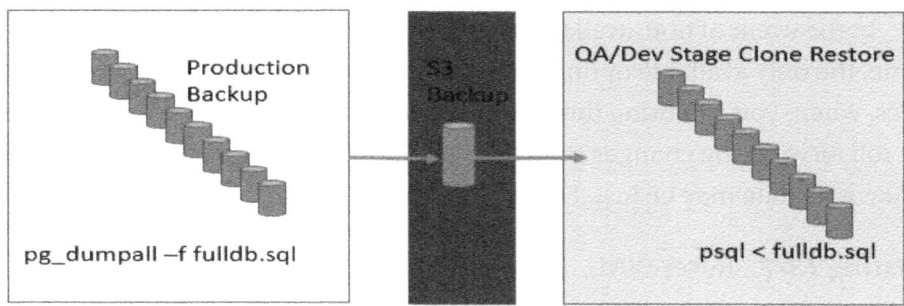

Figure 13-10. pg_dumpall and restore

You can restore a backup on a primary source as well as on remote locations.

Note   pg_dumpall is used in the AWS EC2/Azure VM environment of PostgreSQL. As an RDS/Azure SQL database is a managed service, DBAs do not have access to the pg_auth catalog to back up user logins with the pg_dumpall command.

Restore an Individual Table from a Backup

You can restore a backup from an AWS S3 or Azure Blob location either on the same source of backup or to a remote location. In order to restore individual backups from pg_dump, you have to use the pg_dump -Fc option. See Listing 13-8.

Listing 13-8. pgdump

```
$PGHOME/pg_dump -Fc -d [database] .date.dump
```

Restore command:

```
pg_restore --help
pg_restore restores a PostgreSQL database from an archive
created by pg_dump.
```

```
Usage:
pg_restore [OPTION]... [FILE]
```

```
General options:
-d, --dbname=NAME    connect to database name
-f, --file=FILENAME  output file name (- for stdout)
-F, --format=c|d|t   backup file format (should be
```

```
$PGHOME/pg_restore -a -d [database]  -t [table]  [database]
.date.dump
```

Restore a Database from a Backup

The `pg_dump` or `pg_dumpall` commands can back up large databases with parallel options, based on the CPU count, which saves time for backup as well as for recovery.

```
$PGHOME/pg_restore -d [database] [backupfile]
```

Parallel Restore Job

For large tables, you can utilize the parallel restore capabilities, which have benefits and drawbacks. You should increase the CPU count and adjust `work_mem` for each parallel process. Ensure that you have sufficient physical memory (RAM) because relying on increased swap memory is not recommended due to potential performance degradation

CHAPTER 13 POSTGRESQL RECOVERY

The command to restore using parallel jobs is pg_restore, which takes the CPU count to distribute jobs across each CPU, along with the directory where backups were stored.

Listing 13-9 dynamically allocates available CPUs to the database parameter for parallel restore job processing. The arguments for a parallel restore job are

pg_restore -Fd -j [cpu count] -d [database name] [backup directory name]

Listing 13-9. Parallel Restore

```
#!/bin/bash
# The script, drop the database, set the parallel worker
process and restores from the backup directory.
parallel_restore()
{
echo "enter database to restore"
read db
echo "directory path of restore"
read dir
 psql -c "drop database $db;"
 psql -c "create database $db;"
 parallel_count=$(psql -t -c "show max_parallel_workers;")
 echo "Restoring $db from $dir"
  start_time=$(date +%s)
  pg_restore -Fd -j $parallel_count -d $db $dir
  end_time=$(date +%s)
  echo "Restore completed."
  elapsed_time=$((end_time - start_time))
  echo "Restore completed."
```

```
    echo "Start Time: $(date -d @$start_time)"
    echo "End Time: $(date -d @$end_time)"
    echo "Elapsed Time: $elapsed_time seconds"
 psql -d $db -c " select count(*) From pgbench_accounts;"
}
parallel_restore
```

13.3.13 Remap Schema

There will be requirements to copy database objects from one schema to another schema. The default public schema is not secure as the first thing the hacker would get into this schema. There is no specific option in backup and restore utilities to load data from one schema to another schema. You have to work on the script to move data from another schema. See Figure 13-11.

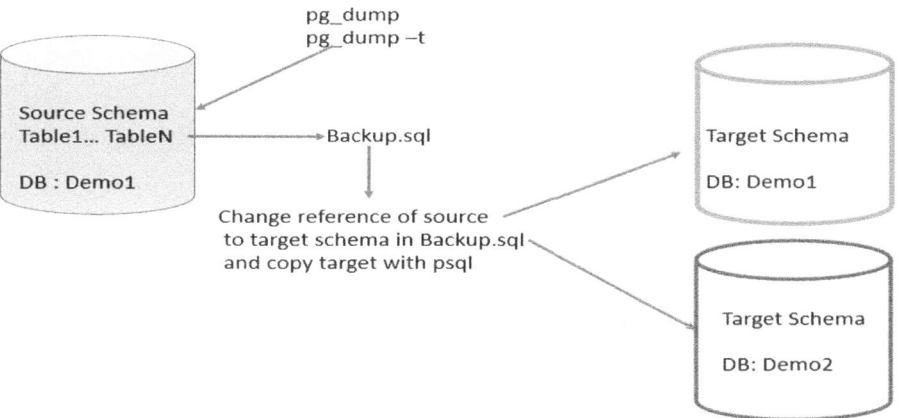

Figure 13-11. *Remap a schema*

13.13.1 Full Database Export for Schema Data Load

To remap a schema, export the database, rename the old schema to a new schema, and load the data from backup. The public schema is renamed to the qa schema with the script in Listing 13-10.

Listing 13-10. Remap a Schema for a Full Database

```
    psql -c " drop database demo1;" # drop test database
createdb demo1;    #create test database
pgbench -i demo1;  #load data with pgbench utility
psql -d demo1 -c "drop schema qa cascade;" #drop test schema
psql -d demo1 -c "create schema qa;" #create test schema
pg_dump -f demo1_full.sql demo1 #backup full database
sed 's/public/qa/g' demo1_full.sql > demo1_DDL.sql  #rename public to qa schema in backup file
psql -d demo1 < demo1_DDL.sql # restore database
psql -d demo1 -c "select count(*) from qa.pgbench_accounts;"
# count the records in qa schema
```

Table Export for a Schema Table Data Load

To remap a schema, export the database, rename the old schema to a new schema, and load the data from a backup. See Listing 13-11.

Listing 13-11. Remap a Schema for Tables

```
psql -d demo1 -c "drop schema qa cascade;"  # drop test schema
psql -d demo1 -c "create schema qa;" # create test schema
pg_dump -f demo1_tab.sql -t pgbench_accounts -t pgbench_branches -t pgbench_history -t pgbench_tellers demo1.
# backup tables
sed 's/public/qa/g' demo1_tab.sql > demo1_tabDDL.sql.
# rename public schema to qa
```

```
psql -d demo1 < demo1_tabDDL.sql. # restore tables from backup
psql -d demo1 -c "select count(*) from qa.pgbench_accounts;"
# validate the row count.
```

Shell Script for a Schema Data Load

The script in Listing 13-12 takes a full backup of database, renames the schema definition in a backup file, and drops the old schema.

Listing 13-12. Remap Schema Shell Script

```
Schema_remap.sh
# enter  database name
echo " enter database name"
# read database name into db variable
read db
# enter the source schena
echo " enter source schema"
# read source schea into a variable
read ssch
# enter target schena
# read target schema into variable
echo " enter target schema"
read tssch

# backup database to disk
pg_dump -f $db.full.sql $db
# rename schemas in backup file
sed "s/$ssch/$tssch/g" $db.full.sql > $db.DDL.sql
# Make sure source schema is not preset on ddl scrpt
grep $ssch $db.DDL.sql
# drop old source schema
psql -d $db -c "drop schema $tssch cascade;"
```

```
# The restore script creates new schema and loads data into
that schema
psql -d $db < $db.DDL.sql
# validate the new schema objects in the database
psql -d $db -c "select * from pg_tables where
schemaname='$tssch';"
```

13.3.14 Restore from an RDS Backup from the Console

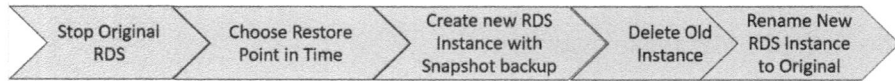

Figure 13-12. *RDS restore*

It is easy and simple to restore from an RDS snapshot backup. See Figure 13-12. Automated backups are made by default and you have to choose the snapshot retention duration, which is typically two weeks for non-prod and four weeks for prod environments. In RDS, you have to create a new instance to restore the database from a backup, where you have to choose the available backups. The newly restored instance will be parallel to your existing instance. You have the option to restore to available WAL files or to a custom timestamp along with the instance model, although it is normal practice to stick to the original instance configuration.

CHAPTER 13 POSTGRESQL RECOVERY

13.14.1 Identify Restore Time

Figure 13-13 shows the restore process to a point in time.

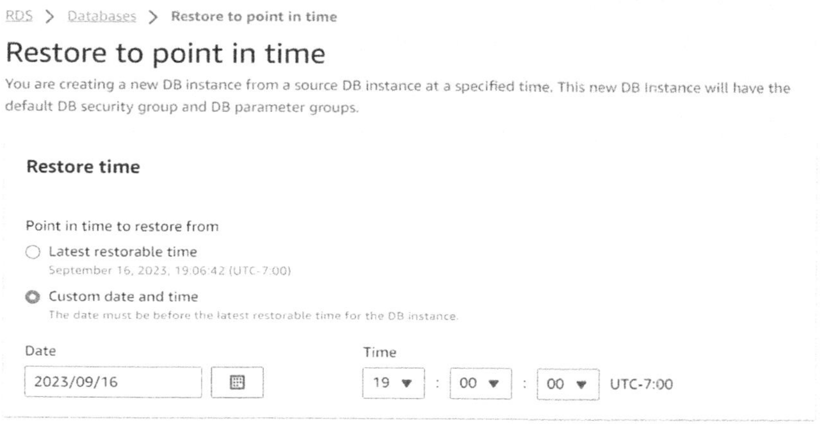

Figure 13-13. Define a new instance name and instance type

You have to create a new instance to restore from the backup. Choose the same instance type for a clone of the database. See Figure 13-14.

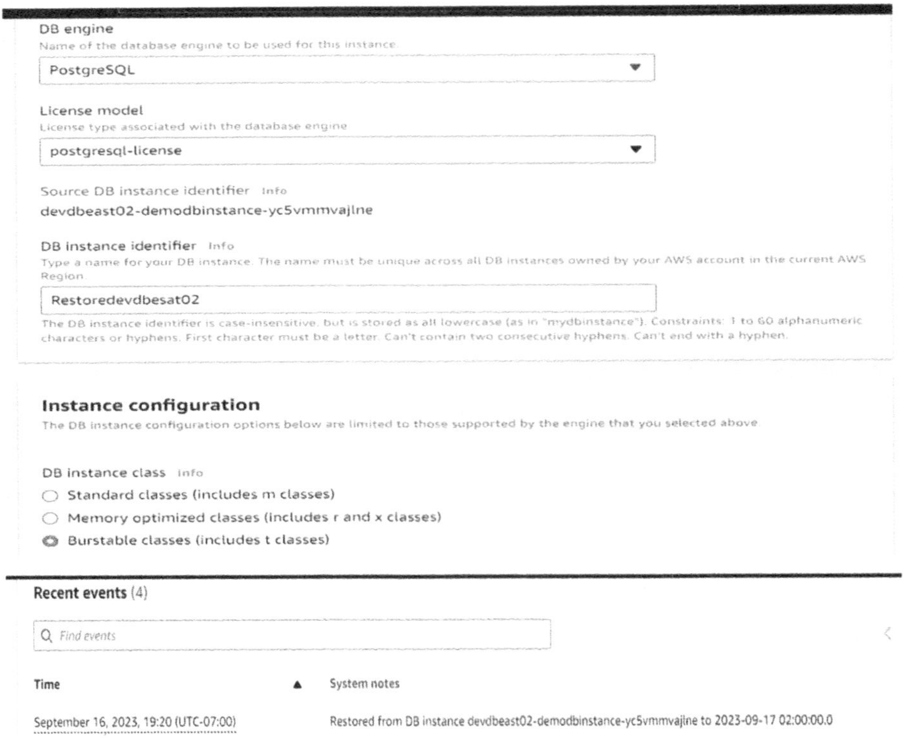

CHAPTER 13 POSTGRESQL RECOVERY

Figure 13-14. Choose the instance

You can choose the same database version or a higher version when restoring the database from the clone. See Figure 13-15.

CHAPTER 13 POSTGRESQL RECOVERY

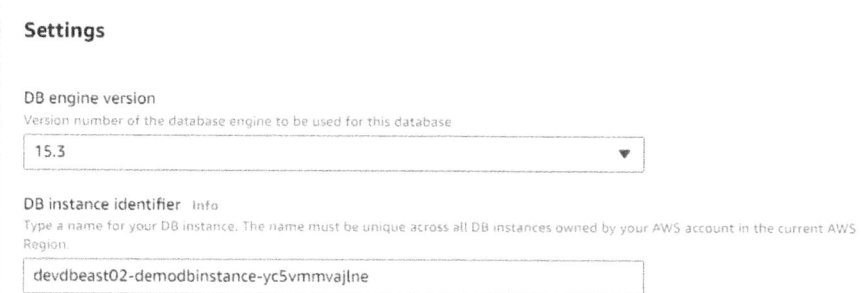

Figure 13-15. Modify the instance

You will notice both instances during the recovery of the database. See Figure 13-16.

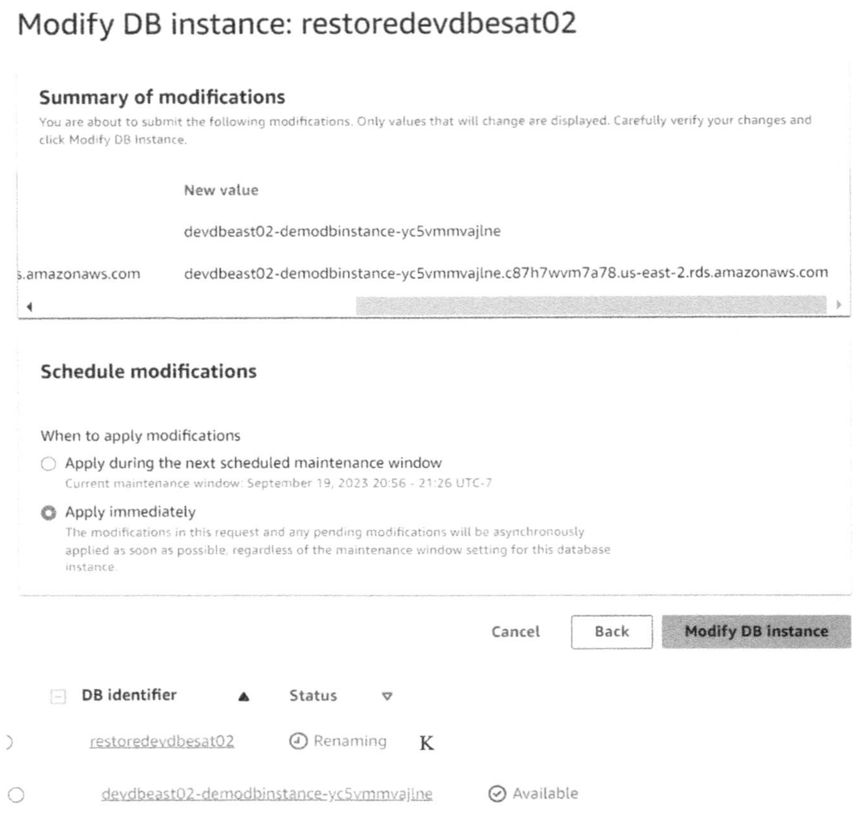

CHAPTER 13 POSTGRESQL RECOVERY

Figure 13-16. Rename the instance

13.3.15 Restore from an Azure SQL Database

Azure Database for PostgreSQL Flexible Server takes automated backups of your entire server. The automated backup includes a daily incremental snapshot of the database. You can restore a database to any Azure PostgreSQL server of a different/same subscription but within the same region of the vault. Furthermore, the DB user whose credentials were chosen via the key vault will have all the privileges over the restored database and any existing DB user boundaries will be overridden [2].

You can restore the PostgreSQL Database in Azure to the desired point in time.

Restore to a Point in Time

Listing 13-13 shows the point-in-time restore procedure from a command line procedure.

Listing 13-13. Azure PostgreSQL Restore

```
az postgres flexible-server  restore -g testgroup -n testsvrnew --source-server testsvr --restore-point-in-time "2024-06-15T13:10:00Z" [3]
```

For console access to the restore, use the link https://learn.microsoft.com/en-us/azure/backup/restore-azure-database-postgresql.

13.4 Keywords

Recovery overview, point-in-time recovery, recovery metadata, restore database from backup, parallel restore, remap schema restore RDS, and Azure SQL restore.

13.4.1 Summary of Learning

All recovery scenarios of a PostgreSQL cluster are covered in this chapter. As DBA, your role is critical in the recovery of a database. You learned the following recovery scenarios:

- Point-in-time recovery using backup from pg_basebackup
- Recovering a database with pg_resetwal

- Recovering an individual table
- Recovering an individual database
- Recovering all databases locally and at a remote location
- Backup and restore of data between schemas
- Log sequence number recovery
- Transaction ID-based recovery
- Complete/latest Recovery
- Database Parameter setting to utilize CPUs
- Remap schema example
- RDS recovery procedures
- Azure recovery procedures

13.4.2 Questions Chapter 13

1. What are RPO and RTO?
2. What is the backup and recovery strategy with 30 minutes of SLA?
3. How do you identify `pg_basebackup` metadata?
4. What is the procedure to perform parallel backup with `pg_dump`?
5. From which version do you have the ability to perform log sequence recovery?
6. Which file do you edit for recovery parameter configuration?
7. How do you determine the restore point in RDS recovery?

8. What steps do you follow to remap a schema for data copy between schemas?

9. What are the contents of pg_waldump?

10. What is the command to restore from Azure?

13.4.3 Practice

1. Recover point-in-time of a PostgreSQL cluster from the backup of pg_basebackup.

2. Recover until a specific transaction of a PostgreSQL cluster from the backup of pg_basebackup.

3. Recover a PostgreSQL cluster until the backup time of pg_baesbackup.

4. Recover a PostgreSQL cluster from a pg_dumpall backup.

5. Recover a table from a backup.

6. Recovery a database from a backup.

References

1. www.postgresql.org/docs/current/app-pgbasebackup.html
2. https://learn.microsoft.com/en-us/azure/backup/restore-azure-database-postgresql
3. https://learn.microsoft.com/en-us/cli/azure/postgres/server?view=azure-cli-latest#code-try-17

Additional References:
www.postgresql.org/docs/current/backup.html
www.postgresql.org/docs/current/continuous-archiving.html

CHAPTER 13 POSTGRESQL RECOVERY

Point-in-time recovery video:
https://us02web.zoom.us/rec/share/D5K7-GFhshgubIUPRneGM-fwj
i8EGb8AQ8J1yhvct8yGmc3HTLTfnQQxoek5oeCr.-kFklt__1oJZzHPE

Database table recovery video:
https://us02web.zoom.us/rec/share/JSTVMJDqqRtDc2a4NS-N6Pcr7
Q3o5wXN61af7nZQq9me1B44QmwwfSdj3hO8y88Z.1JHVROYCbGOapoj1

CHAPTER 14

PostgreSQL High Availability

14.1 Abstract

PostgreSQL cluster software provides robust solutions for high availability (HA) for critical business applications with log shipping and streaming replication methods, ensuring data redundancy and availability in local as well as in remote locations. In the AWS EC2/Azure VM environment, you must configure all redundancy for high availability by setting up one or many replicated standby instances, whereas in AWS RDS/Azure SQL Database, single or multiple availability zones for redundancy and fault tolerance are built into the product. Both EC2/Azure VM and RDS/Azure SQL Database replication environments follow the underlying pg_basebackup or snapshot procedures for setup of PostgreSQL replication. You have to check the status of the primary periodically with scripting methods in AWS EC2/Azure environments and the standby will be promoted to primary in the event of an outage to the primary site, whereas promotion to primary of a standby site is performed automatically by the managed database service. There are several third-party tools and extensions that help in promoting the standby to the primary role in the event of an outage to the primary site.

The original version of the chapter has been revised. A correction to this chapter can be found at https://doi.org/10.1007/979-8-8688-0817-3_18

CHAPTER 14   POSTGRESQL HIGH AVAILABILITY

14.2 Learning Objectives

- Understand database replication and high availability.
- Configure PostgreSQL database replication on AWS/EC2 and Azure VM.
- Set up AWS RDS and Azure SQL Database clones with scripting solutions.
- Set up and configure PostgreSQL high availability solutions with the WAL method and perform a database role change.

14.3 Introduction

PostgreSQL cluster replication is configured to provide HA to support business continuity in the event of disaster of the primary database. PostgreSQL cluster has a robust mechanism to configure HA to support real-time data synchronization between the primary and replicas. The replication is configured in two methods: AWS EC2/Azure VM with log shipping and RDS/Azure SQL Database read replica configuration which in turn configures log shipping. Both methods provide robust options for database replication, ensuring data redundancy and availability. AWS EC2/Azure PostgreSQL instances are deployed on separate AWS EC2/Azure VM instances or virtual machines for standby requirements.

When you configure Amazon RDS multi-AZ with one standby, the automatic failover completes in as quickly as 60 seconds with zero data loss and no manual intervention. (https://aws.amazon.com/rds/features/multi-az/).

When you configure PostgreSQL with Azure Flexible Server high availability, the committed data is never lost in the case of failures. (https://learn.microsoft.com/en-us/azure/reliability/reliability-postgresql-flexible-server).

The replication is started by a full database backup from a standby site from the live system of the primary site to initiate replication, followed by write ahead log (WAL) shipping from the primary site to a standby site, which are replayed to apply all committed transactions on the standby site. After enabling database parameters to support replication, the replication is started with the command `alter system set hot_standby=on`, after adding the primary site details in the `postgresql.conf` file at the standby site.

When using Amazon RDS/Azure SQL Database for PostgreSQL, read replicas are configured to provide high availability and scalability in addition to inbuilt failover of instances in the multi-AZ environment with standby replicas. You can create replication in one or many availability zones. When you choose Amazon RDS with multi-AZ, automatic failover is guaranteed, whereas with a single AZ, you must create a read replica and manually promote the role in the event of primary failover. The read replica site is accessible in read-only mode, which prevents DDL and DML being executed due to the read-only transaction nature of the database. Both EC2/Azure VM and RDS/Azure SQL Database offer replication in read-only mode, which helps to offload the reporting requirements of the business applications.

The primary server operates in continuous archiving mode, while each standby server operates in continuous recovery mode, reading the WAL files from the primary. No changes to the database tables are required to enable this capability, so it offers low administration overhead compared to some other replication solutions. This configuration also has a relatively low performance impact on the primary server.

Figure 14-1 shows the diagram of PostgreSQL replication utilizing the WAL files method. After an initial full backup of the database from the standby site and the setup of replication, the WAL files are shipped from the primary to the standby site.

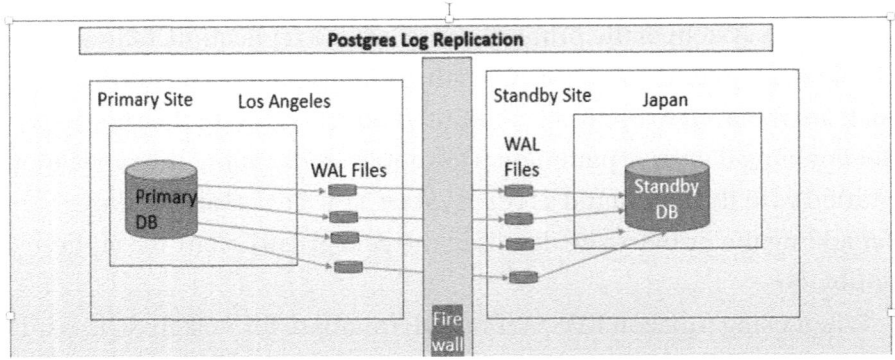

Figure 14-1. Warm standby replication

The first step is to make sure you connect to the standby site from the primary location as well as from the standby site to the primary site. You enable connectivity by adding host names in the pg_hba.conf file on both sites. The replication configuration tasks between the two sites are illustrated in the flow chart in Figure 14-2.

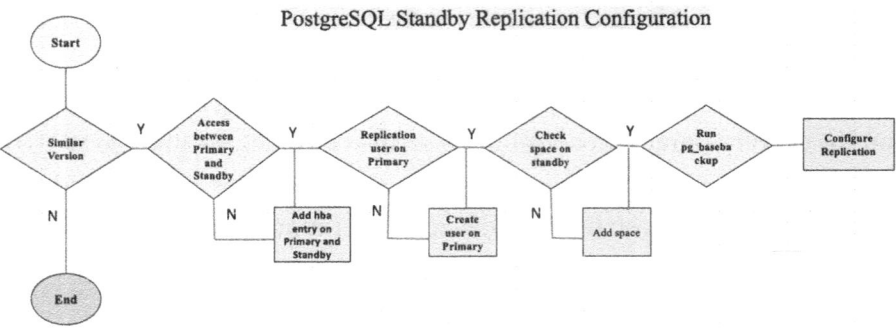

Figure 14-2. Standby replication process

14.4 Set Up Replication Configuration

Create an AWS EC2 or AZURE VM and install the PostgreSQL software before proceeding with replication setup.

The database parameter changes on the primary site are as follows:

wal_level = replica, archive_mode = on, archive_command = 'cp %p /archivepath/%f', and max_wal_senders = 4.

As per the above flow chart, take the following steps to configure replication:

> 1. Set up the replication user in the primary database.
>
> 2. Enable the standby server name or IP address in pg_hba.conf on the primary server.
>
> 3. Enable the primary server name in pg_hba.conf on the standby site.
>
> 4. Configure the primary site parameters to enable WAL.
>
> 5. Run pg_basebackup from the standby site.
>
> 6. Start the replication from the standby site.

14.4.1 Primary pg_hba.conf

You have to add three entries in the pg_hba.conf file at the primary site: access to the primary from the standby site, access to the replication user from the standby site, and allow all users to access the primary site. Replace public address of 0.0.0.0/0 with your own IP address. Use the file from Listing 14-1 on the primary site. You can configure multiple standby sites from the primary database by adding multiple IP addresses of the standby sites.

CHAPTER 14   POSTGRESQL HIGH AVAILABILITY

Listing 14-1. Primary Site pg_hba.conf

```
#
TYPE    DATABASE        USER            ADDRESS                 METHOD

# "local" is for Unix domain socket connections only
local   all             all                                     trust
# IPv4 local connections:
#access to postgres from a remote host . Change with your IP
host    all             all
127.0.0.1/32                    scram-sha-256. # local host with password access
host    all             all             172.31.2.168/32
scram-sha-256# standby  host with password
host    all.            postgres        172.31.2.168/32         trust
# trust postgres user from standby site
host    all             all             ::1/128                 trust
# Allow replication connections from localhost, by a user with the
# replication privilege.
local   replication     all                                     trust
   # access replication user from remote . change with your IP
host    replication     all             172.31.2.168/32         trust # Replication user access from standby
host    replication     all             ::1/128                 trust
host    all all         0.0.0.0/0       scram-sha-256. # allow all hosts with password authentication
```

14.4.2 Standby pg_hba.conf

At the standby site, add the primary site IP address for the replication user and allow all connections from the primary site. Use the file in Listing 14-2 at the standby site.

Listing 14-2. Standby Site pg_hba.conf

```
# "local" is for Unix domain socket connections only
local   all          all                                 trust
# IPv4 local connections:
host    all          all      127.0.0.1/32       scram-sha-256

# IPv6 local connections:
host    all          all      ::1/128                    trust
# Allow replication connections from localhost, by a user with the
# replication privilege.
local   replication  all                                 trust
host    replication  all      172.31.37.213/32           trust
#primary IP address for replication user
host    replication  all
::1/128                 trust
host all 172.31.37.213/32        scram-sha-256
# access from primary host.
```

14.4.3 Validate Primary Site Replication Access

After setting up the replication parameters, the first step is to validate access from the standby host to the primary site and validate the replication user. See Figure 14-3.

```
[postgres@ip-172-31-37-213 ~]$ psql -h 172.31.2.168
psql (16.2)
Type "help" for help.

postgres=# \conninfo
You are connected to database "postgres" as user "postgres" on host "172.31.2.168" at port "5432".
```

Figure 14-3. Validate access to the primary site from the standby

14.4.4 Perform Backup From the Standby Site

Perform a backup of the primary database cluster from the standby site with the command pg_basebackup by providing -D for the data directory location and the replication username along with -X (include WAL files for recovery), s (status interval), and -R (write recovery file) arguments. In Listing 14-3 and Figure 14-4, the backup of the primary site from IP address 172.31.2.168 is performed from standby site IP 172.31.37.213.

Listing 14-3. 14-1 pg_basebackup

pg_basebackup -D /var/lib/pgsql/data1 -h 172.31.2.168 --username=replication -X s -R

```
[postgres@ip-172-31-37-213 ~]$ pg_basebackup -D /var/lib/pgsql/data1 -h 172.31.2.168 --username=replication -X s -R
[postgres@ip-172-31-37-213 ~]$ ls -ltr /var/lib/pgsql/data1
total 196
-rw-------. 1 postgres postgres  225 May 19 00:16 backup_label
drwx------. 3 postgres postgres   60 May 19 00:16 pg_wal
```

Figure 14-4. pg_basebackup command

After completion of the backup, secure the data directory with 0750 (owner all, group read and write, others none permission), as shown here and in Figure 14-5:

Chmod 0750 -R /var/lib/pgsql/data1

```
[postgres@ip-172-31-37-213 ~]$ chmod 0750 -R /var/lib/pgsql/data1
```

Figure 14-5. PGDATA directory permission

CHAPTER 14   POSTGRESQL HIGH AVAILABILITY

14.4.5 Set Up Replication

Set up replication by specifying primary host info, port number, and replication username and then reboot the server (see Figure 14-6).

    alter system set primary_conninfo='host=172.31.2.168 port=5432 user=replication'; # change to your IP address

```
postgres=# alter system set primary_conninfo ='host=172.31.2.168 port=5432 user=replication';
ALTER SYSTEM
postgres=# alter system set hot_standby='on';
ALTER SYSTEM
postgres=# exit
[postgres@ip-172-31-37-213 ~]$ pg_ctl restart -D /var/lib/pgsql/data1
waiting for server to shut down.... done
```

Figure 14-6. *Standby parameter configuration*

14.4.6 Validate Replication

Validate replication by calling the function pg_is_in_recovery and checking the read-only status in the log file (see Figure 14-7).

    psql -c "SELECT pg_is_in_recovery();

```
[postgres@ip-172-31-37-213 log]$ psql -c "SELECT pg_is_in_recovery();"
 pg_is_in_recovery
-------------------
 t
```

Figure 14-7. *Check recovery status*

View the log file to identify the read-only status. See Figure 14-8.

```
2024-05-19 00:22:50.600 UTC [2163] LOG:  consistent recovery state reached at 0/3000110
2024-05-19 00:22:50.601 UTC [2156] LOG:  database system is ready to accept read-only connections
```

Figure 14-8. *Read-only connection status in the database log file*

Standby Process for Recovery

Identify the standby recovery process with command `ps -ef | grep -i recovering`. See Figure 14-9.

```
postgres   2163   2156  0 00:22 ?        00:00:00 postgres: startup recovering 000000010000000000000003
```

Figure 14-9. *View recovering status on the standby site*

Identifying Replication From Primary Site

Identify the walsender process and `pg_stat_replication` view from the primary site. See Figures 14-10 and 14-11.

```
postgres   2127   1620  0 00:22 ?        00:00:00 postgres: walsender replication 172.31.37.213(44758) streaming 0/3000148
```

Figure 14-10. *Primary site WAL sender process*

```
postgres=# select * from pg_stat_replication;
-[ RECORD 1 ]----+------------------------------
pid              | 2127
usesysid         | 16389
usename          | replication
application_name | walreceiver
client_addr      | 172.31.37.213
client_hostname  |
client_port      | 44758
backend_start    | 2024-05-19 00:22:50.606679+00
backend_xmin     |
state            | streaming
sent_lsn         | 0/3000148
```

Figure 14-11. *pg_stat_replication view*

14.4.7 Replication Configuration Script

For mass deployment, you can use the code in Listing 14-4 to perform the following: stop the database on the standby site; connect to the primary site to check `pg_hba.conf` rules for standby access; check for a replication user and create one if not present; create a new data directory; perform pg_base backup; set up the replication; and validate the replication. The script takes two arguments: the primary server hostname and the location of PGDATA for standby.

Listing 14-4. Replication Script

```bash
#!/bin/bash

function rep() {

  # Clear the terminal
  clear
  lhost=172.31.37.213   #enter your standy host ip
  echo  "standby host :::$lhost"
  # Get the current data directory of the old instance
  export ddirold=$(ps -ef | grep -i pgsql | grep -i d | awk '{print $10}')
  echo "Current Data Directory: $ddirold"

  # Stop the old instance if the data directory exists
  if [ ! -z "$ddirold" ]; then
    echo "Stopping old instance"
    $PGHOME/pg_ctl stop -D $ddirold
  fi

  # Read primary host IP and data directory from the user
  echo "Enter Primary Host IP (Tip: 172.31.2.168):" # enter your  remote IP
  read host
  echo "Enter data directory (Tip: /appl/postgres/dev):"
  read datadir

  # Read hba rules and recovery status from the primary
  echo "Reading the hba rules files on the primary with permission from client:"
  hba_rules=$(psql -h $host -t -c "select * from pg_hba_file_rules;")
```

```
# Check if there are no rules related to the standby host
standby_rule=$(echo "$hba_rules" | grep -i "$lhost") # Replace
"standby_host_ip" with actual IP if known
if [ -z "$standby_rule" ]; then
  echo "No pg_hba.conf rules found on primary for the
  standby host."
  echo "No action taken."
  return
else
  echo "$hba_rules"
fi

recovery_status=$(psql -h $host -t -c "select pg_is_in_
recovery();")
echo "Recovery status of primary: $recovery_status"

# Check if replication user exists on the primary
echo "Replication user is required on primary: Checking if
user exists on primary"
repuser=$($PGHOME/psql -t -X -w -h $host -c "select usename
from pg_user where usename='replication';")
echo $repuser

if [ -z "$repuser" ]; then
  echo "Creating replication user on primary..."
  $PGHOME/psql -h $host -c "create user replication with
  login password 'My/srtong';"
  $PGHOME/psql -h $host -c "alter user replication with
  superuser;"
else
  # Create the data directory if it does not exist
  mkdir -p $datadir
```

```
    # Copy data files from primary to the new data directory
    echo "Datafile copy from Primary is in progress..."
    $PGHOME/pg_basebackup -D $datadir -h $host
--username=replication -X s -R
    if [ $? -ne 0 ]; then
      echo "Check data file backup status"
    fi
    echo "Datafile copy from Primary completed..."

    # Set permissions and update configuration for the
    standby server
    chmod 0750 $datadir
    echo "primary_conninfo = 'host=$host port=5432
    user=replication'" >> $datadir/postgresql.conf
    echo "hot_standby = 'on'" >> $datadir/postgresql.conf

    # Start the standby server
    echo "Starting the standby server"
    $PGHOME/pg_ctl start -D $datadir

    # Check the status of the standby server
    echo "Checking the standby status"
    $PGHOME/psql "dbname=postgres replication=database" -c
    "IDENTIFY_SYSTEM;"
    echo "No DDL or DML allowed on standby database"
    $PGHOME/psql -c "create database demo;"
  fi

# Create and check the finance2 database on the primary
and standby
echo "Creating database on primary: finance2, checking on
this standby"
psql -h $host -c "drop database finance2;"
psql -h $host -c "create database finance2;"
```

```
    # Wait for changes from primary to standby
    echo "Wait for changes from primary to standby: Around 2
    seconds"
    sleep 2

    # Verify changes on the standby server
    psql -c "select datname from pg_database where
    datname='finance2';"
    psql -c "SELECT pg_is_in_recovery();"

    # Prompt user to return to the main menu
    echo "Enter to Main Menu"
    read x
}
rep;
```

Listing 14-5 shows the output.

Listing 14-5. Replication Configuration Log

```
standby host :::172.31.37.213
Current Data Directory:
Enter Primary Host IP (Tip: 172.31.2.168):
172.31.2.168. # Enter Primary Host name
Enter data directory (Tip: /appl/postgres/dev):
/appl/postgres/demo001. # Enter standby data directory(PGDATA)
location.
Reading the hba rules files on the primary with permission
from client:
```

:::::: partial outout
          6 | /postgres/pgdata16/pg_hba.conf | 17 |
host | {replication} | {all} | 172.31.37.213 | 255.255.25
5.255 | trust | |
Recovery status of primary: f
Replication user is required on primary: Checking if user exists on primary
replication
Datafile copy from Primary is in progress...
Datafile copy from Primary completed...
Starting the standby server
::: Lines truncated
pg_is_in_recovery
----
 t
(1 row)

14.4.8 Replication Status Check Script

PostgreSQL designates the standby server by creating a standby.signal file in $PGDATA. After promoting the role to stand-alone server, the standby.signal file is removed.

The replication status is identified by two main views: pg_stat_replication from the primary site and pg_stat_wal_receiver from the standby site.

The script in Listing 14-6 takes one argument: the standby hostname. It checks for the replication configuration and displays the primary and standby replication status.

Listing 14-6. Replication Status Details

```bash
#!/bin/bash

function replication_status() {
  # Clear the terminal
  clear

  # Prompt user for the replication host IP
  echo "Enter replication host IP: "
  read rhost

  # Check replication status from the primary
  echo "Checking replication status from primary"
  replist=$($PGHOME/psql -t -X -w <<EOF
select count(*) from pg_stat_replication;
EOF
)

  # Check if replication is not set up
  if [ -z "$replist" ]; then
    echo "Replication not set up"
    read x
  else
    # Display primary replication status
    echo "Primary Replication Status"
    $PGHOME/psql "dbname=postgres replication=database" -c "IDENTIFY_SYSTEM;"

    # Display standby replication status
    echo "Standby Replication Status"
    $PGHOME/psql -h $rhost "dbname=postgres replication=database" -c "IDENTIFY_SYSTEM;"
```

```
  # Check if the previous command was not successful
  if [ $? -ne 0 ]; then
    echo "Check standby host"
  fi

  # Display primary pg_stat_replication details
  echo "Primary: pg_stat_replication:"
  $PGHOME/psql -c "select write_lsn as pg_lsn, reply_time
  from pg_stat_replication;"

  # Display standby pg_stat_wal_receiver details
  echo "Standby: pg_stat_wal_receiver:"
  $PGHOME/psql -h $rhost -c "select status, written_lsn as
  pg_lsn, last_msg_receipt_time from pg_stat_wal_receiver;"
fi

# Prompt user to return to the main menu
echo "Press Enter to return to the main menu"
read x
}
```

14.4.9 Replication Status Script Execution

In the output in Figure 14-12, the WAL file sequence number is fully in sync with the primary server as the log number is same across both primary and standby sites.

```
Enter replication host IP:tip 172.31.37.213
172.31.37.213
Checking replication status from primary
Primary Replication Status
        systemid       | timeline |  xlogpos  |  dbname
---------------------+----------+-----------+----------
 7364987210758097065 |        1 | 0/C42D2A0 | postgres
(1 row)

Standby Replication Status
        systemid       | timeline |  xlogpos  |  dbname
---------------------+----------+-----------+----------
 7364987210758097065 |        1 | 0/C42D2A0 | postgres
(1 row)

Primary: pg_stat_replication:
  pg_lsn   |          reply_time
-----------+------------------------------
 0/C42D2A0 | 2024-05-19 19:57:39.065693+00
(1 row)

Standby: pg_stat_wal_receiver:
  status   |  pg_lsn   |     last_msg_receipt_time
-----------+-----------+------------------------------
 streaming | 0/C42D2A0 | 2024-05-19 19:57:29.059547+00
(1 row)
```

***Figure 14-12.** Replication status output*

The replication is validated by identifying the WAL sequence number on both primary and standby servers. In Figure 14-12, the log sequence number generated on primary 0/C42D2A0 is applied on the standby server. The standby error log constantly displays the applied log sequences to the database.

14.4.10 Replication Slot

A replication slot prevents the deletion of WAL from the primary database cluster unless it is applied to the standby site. You have to be a superuser to work with the replication slot. You can specify a name for the replication slot and you can configure up to 10 replication slots to retain WAL files until the changes are applied on the standby site.

Listing 14-7 shows the command to set up the replication slot on the primary site.

Listing 14-7. Replication Slot Configuration

```
psql -c "pg_replication_slots=replica(select * from pg_create_physical_replication_slot('replica'));"
```

14.4.11 Promote Standby to Standalone Role

There are no automatic failover tools available with the native PostgreSQL open source version. You have to detect the primary failure with your own scripting or notification methods. Upon noticing the primary failure, you can promote the standby to the primary role on AWS EC2 by running the SELECT pg_promote() function from psql. You have to rename the standby host name to the primary name after completion of the role change. In Azure SQL databases, the host is resolved by the virtual IP (VIP) in the Flex Server configuration.

14.5 RDS Read Replica

In an Amazon RDS environment, you can create a read replica configuration to set up replication between a master database and a replica database. Amazon takes care of creating the additional hardware and software necessary for the replication, and the application can connect to the replica site and query a read-only database. This is similar to the log shipment method used in EC2 standby setups, but with RDS, Amazon takes care of setting up the standby cluster.

For critical production systems, you can configure replicas in different regions other than the primary for high availability of databases with cross-regional replicas. You can configure read replicas in different geographical regions, allowing due consideration for network latency. See Figure 14-13.

14.5.1 Read Replica Diagram

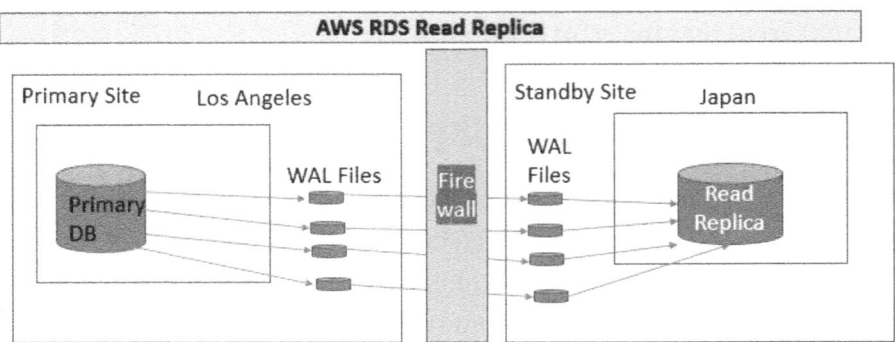

Figure 14-13. AWS RDS read replica

14.5.2 Create a Read Replica from AWS CLI

Unlike EC2, where there are several steps required to configure replication, the RDS replication process takes only two arguments: the new name for the replicated instance and the source instance name. Listing 14-8 creates a read replica with t3.micro by default.

Listing 14-8. RDS Read Replica Creation

```
$ aws rds create-db-instance-read-replica --db-instance-
identifier standby-clonerds1-demodbinstance-jnfqha7is9vn \
 --source-db-instance-identifier clonerds1-demodbinstance-
jnfqha7is9vn=
{
"DBInstance": {
"DBInstanceIdentifier": "standby-clonerds1-demodbinstance-
jnfqha7is9vn",
```

```
"DBInstanceClass": "db.t3.micro",
:::: Lines omitted

"LicenseModel": "postgresql-license",
"
}
```

You can examine the status of replication in the database log in the replicated site.

14.5.3 Standby Recovery Log

From the standby recovery log you can identify tasks related to replication recovery.

14.5.4 Standby Clone AWS Console View

From the AWS console you can identify the primary and standby RDS instances. The recovery time depends on the size of the database and network bandwidth. See Figure 14-14.

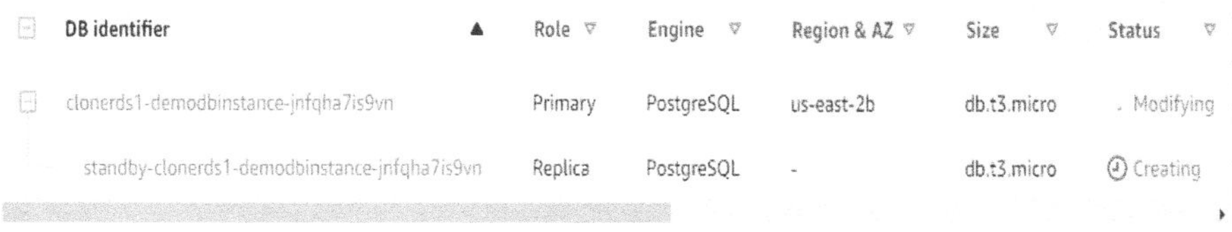

DB identifier	Role	Engine	Region & AZ	Size	Status
clonerds1-demodbinstance-jnfqha7is9vn	Primary	PostgreSQL	us-east-2b	db.t3.micro	Modifying
standby-clonerds1-demodbinstance-jnfqha7is9vn	Replica	PostgreSQL	-	db.t3.micro	Creating

Figure 14-14. Create a replica

14.5.5 RDS Replica Clone Completed View

Depending on the size of the primary database, the standby site is configured. Upon the setup of the replication, you can see the status of availability on both primary and replicas. See Figure 14-15.

CHAPTER 14 POSTGRESQL HIGH AVAILABILITY

Figure 14-15. Read replica creation view

14.5.6 Connect to a Replica from a Linux Host

After completion of the read replica, check the recovery status with this command:

psql -c " select pg_is_in_recovery();"

14.5.7 Promote a Replica to a Standalone Cluster

Automatic failover is not available. You have to manually promote the standby role to primary. You have to rename the replica to the primary site name after failover. You can promote the standby to the primary role from the AWS console or from command line (shown in Figure 14-16):

SELECT pg_promote() function

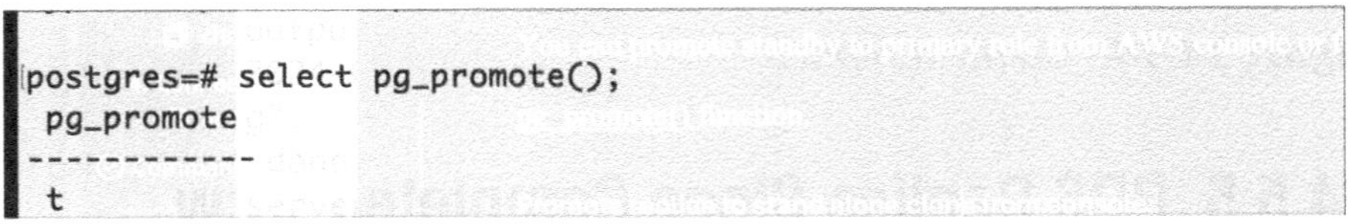

```
postgres=# select pg_promote();
 pg_promote
------------
 t
```

Figure 14-16. Promote a replica to the primary role

14.5.8 Connect to Promoted Standby Clone

After promoting the standby as a standalone role, you can validate the DDL commands on the promoted server. See Listing 14-9.

Listing 14-9. Promoted Replica Access

```
[postgres@node1172 work]$ psql -h standby-clonerds1-
demodbinstance-jnfqha7is9vn.c87h7wvm7a78.us-east-2.rds.
amazonaws.com -U USER1   -d postgres
Password for user USER1:
psql (13.9, server 14.6)
postgres=> create table  t1(id integer);
CREATE TABLE
postgres=>
```

> **Note** When you configure an RDS replica in a single availability zone, you have to manually change the end point (hostname) after promoting the replica to the primary role, whereas with multi-AZ configuration, AWS seamlessly maintains the endpoint name across instances during failover process.

14.6 Azure Read Replica

With a few mouse clicks or with an API, you can set up a standby database, which is called a read replica. After connecting to the Azure console, choose the PostgreSQL Data Service and Properties tab to set up replication in the Properties tab. You can create one or many replicas from the primary database in the same availability zone or in another availability zone. An additional level of protection is provided by adding replicas in another region. The cross-region replication allows users to read the database in another region to reduce the network latency. For instance, users in Europe benefit from replicas from the primary site in the USA. FlexServer offers a virtual IP (VIP) concept for resolving the host name for the role change between the primary standby systems as this dynamic change is internally managed by Azure.

14.6.1 Replication from Azure CLI

For mass deployment, you can use AWS CLI to configure read replication. The command is az Postgres server replica create. See Listing 14-10.

Listing 14-10. *Azure Server Replica Help Command*

```
az postgres flexible-server  replica create --help
Command
    az postgres flexible-server replica create : Create a read
replica for a server.
Arguments
    --replica-name     [Required] : The name of the server to
restore to.
    --resource-group -g [Required] : Name of resource group.
You can configure the default  group  using 'az configure
--defaults group=<name>'.
    --source-server    [Required] : The name or resource ID of
the source server to restore from.
:::::Continued::::::::::
```

Azure flexible deployment options include deploying of networking, maintenance, and setup of high availability to streamline the replica management.

You have to provide three arguments to an AZ Postgres flexible cluster: the name of the replica, resource group name, and source Azure SQL database. See Listing 14-11.

Listing 14-11. Create an Azure Replica

```
az postgres flexible-server replica create --replica-name \
palosdemorep --resource-group demo --source-server palosdemo
```

14.6.2 Validate Read Replica

You have reviewed the views `pg_stat_replication` from the primary site and `pg_stat_wal_receiver` from the standby site, which are discussed in section 14.1.4.

14.6.3 Connection to Read Replica

After the successful setup of replication, connect to the replication instance with this command:

```
psql -h palosdemorep.postgres.database.azure.com -U postdev
-d sales
Password for user postdev:
sales=>
```

The command to validate configuration and working of read replica is with the function `pg_is_in_recovery`. If the function returns t(true), it is confirmed that read replica is configured successfully. Examine the wait events of Recovery WAL and WAL Receiver for replication. See Listing 14-12.

Listing 14-12. Azure Replication Status Check

```
postgres=> \conninfo
sales=> \conninfo
You are connected to database "sales" as user "postdev" on
host "palosdemorep.postgres.database.azure.com" (address
"52.170.112.78") at port "5432".
postgres=> SELECT pg_is_in_recovery();
 pg_is_in_recovery
-------------------
 t
(1 row)
postgres=> sales=>     select wait_event_type,wait_
event,backend_start From pg_stat_activity;
 wait_event_type |    wait_event     |        backend_start
-----------------+-------------------+------------------------------
 Activity        | RecoveryWalStream | 2024-06-02 00:34:49.80818+00
 Activity        | WalReceiverMain   | 2024-06-02 00:35:00.605247+00
```

14.6.4 Read Replica View from the Primary Database

To identify the replication status from the primary database, you can check the view pg_stat_activity for the write ahead send wait event. See Listing 14-13.

Listing 14-13. Replication View from the Primary Site

```
venkat [ ~ ]$ psql -h palosdemo.postgres.database.azure.com  -U postdev -d postgres
Password for user postdev:
psql (14.8, server 15.3)
postgres=> select wait_event_type,wait_event,backend_start From pg_stat_activity;
 wait_event_type |      wait_event      |       backend_start
-----------------+----------------------+----------------------------
  Activity       | WalSenderMain        | 2023-09-21 22:45:03.280332+00
```

14.6.5 Promote Read Replica

You can promote the standby or read replica to the primary role caused by planned and unplanned outages. The `az postgres flexible-server` takes two arguments: the resource group name and the read replica name. The following is the command and partial output (see Figure 14-17):

```
az postgres flexible-server replica promote --resource-group [name]  --name [replicaname]
```

```
venkat [ ~ ]$ az postgres flexible-server replica promote \
> --resource-group demo --name palosdemorep1
Are you sure you want to perform this operation? (y/n): y
{
  "administratorLogin": "postadmin",
  "administratorLoginPassword": null,
```

Figure 14-17. Promote read replica

No user input is required for multi-AZ failover in AWS and Azure. It is worth noting the difference between standby replica and read replica. The standby replica is a synchronous copy of the primary database replica, which is located in the same or another availability zone and can't be used for read queries. In contrast, the read replica can be used to read queries, offloading application queries from the primary to the standby site.

After the role FlexServer is promoted, check the status of recovery with the pg_is_in_recovery function. See Listing 14-14.

Listing 14-14. Recovery Status Check After Promoting to Primary

```
postgres=> \conninfo
You are connected to database "postgres" as user "postadmin" on host "palosdemorep1.postgres.database.azure.com" (address "13.68.212.121") at port "5432".
SSL connection (protocol: TLSv1.3, cipher: TLS_AES_256_GCM_SHA384, bits: 256, compression: off)
postgres=> SELECT pg_is_in_recovery();
 pg_is_in_recovery
-------------------
 f
```

Note Azure SQL Database for Postgres Flexible Server does not support the SELECT pg_promote() function.

14.7 Keywords

High availability, warm standby log replication, RDS read replica, RDS promote replica, Azure read replica, and Azure promote replica

14.8 Summary of Learning

You reviewed the steps to configure warm standby between the primary and standby sites. You now know about the read replication procedures offered by the AWS and Azure cloud providers, as well as how to promote the standby to read write mode.

14.9 Practice Chapter 14

1. Configure a warm standby between two instances of a Postgres cluster.
2. Configure read replica from RDS.
3. Configure read replica from Azure Data Service.
4. Promote the read replica to primary.

14.10 Questions Chapter 14

1. What are the preparatory steps for configuring log file replication in PostgreSQL?
2. Can you explain how to set up log file replication between two different instances of a PostgreSQL cluster?
3. How can you set up replication between hosts in Amazon EC2 for PostgreSQL?
4. Can you provide a step-by-step guide on setting up an RDS replica option in PostgreSQL?

5. What are the different types of replications available in PostgreSQL?

6. How does logical replication differ from physical replication in PostgreSQL?

7. What are the prerequisites for setting up streaming replication in PostgreSQL?

8. Can you explain the concept of replication slots in PostgreSQL?

9. How do you monitor the status and health of a PostgreSQL replication setup?

10. What are the considerations for setting up replication with high availability in PostgreSQL?

References

www.postgresql.org/docs/current/warm-standby.html
www.postgresql.org/docs/current/warm-standby.html#STANDBY-SERVER-SETUP
https://learn.microsoft.com/en-us/azure/postgresql/single-server/how-to-read-replicas-cli

CHAPTER 15

Table Partitions

15.1 Abstract

As a DBA, you are responsible for managing all tasks related to partition creation, data migration to partitions, partition maintenance, and the archival of old data to cloud storage.

From version 10 onwards, Postgres made several enhancements to its partitioning strategy. In each release after 10, Postgres continued to add more features and functionalities to partition methods, along with parallel computing capabilities across partitions. The industry-standard features such as partitioning by hash key, primary key, foreign key indexes, and triggers on partitioned tables, updating a partition key to move data to the correct partitions tree, and parallel index build are available from version 11 onwards.

Be aware that the application comes to a grinding halt if partitions are not created ahead of time. For instance, if the monthly or quarterly partition is not created before the preceding month or quarter ends, the database transactions will fail. As an example, the April partition must be created ahead of time, before April 1st.

The original version of the chapter has been revised. A correction to this chapter can be found at https://doi.org/10.1007/979-8-8688-0817-3_18

CHAPTER 15   TABLE PARTITIONS

15.2 Objectives of Learning

- Table partition methods
- Table partition procedures
- Table partition scripts

15.3 Introduction

Table partitioning is a way to divide a large table into smaller child tables with a similar structure, where the child table will inherit the structure of the parent. Optionally, it can have additional columns. See Figure 15-1.

| Table Partition Methods | Table data copy to Partitions | Partition data copy to Cloud | Partition scripts and catalog views |

Figure 15-1. *Partition process*

A table can have multiple partitions and can be a part of referential integrity through foreign key constraints of other tables in the schema. The partitioning technique improves database performance by allowing the database to search only the required partitions based on partition search criteria, instead of searching the entire large table. Partitions allow you to work on a part or subset of data, utilizing parallel operations to enhance the throughput of query processing and also improve performance in reporting for faster queries of large tables. They require less I/O and offer improved throughput for ranges such as hourly, daily, weekly monthly, quarterly, and yearly. By partitioning the input data among multiple processors and memories, an operator can often be split into many independent operations, each working on a part of the data [1].

The advantage of the partitions approach is you can delete the old or historical data that is not required to support business use cases. There are two options for deleting old or archived data from a partitioned table: the delete option and the purge/delete partition option. The delete option is a DML command, while the purge/delete partition option is a DDL command. If you delete old data based on archival or retention criteria, there will be hot spots and fragments in the datafile, which can cause performance issues for large data sets. However, if you use the partition delete option, the database will truncate the old partitions, reclaiming the allocated space to the free space list of the database. which will not cause any hot spots in the data files as this is a DML operation.

Starting with PostgreSQL version 13, you can also detach a partition from the table and attach a table into the partition parent table. The attach partition feature allows you to exchange table data with a partition table. For example, in a data warehousing environment, after loading monthly data into individual tables, you can merge these partitions with a partition table.

15.4 Partition Table Methods

Figure 15-2 shows the partition table methods.

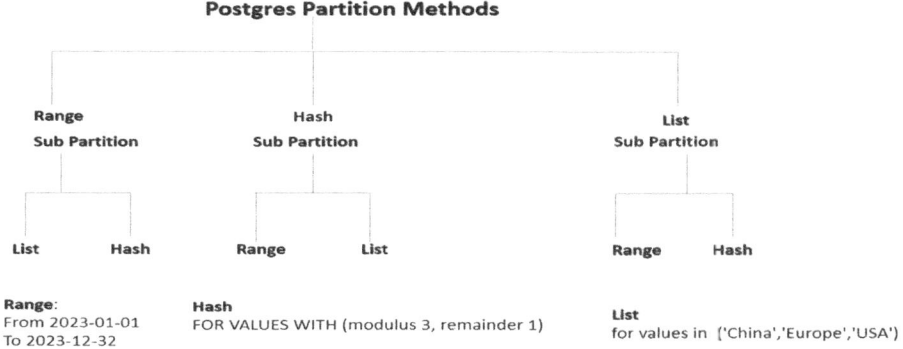

Figure 15-2. *PostgreSQL partition methods*

15.4.1 Table Partition Creation Options

PostgreSQL offers different methods for creating partitions in a database. It is worth mentioning all the available partitioning methods for learning objectives. The most common approach is the declarative method, which involves manually or automatically creating partitions for tables. Another method is using table inheritance, where database constraints are used to create table partitions. See Figure 15-3.

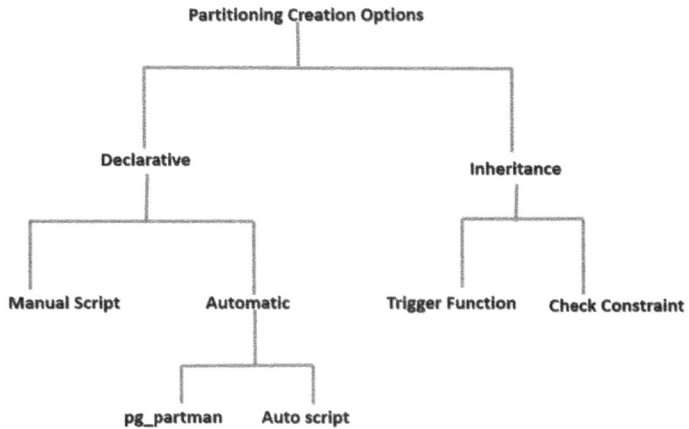

Figure 15-3. Partition creation options

15.4.2 Partition Table Structure

In the following example, notice the partition table structure, partition ranges, partition upgrade method, and sample query from the partitioned table. Declarative partitioning involves explicitly defining partitions for a table. You can create a partitioned table and define partition ranges based on specific criteria, such as a date range or other relevant columns. The most used method of partitioning is by date range with monthly and quarterly methods. With partitioning, you can detach a partition as a normal table as well as attach a table to the partition table, where you can create individual tables with a monthly date range and attach them to partition table.

There are three types of partition methods: range, list, and hash, along with the sub partitions. By setting enable_partition_pruning=on, enable_partitionwise_join=on, and enable_partitionwise_aggregate=on either at the session or system level, you can leverage the parallel processing capabilities of PostgreSQL.

15.4.3 Partition DDL Scripts

To create a partition, you must define a partition column in the table. If you have a primary key for the table, the partition column should be a part of the primary key. If you choose the primary key not as a part of the partition column, create the primary key on the child table. See Listing 15-1.

Listing 15-1. Partitioning

```
CREATE TABLE LOG(log_id integer, logtext  char(30),log_date date
)partition by range(log_date);
CREATE TABLE log_q2_2024 PARTITION OF log
(
    CONSTRAINT pk_log_q2_2024 PRIMARY KEY(log_id)
)
FOR VALUES FROM ('2024-04-01 00:00:00') TO ('2024-06-30 23:59:59');
```

Listing 15-2 creates a partition table and then detaches, attaches, and upgrades with range partitions. Note: When attaching the partition, you have to define the partition range.

Listing 15-2. Partition Table Creation and Exchange Partition

```
    Drop table if exists log cascade;
 CREATE TABLE log (
log_id integer NOT NULL GENERATED ALWAYS AS IDENTITY,
log_date date not null,
log_text char(10),
constraint pk_log primary key(log_id,log_date)
) PARTITION BY RANGE (log_date);
------- Creation of Parent Table
     CREATE TABLE log2023_m1 PARTITION OF log
    FOR VALUES FROM ('2023-01-01') TO ('2023-01-31');---
    Creation of  Child table
CREATE TABLE log2023_m2 PARTITION OF log
    FOR VALUES FROM ('2023-02-01') TO ('2023-03-01');
CREATE TABLE log_default PARTITION OF log DEFAULT ;  --Default
 INSERT INTO log(log_date,log_text) values('2023-01-01','l
og010123');
INSERT INTO  log(log_date,log_text) values('2023-04-01','l
og010123');
ALTER TABLE log DETACH PARTITION log2023_m1; ---- Detach
Partition
ALTER TABLE log  ATTACH PARTITION log2023_m1 -----Attach
Partition
    FOR VALUES FROM ('2023-01-01') TO ('2023-02-01');
SELECT tableoid, tableoid::regclass, * FROM  log;
tableoid | tableoid | log_id | log_date | log_text
----------+-------------+--------+------------+------------
16439 | log2023_m1 | 1 | 2023-01-01 | log010123
16449 | log_default | 2 | 2023-04-01 | log010123
(2 rows)
UPDATE log
```

```
set log_date='2023-08-01';
SELECT tableoid, tableoid::regclass, * FROM  log;
UPDATE log
set log_date='2023-07-01';
SELECT tableoid, tableoid::regclass, * FROM  log;
```

15.4.4 PostgreSQL Extension pg_partman

In PostgreSQL, the partition creation must be done manually, either by creating all the partitions ahead of time or by creating them as needed. The pg_partman extension provides automation for creating and managing partitions based on predefined criteria, such as date or numeric ranges. However, it still requires some initial setup and configuration.

pg_partman Script

The following is the script to create partitions with pg_partman, along with execution details. See Figure 15-4.

For each database:

```
CREATE SCHEMA partman;
CREATE EXTENSION pg_partman WITH SCHEMA partman;
CREATE SCHEMA mk;         ------- create user your schema
CREATE TABLE mkt.sales(
        sale_id         int,
        sales_cout      int,
        prod            char(20),
        create_dt       timestamp,
        CONSTRAINT pk_mkt_event PRIMARY KEY (sale_id, create_dt)
            ) PARTITION BY RANGE (create_dt);
---Create Interval partition: The default is for 7 days
```

CHAPTER 15 TABLE PARTITIONS

```
SELECT partman.create_parent('mkt.sales', 'create_dt','1 day');
create_parent
---------------
t
```

```
postgres=> SELECT partman.create_parent('mkt.sales', 'create_dt','1 day');
 create_parent
---------------
 t
(1 row)

postgres=> \d+ mkt.sales
                                     Partitioned table "mkt.sales"
   Column   |            Type             | Collation | Nullable | Default | Storage  | Stats target | Description
------------+-----------------------------+-----------+----------+---------+----------+--------------+-------------
 sale_id    | integer                     |           | not null |         | plain    |              |
 sales_cout | integer                     |           |          |         | plain    |              |
 prod       | character(20)               |           |          |         | extended |              |
 create_dt  | timestamp without time zone |           | not null |         | plain    |              |
Partition key: RANGE (create_dt)
Indexes:
    "pk_mkt_event" PRIMARY KEY, btree (sale_id, create_dt)
Partitions: mkt.sales_p20240607 FOR VALUES FROM ('2024-06-07 00:00:00') TO ('2024-06-08 00:00:00'),
            mkt.sales_p20240608 FOR VALUES FROM ('2024-06-08 00:00:00') TO ('2024-06-09 00:00:00'),
            mkt.sales_p20240609 FOR VALUES FROM ('2024-06-09 00:00:00') TO ('2024-06-10 00:00:00'),
            mkt.sales_p20240610 FOR VALUES FROM ('2024-06-10 00:00:00') TO ('2024-06-11 00:00:00'),
            mkt.sales_p20240611 FOR VALUES FROM ('2024-06-11 00:00:00') TO ('2024-06-12 00:00:00'),
            mkt.sales_p20240612 FOR VALUES FROM ('2024-06-12 00:00:00') TO ('2024-06-13 00:00:00'),
            mkt.sales_p20240613 FOR VALUES FROM ('2024-06-13 00:00:00') TO ('2024-06-14 00:00:00'),
            mkt.sales_p20240614 FOR VALUES FROM ('2024-06-14 00:00:00') TO ('2024-06-15 00:00:00'),
            mkt.sales_p20240615 FOR VALUES FROM ('2024-06-15 00:00:00') TO ('2024-06-16 00:00:00'),
            mkt.sales_default DEFAULT
```

Figure 15-4. pg_partman example

Note If the data does not confirm the partition range, it will go to the default partition, which is `mkt.sales_default`, without throwing errors while loading data into non-existing partitions.

15.4.5 Partition a Non-Partitioned Table

For performance reasons, you must partition a large table so that you can query the data in the specified partition. The steps are to rename the original table and original sequence, create a table with the partition structure, and copy the data from original table. See Listing 15-3.

CHAPTER 15 TABLE PARTITIONS

Listing 15-3. Non-Partition to Partition Move Example

```
drop table if exists employee_old cascade;
DROP TABLE if exists dept cascade;
drop table if exists employee cascade;
CREATE TABLE dept(dept_number integer,
dept_loc      varchar(20),
create_ts timestamp not null,
CONSTRAINT pk_dept PRIMARY KEY(dept_number)
);
CREATE TABLE employee
(
emp_number                            integer,
dept_number                           integer,
sale_amount                           integer,
create_ts                             timestamp     NOT NULL,
CONSTRAINT pk_emp PRIMARY KEY(emp_number),
CONSTRAINT fk_dept foreign key(dept_number) references
dept(dept_number)
);
INSERT INTO dept values(10,'nyc','2023-01-01');
INSERT INTO  dept values(20,'boston','2023-01-01');
INSERT INTO  employee values(1,10,100,now());
INSERT INTO employee values(2,20,300, '2023-01-01');
ALTER TABLE employee rename to employee_old;   --- rename
original table

CREATE TABLE employee
(emp_number                           integer,
 dept_number                          integer,
 sale_amount                          integer,
 create_ts                            timestamp     NOT NULL
```

```
)PARTITION BY RANGE(create_ts);
CREATE TABLE emp_jan_2023 PARTITION OF employee
(
CONSTRAINT pk_emp_jan_2023
PRIMARY KEY(emp_number),
CONSTRAINT fk_pk_dept FOREIGN KEY (dept_number)
REFERENCES dept(dept_number)
 ON UPDATE NO ACTION
ON DELETE NO ACTION
)FOR VALUES FROM ('2023-01-01 00:00:00') TO ('2023-01-31 23:59:59');
CREATE TABLE employee_default PARTITION OF employee DEFAULT;
 employee select * From employee_old;
SELECT tableoid, tableoid::regclass, * from employee;
tableoid |     tableoid     | emp_number | dept_number | sale_amount |      create_ts
----------+------------------+------------+-------------+-------------+---------------------------
    35075 | emp_jan_2023     |          2 |          20 |         300 | 2023-01-01 00:00:00
    35085 | employee_default |          1 |          10 |         100 | 2024-04-12 16:42:40.338549
```

15.4.6 Non-Partitioned to Partitioned Table with Sequences

The procedure is the same as in the above section, except that you have to manually increment the sequence value.

15.4.7 Partition Indexes

When you create an index on the parent table, indexes are created on partitioned tables (see Listing 15-4).

```
postgres=# create index idx_emp_sales on employee(sale_amount);
```

Note This index is created for all partitioned tables.

Listing 15-4. Partition Index Creation

```
CREATE INDEX
postgres=# CREATE INDEX idx_emp_sales on employee(sale_amount);
CREATE INDEX
postgres=# \di
                            List of relations
 Schema |            Name              |     Type      
 |  Owner   |    Table
--------+------------------------------+-------------------+---
-------+--------------
 public | emp_feb_2023_sale_amount_idx | index             |
postgres | emp_feb_2023
 public | emp_jan_2023_sale_amount_idx | index             |
postgres | emp_jan_2023
 public | emp_mar_2023_sale_amount_idx | index             |
postgres | emp_mar_2023
(9 rows)
```

15.4.8 List with Range Subpartition

To create a list partition with range subpartitions in PostgreSQL, you need to follow these steps: first, you create a table that is partitioned by a list; next, you create child tables that serve as partitions of the parent table; and finally, you create range subpartitions within those list-partitioned. See Listing 15-5.

Listing 15-5. List with Range Subpartition

```
DROP TABLE if exists global;
CREATE TABLE global
 (
 countryid integer,
Region     varchar,
country    varchar,
date_cr    date,
rank       integer)
 PARTITION BY list  (country);   -- Parent Table
---  Child Table with List values
CREATE TABLE country_list
PARTITION OF global
FOR VALUES IN  ('China','Europe','USA')
PARTITION BY RANGE(date_cr);
----Child table based on list with range
 CREATE TABLE country_jan_2021
 PARTITION OF country_list
FOR VALUES FROM  ('2021-01-01 00:00:00') TO ('2021-01-31 23:59:59');
INSERT INTO global values(1,'East','USA','2021-01-01 00:00:00',100);
INSERT INTO global values(2,'East','China','2021-01-01 00:00:00',90);
```

15.4.9 Range with Hash Subpartition

To create a table with range partitions and hash subpartitions in PostgreSQL, start by creating a table partitioned by a range. Next, create child tables that are partitioned by hash within each range partition. Finally, create hash partitions within these hash-partitioned child tables. See Listing 15-6.

Listing 15-6. Range with Hash Subpartition

```
Drop table if exists global1 cascade;
CREATE TABLE global1
(
countryid   integer,
Region      varchar,
country     varchar,
date_cr     date,
amount      integer
)
PARTITION BY RANGE  (date_cr);   -- Parent table partitioned on range
\echo  Child table based on range and partitioned by hash
CREATE TABLE country_dates_2020
PARTITION OF global1
FOR VALUES FROM  ('2020-01-01 00:00:00') TO ('2020-12-31 23:59:59')
PARTITION BY HASH (amount);
CREATE TABLE hash_p0_2020 PARTITION OF country_dates_2020  -- Child table of hash
FOR VALUES WITH (modulus 3, remainder 1);
INSERT INTO global1 values(1113,'East','China','2020-01-01 00:00:00',3000);
```

CHAPTER 15 TABLE PARTITIONS

```
INSERT INTO global1 values(11121,'East','japan','2020-01-01 00:00:00',30000);
INSERT INTO global1 values(1115,'East','USA','2020-02-01 00:00:00',3000);
SET enable_partition_pruning = on;
explain
SELECT * FROM global1
where date_cr='2020-01-01' AND country='China' and amount > 300;
 SELECT    relname as partition_table,
    pg_get_expr(relpartbound, oid) as partition_range
FROM pg_class
WHERE relispartition
and relkind = 'r';
SELECT tableoid::regclass, * FROM global1;
SELECT * FROM pg_partition_tree('global1');
```

15.4.10 Range with List and Hash Partition

To create a table with range partitions with list and hash subpartitions in PostgreSQL, start by creating a table partitioned by a range. Next, create child tables that are partitioned by hash within each range partition. Finally, create list partition within these hash-partitioned child tables. See Listing 15-7.

Listing 15-7. Range with List and Hash Partition

```
Drop table if exists global1 cascade;
CREATE TABLE global1
(
countryid integer,
Region    varchar,
country   varchar,
```

```
date_cr        date,
amount         integer
)
PARTITION BY range  (date_cr);
CREATE TABLE country_dates_2020
PARTITION OF global1
FOR VALUES FROM  ('2020-01-01 00:00:00') TO ('2020-12-31
23:59:59');
CREATE TABLE hash_p0_2020 PARTITION OF country_dates_2020
FOR VALUES WITH (modulus 3, remainder 1);
CREATE TABLE country_list_2023
PARTITION OF global1
FOR VALUES FROM  ('2019-01-01 00:00:00') TO ('2019-12-31 23:59:59')
PARTITION BY LIST(country);
CREATE INDEX idx_id_country1 on global1(countryid);
CREATE INDEX idx_country1 on global1(country);
INSERT INTO global1 values (1113,'East','China','2020-01-01
00:00:00',3000);
INSERT INTO  global1 values(1112,'East','usa','2021-01-01
00:00:00',300);
INSERT INTO global1 values(11121,'East','japan','2020-01-01
00:00:00',30000);
SET enable_partition_pruning = on;
SELECT * FROM global1;
```

15.4.11 List Partition with Range and Hash Subpartition

To create a table with list partitions with range and hash subpartitions in PostgreSQL, start by creating a table partitioned by a list. Next, create child tables that are partitioned by a range within each range partition. Finally, create hash partition within these range partitioned child tables. See Listing 15-8.

CHAPTER 15 TABLE PARTITIONS

Listing 15-8. List Partition with Range and Hash Subpartition

```
DROP TABLE IF EXISTS global1 CASCADE;
-- Create the main table with RANGE partitioning on date_cr
CREATE TABLE global1
(
    countryid integer,
    region varchar,
    country varchar,
    date_cr date,
    amount integer
)
PARTITION BY RANGE (date_cr);
CREATE TABLE country_dates_2020
PARTITION OF global1
FOR VALUES FROM ('2020-01-01') TO ('2021-01-01');
CREATE TABLE country_dates_2020_p0
PARTITION OF country_dates_2020
FOR VALUES WITH (MODULUS 3, REMAINDER 0)
PARTITION BY LIST (country);
CREATE TABLE country_dates_2020_p0_list1
PARTITION OF country_dates_2020_p0
FOR VALUES IN ('USA', 'JAPAN', 'CHINA');
CREATE TABLE country_dates_2020_p0_list2
PARTITION OF country_dates_2020_p0
FOR VALUES IN ('UK', 'FRANCE', 'GERMANY');
CREATE TABLE country_dates_2020_p0_list3
PARTITION OF country_dates_2020_p0
FOR VALUES IN ('INDIA', 'BRAZIL', 'AUSTRALIA');
INSERT INTO global1 (countryid, region, country, date_cr, amount) VALUES
(0, 'North America', 'USA', '2020-05-15', 1000),
```

```
(3, 'Asia', 'JAPAN', '2020-06-10', 2000),
(6, 'Europe', 'UK', '2020-08-25', 1800);
SELECT * FROM global1;
```

The table inheritance for partitioning tables is the old way of table partition, before version 10, where you had to programmatically partition data with functions and triggers. However, this approach requires more maintenance and development effort than declarative partitions. The partition data is not automatically distributed to appropriate partitions after update of partition data.

Listing 15-9 shows the script to create partitions with inheritance to create partitions dynamically.

15.4.12 Partitions with Inheritance

With the inheritance method, you have to insert data into partitions by triggers. This method is for downward compatibility. This method does not update the partitions for the data movement by the upgrade command. Listing 15-9 creates tables with the specified partition range using generate series function and dynamic SQL.

Listing 15-9. Partitions with Inheritance

```
    drop table if exists weather_data cascade;
    CREATE TABLE weather_data (
    location_id   int not null,
    entrydate     date not null,
    avg_temp      int,
    rainfall      int
);
-- Create table for each day
    DO $$
DECLARE
```

```
        day DATE;
BEGIN
    FOR day IN SELECT generate_series('2024-06-01'::DATE,
    '2024-06-7'::DATE, '1 day'::INTERVAL)::DATE
    LOOP
        EXECUTE 'CREATE TABLE weather_data_' || to_char(day,
        'YYYYMMDD') || ' () INHERITS (weather_data)';
    END LOOP;
END $$;
```

Note You have to write a function and trigger to insert data into respective partitions with new values (New.). See Listing 15-10.

Listing 15-10. Partition Insert Procedure

```
CREATE OR REPLACE FUNCTION weather_insert_trigger()
RETURNS TRIGGER AS $$
BEGIN
    IF (NEW.entrydate >= '2024-06-01'AND NEW.entrydate <
'2024-06-02') THEN
        INSERT INTO weather_data_20240601 VALUES (NEW.*);
      ELSIF (NEW.entrydate >= '2024-06-02' AND NEW.entrydate<
      '2024-06-03') THEN
        INSERT INTO weather_data_20240602 VALUES (NEW.*);
     ELSIF (NEW.entrydate >= '2024-06-03' AND NEW.entrydate<
      '2024-06-04') THEN
        INSERT INTO weather_data_20240603 VALUES (NEW.*);
    ELSIF (NEW.entrydate >= '2024-06-04' AND NEW.entrydate<
      '2024-06-05') THEN
        INSERT INTO weather_data_20240604 VALUES (NEW.*);
```

```
        ELSIF (NEW.entrydate >= '2024-06-05' AND NEW.entrydate<
        '2024-06-06') THEN
            INSERT INTO weather_data_20240605 VALUES (NEW.*);
        ELSIF (NEW.entrydate >= '2024-06-06' AND NEW.entrydate<
        '2024-06-07') THEN
            INSERT INTO weather_data_20240606 VALUES (NEW.*);
        ELSE
            RAISE EXCEPTION 'Date out of range for weather_insert_
            trigger() function!';
        END IF;
        RETURN NULL;
END;
$$ LANGUAGE plpgsql;
CREATE TRIGGER insert_weather_data_trigger
BEFORE INSERT ON weather_data
FOR EACH ROW EXECUTE FUNCTION weather_insert_trigger();
```

15.5 PostgreSQL Partition Copy to Cloud Storage

It is common practice in corporate IT data procedures to purge old partitions that are no longer required for business reporting. With simple Linux shell scripting, you can back up partitions, copy them to S3, and delete the copied partitions to release space from the database.

Azure Database for PostgreSQL connector in copy activity provides built-in data partitioning to copy data in parallel. Refer to this URL for details: https://learn.microsoft.com/en-us/azure/data-factory/copy-activity-performance-features#parallel-copy.

Amazon RDS provides a set of API calls to back up PostgreSQL partitions to an S3 bucket. You learned how to copy data to S3 or Azure

CHAPTER 15 TABLE PARTITIONS

Blob in Chapter 3. Use the scripting examples to copy partition data to cloud storage for long-term archival retention.

15.5.1 PostgreSQL Partition Shell Script to S3 Copy

```
function part_s3() {
  clear
  dd=`date +%m%y%d%S`
  dbname=`$PGHOME/psql -A -F -v -q -t -X -w <<eof
select datname from pg_database
where datname not like '%temp%';
:::::::::::::::::::::::::::::::::::::::::::::
```

Refer to AMI for the full script description.

15.5.2 Partition Catalog Metadata Views

The function pg_partition_tree displays the parent and child partition levels in the database.

```
postgres=#      select * from pg_partition_tree('log');
    relid    | parentrelid | isleaf | level
-------------+-------------+--------+-------
 log         |             | f      |   0
 log_q1_2024 | log         | t      |   1
 log_q2_2024 | log         | t      |   1
```

The partition range details are obtained from the pg_get_expr function.

```
SELECT
    relname as partition_table,
```

```
        pg_get_expr(relpartbound, oid) as partition_range
        FROM pg_class
WHERE relispartition
AND relkind = 'r'
;
 partition_table |                    partition_range
-----------------+-------------------------------------------
 log_q2_2024     | FOR VALUES FROM ('2024-04-01') TO
('2024-06-30')
 log_q1_2024     | FOR VALUES FROM ('2024-01-01') TO
('2024-03-31')
```

The partition table object id(oid) is converted to tablename by the ::regclass typecase operator.

```
SELECT tableoid::regclass, * FROM log;
   tableoid   | log_id |           logtext           | log_date
--------------+--------+-----------------------------+------------
 log_q1_2024  |   200  | test                        | 2024-03-20
 log_q2_2024  |   100  | test                        | 2024-06-21
```

15.6 Keywords

Table partition methods, table partition options, table partition scripts, table partition with inheritance, table partition copy to S3, and table partition copy to Azure Blob.

You can find a partition copy video here:

https://us02web.zoom.us/rec/share/vNdf_4sty2H-Vzc2bVeSPDy-cuTy9bZGQak7Fnn5bSQbtAck6JwTYsaLtYPf613H.4jL8EbmBǝUbLB3SI

15.7 Summary of Learning

You reviewed different partition methods. You learned how to create partitioned tables, how to detach and attach partitions, how to update partition data, and how to view the partition details from the PostgreSQL catalog.

15.8 Practice Chapter 15

1. Create a range partitioned table for four quarters and insert the data.

2. Detach and attach partitions.

3. Copy data from a non-partitioned table to a partitioned table with and without a primary key.

4. Create a trigger function to load data into a partitioned table.

15.9 Question Chapter 15

1. How do you create a table partition using the Hash method? Can you provide an example?

2. Can you explain the steps involved in detaching and attaching partitions?

3. How do you install and configure the `pg_partman` extension?

4. What is the procedure to view partition DDL (Data Definition Language) and DML (Data Manipulation Language) details in PostgreSQL?

5. How can you copy data between multiple schemas?

6. Can you provide an example of creating sub partitions with a hash partition in PostgreSQL?

7. How do you create declarative partitions with check constraints? Can you provide an example?

8. Where can you find the partition metadata catalog scripts?

9. How do you create a table partition using the list method? Can you provide an example?

10. What are the advantages of using partitioning?

References

1. David Dewitt and Jim Gray. *Parallel Database Systems: The Future of High-Performance Database Systems*, page 86. https://github.com/pgpartman/pg_partman/blob/master/doc/pg_partman.md

CHAPTER 16

Postgres Tablespaces

16.1 Abstract

By default, PostgreSQL cluster datafiles, configuration files, and transaction log files are stored in the operating system directory and refer to the environmental PGDATA, which is located in the operating system root directory. Tables and other objects are created within this directory, which is referred to as the default data directory. With the creation of PostgreSQL tablespaces, you can distribute table and index data into separate tablespaces residing at different disk locations to take advantage of parallel I/O on multiple drives. Furthermore, you can define different schemas residing at separate storage locations for effective balancing of I/O to improve overall performance. The PostgreSQL cluster includes the backup of files residing on file systems along with the backup of the PGDATA directory

16.2 Objectives of Learning

- Tablespaces overview
- OS configuration for the tablespace
- Data copy procedures for the tablespace
- Backup of the tablespaces

CHAPTER 16   POSTGRES TABLESPACES

16.3 Introduction

By default, PostgreSQL stores its data in a directory that is defined in the environmental variable called PGDATA. Tables and other objects are created within this directory in a separate file. You can create tablespaces outside of the default PGDATA data directory for larger systems, to isolate data from indexes, to create storage for application-related subject areas, to improve performance by creating tables on SSD devices, and to specify separate storage for partitions. To create a tablespace in PostgreSQL, you can use the CREATE TABLESPACE command, specifying the name and location of the tablespace. Tablespaces in PostgreSQL allow database administrators to define locations in the file system where the files representing database objects can be stored [1].

When you create tablespace(s), the database files are created outside the default data directory; however, there is a symbolic link from the data directory to the location of the tablespace data file location. During the backup, PostgreSQL backs up all the data from the tablespaces. There are two default tablespaces: the default for user data and the system catalog data. There is a symbolic link from the pg_tblspc to the filesystem. See Figure 16-1.

Postgres Tablespaces

Postgres Cluster	
Default Tablespace	Non Default Tablespaces
Tables A/B/C/D/E/F/G/H/I/J/K/L	Tables M/N/O/P/Q/R/S/T/V/W/X
mounted on directory /data	mounted on /datasales /datafin /datamkt
Table data location: data_directory/base	Table data location: data_directory/pg_tblspc

Default Tablespace
In base directory of PGDATA
Table: log
Path: base/13748/16409

Tablespace Data01
On file system /datasales/dev'
Table: 'log2023_m1'
Path:pg_tblspc/16384/PG_14_202107181/13748/16399

Figure 16-1. *Default and non-default tablespace objects*

16.4 Tablespace Creation Procedures

Tablespace creation is a two-step process: you create an operating system directory and you create a tablespace from the database.

16.4.1 Create an Operating System Directory

The first task after logging onto a Linux host is to set the profile to the reference of PGHOME to the PostgreSQL binaries location and PGDATA to the data directory.

Then you create directories at the operating system level with following make directory command. Refer to examples in Chapter 3 to allocate the storage and creation of directories.

```
sudo mkdir -p /pgtblespace/dev
sudo mkdir -p /pgtblespace/dev1
```

16.4.2 Create a Tablespace

After the creation of directories, the next step is to create a tablespace in the database with the following command. Run it from the shell.

```
psql -c "create tablespace data01 location '/pgtblespace/dev';"
psql -c "create tablespace data02 location '/pgtblespace/dev1';"
```

16.4.3 Create Tables in a Tablespace

The final step is to create a table in the tablespaces. You can assign the tablespace in the table DDL command or set the tablespace name at the psql command. See Listing 16-1.

Listing 16-1. Create a Table in a Non-Default Tablespace

```
     DROP TABLE IF EXISTS log;
CREATE TABLE log (
log_id        integer NOT NULL GENERATED ALWAYS AS IDENTITY,
log_date       date not null,
log_text       char(10),
constraint pk_log primary key(log_id,log_date)
) PARTITION BY RANGE (log_date);
 CREATE TABLE log2023_m1 PARTITION OF log
 FOR VALUES FROM ('2023-01-01') TO ('2023-02-01')
 tablespace data01;
```

16.4.4 Create a Table in a Tablespace with the set Command

Listing 16-2 shows the script to assign tables to the different tablespaces.

Listing 16-2. Set Tablespace Command

```
 SET default_tablespace =data01;
DROP TABLE IF EXISTS log2023_m1;
CREATE TABLE log2023_m1 PARTITION OF log
FOR VALUES FROM ('2023-01-01') TO ('2023-02-01');
SET default_tablespace =data02;
CREATE TABLE log2023_m2 PARTITION OF log
FOR VALUES FROM ('2023-02-01') TO ('2023-03-01');
```

16.4.5 Create a Table in a Default Tablespace

You can also use the default $PGDATA to assign storage to the table. The following is the command to create a table in a default tablespace:

```
CREATE TABLE log_default PARTITION OF log DEFAULT ;
```

16.4.6 Load Sample Data

You can load sample data which will be copied to partitions, based on the data distribution. See Listing 16-3.

Listing 16-3. Insert Command

```
INSERT INTO log(log_date,log_text) values('2023-01-01','log010123');
INSERT INTO log(log_date,log_text) values('2023-01-02','log010123');
```

16.4.7 Query the Location of a Table in a Tablespace

You can identify the physical location of the partitioned tables with the pg_relation_filepath command. In the select statement with the pg_relation_filepath function, you can identify the table data location on the computer hard disk. See Listing 16-4.

Listing 16-4. Table to File Mapping

```
      SELECT pg_relation_filepath('log2023_m1');
           pg_relation_filepath
------------------------------------------------
 pg_tblspc/16384/PG_14_202107181/13748/16399
(1 row)
postgres=# SELECT pg_relation_filepath('log');
 pg_relation_filepath
----------------------
postgres=# SELECT pg_relation_filepath('log_default');
 base/13748/1640
```

16.4.8 Non-Default Tablespaces Creation Summary

Set the environmental variable to the location of the data directory by exporting PGDATA=[location of Data Directory]. Listing 16-5 shows the summary steps to create a non-default tablespace. See Figure 16-2.

Listing 16-5. Summary of Tablespace Creation Procedures

```
1) df -h
2) psql -c "create tablespace data01 location /
pgtablespace/dev;"
3) psql -c "create table log(id integer, name location,
crdate date;"
4) ls -l $PGDATA/pg_tblspc
5) psql -c "select pg_reation_filepath('log');"
6) pg_basebackup /tmp -F t.  # adjust to your backup path
7) cat /tmp/backup_manifest
```

CHAPTER 16 POSTGRES TABLESPACES

Non-Default tables space in Postgres Creation and Backup

1. **df -h** # Identify the file system
   /pgtablesace/dev
2. **Create tablespace data01** # create tablespace
       location /pgtablespace/dev
3. **Create table log** # create table on data01 tablespace
       tablespace data01
4. **ls -l $PGDATA/pg_tblspc** # Identify tablespace symbolic link
       lrwxrwxrwx. 1 postgres 16 May 6 03:00 16384 -> /pgtblespace/dev
5. **SELECT pg_relation_filepath**('log'); # check the log table disk path

   pg_relation_filepath
   ----
   pg_tblspc/16384/PG_14_202107181/13748/16399

6. **pg_basebackup** [backupdir] –F t # Backup Cluster
7. Identify Backup manifest file: **backup_manifest** # Identify the tablespace
8. { "Path": "pg_tblspc/16384/PG_14_202107181/13748/16399"

Figure 16-2. Tablespace creation summary

When making a backup of a PostgreSQL database, the data directory $PGDATA and all the files and directories within it are backed up. This includes the default tablespace as well as any additional tablespaces created in the database.

When you create tablespaces, symbolic links are created in the $PGDATA/pg_tblspc directory that point to the individual directories of each non-built-in tablespace defined in the cluster. The pg_basebackup command includes symbolic links in the backup, allowing the tablespaces to be restored along with the main database for recovery requirements.

CHAPTER 16 POSTGRES TABLESPACES

When restoring a backup, check that the symbolic links in the $PGDATA/pg_tblspc directory are restored along with the backup of the tablespaces themselves. This will ensure that the symbolic links point to the correct locations of the restored tablespaces. All tablespace details are viewed from the \db meta command or from select * From pg_catalog.pg_tablespace.

The table data is moved from the default to new tablespace with the command ALTER TABLE [tablename] SET TABLESPACE [new tablespace]. Listing 16-6 shows an example.

Listing 16-6. Table Move Procedure

```
$mkdir -p /postdata16/data
$psql -c "CREATE TABLESPACE data1 location '/postdata16/data';"
$psql -c "CREATE TABLE test1 as select * From pg_tables;"
$psql -c "SELECT pg_relation_filepath('test1');"
 base/5/16568
$psql -c "ALTER TABLE test1 set tablespace data1;"
$psql -c "SELECT pg_relation_filepath('test1');"
         pg_relation_filepath
------------------------------------------
 pg_tblspc/16567/PG_16_202307071/5/16571
(1 row)
```

The following is an example of identifying symbolic links:

```
$ ls -l $PGDATA/pg_tblspc
total 0
lrwxrwxrwx. 1 postgres 16 May  6 03:00 16384 -> /pgtblespace/dev
lrwxrwxrwx. 1 postgres 17 May  6 03:01 16386 -> /pgtblespace/dev1
```

16.4.9 pg_basebackup

After completing the backup with the pg_basebackp command, you can examine the reference to the Postgres custom created tablespaces. Listing 16-7 shows the backup command along with base.tar and pg_wal.tar files, created in the backup directory.

Listing 16-7. Backup Manifest File

```
$ pg_basebackup  -D /pgdata15/'hostname'$dd  -F t
$ ls -ltr /pgdata15
16384.tar  16386.tar  backup_manifest  base.tar  pg_wal.tar
$ cat backup_manifest
{ "PostgreSQL-Backup-Manifest-Version": 1,
"Files": [
{ "Path": "pg_tblspc/16384/PG_14_202107181/13748/16387",
"Size": 8192, "Last-Modified": "2023-05-06 03:C5:12 GMT",
"Checksum-Algorithm": "CRC32C", "Checksum": "3aea70d3" },
"Manifest-Checksum": "2be6fd49c733403a3aad17bc1a2b2803e843a73
5cc16bb0c85957b7a113d4f31"}
```

If you examine the backup manifest command, you will notice the reference to default tablespaces.

16.5 Keywords

Create directory, create tablespace, create table and tablespaces in backup

16.6 Summary of Learning

You learned how to create directories for PostgreSQL tablespaces, identified the custom tablespace in the data dictionary, reviewed DDL for creation of tablespaces, and reviewed the backup manifestation.

16.7 Practice Chapter 16

1. Create a tablespace on a separate filesystem.
2. Create a table in the tablespace.
3. Validate a tablespace in the `pg_basebackup`.
4. Move tables from the base data directory to a tablespace.

16.8 Questions Chapter 16

1. What are the main benefits of creating separate tablespaces in PostgreSQL?
2. How can you identify tablespaces that are located outside of the default PGDATA directory?
3. What are the steps involved in creating and mounting file systems for tablespaces in PostgreSQL?
4. Can you provide a detailed procedure for migrating table data to tablespaces in PostgreSQL?
5. How can you identify the tablespaces associated with backup metadata?
6. What methods can be used to specify tablespaces for tables, partitions, and indexes in PostgreSQL?
7. What is the significance of the `pg_default` and `pg_global` tablespaces?
8. How can you view the current tablespaces in a database?

CHAPTER 16 POSTGRES TABLESPACES

9. Can you explain the concept of tablespace inheritance?

10. What happens if a tablespace runs out of disk space?

11. Is it possible to move a table from one tablespace to another? If so, how?

12. How can you change the default tablespace for a table?

Reference

1. www.postgresql.org/docs/current/manage-ag-tablespaces.html

CHAPTER 17

MVCC

17.1 Abstract

The core competency of the database engine is gauged by its adherence to multi-version concurrency control (MVCC) transaction processing procedures and protocols. MVCC enables multiple user transactions to access the data concurrently for select, insert, update, and delete operations using ANSI-compliant isolation levels, which include READ UNCOMMITTED, READ COMMITTED, REPEATABLE READ, or SERIALIZABLE. Dirty reads are possible with READ UNCOMMITTED transactions, whereas READ COMMITTED reads committed data, avoiding dirty reads.

Non-repeatable reads are prevented with REPEATABLE READ. SERIALIZATION is the ideal form with high level isolation.

Although no specific setting is required for the default READ COMMITTED isolation level, you have to modify database parameters to support other isolations. PostgreSQL employs locking mechanisms to support data integrity during DDL and DML operations. PostgreSQL provides a rich set of database catalog views to identify locking conflicts, aiding DBAs in supporting critical production environments.

CHAPTER 17 MVCC

17.2 Objectives of Learning

- Multi-version concurrency control overview
- Isolation levels
- Data integrity
- Database locks

17.3 Multi-Version Concurrency Control

MVCC is implemented by creating multiple versions of individual transaction data with two virtual columns, xmin and xmax. xmin has the identity (transaction ID) of the inserting transaction for this row version and xmax has the identity (transaction ID) of the deleting transaction, or zero for an undeleted row version [1]. With these virtual columns, PostgreSQL tracks changes that occurred during insert, updates, and deletes inside the transaction block for commit as well as for rollback and to provide a consistent view of data for select statements used for long-running reports. The WAL files are used for rollback and recovery, which roll backs aborted transactions and replays the committed transactions. The main advantage of MVCC concurrency control is that its readers don't block writers and vice versa where user action is not required and is managed by PostgreSQL Server.

17.3.1 ANSI SQL Isolation Levels

A SQL transaction has an isolation level that is READ UNCOMMITTED, READ COMMITTED, REPEATABLE READ, or SERIALIZABLE.

PostgreSQL offers all the four isolation levels specified by ANSI SQL standards. The possibilities of the read transaction behavior are defined in Figure 17-1, defined in the PostgreSQL documentation

CHAPTER 17 MVCC

Isolation Level	Dirty Read	Nonrepeatable Read	Phantom Read	Serialization Anomaly
Read uncommitted	Allowed, but not in PG	Possible	Possible	Possible
Read committed	Not possible	Possible	Possible	Possible
Repeatable read	Not possible	Not possible	Allowed, but not in PG	Possible
Serializable	Not possible	Not possible	Not possible	Not possible

Figure 17-1. *ANSI/ISO SQL isolation levels [2]*

Starting with PostgreSQL 9.1, SERIALIZABLE is merged with the snapshot isolation methodology.

17.3.2 Read Anomaly

There are three categories of read anomalies that can cause data inconsistency during SQL statement retrieval in transactions: dirty reads, non-repeatable (or fuzzy) reads, and phantom reads. MVCC helps eliminate these read anomalies by preserving the old image of the data during the duration of the select statement. See Figure 17-2.

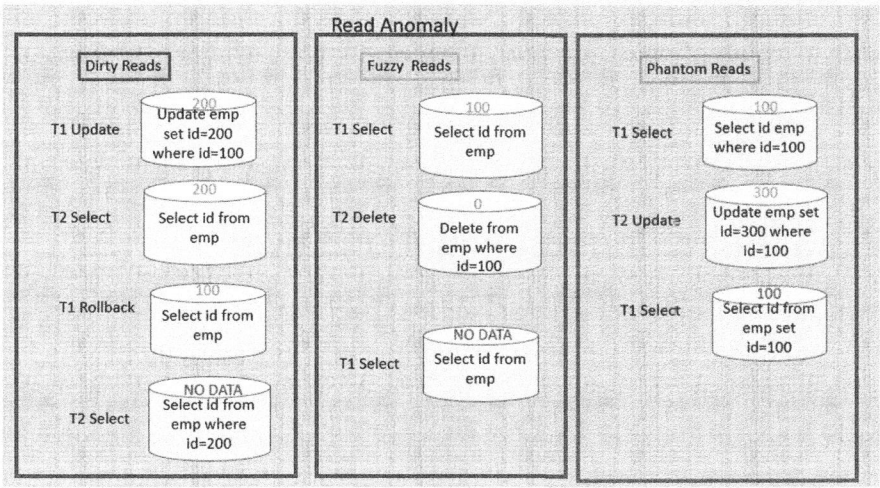

Figure 17-2. *Read anomaly*

- **Dirty reads anomaly**: This occurs when a transaction t2 reads an uncommitted data from transaction t1; when t1 rolls back the data, the original data is not visible to t2. It's not possible in PostgreSQL.

- **Fuzzy read anomaly**: This arises when a transaction, t1, reads data but before completing, another transaction, t2, deletes that same data. If t1 attempts to read the data again, it might encounter a different value or discover that the data is no longer present.

- **Phantom reads anomaly**: This happens when a transaction, t1, reads a set of rows that match a certain condition. Then another transaction, t2, inserts, deletes, or updates some rows, which causes them to now match or no longer match the condition. If t1 re-executes the reading query, it gets a different set of rows.

Note Assumption of one row in the emp table with the id value of 100 in Figure 17-2.

17.3.3 Read Commit Isolation Level

The default isolation in PostgreSQL is READ COMMITTED. The select statement may exhibit data inconsistency within its transaction, particularly for uncommitted data. During an update statement, if multiple transactions are updating a row concurrently, the update transaction will wait for the commit or rollback of the other transaction. The behavior of the delete statement is like the select statement. The insert statement has two additional arguments for conflict action: (1) do nothing and (2) do update set. The conflict do update is the same as the insert statement, whereas with a conflicting do nothing, it waits for the outcome of the dependent transaction [3]

17.3.4 Repeatable Read Isolation Level

In the REPEATABLE READ isolation level, the DML changes made to data are not visible to other sessions. For example, if you delete two rows from a table, these changes won't be visible to other sessions. This behavior can be observed in the MVCC simulation script shown later in the chapter.

17.3.5 Serializable Isolation Level

The SERIALIZABLE isolation level in PostgreSQL uses serializable snapshot isolation (SSI), which employs predictive locking. Instead of executing all transactions purely serially, it uses non-blocking predictive locks to prevent data inconsistencies, ensuring that the effect of concurrent transactions is as if they were executed one after another. The predicate locking mechanism is employed to detect and prevent anomalies without relying on traditional locks. Furthermore, PostgreSQL uses SSI locks during the pg_dump backup activity to guarantee a consistent state of the database throughout the backup process.

MVCC boosts concurrency without relying on exclusive table locks by using row-level versioning, not necessarily locking at the block or page level. Essentially, MVCC ensures that each user's access to data remains isolated from other users. This guarantees that writers never block readers and vice versa. The detailed mechanics of how isolation levels are implemented are beyond the scope of this book.

Beginning from version 9, PostgreSQL included snapshot isolation, which allows transactions to view consistent snapshot of the database at the start of the transaction.

17.4 MVCC and Database Blocks

While MVCC uses row-level versioning to manage concurrency, the physical storage in terms of database blocks or pages plays a significant role in the transactional workflow. The database block is the lowest unit of data storage in the operating system, and pages are managed by the database system. Considerations related to a database block include the following:

- How many blocks are required for the transaction
- The specific location of the data block
- Whether the block is located on disk or in memory
- The number of transactions and user sessions accessing these blocks
- The state and type of locks on these blocks

PostgreSQL efficiently manages concurrent access to these database blocks with its robust transaction management system.

By using MVCC and offering different isolation levels, PostgreSQL permits concurrent transactions to access data in a controlled manner.

17.5 Linux and Database Concurrency

In the Linux operating system, elements such as the file system cache contribute to a database's efficient functioning by speeding up data access. Within database systems, mechanisms like page-level locking, lightweight buffer locks, and record-level locking in the snapshot of the data allow reads and writes to occur independently. These mechanisms ensure that operations don't block each other simultaneously, leading to increased concurrency. This results in reduced chances of conflicts while ensuring data integrity and consistency.

17.6 DBA Tasks

As a DBA, you may need to collaborate with the application team to recommend non-default isolation levels, such as READ UNCOMMITTED, REPEATABLE READ, and SERIALIZABLE. No action is needed with the default read commit isolation. The DBA's responsibility is to understand the read anomalies associated with transactions, examine the locking mechanisms to resolve performance issues, set up appropriate values for parameters that govern the isolation levels, and support the normal functioning of the database system. All you need to understand is the commands and how to execute these commands in support of database administration. These can be set at the individual session level. Before engaging with the application team, it's essential to have a deep understanding of MVCC and its practical applications.

The default isolation level is READ COMMITTED.

For the alter system command, the scope is for the entire database, and with the set transaction command, the scope is for individual sessions. Here are examples:

```
postgres=# ALTER SYSTEM SET default_transaction_isolation TO 'REPEATABLE READ';
postgres=# ALTER SYSTEM SET default_transaction_isolation TO 'SERIALIZABLE';
```

To set isolation level for the session or for individual transactions, you must use the command inside a translation block of begin and end. Here is an example:

```
BEGIN;
SET TRANSACTION ISOLATION LEVEL SERIALIZABLE;
- Run transactions
END;
```

CHAPTER 17 MVCC

If you do not set inside the block, you will receive this error:

```
postgres=# SET TRANSACTION ISOLATION LEVEL SERIALIZABLE;
WARNING: SET TRANSACTION can only be used in transaction blocks
```

The default transaction level is displayed with the show command:

```
postgres=# SHOW default_transaction_isolation;
default_transaction_isolation
-------------------------------
read committed
```

With Postgres catalog views, pg_locks, pg_blocking_pids(), pg_blocked_pid(), pgrowlocks, and pg_stat_activity, you can identify the row level, table level, page level, and block level lock.

You have to determine the age of the long-running transactions and advise the application team to disconnect or terminate long-running queries to avoid "oldest x min is far in the past." You can determine the long-running query by subtracting the current time with xact_start in the view pg_stat_activity. The SQL to check long running transactions is shown in Listing 17-1.

Listing 17-1. Long-Running Status Check

```
SELECT substr(query,1,40),pid,backend_start,xact_start,now()-
xact_start seconds from pg_stat_activity where xact_start is
not null;
```

As a DBA, you are responsible for reviewing database locking activity. Consider the delete statement in Listings 17-2 and 17-3 to understand the database locking behavior.

Note To view the pgrolocks, you have to install the extension pgrolocks.

Session 1

Listing 17-2. Repeatable Read Isolation Level

```
postgres=#  BEGIN TRANSACTION ISOLATION LEVEL REPEATABLE READ;
# CREATE TABLE emp(id INT);
postgres=# INSERT INTO emp VALUES(100),(200),(300);
postgres=*# DELETE FROM emp where id=300;
```

Session 2

Listing 17-3. Database Row Level Locks

```
SELECT a.pid,a.mode, a.transactionid, a.relation, b.relname,
s.usename
FROM pg_locks a
JOIN pg_class b ON a.relation = b.oid
JOIN pg_stat_activity s ON a.pid = s.pid
 where b.relname='emp';
 pid  |       mode       | transactionid | relation | relname
 | usename
------+------------------+---------------+----------+---------
+----------
 1853 | RowExclusiveLock |               |    34159 | emp      |
postgres
(1 row)
CREATE EXTENSION pgrowlocks;

postgres=# SELECT pgrowlocks('emp');
                pgrowlocks
---------------------------------------------
 ("(0,2)",114163,f,{114163},{Update},{1853})
(1 row)
```

If you examine the above image, the shared locks were granted for the emp table. By default, PostgreSQL acquires an AccessShareLock on `pg_database`, `pg_authid` indexes, and `pg_class` indexes. Using the query mentioned earlier, you can monitor the database's locking activity. This information can be vital when collaborating with application developers to address performance issues related to database locks

17.7 Serializable Isolation Configuration

If you choose to override the default read commit isolation level, for the setup of the non-default isolation level of SERIALIZABLE, for optimal database performance, you have to tune parameters such as `idle_in_transaction_session_timeout`, `max_pred_locks_per_transaction`, `max_pred_locks_per_relation`, `max_pred_locks_per_page`, `random_page_cost`, and `cpu_tuple_cost` are necessary [4].

17.8 MVCC and Implicit Locks

In PostgreSQL, for Data Definition Language (DDL) commands such as `CREATE TABLE`, `ALTER TABLE`, `TRUNCATE TABLE`, and `CREATE INDEX`, the system imposes default locks. These are commonly referred to as "pessimistic locks" and "implicit locks." Such locks prevent other operations from accessing the relevant data structures during the execution of the DDL command.

17.9 MVCC and Explicit Locks

Explicit locks in PostgreSQL encompass table-level, row-level, page-level locks, and deadlocks. Table-level locks include ACCESS SHARE, ROW SHARE, ROW EXCLUSIVE, SHARE UPDATE EXCLUSIVE, SHARE, SHARE

ROW EXCLUSIVE, EXCLUSIVE, and ACCESS EXCLUSIVE. Row-level locks feature FOR UPDATE, FOR NO KEY UPDATE, FOR SHARE, and FOR KEY SHARE. Page-level locks are managed internally by the PostgreSQL database. Notably, deadlocks can arise due to these explicit locking mechanisms [5].

As reviewed earlier in this chapter, PostgreSQL creates xmin and xmax virtual columns to track the changes to the row of the table for update and delete operations. The data elements with xmin and xmax are identified in the section.

17.10 Understanding MVCC Scenarios in the Real World

While theory, concepts, and implementation offer foundational knowledge, how do you truly understand MVCC scenarios in a real-world context? Should you wait until you face transaction processing challenges or errors? A practical way to address these questions is to simulate MVCC behavior using a Linux shell script. Through this method, different isolation levels can be tested and demonstrated.

Please refer to the AMI example to simulate the isolation level anomalies.

In the REPEATABLE READS isolation level, a consistent snapshot of the data is taken at the beginning of the transaction. For instance, under the REPEATABLE READS isolation level, if one session deletes certain rows in a table, these rows remain visible to other user sessions with different xmax values for each row.

REPEATABLE READ isolation level and xmin virtual column details are in Listing 17-4.

CHAPTER 17 MVCC

Listing 17-4. REPEATABLE READ Isolation Level

```
Session 1
postgres=# BEGIN TRANSACTION ISOLATION LEVEL REPEATABLE READ;
BEGIN
postgres=*# select xmin,xmax,* From emp;
 xmin | xmax | id  | fname | lname
------+------+-----+-------+--------
 2548 |    0 | 101 | john1 | bogus1
 2549 |    0 | 200 | john2 | bogus2

postgres=*# update emp
set id=9999
where id=101
postgres-*# ;
UPDATE 1
postgres=*# select xmin,xmax,* From emp;
 xmin | xmax |  id  | fname | lname
------+------+------+-------+--------
 2549 |    0 |  200 | john2 | bogus2
 2553 |    0 | 9999 | john1 | bogus1
```

In Listing 17-4, when the column id 101 value is updated, PostgreSQL created new min value to 2553. See Listing 17-5.

Listing 17-5. xmin and xmax Values

```
Session 2
postgres=# BEGIN TRANSACTION ISOLATION LEVEL REPEATABLE READ;
select xmin,xmax,*  From emp;
BEGIN
```

```
 xmin | xmax | id  | fname | lname
------+------+-----+-------+--------
 2548 | 2553 | 101 | john1 | bogus1.  ← New changed values in
xmax. The original 2548
 2549 |    0 | 200 | john2 | bogus2
```

From the second session, the original and changed xmin values are visible. The original value is 2548 and the new value is 2553.

In the above image, as rows are deleted by session 2, the xmax is set to 10555 for unique version identification.

17.11 Serializable Concurrent Transaction Issue

Although the isolation level of SERIALIZABLE does not exhibit any read anomalies, it can present transaction errors in concurrent access to the data. Application developers should have appropriate levels of commits in their code to avoid serialization issues. When two transactions are simultaneously deleting in the SERIALIZABLE isolation level, "ERROR: could not serialize due to concurrent delete" will be shown. Figure 17-3 exhibits this behavior.

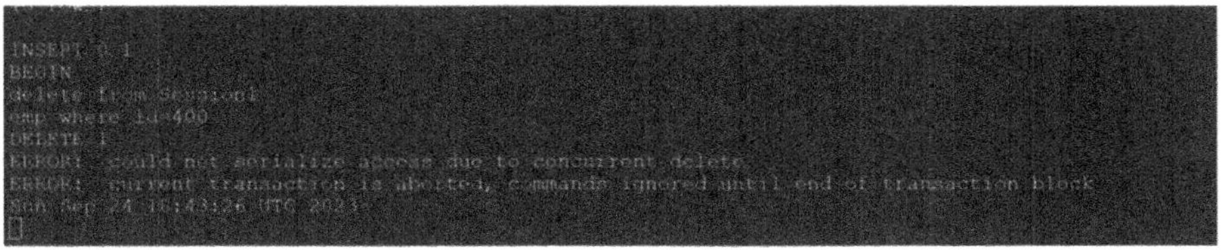

Figure 17-3. Serialization error

Effective application design, particularly regarding database interactions, can indeed prevent data inconsistencies.

CHAPTER 17   MVCC

17.12 Keywords

Isolation levels, read anomaly, READ COMMIT isolation level, REPEATABLE READ isolation level, SERIALIZABLE isolation level, and MVCC locks.

17.13 Summary of Learning

- You identified all isolation levels: READ UNCOMMITTED, READ COMMITTED, REPEATABLE READ, and SERIALIZABLE
- You learned how to set isolation levels for the system and transaction.
- You reviewed the read anomaly data.
- You identified parameters `max_pred_locks_per_transaction`, `max_pred_locks_per_relation`, `max_pred_locks_per_page`, `random_page_cost`, and `cpu_tuple_cost`.
- You saw a simulation of data for isolation errors.
- You learned about optimistic locks, pessimistic locks, explicit locks, and implicit locks.
- You used the `xmin` and `xmax sudo` columns.
- You used the `CURRENT_TIMESTAMP` and `pg_backend_pid()` variables.

17.14 Questions Chapter 17

1. What are the default ANSI isolation levels?
2. How many isolation levels are present in PostgreSQL?
3. Which version of PostgreSQL included the snapshot isolation method?
4. What are the main views to determine the locks in the PostgreSQL database?
5. What is the command to end the isolation level?
6. How do you check blocking and blocked user sessions?
7. What are the differences between optimistic and pessimistic locks?
8. What are the differences between implicit and explicit locks?
9. What role do the xmin and xmax system columns play in MVCC in PostgreSQL?
10. How does PostgreSQL handle deadlocks?
11. What is the purpose of the pg_stat_activity view in PostgreSQL?

References

1. www.postgresql.org/docs/current/ddl-system-columns.html
2. www.postgresql.org/docs/16/transaction-iso.html
3. www.postgresql.org/docs/current/sql-insert.html
4. www.postgresql.org/docs/current/runtime-config-locks.html
5. www.postgresql.org/docs/current/explicit-locking.html

Correction to: PostgreSQL Software Installation on Amazon EC2/Azure VM Linux

Correction to:

Venkateswara Vadlamani, *PostgreSQL Skills Development on Cloud*,
https://doi.org/10.1007/979-8-8688-0817-3

This book was inadvertently published with the below corrections not carried out, which have now been incorporated.

The updated version of these chapters can be found at
https://doi.org/10.1007/979-8-8688-0817-3_1
https://doi.org/10.1007/979-8-8688-0817-3_2
https://doi.org/10.1007/979-8-8688-0817-3_4
https://doi.org/10.1007/979-8-8688-0817-3_7
https://doi.org/10.1007/979-8-8688-0817-3_14
https://doi.org/10.1007/979-8-8688-0817-3_15
https://doi.org/10.1007/979-8-8688-0817-3

© Venkateswara Vadlamani 2025
V. Vadlamani, *PostgreSQL Skills Development on Cloud*,
https://doi.org/10.1007/979-8-8688-0817-3_18

CORRECTION TO: POSTGRESQL SOFTWARE INSTALLATION ON AMAZON EC2/AZURE VM LINUX

On page xxxvi, update in Table 1, Week 2 (Chapters 3/4/5) as "Postgres pre-install tasks, installation and configuration of Postgres Cluster with Red Hat RPM method"

On page 3, update in 2nd para, 3rd sentence, as "PostgreSQL is a widely used database in the cloud infrastructure due to its scalability and portability"

On page 62, citation 17 corrected as "S3 Glacier and S3 Glacier Deep Archival for lastly used objects such as videos and photos [16]"

On page 67, citation 17 corrected as "The az is a program that takes several arguments to manage the Data Blob service [17]:"

On page 140, changed the caption of Figure 4-5 as "PostgreSQL Security Access"

On page 148, changed the caption of Figure 4-6 as "Host based file access rules"

On page 150, Figure 4-7 updated with below image and caption as "Host based file access"

```
# TYPE  DATABASE    USER        ADDRESS              METHOD
# "local" is for Unix domain socket connections only
local    all         all                              trust
# IPv4 local connections:
host     all         all         127.0.0.1/32         trust
# IPv6 local connections:
host     all         all         ::1/128              trust
# Allow replication connections from localhost, by a user with the
# replication privilege.
local    replication all                              trust
host     replication all         127.0.0.1/32         trust
host     replication all         ::1/128              trust
host     all         all         0.0.0.0/0            scram-sha-256
```

On page 154, changed the section title as "4.6.4 New Parameters Between Versions 14-16"

CORRECTION TO: POSTGRESQL SOFTWARE INSTALLATION ON AMAZON EC2/AZURE VM LINUX

On page 155, retained Figure 4-8 as is and updated the caption as "PostgreSQL parameters"

On page 155, updated Figure 4-9 as below and updated the caption as "pg_stat_statements in postgresql.conf"

```
pg_stat_statements.track = all
shared_preload_libraries = 'pg_stat_statements'
pg_stat_statements.max = 10000
```

On page 156, Figure 4-10's caption changed to "Explain command"

On page 158, Figure 4-11's caption changed to "The timing command"

On page 158, Figure 4-12's caption changed to "PostgreSQL OS processes"

On page 159, Figure 4-13's caption changed to "systemctl details of PostgreSQL process"

On page 163, replaced Figure 4-15 with Figure 4-16

```
c:\Users\pvad1\Downloads>"c:\Program Files\PostgreSQL\16\bin\psql" -h 3.149.235.237 -U devuser -d sales
Password for user devuser:
psql (16.1, server 16.2)
WARNING: Console code page (437) differs from Windows code page (1252)
         8-bit characters might not work correctly. See psql reference
         page "Notes for Windows users" for details.
Type "help" for help.

sales=> \conninfo
You are connected to database "sales" as user "devuser" on host "3.149.235.237" at port "5432".
sales=> \! hostname
ven
```

On page 164, replaced Figure 4-16 with Figure 4-15

```
[postgres@PGdev data]$ psql -p 5433
psql (16.3)
Type "help" for help.

postgres=#
```

In the back cover text, under "What You Will Learn," the third bullet point updated as "Access sample references to scripting solutions and database management tools for working with Postgres, Redshift (based on Postgres 8.0.2), and Docker"

CORRECTION TO: POSTGRESQL SOFTWARE INSTALLATION ON AMAZON EC2/AZURE VM LINUX

On page 272, the content "Note: In the Crunchy Data example in the Appendix, you can work on open shift container tasks with shell scripting" has been removed

On page 510, the References section has been unnumbered and hyperlink retained

On page 533, Reference no. 2 has been unnumbered and hyperlink retained

APPENDIX A

Project Work: Amazon AMI

With Amazon AMI, you can deploy a fleet of EC2 instances prebuilt with PostgreSQL Cluster Software, database management utilities, and scripts, which is a repository of software to manage all aspects of PostgreSQL Database in an Amazon Cloud environment. See Figure A-1.

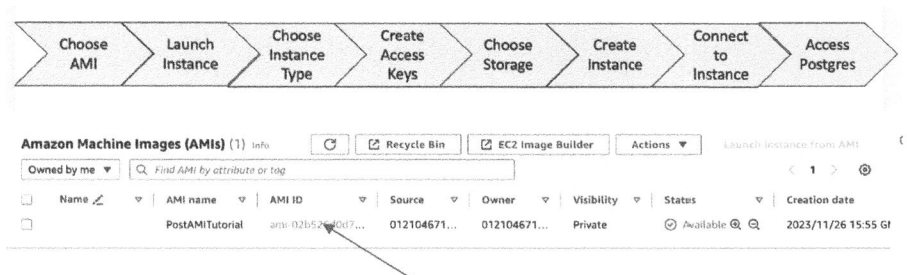

Figure A-1. AMI image

APPENDIX B

DBA Tool in AMI

The DBA tool in AMI will work with over 50 database tasks of PostgreSQL on Red Hat Linux along with Docker via a menu-driven interface, where the underlying commands are taken care of by the DBA tool (Figures B-1 and B-2). The main sections are as follows:

- Create EC2
- Create RDS
- Create Redshift
- Create PostgreSQL cluster
- Create databases, users, and data load with pgbench
- Backup and recovery
- Log dump review
- Install and configure /dockers

APPENDIX B DBA TOOL IN AMI

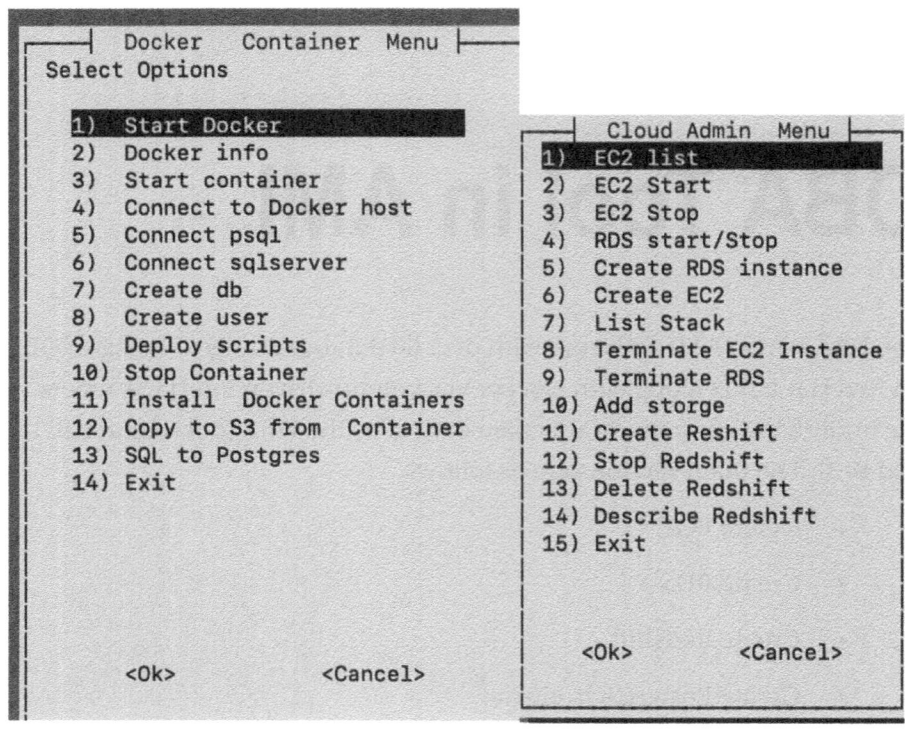

Figure B-1. *DBA tool to manage Docker, EC2, and RDS*

APPENDIX B   DBA TOOL IN AMI

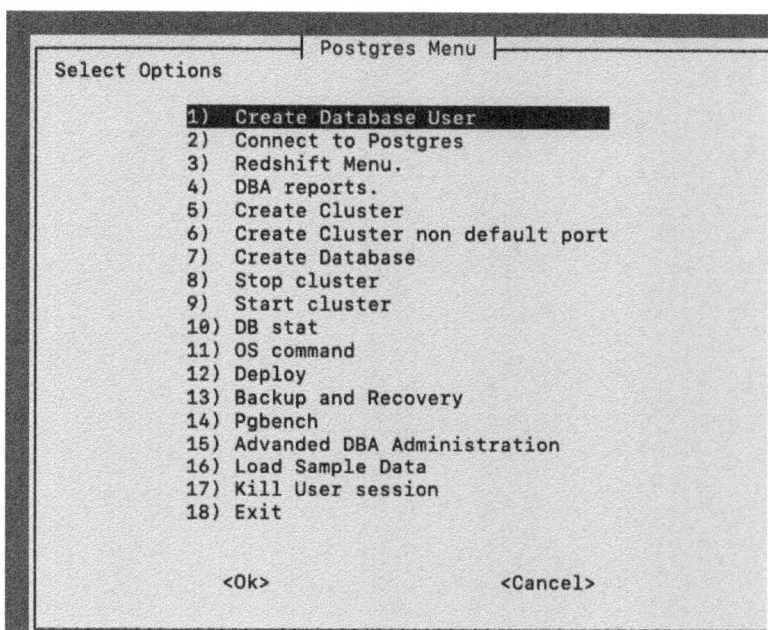

Figure B-2. *PostgreSQL admin options*

Amazon PostgreSQL AMI Reference Document link:
https://docs.google.com/document/d/15ts-6icxNGnOXaLV2hLjSL_bO4i7MlpP/edit?usp=sharing&ouid=117618855868897795502&rtpof=true&sd=true.

Azure PostgreSQL AMI Reference Document link:
https://docs.google.com/document/d/1CGb2Y-IutUzc-WpK16iPkvkcEWQJo7lf/edit?usp=drive_link&ouid=117618855868897795502&rtpof=true&sd=true.

APPENDIX C

RDS Proxy

Amazon RDS Proxy is a managed database service which is designed to improve application scalability by optimizing database connections by pooling and sharing connections; this significantly reduces the overhead associated with opening and closing connections for each user request. By reusing a smaller pool of database connections, RDS Proxy also terminates idle connections and clears up resources to be used for future sessions.

The steps to create a proxy are to create database secrets, create a proxy IAM policy, create a proxy, and modify the proxy to add users.

C.1 Create the AWS Secret for User Passwords

AWS stores user credentials with the secret manager service. Listing C-1 shows the necessary commands.

Listing C-1. AWS secretmanager create

```
$aws secretsmanager create-secret --name dev-user004
--description " RDS Proxy Credential" --secret-string
'{"username":"USER1","password":"Monitor10177"}'
```

APPENDIX C   RDS PROXY

C.2 Create the Policy for the Proxy

After storing the user credentials in secrets, the next step is to create an IAM policy for RDS Proxy. AWS uses two services to create a proxy policy for RDS Proxy. The services are Key Management Service (KMS) and secret manager. The secret manager keys are unique to your account. Identify the secret manager keys from KMS service ➤ AWS managed keys section. Identify and use the secret Amazon resource number (ARN) from AWS secret manager ➤ secrets.

With these two values, create an IAM policy for RDS Proxy.

(1) From the AWS Console, choose KMS and click aws/secretsmanager, which will display the key. See Figure C-1.

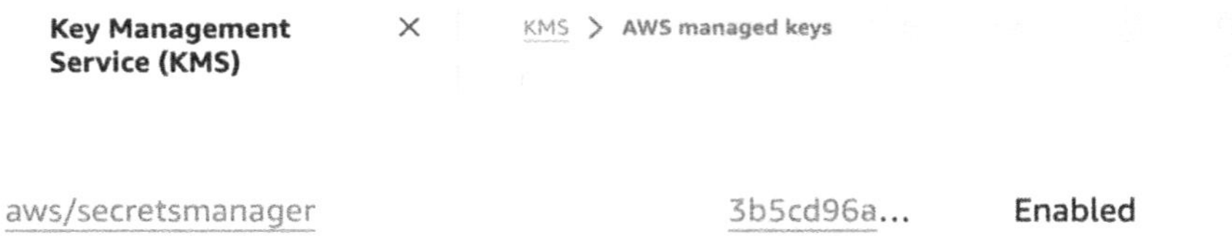

Key Management Service (KMS)	×	KMS > AWS managed keys		
aws/secretsmanager			3b5cd96a...	Enabled

Figure C-1. *KMS keyview*

(2) From AWS Console, go to AWS Secrets Manager ➤ Secrets ➤ demo[username] Secret ARN

```
arn:aws:secretsmanager:us-east-2:12345678901:secret:demo-GVQzxd
```

Create the policy RDS-Proxy-Dev JSON script with KMS and secrets as shown in Listing C-2.

Listing C-2. Create the Proxy Policy

```
aws iam create-policy --policy-name MyDevRDS --policy-document '{
    "Version": "2012-10-17",
```

```
    "Statement": [
        {
            "Sid": "GetSecretValue",
            "Effect": "Allow",
            "Action": [
                "secretsmanager:GetSecretValue"
            ],
            "Resource": "arn:aws:secretsmanager:us-east-2:12345
            678901:secret:demo-GVQzxd"
        },
        {
            "Sid": "DecryptSecretValue",
            "Effect": "Allow",
            "Action": [
                "kms:Decrypt"
            ],
            "Resource": "arn:aws:kms:us-east-2:12345678901:key
            /3b596a........",
            "Condition": {
                "StringEquals": {
                    "kms:ViaService": "secretsmanager.us-
                    east-2.amazonaws.com"
                }
            }
        }
    ]
}'
```

Create a shell script with the above proxy policy script and execute it. Listing C-3 shows the successful output of the script.

Listing C-3. Policy Creation Output

```
./policy.sh
{
    "Policy": {
        "PolicyName": "MyDevRDS",
        "PolicyId": "ANPAQFUL6UAV6EBFUDACV",
::::: Lines truncated
    }
}
```

Upon completion of the AWS secrets for the user account and IAM policy, you are ready to create RDS Proxy.

C.3 Create the Proxy Command

The command is aws rds create-db-proxy, which takes six mandatory arguments (proxyname, account number, policy, subnets, secrets, engine, and timeout). See Listing C-4.

Listing C-4. Proxy Creation

```
aws rds create-db-proxy --db-proxy-name dev --role-arn arn:aws:iam::012177777775:policy/MyDevRDS --vpc-subnet-ids subnet-b3dcbac9,subnet-d506cf99 --vpc-security-group-ids sg-0d7e4fce4a4eb8e1a --auth '[{"AuthScheme":"SECRETS","SecretArn":"arn:aws:secretsmanager:us-east-2:012177777775:secret:demo-MJUIzxd:dev-user1","IAMAuth":"DISABLED"}]' --engine-family POSTGRESQL --require-tls --idle-client-timeout 10
```

Listing C-5 shows the output.

Listing C-5. AWS Proxy Creation Output

```
{
    "DBProxy": {
        "DBProxyName": "dev",
        "DBProxyArn": "arn:aws:rds:us-east-2:01210
:::: Lines truncated
        "CreatedDate": "2024-06-09T20:36:18.734000+00:00"
    }
}
```

C.4 Modify Proxy

To add users, the process is to modify the proxy with definitions of the secrets manager. The proxy should be created before modifying to add users, like so:

```
aws rds modify-db-proxy \
    --db-proxy-name dev\
    --auth '[{"AuthScheme":"SECRETS","SecretArn":"arn:aws:secretsmanager:us-east-2:012177777775:secret:dev-user01-FIIxlE",
    "IAMAuth":"DISABLED"}]'
```

See Listing C-6 for the output.

Listing C-6. Modify Proxy to Add Users

```
{
    "DBProxy": {
        "DBProxyName": "dev",
::::: Lines truncated
}
```

C.4.1 Describe Proxies

You can describe the attributes of the proxy with `describe proxy` command, as follows:

```
$aws rds describe-db-proxies  --db-proxy-name dev
```

Listing C-7 shows the output.

Listing C-7. Describe Proxy

```
{
    "DBProxies": [
        {
            "DBProxyName": "dev",
            "DBProxyArn": "arn:aws:rds:us-east-2:012177777775:db-
            proxy:prx-038ddc5188312cabe",
 ::: Lines truncated
}
```

C.5 Describe Proxy Targets

Yon can describe `proxy-target` with the `describe-targets` command, as shown in Listing C-8.

Listing C-8. Describe Proxy Targets

```
$aws rds describe-db-proxy-targets --db-proxy-name dev
```

C.6 Connect to the RDS Database with Proxy Access

Connect to the console and receive the endpoint details:

```
psql  'host=test.proxy-c8uiiuui788.us-east-2.rds.amazonaws.com user=user01 dbname=postgres password=Monitor10177'
```

APPENDIX D

Postgres with Apache/PHP

Create EC2/VM → Install Red Hat OS → Install Apache Web Seerver → Install PHP App Server → Install Posgres Cluster → Deploy PHP App

D.1 Learning Objectives

1. Revisit CloudFormation.
2. Review the JSON template.
3. Create an EC2 VM and deploy Red Hat, Apache, PHP, and PostgreSQL software.
4. Describe the CloudFormation stack.
5. Review the configuration status and log files.
6. Deploy PHP code.
7. Validate the PHP website.

APPENDIX D POSTGRES WITH APACHE/PHP

D.2 Scripting

With the JSON, YAML, or Bicep scripting languages, you can deploy all the software components for the deployment of web applications created by PHP programs.

The first step is to create the required security groups for access to SSH, the web server, and the database server. After creating the necessary security groups, the next steps involve selecting the virtual machine, the required operating system, Apache HTTP server, PHP app server, and PostgreSQL database cluster.

The JSON script consists of three main components: 1) Define the resources, 2) create the resources, and 3) user data.

The resource definition for the PostgreSQL cluster includes the database cluster, which comprises the primary cluster along with a bunch of standby clusters, cluster configuration parameters, and database monitoring tools such as Patroni. After defining the resources, you can create the resources along with specific scripts defined in the user data section. The user data includes the scripts that are passed to the EC2 instance at the launch state, following VM and OS tasks.

> **Note** JSON, YAML, or Bicep scripts often run into hundreds of lines of code to deploy a large application along with all the dependencies in the cloud.

The following is the simple script to deploy PHP applications on the cloud:
   demo.json

```
{
  "AWSTemplateFormatVersion": "2010-09-09",
  "Resources": {
    "MySecurityGroup": {
```

```
      "Type": "AWS::EC2::SecurityGroup",
      "Properties": {
        "GroupDescription": "My Security Group",
        "SecurityGroupIngress": [
          {
            "IpProtocol": "tcp",
            "FromPort": 22,
            "ToPort": 22,
            "CidrIp": "0.0.0.0/0"
          },
          {
            "IpProtocol": "tcp",
            "FromPort": 5432,
            "ToPort": 5432,
            "CidrIp": "0.0.0.0/0"
          },
          {
            "IpProtocol": "tcp",
            "FromPort": 80,
            "ToPort": 80,
            "CidrIp": "0.0.0.0/0"
          }
        ]
      }
    },
    "MyEC2Instance": {
      "Type": "AWS::EC2::Instance",
      "Properties": {
        "ImageId": "ami-02b8534ff4b424939",
        "InstanceType": "t2.micro",
        "KeyName": "dev",
```

APPENDIX D   POSTGRES WITH APACHE/PHP

```
    "SecurityGroups": [
      {
        "Ref": "MySecurityGroup"
      }
    ],
    "UserData": {
      "Fn::Base64": {
        "Fn::Join": [
          "",
          [
            "#!/bin/bash\n",
            "sudo dnf install -y httpd mod_ssl\n",
            "sudo systemctl enable --now httpd\n",
            "sudo systemctl status httpd\n",
            "sudo systemctl stop httpd\n",
           "sudo setsebool -P httpd_can_network_connect 1\n",
            "sudo systemctl start httpd\n",
            "sudo dnf module reset -y php\n",
            "sudo dnf module install -y php\n",
            "sudo dnf install -y php php-cli php-fpm php-mysqlnd php-pgsql php-sqlite3 php-json php-xml php-gd php-mbstring php-json php-zip php-curl\n",
            "sudo systemctl restart httpd\n",
            "sudo systemctl status httpd\n",
            "sudo echo '<?php phpinfo(); ?>' > /var/www/html/index.php\n",
            "php -v\n",
            "sudo dnf install -y https://download.postgresql.org/pub/repos/yum/reporpms/EL-8-x86_64/pgdg-redhat-repo-latest.noarch.rpm\n",
```

```
          "sudo dnf -qy module disable postgresql\n",
          "sudo dnf install -y postgresql16-server\n",
          "sudo /usr/pgsql-16/bin/postgresql-16-setup
          initdb\n",
          "sudo systemctl enable postgresql-16\n",
          "sudo systemctl start postgresql-16\n",
          "sudo yum install -y postgresql16-contrib\n",
           sudo su - postgres -c "echo 'host all all
           127.0.0.1/32 trust' >> /var/lib/pgsql/16/data/
           pg_hba.conf"\n,
          sudo systemctl restart postgresql-16\n"
        ]
      ]
    }
   }
  }
 }
}
}
```

D.3 Script Cloudformation

Lisitng D-1 is the Cloudformation deployment code.

Listing D-1. Cloudformation Completion

```
aws cloudformation deploy --template-file /home/clouduser/
scripts/demo.json --stack-name demophp1

$aws cloudformation describe-stacks --stack-name demophp1
{
    "Stacks": [
```

```
    {
        "StackId": "arn:aws:cloudformation:us-
        east-2:12345678909:stack/
        demophp1/978bce70-7bf5-11ee-aacf-0679b4f0dec3",
        "StackName": "demophp1",
::::: Lines omitted
            "StackDriftStatus": "NOT_CHECKED"
        }
    }
  ]
}
```

D.4 Validation of Services After Deployment

Figure D-1 shows screen images of the validation of successful deployment of PHP, Apache, and Postgres clusters.

APPENDIX D POSTGRES WITH APACHE/PHP

```
[ec2-user@ip-172-31-14-248 html]$ sudo systemctl status httpd
● httpd.service - The Apache HTTP Server
     Loaded: loaded (/usr/lib/systemd/system/httpd.service; enabled; preset: disabled)
    Drop-In: /usr/lib/systemd/system/httpd.service.d
             └─php-fpm.conf
     Active: active (running) since Sun 2023-11-05 03:17:28 UTC; 19min ago
```

```
[ec2-user@ip-172-31-14-248 html]$ sudo systemctl status php-fpm.service
● php-fpm.service - The PHP FastCGI Process Manager
     Loaded: loaded (/usr/lib/systemd/system/php-fpm.service; disabled; preset: disabled)
     Active: active (running) since Sun 2023-11-05 03:17:27 UTC; 18min ago
```

```
[ec2-user@ip-172-31-14-248 html]$ sudo systemctl status postgresql-15
○ postgresql-15.service - PostgreSQL 15 database server
     Loaded: loaded (/usr/lib/systemd/system/postgresql-15.service; enabled; preset: disabled)
```

```
│ ├─httpd.service
│ │ ├─14483 /usr/sbin/httpd -DFOREGROUND
│ │ ├─14484 /usr/sbin/httpd -DFOREGROUND
│ │ ├─14486 /usr/sbin/httpd -DFOREGROUND
│ │ ├─14487 /usr/sbin/httpd -DFOREGROUND
│ │ ├─14488 /usr/sbin/httpd -DFOREGROUND
│ │ └─16463 /usr/sbin/httpd -DFOREGROUND
│ ├─php-fpm.service
│ │ ├─14475 "php-fpm: master process (/etc/php-fpm.conf)"
│ │ ├─14476 "php-fpm: pool www"
│ │ ├─14477 "php-fpm: pool www"
│ │ ├─14478 "php-fpm: pool www"
│ │ ├─14479 "php-fpm: pool www"
│ │ └─14480 "php-fpm: pool www"
│ ├─polkit.service
│ │ └─899 /usr/lib/polkit-1/polkitd --no-debug
│ ├─postgresql-15.service
│ │ ├─15416 /usr/pgsql-15/bin/postmaster -D /var/lib/pgsql/15/data/
│ │ ├─15417 "postgres: logger "
│ │ ├─15418 "postgres: checkpointer "
│ │ ├─15419 "postgres: background writer "
│ │ ├─15421 "postgres: walwriter "
│ │ ├─15422 "postgres: autovacuum launcher "
│ │ └─15423 "postgres: logical replication launcher "
```

Figure D-1. *Successful deployment*

D.5 PHP Script Deployment

There are four steps to creating a PHP program.

1. Connect to a database.
2. Query the database,
3. Fetch results and display the result set.
4. Close the program.

APPENDIX D   POSTGRES WITH APACHE/PHP

You connect with the pg_connect function, which is overloaded to take multiple arguments.

The query is done with the pg_query function, which takes two arguments: the connection details and the SQL query. The result set is returned with the pg_fetch_assoc function and the results are displayed in the HTML format.

D.6 Sample PHP Program

```php
<?php
error_reporting(E_ALL);
ini_set('display_errors', 1);
// Database connection details
$dbHost = 'localhost';
$dbName = 'postgres';
$dbUser = 'postgres';
// PostgreSQL database connection
$conn = pg_connect("host=$dbHost dbname=$dbName user=$dbUser");
// Check if the connection is successful
if (!$conn) {
    echo "An error occurred.\n";
    exit;
}
// Query to retrieve data from the pg_database table
$result = pg_query($conn, "SELECT datname from pg_database;");
if (!$result) {
    echo "An error occurred.\n";
    exit;
}
// Start an HTML table
echo "<table border='1'>
```

APPENDIX D POSTGRES WITH APACHE/PHP

```
            <tr>
                <th>datname</th>
            </tr>";
// Fetch and display the data
while ($row = pg_fetch_assoc($result)) {
    echo "<tr>";
    echo "<td>" . $row['datname'] . "</td>";
    echo "</tr>";
}
pg_close($conn);
?>
```

After successfully validating the services, copy the following file to /var/www/html and validate the PHP program with the php db.php command, as follows (see Figure D-2):

```
php db.php
<table border='1'>
            <tr>
                <th>datname</th>
            </tr><tr><td>postgres</td></tr><tr><td>demo</td>
            </tr><tr><td>template1</td></tr><tr><td>template0
            </td></tr></table>
```

← → C 🌐 3.145.4.135/db.php
Ⓜ Gmail ▶ YouTube ❓ Maps ⓖ GPT-4

datname
postgres
demo
template1
template0

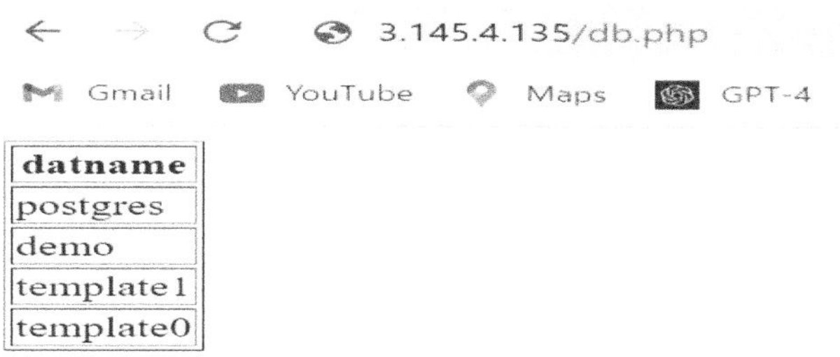

Figure D-2. *Successful validation*

D.7 Log File Apache

In the Apache web server log, note the client machine as well as the server host IP addresses along with the PHP URL:

tail /var/log/httpd/access_log

49.22.119.107 - - [06/Nov/2023:23:24:01 +0000] "GET /favicon.ico HTTP/1.1" 404 196 "http://3.144.249.19/" "Mozilla/5.0 (Macintosh; Intel Mac OS X 10_10_5) AppleWebKit/537.36 (KHTML, like Gecko) Chrome/87.0.4280.88 Safari/537.36"
42.22.119.107 - - [06/Nov/2023:23:24:11 +0000] "GET /db.php HTTP/1.1" 200 175 "-" "Mozilla/5.0 (Macintosh; Intel Mac OS X 10_10_5) AppleWebKit/537.36 (KHTML, like Gecko) Chrome/87.0.4280.88 Safari/537.36"

D.8 Log File PHP

 tail -2 /var/log/php-fpm/error.log
[06-Nov-2023 23:03:50] NOTICE: ready to handle connections
[06-Nov-2023 23:03:50] NOTICE: systemd monitor interval set to 10000ms

D.9 Stop Services

systemctl stop httpd. # stop Apache
systemctl stop php-fpm. # stop PhP
systemctl stop postgresql-15. # stop PostgreSQL

D.10 Delete Stack

aws cloudformation delete-stack --stack-name demophp1

References:

www.php.net/manual/en/ref.pgsql.php

https://aws.amazon.com/cloudformation/

APPENDIX E

pgBouncer

As individual connections to a database are expensive in terms of resources, you can configure pgBouncer where user connections are kept alive for reuse of user sessions. pgBouncer has several configuration parameters, which you can obtain from the help command. With `auth_file`, you can define usernames and encrypted passwords for primary as well as standby roles. See Listing E-1.

Listing E-1. pgBouncer Configuration

```
Preparation:
sudo yum install -y pgbouncer
edit /etc/pgbouncer/pgbouncer.ini file, add below values.
 [databases]
* = host=node2 port=5432 user=user01
[pgbouncer]
listen_addr = *
listen_port = 6432
auth_type = md5
auth_file = /tmp/userlist.txt
admin_users = postgres

Add the following value in /tmp/userlist.txt:
"user01" "Temp001"
"user02" "\xb92fa3b1e668ac0b18ce9c6125fa914a"
```

APPENDIX E   PGBOUNCER

After configuration, star the services with the command `sudo systemctl start pgbouncer`.

Connect to psql from a Windows client from port 6432. See Figure E-1.

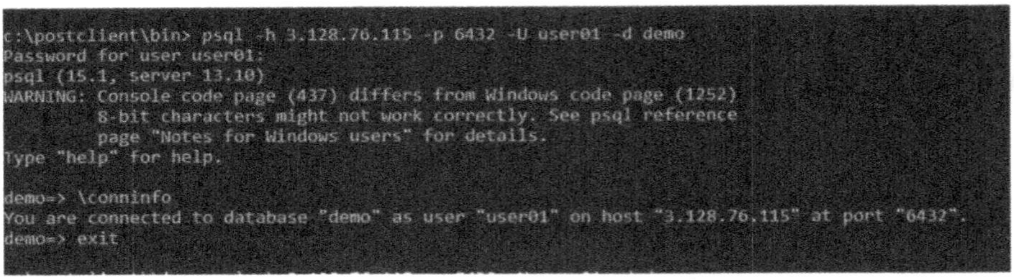

Figure E-1. pgBouncer access from a Windows PC

APPENDIX F

Red Hat Pacemaker HA

This is a high-level overview of how to set up a PostgreSQL high-availability cluster with Red Hat's Pacemaker Cluster Suite (PCS) to make PostgreSQL available due to node failure.

Install pacemaker → Password HA cluster → Authenticate pc cluster from both nodes → Setup name for 2 clusters → Start the cluster → Add Postgres resource to cluster → Create vip and fense for the cluster → Add constraint and start resource

The high-level steps to configure Pacemaker after creating two PostgreSQL instances called node1 and node2 are as follows:

1. `sudo yum install pacemaker pcs`
2. `sudo passwd hacluster`
3. `sudo pcs cluster auth node1 node2`
4. `sudo pcs cluster setup --name demopost node1 node2`
5. `sudo pcs cluster start -all`
6. `sudo systemctl enable pacemaker`
7. `sudo systemctl enable corosync`
8. `sudo systemctl start pacemaker`
9. `sudo systemctl start corosync`

10. sudo pcs resource create pgsql ocf:heartbeat:pgsql \
    pgctl="/usr/bin/pg_ctl" \
    psql="/usr/bin/psql" \
    pgdata="/var/lib/pgsql/15/data" \
    rep_mode="sync" \
    node_list="node1 node2" \
    op start timeout=60s \
    op stop timeout=60s \
    op monitor timeout=60s
11 sudo pcs stonith create fence_node1 fence_pcmk \
    pcmk_host_list="node1" \
    ipaddr="node1_ip_address" \
    pcmk_reboot_action="reboot" \
    pcmk_reboot_timeout="60"
12 sudo pcs stonith create fence_node2 fence_pcmk \
    pcmk_host_list="node2" \
    ipaddr="node2_ip_address" \
    pcmk_reboot_action="reboot" \
    pcmk_reboot_timeout="60"
13 sudo pcs status
14 sudo pcs cluster stop node1
15 sudo pcs cluster start node1

Reference: https://access.redhat.com/solutions/7002546

APPENDIX G

Python with PostgreSQL

Root user
sudo dnf update or sudo yum install python3
 python --version
 sudo yum install python3-pip
 pip3 install psycopg2-binary or python3 -m pip install psycopg2-binary
sudo dnf install -y https://download.postgresql.org/pub/repos/yum/reporpms/EL-8-x86_64/pgdg-redhat-repo-latest.noarch.rpm
    sudo dnf -qy module disable postgresql
   sudo dnf install -y postgresql16-server
   sudo /usr/pgsql-16/bin/postgresql-16-setup initdb
   sudo systemctl enable postgresql-16
   sudo systemctl start postgresql-16
   sudo yum install postgresql16-contrib
      Postgres user
    sudo su - postgres

APPENDIX G   PYTHON WITH POSTGRESQL

```
     /usr/pgsql-16/bin/psql -U postgres -c "create user user1
     with password 'StrongPwd#;'"
   echo "host all    0.0.0.0/0 md5" >> /var/lib/pgsql/16/data/
   pg_hba.conf
         /usr/pgsql-16/bin/pg_ctl restart -D /var/lib/
         pgsql/16/data
conn.py
$ cat con.py
import psycopg2
def connect_to_postgres():
    # Modify these variables with your database credentials
    HOST = "localhost"
    PORT = "5432"
    USER = "user1"
    PASSWORD = "'StrongPwd#"
    DBNAME = "postgres"

    try:
        # Connect to the PostgreSQL database
        connection = psycopg2.connect(
            host=HOST,
            port=PORT,
            user=USER,
            password=PASSWORD,
            dbname=DBNAME
        )
        cursor = connection.cursor()
        # Execute a query to fetch database names
        cursor.execute("SELECT datname FROM pg_database;")
        # Fetch all database names
        db_names = cursor.fetchall()
        # Print each database name
```

```
            print("Databases:")
            for db in db_names:
                print(db[0])
        except (Exception, psycopg2.DatabaseError) as error:
            print("Error:", error)
        finally:
            # Close the cursor and connection
            if cursor:
                cursor.close()
            if connection:
                connection.close()
                print("Connection closed.")
if __name__ == "__main__":
    connect_to_postgres()
python3 con.py
Databases:
postgres
template1
template0
demo
Connection closed.
```

APPENDIX H1

Incremental Backup

Available from version 17 which copies only changed blocks since last full backup with pg_basebackup command. Preparation: Enable archive log of the server, followed by enabling summarize_wal and reload the configuration.

Following are the steps:

```
psql -c "ALTER system SET summarize_wal = ON;"
psql -c " SELECT pg_reload_conf();"
export sdate=$(date "+%m%d%Y%H%M%S")
echo "Start Backp:::$sdate" > /tmp/bk
pg_basebackup -D /appl/postgres/backup/full_$sdate -Ft # full backup
pg_basebackup --i /appl/postgres/backup/full_$sdate/backup_manifest -D /appl/postgres/backup/inc_01_$sdate -Ft
# incremental backup
export edate=$(date "+%m%d%Y%H%M%S")
echo "End Backup :::$edate" >> /tmp/bk
```

APPENDIX H2

Incremental Backup Restore

Database backup restore with incremental backup files

The procedure is to extract files from the full and incremental backups and combine them into one file. A new program, pg_combinebackup, is created to combine the full backup with incremental backups. After restoring backup files from backup to operating system perform below steps.

1. Create the original PGDATA directory.

   ```
   mkdir -p /pgdata/devdb
   # create your own PGDATA directory
   chmod 0750 /pgdata/devdb
   # Set the permissions of PGDATA
   chown postgres:postgres /pgdata/dbdev
   ```

2. Extract base backup file from full backup.

   ```
   tar -xvf /appl/postgres/backup/full/base.tar
   # Choose your restore directory
   ```

APPENDIX H2   INCREMENTAL BACKUP RESTORE

2.1. Extract pg_wal file.

mv /appl/postgres/backup/full/pg_wal.tar /appl/postgres/backup/full/pg_wal
tar -xvf /appl/postgres/backup/full/pg_wal/pg_wal.tar -C /appl/postgres/backup/full/pg_wal

2.2. Remove backup files # remove base.tar and pg_wal.tar as these file are not registered with backup manifest file rm /appl/postgres/backup/full/pg_wal/pg_wal.tar

rm /appl/postgres/backup/full/base.tar

3. Extract files from incremental backup.

tar -xvf /appl/postgres/backup/inc_01/base.tar

3.1. Extract pg_wal file.

mv /appl/postgres/backup/inc_01/pg_wal.tar /appl/postgres/backup/inc_01/pg_wal
tar -xvf /appl/postgres/backup/inc_01/pg_wal/pg_wal.tar -C /appl/postgres/backup/inc_01/pg_wal

3.2. Remove backup files # remove base.tar and pg_wal.tar as these file are not registered with backup manifest file rm /appl/postgres/backup/inc_01/pg_wal/pg_wal.tar

rm /appl/postgres/backup/inc_01/base.tar

4. Combine full and incremental backups into a directory.

pg_combinebackup -o /pgdata/devdb /appl/postgres/backup/full /appl/postgres/backup/inc_01

APPENDIX H2   INCREMENTAL BACKUP RESTORE

5. Start the PostgreSQL Cluster

    $pg_ctl start -D /pgdata/devdb

    waiting for server to start....2024-10-01 14:42:46.123 UTC [53003] LOG:

    redirecting log output to logging collector process

APPENDIX I

Answers to Chapter Questions

https://docs.google.com/document/d/1RLpFiTnJicDUqd_mGKreVMFYll7VTXci/edit?usp=sharing&ouid=117618855868897795502&rtpof=true&sd=true

Index

A

Amazon EKS, 272
Amazon S3, 62
Analytics workspace, 243
Analyze databases, 433
Attach Instance to Volume, 119
aws ce get-cost-and-usage, 113
AWS CLI install on Linux, 188
AWS CLI on MAC, 188
AWS CloudFormation, 94
aws cloudformation create-stack, 96
aws cloudformation deploy, 97, 99, 214
AWS CloudFormation deployment from JSON, 97–99
aws cloudformation describe-stacks, 96
aws cloudformation list-stacks, 121
AWS Cloud Shell, 45
aws cloudwatch get-metric-statistics, 231
aws cloudwatch list-metrics, 228
AWS command line interface on Windows, 185–188
aws ec2 attach-volume, 119
aws ec2 authorize-security-group-ingress, 94, 162
aws ec2 create-key-pair, 93
aws ec2 create-security-group, 93, 162
aws ec2 create-volume, 119
aws ec2 describe-images--owners amazon, 316
aws ec2 describe-instances, 118
aws ec2 describe-instances--query, 121
aws ec2 describe-instance-type-offerings, 46
aws ec2 describe-instance-types, 46
aws ec2 describe-regions, 47
aws ec2 describe-security-groups, 162
aws ec2 modify-instance-attribute, 162
aws ec2 run-instances, 94
aws ec2 start-instances, 121
aws ec2 stop-instances, 324
AWS hardware configuration, 51, 52
AWS instance creation, 85–92
AWS Performance Insight, 224
AWS RDS, 205

INDEX

aws rds create-db-instance, 211
aws rds create-db-instance-read-replica, 500
aws rds create-db-parameter-group, 221
aws rds create-db-snapshot, 305
aws rds create-option-group, 222
aws rds describe-db-instances, 210
aws rds describe-db-log-files, 223
aws rds describe-db-parameters, 221
aws rds download-db-log-file-portion, 432
aws rds modify-db-instance, 219, 221, 430
aws rds modify-db-parameter-group, 221
aws s3api list-objects, 63
AWS Security Group Networking configuration, 90–92
AWS Web Services, 44–46
az account list-locations, 49
az deployment group create, 241
az group create, 318
az network nsg rule create, 163
az postgres flexible-server, 477
az postgres flexible-server create, 237
az postgres flexible-server replica, 504
az postgres flexible-server replica promote, 507
az storage account create, 66
az storage account keys list, 66
az storage blob upload, 307
az storage container, 66
Azure Client, 199, 200
Azure Cloud Shell, 48, 49
Azure Hardware Configuration, 53
Azure PostgreSQL Flexible Server commands, 236
Azure Security Group, 162
Azure SQL Database, 232–245
az vm create, 104, 319
az vm list-skus, 50

B

backup_manifest, 452
Bicep template, 238, 239

C

CLOUDFORMATION, 96
Cloud Services, 42–70
Cloud VM creation, 84–99
Configuration of putty, 106–109
Configuration option, 136–139
Connect to Azure Portal, 100–103
Connect to EC2/Azure VM, 105
Contributory Packages, 132
Copy, 370, 371
Create Azure VM from Command line, 104

INDEX

createdb, 164
Create Extension, 155–158
Create IAM user account, 186, 187
Create non default security group, 162–164
CREATE PUBLICATION, 436
Create RDS from command line, 210
Create RDS from YAML template, 212–216
Create schema, 355
create sequence, 380
CREATE SUBSCRIPTION, 436, 437
create tablespace, 536, 537

D

Database management system, 12–17
Data encryption policies, 58
Data masking, 58
default_tablespace, 538
dnf install, 131
Docker, 250
Docker compose, 257–259
docker-compose.yaml, 257
Docker Desktop, 273–276
docker exec-it, 255
docker export, 263
Docker images, 253
docker info, 252
docker load, 264
Docker Platform, 251–262
docker ps-a, 255
docker pull, 253
docker rm, 266
docker run, 254
Dynamic SQL, 361

E

EC2/Azure VM Installation Methods, 84
EC2 Deployment with CloudFormation, 94–97
Expand shared buffers memory, 152

F

File copy to S3, 62
First Normal Form, 15, 16
forfiles, 332

G, H

Git Bash, 189–191

I, J

IDENTITY, 400
initdb, 143
Initialize PostgreSQL cluster, 141–151

INDEX

Install postgres odbc, 192
Install PostgreSQL Cluster on MAC, 26–30
Introduction to Linux Operating System, 76–82
Introduction to Linux Shell, 78

K

KQL, 244
kubectl apply, 271
Kubernetes, 266–268

L

last_value, 383
Launch EC2 Instances from AWS console, 86
libpq, 5
Linux huge pages, 111, 112
Linux Kernel, 110
Linux variable, 342
Logical replication procedure, 435
Logical volume setup commands, 114
Log sequence recovery, 459, 460
lvcreate, 114

M

Major features of Linux operating system, 77
Major features of PostgreSQL, 9–10
Microsoft Azure Web Service, 47–50

mkfs, 119
Modify parameter in postgresql.conf, 153

N

New parameters between versions 10-16, 154

O

Object relational model, 23–25
Open Database Connectivity (ODBC), 191–196
OpenShift, 271
Overload function, 372–375

P, Q

Parallel Backup Configuration, 290, 291
Parameter group, 219
Partitions with Inheritance, 527–529
pgAdmin, 175
pg_basebackup, 299–301
pg_create_logical_replication_slot, 437, 438
pg_ctl, 144
pg_dump, 286–293
pg_dumpall, 294–298
pg_get_serial_sequence, 384
pg_hba.conf, 148
pg_is_in_recovery, 489
pg_partman, 517–520

INDEX

pg_promote(), 502, 508
pg_resetwal, 464
pg_restore, 199, 289, 290, 468
pgrowlocks, 554, 555
pg_stat_activity, 226, 506, 554
pg_upgrade, 415–421
pg_waldump, 453
Pod, 268
PostgreSQL client on Linux, 197, 198
PostgreSQL cluster installation directories, 140
PostgreSQL cluster install on Windows PC, 30–33
PostgreSQL cluster origin, 3–7
PostgreSQL cluster provisioning methods, 60
PostgreSQL cluster resource managers, 6
postgresql.conf, 146
PostgreSQL partition methods, 513
PostgreSQL server architecture, 6
PostgreSQL server operating system resources, 7–9
PostgreSQL software for installation on Linux, 130
PostgreSQL wait event types, 227
PowerShell, 327
Primary pg_hba.conf, 485, 486
psql, 340–349
PSQL, 178
psql client on windows, 179, 180
psql shell, 324
pvcreate, 115

R

RDS availability zones and failover, 206
RDS backup, 303–309
RDS Creation Procedure from Console, 208, 209
RDS PostgreSQL creation methods, 207
RDS Proxy, 566, 569–575
Read Anomaly, 549, 550
Recovery Point Objective (RPO), 284
recovery_target_time, 461
Recovery Time Objective (RTO), 284
Red Hat package manager (RPM), 129
Registry Entry, 330
Relational data model, 19–21
Replication slot, 498–499
restore_command, 457

S

search_path, 352
Second Normal Form, 16, 17
Serializable isolation level, 551
Set PATH windows, 32, 33
Setval, 392, 393
SQLJ Workbench, 180–184
Standby pg_hba.conf, 487
standby.signal, 495
Star schema, 21–23
Stop-Process, 334

T, U

Third Normal Form, 17
Time based recovery, 461
Transaction ID recovery, 461

V, W, X, Y, Z

vgcreate, 114
Volume group
    creation, 114–117

The manufacturer's authorised representative in the EU is Springer Nature Customer Service Centre GmbH, Europaplatz 3, 69115 Heidelberg, Germany. If you have any concerns regarding our products, please contact ProductSafety@springernature.com

Printed and bound by CPI Group (UK) Ltd, Croydon, CR0 4YY

25/03/2026

02078192-0018